Nationalism and Human Rights

Series in Issues Studies (USSR and East Europe)

No. 1

Nationalism and Human Rights

Processes of Modernization in the USSR

Edited by Ihor Kamenetsky

Published for the Association
for the Study of the Nationalities
(USSR and East Europe) Inc. by
Libraries Unlimited, Inc.

Littleton, Colo.

1977

LIBRARIES UNLIMITED, INC.
P.O. Box 263
Littleton, Colorado 80160

Library of Congress Cataloging in Publication Data

Main entry under title:

Nationalism and human rights.

Includes index.
1. Minorities--Russia--Addresses, essays, lectures. 2. Civil rights--Russia--Addresses, essays,
lectures. 3. Nationalism and socialism--Addresses,
essays, lectures. I. Kamenetsky, Ihor, 1927–
JN6520.M5N26   323.42'3'0947   77-1257
ISBN 0-87287-143-6

TABLE OF CONTENTS

39578

PART III–FERMENT AND DISSENT IN THE
WESTERN PART OF THE USSR

PART IV–THE SEARCH FOR IDENTITY AMONG
SOME NON-WESTERN SOVIET NATIONALITIES

PART V–THE CASE OF SOME PERSECUTED MINORITIES

ACKNOWLEDGMENT

I would like to thank the contributors to this volume for sharing with us their expert knowledge and advice, and for extending to us their cooperation and patience. Further, I would like to express my sincere appreciation to Dr. Stephan Horak, President of the Association for the Study of the Nationalities (USSR and East Europe) Inc., for his tireless support and encouragement in this project, and for his help in the technical and administrative arrangements made for this publication. Special thanks are due also to the editors of the *Canadian Slavonic Papers* for giving us their kind permission to reprint three articles relevant to our symposium.

Ihor Kamenetsky

PREFACE

Ihor Kamenetsky
Central Michigan University
Mount Pleasant, Michigan

The essence of modernization as it emerged in the West means, in human terms, first of all the liberation of man from the shackles and limitations of a traditional society. In its logical consequence and in the final analysis, this represented a growing opportunity for the common man to develop his potentialities in the political, economic, and social sense. Politically speaking, modernization originally referred to a system in which the government was expected to represent the interests of the majority of a nation and to be accountable to it. Socially, it meant equality before the law. Economically, it meant legal freedom for each citizen to pursue his economic self-reliance and interest, without undue interference by his government.

These political, social, and economic changes did not happen in a vacuum. The legitimate basis for a majority rule was seen in a nation which, at least theoretically, was supposed to represent the common denominator of interests of a people united by heritage, traditions, culture, a common political experience, and goals which they cherished and with which they identified. It is interesting that the growing importance of the dignity and freedom of the common man originally coincided with the concern for the freedom and destiny of a nation—a concern which became broader and more popular as the modernization processes developed. The implications of most of these ideas were revolutionary in nature and in many cases conflicted with the status quo. Frequently, they led to violent changes and revolutions within the framework of wars of liberation, national unification, irredenta, etc., but in most cases, the violence involved seemed to be corrective and temporary in nature. It cannot be denied that the newly emerging political principles, like sovereignty of the people and the principle of national self-determination, provided potentialities for the elimination of many traditional causes for going to war.

But the greatest, the most revolutionary, and the longest lasting impact of the launching stage of modernization in the West was the crystallization of the concept of universal human rights. Whatever we may think about the practical implementations of the American Declaration of Independence, the American Bill of

9

Rights, or the French Declaration of the Rights of Man and of the Citizen, it must be admitted that, basically, they have provided an important and universal point of reference for the delicate balance between the rights of the individual and the rights of a nation. Also, they could be considered a moral bulwark for the civilized states against man's inhumanities to man.

The impact of the industrial, scientific, and technological revolution in the nineteenth century added new dimensions to the concern for human rights. In the long run, the industrial revolution not only eliminated hard physical work and long working hours, but it provided also an unprecedentedly high standard of living for the workers in the advanced countries of the West. Further, it created a basis for a better educated and less parochially oriented citizenry, which of itself must be considered as an asset for a modern nation state. We must keep in mind that industrialization provided a fertile soil for a more extensive and potentially more profitable international trade, cultural and scientific exchanges, and other forms of useful and peaceful international interactions. But the dangers emanating from the same processes were not less impressive. The industrial revolution in general created an unprecedented number of economic power centers affecting employment, access to raw materials, vital trade, and the necessities of national development, all of which frequently eluded the democratic rules and humanitarian considerations. In other words, the economic, scientific, and technological interdependence, without equitable regulations and arrangements, potentially threatened to undermine those civil liberties which, at least in principle, had been established in the pre-industrial age.

As it happened, with the progress of industrialization, those states in which civil rights, a concern for human values, and democratic principles were more or less firmly rooted eventually established democratic controls over intractable economic forces, and various social welfare programs helped secure those individual rights that were in danger of erosion. On the other hand, in countries like Italy, Germany, and Japan, where the emergence of a nation state coincided with industrialization but where the democratic principles and individual rights were weak or non-existent, the modernization trends strengthened the traditional authoritarian political culture. Even if here and there paternalistic social welfare programs were introduced, the system as such eluded popular control. It took a crushing military defeat, ideological bankruptcy of the various authoritarian schemes, and a Western "re-education policy" after World War II to provide democratic controls for the modernization processes.

More complicated was the impact of industrialization on human rights and the principle of national self-determination in the field of international relations. The new economic incentives and economic insecurity turned out to be stronger than the cause of universal freedom and humanity. Even such democratic nations as Great Britain, France, and the United States succumbed to expansionism and double standards, preaching democracy at home while applying imperialistic methods and objectives in overseas colonies and economically dependent countries. However, the political commitment of the Western states to the democratic principles was not without an influence on the attempts to eliminate such discrepancies in the long run. During World War I and afterwards, the Western Powers accepted President Wilson's ideas concerning the universality of the principle of national self-determination and equal access of all nations to world resources and the world market, as well as the idea of a mandate system, which aimed at the ultimate decolonization of the dependent areas.

Although around 1918 the victorious Western Powers were not ready to abandon their colonial possessions or to share with the other nations their economic assets, the new set of principles built around the Covenant of the League of Nations proved to become for them, in the long run, a point of no return, insofar as their theoretical commitments were concerned. Further, as it turned out, the principles of a more democratic world order visualized by President Wilson and his allies created rising expectations among the nations around the world, which, in turn, led to pressures that by themselves could be considered as new factors of political power. Nevertheless, it took primarily the shock of World War II to move the Western states closer to those principles of international order which they supported in theory.

The opposite alternatives pursued between two world wars by Nazi Germany, Fascist Italy, and Imperial Japan, aiming basically at economic autarky and the building of extensive empires by conquest, failed and left the road open to the ideas of the United Nations, which could be considered essentially as revived and extended ideas of President Wilson. There were two particular principles within the framework of the United Nations that did emerge in a stronger form than was the case under the League of Nations and that, in the long run, proved to have a lasting effect:

1. That a just and peaceful world order depends not only on free world markets and free transit of goods and ideas, but also on the commitment of advanced nations to help the underdeveloped needy nations to reach a balanced growth and a capability to help themselves.
2. That basic human rights must become a universal concern.

It is true that the institutional weakness of the United Nations did not permit the enforcement of these principles in any impressive way, but it cannot be denied that by keeping these issues alive, providing an international forum for discussions, and inspiring the creation of official and semi-official specialized agencies, certain norms for an internal and an external policy were created along the lines of modernization which no state can easily or safely disregard. Such standards could be subdivided basically into the following groups:

1. That each people, ethnic group, or minority is entitled to the preservation and development of its identity and culture.
2. That there must be an increasing identification between the policy of a government and the interests of the common man, with an allowance made for safeguarding the basic human rights of everyone concerned.
3. That the growing economic, scientific, and technological interdependence of nations should lead to a cooperation of the nations on an equitable basis, but that it should not be used as a justification for a foreign control, imperialistic expansion, or the denial of chances for a free development of other nations, however weak or underdeveloped they may be.

This orientation had its bearing also upon the nature of international crises after World War II. Thus, without minimizing the significance of super-power rivalry, population explosion, economic confrontations, etc., it must not be overlooked that the origin of major internal and international difficulties of the existing states in this period could not be separated from the issues of national self-determination, national identity, the status of minorities, and human rights in general. When we take such examples as the creation of the state of Israel, the status of the Palestinians, the status of the South African majority, the Berlin Blockade, the Hungarian Uprising, the Arab oil embargo against the West, and Vietnam, we realize that one or more of these issues were involved in the crises and tensions connected with them.

If we look upon the removal of arbitrary foreign control and of a discriminatory treatment of citizens by a state as one of the pre-requisites for modern development, then it is inevitable that we should look upon the twentieth century, despite its excesses and its two world wars, as a century of progress. Hardly any other century witnessed the dissolution of so many empires within a relatively short span of time. Thus, around 1918, Imperial Germany, the Austro-Hungarian Monarchy, the Tsarist Empire, and the Ottoman Empire dissolved as a result of military defeats in World War I. The same fate befell the Third Reich, Imperial Japan and Fascist Italy as a consequence of a military disaster during World War II. Then, in the years following the end of World War II, we witnessed a startling dissolution of the colonial possessions of the victorious Western states, as a result of economic and diplomatic pressures and a sensitivity to public opinion at home and abroad. The most recent colonial empire to topple was that of Portugal, which occurred after a successful democratic revolution in the mother country itself.

The last multinational empire in existence, which not only did not indicate signs of shrinkage but, contrary to the other empires, experienced an expansion in terms of territory and spheres of influence, is that of the Soviet Union. As it represents a certain anomalism in terms of existing international trends of modernization, several questions do arise. First, we may ask, in which way did the Russian historical heritage and the circumstances under which Russia encountered the challenges of modernization favor the idea of a continuation of a multi-national empire? Secondly, we may explore the question of the conceptual basis on which the Bolshevik leaders were able to substitute for the defunct traditional Tsarist Empire a modernized multi-national Soviet empire. Third, how do more contemporary modern changes in the Soviet Union and around the world affect, or how are they likely to affect, their political system?

Turning to the Russian historical background, we will notice that the first modernizing ideas made their appearance in the Russian Empire not as a result of a national internal development, but as an import from the outside in form of the modernization of the army, bureaucracy, etc. Thus, they serve as one of the additional means for the strengthening of an authoritarian, traditional establishment. This was the case in Tsarist Russia under Peter the Great and Catherine the Great, for instance, and this orientation was predominating in the ruling circles when Russia started to industrialize by the end of the nineteenth century. But, as in many similar cases, it proved to be impossible for the Tsarist administration to stop those political, social, and humanitarian ideas which accompanied the modernization processes in the West and which gravitated toward a democratic solution of human problems. Thus, since the beginning of the nineteenth century, the most significant and most influential portion of the Russian intelligentsia disassociated itself politically from the Tsarist autocracy, embracing a creed which could be broadly described as populist and humanitarian. While opposing the outdated Tsarist system, the Russian intelligentsia eventually faced some difficulty in finding a practical alternative for the implementation of their ideas. One of the difficulties was that, socially, modernization touched upon a very insignificant portion of the masses.

One of the limitations for a political enlightenment action of the Russian intelligentsia was the illiteracy and ignorance of the peasant masses, which represented an overwhelming majority of the population. Another handicap was the prohibition of open political meetings which, within the framework of the Tsarist police system, was rather efficiently enforced. Secondly, the Tsarist Empire consisted of a mosaic of nationalities of various cultures and different stages of development, and these nationalities were frequently hostile to the idea of Russian political, social, and economic control. Like their Western counterparts at that time, who were liberal at home but supported the "white man's burden" in overseas colonies, the Russian intelligentsia in most cases found it difficult to reconcile the idea of a democratic system with the idea of the dissolution of the Russian Empire. But we cannot ignore the different political environments in which the pre-Revolutionary Russian intelligentsia crystallized its ideas. While in the West the pressures of an open pluralistic society helped to expose the discrepancy between democratic ideals and a glorification of imperialism, the Tsarist system did not provide such corrective devices. Nor did the coexistence with the Ottoman Empire, the Austro-Hungarian Monarchy, and Imperial Germany in East Central Europe contribute to a liberalization of Russian attitudes to the nationality question. Politically, Turkey, Austria, and Prussia (later Imperial Germany) were committed to the preservation of the status quo in Eastern Europe, and their impact was basically a conservative one. Ideologically, the rise of Pan-Germanism and modern anti-Semitism in Germany and Austria during the nineteenth century had an impact upon a growing Pan-Slavism and modern anti-Semitism in Tsarist Russia. This, in turn, eventually contributed to a fragmentation of the Russian liberal intelligentsia in their opposition to autocracy and drove some sections of them in a conservative direction.

Also, the national awakening of the submerged nations in the Tsarist Empire and the remaining parts of Eastern Europe was not unaffected by the contradictions between the yearning for domination and the principle of self-determination. The striving for national independence, stimulated by powerful Western ideas, unfortunately did not always coincide with a recognition of similar rights of the other submerged nations, whenever and wherever historical boundaries, territorial disputes, cultural superiority, and similar factors became an issue.

The Soviet system, which prevailed on the ruins of the Tsarist Empire, generally is considered another example of the modernization in Eastern Europe within roughly the same span of time. Milovan Djilas, in his work, *The New Class*, even attributed the victory of the Bolsheviks to the fact that they were the only party in the Civil War contest that had, and that widely publicized, a concept of industrial transformation of the society in a country that was backward and stagnant.[1] Actually, there is no evidence that the revolutionized masses were looking forward to a rapid industrialization as a wave of the future, and that the Bolsheviks were able to recognize and to utilize this yearning. On the contrary, the popular ideals of the 1917 Revolution had little to do with the pressures of public opinion in favor of the prospects of industrialization. The peasants' pressure for a division of land actually meant a fragmentation of land-holdings to a size where an advanced agricultural production, typical of an industrial society, was, at least initially, impossible. Many non-Russian nationalities considered as their paramount concern first of all the safeguarding of their cultural or political independence, or both. For many members of the Russian intelligentsia the preconcern centered on the civil liberties and the constitutional transformation of the Russian state, while the preservation of territorial integrity of the previous Russian Empire was still an important imperative. If there was some common denominator of the closest revolutionary concern among the various political, social, national, and racial groups following the Revolution of 1917, it could be described as an aversion to an arbitrary and unaccountable authority.

Even though Lenin's policy of the dictatorship of the proletariat interfered with the civil liberties and the principle of national self-determination during the October Revolution and the Civil War, Lenin managed to create an ambiguous legacy which seemed to narrow the gap between the original promises of the Revolution and the realities during the period of "War Communism."

On this account we could mention the following positions expressed by Lenin, which later turned out to be ephemeral and unsubstantiated:

1.   That the civil liberties were suspended temporarily and that they would be restored after the emergency situation receded;
2.   That some institutions of popular control, like the Soviets, would continue to exist, and that within a reasonable time they would gain substantial power over vital decisions;
3.   That unity of interests and cooperation would be established among the peoples of the former Tsarist Empire after the Bolshevik victory, on the basis of their own national identity and on the basis of equal national rights of their peoples.

Although these commitments were marred already in the early state of the Bolshevik rule by many inconsistencies between theory and practice, they had some ideological and psychological effect that helped to secure support for Lenin's cause. One of the reasons for this support was the fact that while the Bolsheviks tried to match the democratic promises of some of their opponents in the Civil War, they appealed on the "all-union" basis to a broader constituency than the one represented by anti-Bolshevik forces, which were fragmented along the lines of nationality, politics, and social issues. The first moment of "truth" for the Soviet modernizers emerged during the last waning years of Lenin's rule. It emerged as the question of the country's direction of social and political transformation came under critical reconsideration.

Whereas the de facto Bolshevik interference with the civil liberties and the rights of the various nationalities during the Civil War could be interpreted as a necessity of "War Communism," no such explanations could be used effectively to explain the ruthless suppression of the Kronstadt Uprising by Trotsky and the elimination of the opposition in Georgia and in the Ukraine, which fell into the after-war period. Lenin, incapacitated physically but alert intellectually, and with more leisure to observe and evaluate the trends of change in the system which he helped to build, came to the conclusion himself that the policy pursued by his associates departed further and further from the original objectives of the Bolshevik Revolution. Isaak Deutscher, who deeply sympathized with the predicament of Lenin, described Lenin's views on these matters in the following words: "Lenin felt guilty before the working class of his country because, so he said, he had not acted with sufficient determination and early enough against Stalin and Dzerzhinsky, against their Great Russian chauvinism, against the suppression of the rights of the small nations, and against the new oppression, in Russia, of the weak by the strong."[2]

Whatever one may think about Lenin's interpretation and application of Marxist teachings, one cannot deny to him the validity of one corrective insight— namely, that a modern human society cannot be built permanently on intimidating the majority and on favoring one nation over another nation. While his steps to correct the course of the Bolshevik leadership at the end of his political career failed and the testament which he left behind was destined to be suppressed for over thirty years, it must be conceded that the revelation of his criticism following Khrushchev's speech in 1956 had a prolonged effect upon the reconsideration of many aspects of Marxism-Leninism in the USSR and in the World Communist movement. This in itself does not prove that Lenin would have acted differently if he had faced the circumstances confronting Stalin, or that he indeed did not pave the way for Stalin's arbitrary rule. It means only that many activists and supporters of the Soviet system operated on the basis that Stalin's measures were just and necessary and dedicated to the welfare of the people, and that he carried out the legacy of Lenin with which he repeatedly identified.[3]

The methods of "social engineering," purges, and terror, as well as the psychologically exploited real fears of foreign invasions (Japan, Nazi Germany) apparently were responsible for the first stage of the modern transformation of the Soviet society. Socially, the Stalinist methods of modernizing society created penetrating human traumas about which we are becoming aware more extensively as the accounts written by Solzhenitsyn and other distinguished survivors of the Soviet penal system become available in increasing numbers. During the processes of modernization initiated by Stalin, the nature of many nations within the Soviet Union also changed significantly. On the one hand, this was an unfavorable change. Pursuing his norm "national in form and socialist in content," Stalin succeeded, first of all, in eliminating or weakening those segments of the non-Russian nationalities that were nationally conscious, and particularly those elements which tried to perpetuate the identity of their people by looking for a synthesis between the national tradition and modernization. This applied specifically to the numerically weak but dedicated and dynamic portion of the intelligentsia which, during the permissive times of the N.E.P., worked and hoped for a national renaissance.

The point which Stalin reached after a prolonged fight against "bourgeois nationalism" was well perceived by Milovan Djilas during his visit to the second largest Soviet Republic, the Ukraine, in the spring of 1945. While referring to the beauty of Kiev and the strength, self-confidence, and humor of Nikita Khrushchev, whom he met, he conveyed the impression of the loss of personality, apathy, and hopelessness which the country left upon him.[4] Also, in his book *The New Class* he referred to this issue when he asked: "Who knows anything nowadays about Ukrainian writers and political figures? What has happened to that nation, which is the same size as France, and was once the most advanced nation in Russia? You would think that only an amorphous and formless mass of people could remain under this impersonal machine of oppression."[5] But he hastened to add that, keeping in mind the transformation of the national base and the spirit of time, such an artificial denationalization could not be successful in the long run:

> Just as personality, various social classes, and ideas still live, so do the nations still live, they function, they struggle against despotism, and they preserve their distinctive features undestroyed. If their conscience and souls are smothered, they are not broken. Though they are under subjugation, they are not yielded. The force activating them today is more than the old or bourgeois nationalism, it is an imperishable desire to be their own masters, and, by their own free development, to attain an increasingly fuller fellowship with the rest of the human race in its eternal existence.[6]

The ironic touch of Stalinization in the USSR was that many aspects of modernization which were practiced under the iron grip of Stalin represented in reality a double-edged weapon for the establishment. While uprooting people and inducing mass migration, particularly of the rural population during the period of a very rapid collectivization and industrialization following the first Five-Year Plan, the Soviet regime expected to establish a basis for its two apparent long-range objectives: to create a programmed man who would internalize the prescribed values and patterns of behavior, and to create an ethnically homogeneous Soviet society. Indirectly, mass education, the mass media, transfers of population, and purges were used to induce on the one hand the social engineering of the modern individual and, on the other hand, a uniformity of the multi-national Soviet society.

But many aspects of modernization also have created factors that were hardly anticipated by Stalin or his heirs. One of the by-products of mass education, mass communication, and an increased opportunity to complete higher education or to be involved in more sophisticated research was the emergence of an increasing number of critically minded, better informed, and more self-conscious individuals. While during the N.E.P. period the native intelligentsia of the various nationalities were numerically weak or, in the case of some Central Asian Soviet republics, hardly existent, this vacuum was filled by the new working intelligentsia, who constitute the most informed and conscious segment of the new Soviet society. They still represent largely a raw material for contervailing forces, but they are beginning to crystallize along the lines of the various Soviet nationalities.

Valentyn Moroz, who symbolizes the regeneration of the nationally conscious younger Ukrainian generation, refers to the broadening base of the intelligentsia that has resulted from modernization. In this connection he writes:

> The process of national reawakening has unlimited resources, for every man—even one thought to be spiritually dead—has within his soul a spark of national identity. We saw an example of this during the recent debates on the expulsion of Ivan Dzyuba from the Writers' Union, when votes against his expulsion were cast by those of whom this was not expected. . . .

The Ukrainian renaissance has yet to become a mass movement; however, do not deceive yourselves that it will remain that way forever. With universal literacy in Ukraine, 800,000 students, and a radio in every home, every socially significant movement becomes a mass movement. Is it possible you do not comprehend that soon you will be dealing with *mass social movements*? New processes are only beginning, and your repressive measures have long ceased to be effective. What of the future?[7]

The main purpose of this symposium is to trace the correlation between the objectives of Marxism-Leninism and the condition of national and human rights in the multi-national state of the USSR. Beginning with the historical background of the Revolution of 1917, and the objectives and methods of the Soviet leaders in building a modern political, social, and economic system, this symposium concentrates on the problems of modernization that have developed in the USSR since the death of Stalin. In addition to an evaluation of the nature of liberalization and of the nonconformist groups that emerged, this study hopes to provide some insights into the reasons for the partial freeze-up and the neo-Stalinist policies that developed under the Brezhnev-Kosygin leadership.

To provide a multi-dimensional insight into the issues involved, the articles have been arranged under three broad topics—the historical-theoretical background, the broader all-Union issues related to nationalities and human rights, and an evaluation of trends in the case of selected non-Russian nationalities and minorities.

It is hoped that this volume, as well as the planned second volume on the Eastern European states, will help strengthen awareness of the urgency of securing also in this part of the world the human rights and principles that are considered self-evident by all concerned. One can hardly overlook the fact that the two world wars started in Eastern Europe and that the political instability promoting their initiation was closely related to the question of national self-determination and the frustrations resulting from an absence of human rights. The recently disclosed Sonnenfeldt Doctrine reveals similar dangers for our time, even though the remedies suggested by those behind it are rather shortsighted.[8]

No permanent peace and social and economic stability seem to have a prospect of survival in our modern world, if they are pursued on a double standard basis, being exposed constantly to the contrasts between professed values and an intolerable reality. Such a duality is inconceivable in the long run, unless the existing international systems are to drift into a kind of global situation along the lines of a *Brave New World* or a *1984*. But humanity has advanced too far in terms of rational thinking and moral sensitivity to succumb to such solutions in the absence of an insurmountable crisis. After all, modernization is a product of human ingenuity and creativity; since it has brought into reality so many human dreams, it may well be able to reconcile the elements of human uniqueness with those of the brotherhood of man.

NOTES

[1] Milovan Djilas, *The New Class* (New York: F. A. Praeger, 1957), pp. 101, 102.

[2] Isaak Deutscher, *Ironies of History* (London: Oxford University Press, 1966), pp. 72-73.

[3] Nikita Khrushchev, *Khrushchev Remembers* (Boston: Little, Brown, and Co., 1970), pp. 26-27, 43, 47, 62-63.

[4] Milovan Djilas, *Gespräche mit Stalin* (Frankfurt a. Main: S. Fischer Verlag, 1962), p. 159.

[5] Djilas, *The New Class*, p. 102.

[6] *Ibid.*

[7] Valentyn Moroz, *Boomerang* (Baltimore: Smoloskyp, 1974), pp. 4-5.

[8] "Sonnenfeldt's Doctrine," Consult: *Herald Tribune* (March 22, 1976) and *New York Times* (April 6 and 7, 1976). "Sonnenfeldt's Doctrine," refers to the secret guidelines on American foreign policy in Eastern Europe stated by a high official of the State Department, Helmut Sonnenfeldt, during a conference of American ambassadors in London, December 1975. Mr. Sonnenfeldt, who is considered to be a mentor of State Secretary Henry Kissinger, insists that Eastern Europe represents an area of vital interest to the Soviet leaders, and that it is in the interest of the Soviet Union, as well as of the United States, to stabilize the Soviet control in this part of the world. According to his theory, the present lack of stabilization in Eastern Europe is due to the fact that Soviet control over other nations in this region depends exclusively on sheer force and an absence of mutual interests. This leads to an encouragement of Eastern Europeans to extricate themselves from the Soviet control, which, in turn, invites a Soviet intervention and potentially, an American involvement leading to World War III. By securing an "organic relationship" between the Eastern European nations and the Soviet leaders, the U.S.A. allegedly then would be in a position to avoid such a danger.

The essence of the problem is that this "organic relationship" is based upon a status of a formal inequality in relation to the Soviet Union—a principle that takes for granted the unaccountability of the Eastern European satellite governments and of the USSR to their own peoples. Yet, in the case of a modernizing society, such an omission of political and human rights seems to be the very factor causing instability.

PART I

MODERNIZATION AND DEMOCRATIZATION IN HISTORICAL PERSPECTIVE

MARXISM-LENINISM AND GERMAN CONSERVATIVE REVOLUTIONARY THOUGHT

Ihor Kamenetsky
Central Michigan University
Mount Pleasant, Michigan

The differences between Marxism-Leninism and German Conservative Revolutionary thought at first glance may seem too great for a meaningful comparison. However, their roots, their anti-establishment approaches, and some of their utopian schemes for the future bring them close enough together in certain points to permit us to draw some parallels.

Both ideologies trace their origins to the second half of the nineteenth century. They emerged as an aftermath of the failure of a democratic effort to establish a popular government, following on the one hand the convocation of the all-German constituent assembly in 1848, and on the other the futile attempt of the Narodnik movement in Russia to build up popular pressures forcing the Tsar to introduce a constitutional type of government. Both ideologies claimed to stand for safeguarding the interests of the working masses in the future society which they proposed to create, and they both expressed opposition to the selfish vested interests of the privileged groups living at the expense of the people. Further, even though for the most part the German Conservative Revolutionaries had a diametrically opposite view of the merits of industrialization, they were equally vehement in the condemnation of economic liberalism, commercial mentality, and democratic parliamentarism.

One of the closest parallels between the German Conservative Revolutionaries and the Marxist-Leninists may be found in their attachment to the mythical and messianic role of a particular class as a redeemer of society. In Germany, the opponents of the Conservative Revolutionary thought, Paul de Lagarde and Julius Langbehn, saw the salvation of the Germans and some other Germanic peoples in the strengthening of the peasant class and their value system, their customs and mores.[1] In Russia, Vladimir Illich Lenin saw the cure of Russian society, and of mankind in general, in the attainment of the dictatorship of the proletariat.[2] These two ideologies emerged in societies beset by ferments and tensions that were rooted in not entirely dissimilar causes. Both countries found themselves under an increasing impact of Western ideas and processes, which revealed the absolute character of their political structure and, in case of Russia, also of her economic and technological backwardness. However, there were also some serious reservations among the enlightened sections of Russian and German society concerning the wholehearted acceptance of Western ideas, either because of traditionalist values which they cherished, or because of objective circumstances in which their countries found themselves.

Insofar as the Germans were concerned, their national aspirations, awakened since the beginning of the nineteenth century, were not fulfilled upon the creation of the Second German Empire in 1871. Nor did the Germans feel that they had found their rightful spot under the sun.[3] The fact that the national unification was brought from above, by a compromise of the various German dynasties and the nobility, which for a prolonged time had opposed the unification, was reason in itself to doubt its genuine character. The nobility's insistence on the perpetuation of their many privileges only accentuated such doubts. While the old divisive class antagonism and prejudice persisted, new social tensions were added by what was thought to be an opportunistic deal of Bismarck, with the growth of modern business and industry in Germany. This growth was responsible for a rapidly increasing and unrestful urban proletariat, which undermined the income and security of the lower middle class and caused a mass migration of the German peasants to the industrial city. In some regions of Germany this led to a virtual land desertion (*Landflucht*).[4] As life was becoming more and more interdependent, the domination by Prussianized bureaucracy was experienced as more stifling in the various parts of unified Germany; many patriotic Germans began to consider this bureaucracy as a "long arm" of the various vested interests, which paralyzed national dynamics and creativity instead of providing a link for closer unity.[5]

In Germany, the extensive economic, social, and political reforms also were not entirely acceptable to many national-minded Germans, because such concepts as individual freedom, equality, free and competitive enterprise by themselves, separated from the interests of the national community, found little understanding among them; they were associated with selfishness, rivalry, and potential disorders, of which Germany had had more than enough in her historical past. The principle of equality added another complication within the framework of German modern nationalism. To a much greater degree than Western nationalism, German modern nationalism was ethnically oriented, rather than politically. Even before the unification, the ethnic Germans frequently enjoyed a dominant position not only in the German states with a mixed population (like Prussia and Austria), but also in some non-German states (for example, in the Baltic provinces of Tsarist Russia). Thus, an equal status of non-German ethnic groups often was considered as detrimental to German national, social, or economic interests. Besides, many issues championed by Western liberalism were viewed by the Germans as the products of the bourgeois class—a class which, because of its alleged philistine and opportunistic ways of life and its limited political role, did not enjoy much prestige or power.

The vacuum of reliable social forces in Germany is well described by Max Weber in one of his speeches in 1895, in which he refers to the dominant German aristocracy as an economically declining class, to the middle class as immature, ethically wavering and waiting for a strong man, and to the proletariat as lacking statesmanlike qualities.[6]

Many of these circumstances and sentiments are applicable at the same period of time to Tsarist Russia. The position of the Russian middle class was even weaker and more compromised, and the aversion of the Russian intelligentsia to the Western bourgeois mentality was even stronger. Alexander Herzen, whose Narodnik conception of revolution Lenin rejected, but whose moral condemnation of Western bourgeois mentality he shared, stated eloquently the reservations of the Russian intelligentsia toward the West:

> What have we to do with your sacred duties, we younger brothers robbed of our heritage? And can we be honestly contented with your threadbare morality, unchristian and inhuman, existing only in rhetorical exercises and speeches for the prosecution? What respect can be inspired in us by your Roman-barbaric system of law, that hollow clumsy edifice, without light and air, repaired in the Middle Ages, whitewashed by the newly enfranchised petty bourgeois? I admit that the daily brigandage in the Russian lawcourts is even worse, but it does not follow from that that you have justice in your laws or your courts . . . Russia will never make a revolution with the object of getting rid of Tsar Nicholas, and replacing him by other Tsars—parliamentary representatives, judges, and police officials. We perhaps ask for too much and shall get nothing. That may be so, but yet we do not despair . . . [7]

Russia also was afflicted, to an even greater degree than Germany, by a social and national split of its society. First, there was the chasm between the Russian upper and middle class on one side and the lower classes on the other. Secondly, there was the fact that Russia was a multi-national empire in which the non-Russians represented about 55 percent of the population; many of these non-Russians started to become nationally conscious and increasingly unrestful under the impact of Western ideas. These conditions made both the Tsarist repressive measures and a complete liberalization of the system appear equally dangerous to many circles of the Russian intelligentsia which, in spite of their aversion to Tsarist despotism, were strongly inclined to preserve the imperial unity, and which believed that the Russians had a leading role to play in a future society that would transcend the confines of the Russian nation. In the decades preceding World War I, when the physical growth of the German and of the Russian Empire coincided with the lack of internal cohesion and the loss of a sense of purpose, the Conservative Revolution in Germany and the Marxist-Leninists in Russia presented an integrated program for the future that would create a feeling of community within society and would secure some qualified measure of freedom, justice, and participation of the masses, in order to assure some basic security for their nations in confrontation with the challenging modern world. The plans and promises of both were such that they might be accomplished within the framework of certain traditional values.

De Lagarde and Langbehn tried to accomplish these objectives by building up a strong image of the peasant way of life, utilizing the fact that the peasant, from the very beginning of modern German nationalism, had been regarded as the most pure and healthy substance of the German nation.[8] They believed that, economically, a widely extended employment of the population in agriculture would be the best way to avoid a dependence on foreign trade and to create an invulnerability to depression. Also, they thought that the availability of land for every citizen would enable Germany to solve the social problems of the unemployed, the handicapped, and the retired soldiers, as well as the problem of an emigration overseas,[9] hoping by these measures to bring about a society that would assure a certain economic independence to each German citizen. It was their belief that providing each "Germanic man" with his own piece of land, regardless of his occupation, would establish a common bond through their closeness to nature.[10]

Lenin originally attributed the mission of establishing a harmonious society to the urban proletariat. However, considering the peculiarly Russian circumstances (in which the industrial proletariat was numerically insignificant, whereas the peasant element was overwhelmingly in the majority), he made some adjustments by including a certain portion of the peasantry as junior partners of the industrial proletariat.[11] Even though Lenin did not particularly care if the work accomplished was connected with the soil or with the factory, he did believe that the right to work should be safeguarded, and that the independence of the common man from the crushing burden of economic insecurity would be an absolute prerequisite for a harmonious society. He also stressed the concepts of the classless society and of the gradual elimination of differences between manual and non-manual work.

These ideas of Lenin were borrowed, of course, from Marx, in the same way that his idea of counting primarily on workers rather than on peasants in revolutionary processes was borrowed from Plekhanov's Russian Social-Democratic Party, which he wholeheartedly supported at the beginning of his career. The Russian Social-Democrats were turning the attention of many members of the Russian intelligentsia to the fact that since the last decades of the nineteenth century Tsarist Russia had been involved in an accelerated process of industrialization with a rising proletariat, arguing that, from the Marxist point of view, this industrialization would make a revolutionary change inevitable. After the failure of the Narodnik movement around 1880, and in view of the rather conservative attitude of the peasant masses toward the revolutionary activities of the Russian intelligentsia, the idea of the inevitability of a revolution, through the apparent and irresistible economic changes and the emergence of a new revolutionary class of an urban proletariat, seemed convincing enough to many disheartened Russian revolutionaries.[12] Yet the expectations of these "orthodox Marxists" also had some considerable flaws. First of all, such expectations would postpone the actual revolution indefinitely, since the revolutionaries would have no control over the pace of industrialization, nor would they have an idea when it might reach the point of making the socialist take-over justifiable. Secondly, it included as its prerequisite the education of the proletariat, to make it aware of its revolutionary mission, which was a difficult task to accomplish within the realities of the Tsarist regime. The third proposition was actually the most difficult one to accept for the Russian revolutionary intelligentsia, as it referred to Marx's theory that the completion of the industrialization and proletarization processes would have to take place under a bourgeois system, and that Russia, standing on the threshold of industrialization, would have to submit voluntarily to Western commercialism, exploitation of the masses, and other inhumanities of the capitalist system. Lenin's original contribution to Marxism, which to a great degree matched the peculiar Russian circumstances and the mood of the Russian intelligentsia, may be summarized in three main points:

1. He rejected the notion that any extensive period of a bourgeois-democratic system would be indispensable on the way towards a proletarian revolution, maintaining that Russia was ready for a revolution because it presented the weakest link in the already mature world-wide capitalist system.
2. He assumed that the masses before the revolution only needed to be revolutionized, and not re-educated.
3. He made the provision that a re-education of the masses should be postponed until after a successful revolution had taken place, and that it should be initiated and supervised by an elitarian party of professional revolutionaries.

The Marxist-Leninists, while differing from the German Conservative Revolutionaries in assigning a special role in the future changing society to the urban proletariat rather than to the peasants, came close to them in the following points: A. Their rejection of some essential Western democratic values and methods. B. Their concept of re-educating the masses and expecting them to participate in public affairs. C. Their concept of an ultimate authority (political and moral) in the society of the future.

Both ideologies, while attacking as hypocrisies the Western democratic principles stating that every citizen is equal before the law and that every nation is equal before international law, provided their own alternatives in their schemes of transition towards a more harmonious future society.

In the Conservative Revolutionary conception, ethnic or racial homogeneity was the prerequisite for acceptance in their anticipated new society. De Lagarde and Langbehn did not consider it essential to give equal protection of rights and welfare to German citizens of Polish, Jewish, or Cashub origin, for example, unless they were fully assimilated—a possibility which was more and more doubted as the Conservative Revolutionary ideology evolved. In case of the Marxist-Leninists, this unequal treatment applied, of course, to the hostile classes who, according to Lenin, could not be integrated with the working classes. This referred, for instance, to the aristocracy, the big land-owners, and the kulaks, to whom the full harshness of the dictatorship of the proletariat was to be applied during and after the revolution. The acceptance of unequal treatment on the basis of nationality or social origin did not imply primarily an economic exploitation; rather, it was aimed at the destruction of certain groups, or their removal, in one or another way, from the framework of the anticipated future society. This line of thought was typical of both ideologies.

A somewhat similar attitude was also applied in their concept of international relations on an inter-state basis. In principle, the Conservative Revolutionaries and the Marxist-Leninists conceded to each nation the right of national self-determination, but then followed various qualifications that would make such a right highly questionable. De Lagarde stated, for instance:

> Because we Germans raise a claim to be permitted to exist as a
> nation, we cannot deny the right to the Poles to raise the same
> claim . . . We will draw boundaries for Poland which will suit us; we
> are going to push over to their territory the Palestinians [Jews], which
> will have a deadening effect on each not yet mature nation; also in the

> East of Poland we will establish a German province and see to it that
> the Poles are Germanized in the end.[14]

Lenin's statement on behalf of this right was equally ambiguous:

> The right of nations for self-determination means only the
> right to independence in a political sense, the right to free,
> political secession from the oppressing nation. Concretely, this
> political, democratic demand implies complete freedom to carry
> on agitation in favor of secession, and freedom to settle the ques-
> tion of secession by means of a referendum of the nation that
> desires to secede. Consequently, this demand is by no means
> identical with the demand for secession, for partition, for the
> formation of small states.[15]

De Lagarde and Langbehn talked about the necessity of German territorial expansion
in order to assure German self-sufficiency in food and to provide an opportunity
for every German citizen to own a piece of land. This applied to the non-German
nationalities of the Austro-Hungarian Empire and to some nationalities inhabiting
the Western provinces of Tsarist Russia.[16] Insofar as these conquered nationalities
were concerned, according to de Lagarde they would be permitted a marginal
existence only. They were supposed to be made aware of the German superiority,
of the German right to rule, but he assumed that their assimilation into the
Germandom would eventually eliminate the problem of inequality. Lenin, who
believed in the emancipation of all nations from foreign oppression, stated his
qualifications of the principle of national self-determination still before the October
Revolution by advocating the view of the integration of the smaller nations into the
larger regional nations (of course, on a voluntary basis). When the disintegration of
the Tsarist Empire generated a much stronger drive for independence also among
the smaller nations under the Russian rule, Lenin modified his theory in order to
adjust to the realities of the political situation. While the Provisionary Government
lasted in Russia, he stressed the universal right for secession, dropping in this connection the distinction between the status of larger nations and smaller nations:

> ... We say to the Russian people: Don't rape Finland; no nation can
> be free if it oppresses other nations. In our resolution concerning
> Borgbjerg, we state: withdraw your armies and let the nation settle
> this question itself. But if the Soviet seizes power tomorrow, it
> will no longer be a "method of socialist revolution". We shall then
> say: Germany, withdraw your armies from Poland; Russia, withdraw
> your armies from Armenia—otherwise, the whole thing will be a
> deception.[17]

Lenin's assumption was, however, that both the smaller and the larger nations
would abstain from secession if the Soviet system would replace the bourgeois
system:

> ... We are for the fraternal union of all nations. If there is a
> Ukrainian republic and a Russian republic, there will be closer

contact, greater confidence between the two. If the Ukrainians see that we have a Soviet republic, they will not break away. But if we retain the Milyukov republic, they will break away.[18]

When the seizure of power by the Bolsheviks did not produce the effect that Lenin had expected, and when a voluntary reunion of the non-Russian republics was not taking place, he did not hesitate to use force in order to reconquer them, whenever he could do so within the limits of his power.[19]

De Lagarde assumed that most of the nations in Central and Eastern Europe would be more or less voluntarily and peacefully arraigned under the leadership of Germany in a federated Middle European state. This he thought indispensable to assure peace and stability in Europe to safeguard Germany's security. When around World War I his dream evolved far enough, in form of a Middle European Customs Union in Germany, to be given a practical trial, the German government found that considerable arm-twisting and sheer force had to be used to prepare the prospective candidates for the acceptance of this scheme. The resistance was understandable. It occurred mainly because the would-be partners, being much weaker than Germany, did not think that German preponderance of power was matched reliably by legal or moral norms to make such a common venture safe for them.[20]

The same may be said about Hitler's concept of the "New Europe," which represented the development of the Conservative Revolutionary idea on a much larger scale, following up all of its possible implications. In general, it may be observed that both the Conservative Revolutionary and the Marxist-Leninist thoughts suggested a concept of larger international complexes in which the nature of the relations and the common interests of the nations involved were actually defined and determined by the strongest nation in a paternalistic way.

Equally strong and very similar in the essence of their criticisms were Lenin's and de Lagarde's attacks on Western parliamentarism and the party system. Both rejected the notion that the parliaments through the elected party representatives actually reflected the views and the interests of the people, or that the people had a chance to participate through them meaningfully in political life. De Lagarde wrote in this connection: "The Government Party consists in contemporary Germany of persons who have to be addressed by their hereditary titles: and this Party assumedly represents the German people! The people, who ought to be the sole concern of the government . . . remain completely outside."[21] He went even further in describing the oligarchical nature of the German government parties,[22] and he also stressed that the representatives elected by a direct vote based on universal suffrage would still represent the vested interests rather than the welfare of the nation, particularly while voting on taxation.[23] And Lenin commented:

The modern wage-slaves, owing to the conditions of capitalist exploitation, are so much crushed by want and poverty that "democracy is nothing to them;" that in the ordinary peaceful course of events, the majority of the population is debarred from participating in social and political life.

The correctness of this statement is perhaps most clearly proven by Germany, just because in this state constitutional legality lasted and remained stable for a remarkably long time—for nearly half a century (1871-1914)—and because Social-Democracy in Germany during that time was able to achieve far more than in other countries in "utilising legality," and was able to organise into a political party a larger proportion of the working class than anywhere else in the world.

What, then, is this largest proportion of politically conscious and active wage-slaves that has so far been observed in capitalist society? One million members of the Social-Democratic Party—out of fifteen million wage-workers! Three million organized in trade unions—out of fifteen million!

Democracy for an insignificant minority, democracy for the rich—that is the democracy of capitalist society.[24]

What remedies did the Conservative Revolutionaries and the Marxist-Leninists offer for safeguarding the interests of the people? Both tried to reduce the significance of the state apparatus, particularly of bureaucracy. Lenin, in classical Marxist fashion, stressed that the state, with the perfection of the socialist society, would gradually fade away completely, and he already took some short-range measures in this direction. He suggested that even the highest official in government should not be paid more than the average factory worker. In this way, he expected to keep the opportunistic elements away, and he hoped to prevent the building of some vested interests in the government. He also expected that even a cook might be capable of being involved in the higher levels of governmental administration, due to a simplification of the accounting procedure. The government, of course, should be under very close supervision, and thus Lenin created the position of a Rabkrin (Commissariat of the Workers' and Peasants' Inspectorate) to check on the performance of government, and of political commissars to supervise the armed forces.[25] Also De Lagarde spoke about a confinement of the role of the state to the tasks absolutely necessary,[26] and his views coincided with Lenin's in that the state should be very closely supervised.[27] However, as to the actual supervision of the government, as well as the final authority on the most important public matters, neither the Conservative Revolutionaries nor the Marxist-Leninists placed them in the hands of the elected representatives of the people. De Lagarde and Langbehn saw the embodiment of the final authority and supervision in a somewhat mystical emperor who would emerge as a natural leader in a free nation, and who would be above the parties and the vested interests, embodying the will and the interests of the nation and enjoying its absolute trust. De Lagarde supplemented his leadership concept by the idea of the creation of an unselfish, ethically motivated, intellectually superior, and economically independent class that would voluntarily render its services for the welfare of the people, and that would be perpetually renewed from the wide ranks of the nation.[28]

Both ideas, that of an infallible leadership on behalf of the people and that of a unique dedicated elite, find their reflection in the concept of the Communist Party as conceived by Lenin. This kind of leadership, combined with a secure economic base for society as a whole, represented a precondition for the re-education and meaningful participation of the people in public affairs. The inherent implication in both concepts was that the talents in the society should be promoted, without consideration of the social background or the financial limitations of an individual—unless, of course, the members of the hostile classes or respectively of undesirable nationalities were involved.[29]

There is also a peculiar similarity in both ideologies with respect to making the educational process relevant to life. This implied the establishment of an organic relationship between the educational system and the needs of the society. Fritz H. Hippler, a Nazi writer who traced the links between the ideas of de Lagarde and the ideology of National Socialism, commented in this connection as follows:

> It is de Lagarde's contribution to education that in his time when a feudal-bourgeois-capitalistic monopoly in education prevailed, he created an awareness of the importance of character building of man, and of his spiritual links with the factors and events of everyday life.

Side by side, Hippler quoted the words of Hitler:

> When the political leadership of a nation overlooks her own related talents among the people, then it must carry the responsibility when the natural talent provides its own sphere of activity, even if only as in the case of Spartacus, for example, to organize an uprising among the slaves.[30]

The criticism of Western liberalism for its misguided educational policy also finds its parallels in the criticism voiced by the Marxist-Leninists:

> Due to the elimination of capitalistic competition, with the jungle laws in our society and the establishment of socialistic industrial relations on the basis of friendship and mutual help, we witnessed the development of talents from among the untapped resources of popular power which capitalism had subdued and oppressed by thousands and millions.[31]

However, the tapping of talents hidden among the popular masses was not supposed to mean an equality of men before the law, or even an equality of opportunity, when it did not coincide with the main principles of the respective ideologies. Taking the Conservative Revolutionary thought as it crystallized in the Third Reich, we may quote Nazi Reichspressechef Dr. O. Dietrich in this connection:

> . . . freedom for creation in the sense of national socialism is readily available in our society and nobody has to press for it. If there is still somebody who calls for freedom, then it must come from the people determined to act in such a way that is not consistent with the interests of our national community but which is opposed to them.
>
> What such people demand is not freedom for a creative cooperation but a work of destruction.

And further:

> There is no freedom of the individual in itself; there is only
> freedom of peoples, nations, and races. . . in freedom of which the
> individuals take part and live, being the members of these units . . .
> The system of Liberalism created an individualistic society—the
> class, which is the element of destruction for this society.
> By contrast, the National-Socialist community creates person-
> ality, a personality which has nothing to do with the arbitrariness,
> selfishness, but which exists for the sake of community and com-
> munity service.[32]

The successors of Lenin developed the concept of freedom along similar lines.
Thus, the Soviet ideologist T. Ivanov wrote:

> Under socialism freedom of society means at the same time
> freedom of each member of the society. In the U.S.S.R., man whose
> activity does not interfere with the interests of the Soviet society,
> is actually free and has all opportunities for development of his
> own individuality. Of course, the socialist community does not
> permit the growth of bourgeois individualism which is directed
> against the interests of the majority of members of the socialist
> community. A person is free not by acting as a counterpoise toward
> a collective of toilers but only then when he toils and struggles with
> them together for the fulfillment of common goals.[33]

The Conservative Revolutionaries and the Marxist-Leninists did not limit
themselves to the creation of the concept of a society-oriented elite. They also
aimed at the participation of the masses in public affairs, partially to counteract
the paralyzing effect of modern bureaucracy, which they viewed as a typical
millstone around the neck of bourgeois liberalism, and partially to create a community spirit which, as they claimed, was a thing of impossibility in an individualis-
tic liberal society dominated by class struggle. A spontaneous, natural, and direct
participation of the masses in public affairs was, of course, out of question. De
Lagarde proposed to revive the estates which were supposed to replace the selfish
and divisive classes. In his estate, an individual was expected to find a range of
activities in economic, social, and political terms that would help him to acquire a
sense of belonging.[34] Besides, the estates were supposed to represent the organic
parts of the national community, and thus to coexist in a reasonable harmony and
with mutual respect. They would have to fulfill many functions performed by the
state apparatus and bureaucracy, and also, they would have an advisory capacity
in relation to the emperor and to the natural elite (natural aristocracy), which
would then make the vital decisions on behalf of the nation.

Marxism-Leninism, of course, would not turn back to the revival of the
medieval estates, but in another form it came close to the idea of mass participation. Lenin first believed that the Soviets would be the most proper channels of the
popular participation, but already in 1919 he started to encounter some difficulties
in connection with this approach. He said:

We can fight bureaucracy to the bitter end, to a complete victory, only when the whole population participates in the work of government. In the bourgeois republics not only was this impossible, *but the very law prevented it*. The best of the bourgeois republics, no matter how democratic they may be, have thousands of legislative hindrances which prevent the toilers from participating in the work of government. We have removed these hindrances, but so far we have not managed to get the toiling masses to participate in the work of government. Apart from the law, there is still the level of culture, which you cannot subject to any law. The result of this low cultural level is that the Soviets, which, by virtue of their program, are organs of government *by the toilers*, are in fact organs of government *for the toilers* by means of the advanced stratum of the proletariat, but not by means of the toiling masses.

Here we are confronted by a problem which cannot be solved except by prolonged education.[35]

The main channels of participation of the masses actually became the labor and trade unions, in which membership for each working citizen was compulsory. They provided the basis for political meetings, political declarations, and resolutions, and for nominating candidates for the various levels of the elective government positions, and they resembled de Lagarde's idea concerning the role of the estates.

We may recall that the new Draft Program of the CPSU adopted by the 22nd Party Congress in 1961 formally referred to a gradual transfer of responsibilities from the state to the mass organizations.[36] In these new arrangements a special role was assigned to the trade unions: "The role of social organizations increases in the period of the full-scale construction of communism. The trade unions acquire particular importance as schools of administration and economic management, as schools of communism."[37] This experiment, it is true, remained largely on paper, but nevertheless, it represented at least a theoretical attempt to revive some of the original concepts of Leninism concerning the interrelationship between the withdrawal of the state and a more active mass participation in administering public affairs.

Conceding some vast ideological differences which do exist between the German Conservative Revolutionaries and the Marxist-Leninists, we may summarize the similarities which they reveal as follows:

1. Before they seriously clashed with each other after having ignored each other for a long time, their main targets were the remnants of an ossified feudalism and particularly the growing liberalism.
2. The disintegrating effect of liberalism was mainly attacked for alienating the individual, and for failing to provide a genuine community interest on the economic, social, and political level.
3. Both ideologies were mass oriented, insofar as they aimed at the regeneration of the whole society, at long-range planning to safeguard economic security, and at a manipulated participation of the people in public affairs.

4.   They were concerned with the preventive measures taken against ethnic, social, or racial groups regarded as foreign bodies in the pre-planned society, and efforts were made to assimilate them or to remove them as groups.

5.   In both cases it was expected that the people representing the raw materials for the pre-planned society would internalize the patterns of the expected behavior through a controlled education and through conditioning processes.

6.   Both ideologies relied upon the concept of an infallible benevolent leadership which would act according to conscious and subconscious desires and interests of the people as they were determined by the leaders.

In the process of their criticism of liberalism, especially of the capitalistic system and some of the shortcomings of the parliamentarian systems, many valid exposures were added by both the German Conservative Revolutionaries and the Marxist-Leninists. However, in seeking alternatives to safeguard the interests of the common people, they both created two particular concepts which, taking everything into consideration, became greater liabilities in internal and external politics of a modern state than the evils of liberalism which they were supposed to overcome. One of these was the acceptance of the principle of inevitability of conflict along the lines of ethnic or social origin. This concept fostered a build-up of a machinery of terror for internal use, and a formidable military establishment for an anticipated encounter with other states, which made precarious the existence not only of those who were born on the wrong side of the ideological fence, but also of those who were regarded worthy to become members of a new and better society.

Another unfortunate concept was that of infallibility and unaccountability of leadership, which became particularly hazardous in the confines of a modern state apparatus. The concept of an undisputable and indefinite guardianship of the people made a meaningful participation of the masses questionable from the very beginning. The criticism which Rosa Luxemburg voiced in connection with Lenin's handling of the masses shortly after the October Revolution is relevant to both ideologies:

> To be sure, every democratic institution has its limits and shortcomings, things which it doubtless shares with all other human institutions. But the remedy which Lenin and Trotsky have found, the elimination of democracy as such, is worse than the disease it is supposed to cure; for it stops up the living source from which alone can come the correction of all the innate shortcomings of social institutions. That source is the active, untrammeled, energetic political life of the broadest masses of the people.[38]

NOTES

[1] See: Paul de Lagarde, *Schriften für Deutschland* (Leipzig, 1933). Also: Julius Langbehn, *Rembrandt als Erzieher* (Weimar, 1922), and Fritz Stern, *The Politics of Cultural Despair: A Study in the Rise of the Germanic Ideology* (Berkeley, 1961).

[2] Nicolas Berdyaev, *The Origin of Russian Communism* (Ann Arbor, 1960).

[3] Fritz Fischer, *Griff nach der Weltmacht; Die Kriegszielpolitik des Kaiserlichen Deutschland 1914/18* (Düsseldorf, 1961), pp. 15-55.

[4] Graf Baudissin-Berlin, "Innere Kolonisation. Grundsätzliches und Praktisches," in Wilhelm Volz, ed., *Der Deutsche Volksboden: Aufsätze zu den Fragen des Ostens* (Breslau, 1922), p. 375, and Gustav Aubin, "Die historische Entwicklung der ostdeutschen Agrarverfassung und ihre Beziehung zum Nationalitätenproblem der Gegenwart," *ibid.*, p. 363.

[5] de Lagarde, pp. 142-43. See also: Arnim Mohler, *Die Konservative Revolution in Deutschland; Grundriss ihrer Weltanschauung* (Stuttgart, 1950), and Stern, *op. cit.*

[6] Max Weber, *Gesammelte Politische Schriften* (München, 1921), pp. 24ff., cited in Stern, pp. xxviii-xxix.

[7] Alexander Herzen, "The Russian People and Socialism," excerpts from a letter to J. Michelet, the French historian. From A. Herzen, *My Past and Thoughts*, cited in Robert A. Goldwin, *et al.*, eds., *Readings in Russian Foreign Policy* (New York, 1959), pp. 58-59.

[8] de Lagarde, p. 80; Langbehn, p. 118.

[9] de Lagarde, pp. 79-80.

[10] *Ibid.*

[11] V. I. Lenin, *Selected Works* III (Moscow, 1943), p. 285.

[12] Berdyaev, pp. 101-102.

[13] de Lagarde, p. 79.

[14] de Lagarde, "Die nächsten Pflichten deutscher Politik," *Schriften für das deutsche Volk*, in *Deutsche Schriften* I (München, Berlin, 1940), p. 468.

[15] Lenin, "The Socialist Revolution and the Right of Nations to Self-Determination" (January/February, 1916), cited in Stefan T. Possony, ed., *Lenin Reader* (Chicago, 1966), p. 248.

[16] de Lagarde (1933 ed.), pp. 82-83. All of the following references to de Lagarde's *Schriften* will be made to this edition, unless otherwise stated.

[17] Lenin, "Speech on the National Question," (May 12, 1917), Possony, p. 254.

[18] *Ibid.*, pp. 254-55.

[19] Jan Librach, *The Rise of the Soviet Empire; A Study of Soviet Foreign Policy* (New York/Washington, 1964), pp. 138-45.

[20] Fischer, pp. 103-104, 202-211, 519-39. See also: J. Rajewski, *Mitteleuropa. Studia z dziejów imperializmu niemieckiego v dobie pierwszej wojny swiatowej* (Study of German Imperialism in the Era of World War I) (Poznań, 1959).

[21] de Lagarde, pp. 142-43.

[22] *Ibid.*, p. 137.

[23] de Lagarde (München, 1940), p. 469.

[24] Lenin, *State and Revolution* (New York, 1943), p. 72.

[25] Isaac Deutscher, *Stalin: A Political Biography* (New York, 1949). Cited in Samuel Hendel, ed., *The Soviet Crucible. The Soviet System in Theory and Practice* (Princeton, 1967), 3rd ed.

[26] de Lagarde, pp. 136-37, 144.

[27] *Ibid.*, p. 90.

[28] *Ibid.*, pp. 142-43.

[29] *Ibid.*, p. 82 and p. 144. Also: Lenin, *State and Revolution*, pp. 54-62.

[30] Fritz H. Hippler, *Staat und Gesellschaft bei Mill, Marx, Lagarde* (Berlin, 1934), p. 234.

[31] T. Ivanov, "Freedom and Necessity in Conditions of Socialist Society," *Communist of Ukraine* (Kiev, October, 1959), p. 67.

[32] Reichspressechef Dr. O. Dietrich, "Revolution des Denkens," *Freude und Arbeit* (Berlin, 1934), p. 234. Monthly, No. 4.

[33] Ivanov, pp. 67-68.

[34] Hippler, p. 167.

[35] Lenin, "On the Party Program" (March, 1919), Possony, p. 188.

[36] Herbert Ritvo, *The New Soviet Society; Final Text of the Program of the Communist Party of the Soviet Union* (New York, 1962), p. 170.

[37] *Ibid.*, p. 178.

[38] Rosa Luxemburg, cited in Sidney Hood, ed., *Marx and the Marxists* (Princeton, 1955), p. 104.

THE QUESTION OF POLITICAL DEVELOPMENT AND NATIONALITIES ISSUES IN RUSSIAN AND EAST EUROPEAN POLITICAL THEORIES

Jurij Borys
University of Calgary
Calgary, Alberta, Canada

POLITICAL DEVELOPMENT AND NATIONALISM

The history of mankind has demonstrated a continuous process of development from primitive, simple relationships to more complex, intricate ones. Development can be described as a process by which the organisms and systems achieve a higher level of control and rationality, complexity and integration. Modernization is defined as a level of economic development or as man's ability to control and exploit his physical and social environment. In this sense modernization demonstrates innumerable variations and nuances; the per capita GNP as a kind of fixed criterion for economic development is both new and illusory. The same could be said about the level of industrialization as an equation of economic development—for example, Denmark seems to be economically among the top nations, whereas its industrial output is insignificant. Thus, it seems that modernization, in an economic sense, implies the adaptation of modern industrial technology and its maximum utilization for the exploitation of natural and human resources.

Political modernization is seen as a condition for industrial modernization. Since economic modernization always takes place within a social context, social mobilization becomes the necessary prerequisite for modernization. A certain amount of *élan*, Weberian "Protestant ethic," "nationalism," or simply "achievement orientation" are among the human determinants of industrialization. The preponderance of the variables is determined by the developmental circumstances. In Western Europe the "Protestant ethic" provided a set of values uniquely suitable to modernization. In other societies, nationalism has been an important motivating force in the transition from traditional to modern industrial society. In Russia, it was a series of military defeats (Crimean War, the Russo-Japanese War, and First World War) that evoked nationalist feelings and a psychological disposition for modernization. Communist China is another case where national humiliation was used to mobilize popular support in the drive for rapid modernization. As

Gunnar Myrdal implies, the lack of "modernization ideals" may be considered as a disfunctional variable in the development of south-eastern Asia. National coherence or national integration is in many cases a pre-condition both for the preservation of the state and for its capability to mobilize the population for modernization.

It has been vaguely assumed that societal modernization, social mobility, a high degree of specialization of roles, urbanization, secularization, and high degree of literacy were preceded by a modernizational ethic among the elites. Political modernization is much more ambiguous and implicitly normative and often even ethnocentric. The "modern" political system has been equated with Western liberal democracy, in which the emphasis is placed on secularization and achievement criteria in political recruitment and role differentiation, group interest articulation by competing voluntary organizations, and the interest aggregation by at least two political parties in a competitive struggle for people's votes. The level of political development can be measured by the degree of role differentiation, subsystem autonomy, and secularization.

Political modernization and nationalism have been approached as two different problems by most students of political systems. Usually the former is treated as something to be desired, the positive, whereas the latter is viewed nearly as the negation of modernization, if not its antipode. Yet there are signs indicating an interrelationship between the two. Some writers consider at least the formative stage of nationalism (e.g., its contribution to the process of integration and nation-building) as almost a necessary pre-condition of political modernization.[1] Samuel Huntington, for example, emphasizes the importance of societal integration by starting one of his innumerable contributions to the discussion with the quotation from de Tocqueville: "If men are to remain civilized or to become so, 'the art of associating together' must grow and improve in the same ratio in which the equality of conditions is increased."[2] "The art of associating together" should not be confused with the degree of political participation which in some political systems turns out to be nothing more than *mobilization* of citizens into "regiments" set up by the system for the fulfillment of certain roles; thus the description of the Soviet political system as an "administered society,"[3] an "organizational society,"[4] or as in its most rigid form, the "totalitarian system."[5]

The concepts of political modernization are numerous. In a sense they all emphasize its dynamic, changing condition. The Western models or paradigms of political modernization usually center around three sets of categories: rationalization, integration and democratization. The first one, based primarily on Talcott Parson's pattern variables, involves development or change from particularism to universalism, from diffuseness to specificity, from ascription to achievement, and from affectivity to affective neutrality.[6] The second set of characteristics involves nationalism and national integration. "Nation-building" is regarded as a basic aspect of political development or perhaps its very beginning. A lack or weak sense of national identity may negatively influence the process of political modernization, especially its third variant, generally expressed as *democratization*, which, among other things, means the competitive struggle for the people's vote. A new dimension to the process of political development has been presented by Huntington, which he conceptualizes as *"institution-building."* This concept, according to Huntington, "liberates development from modernization" with its underlying commitment to the theory of progress, which does not account for a reversible political process, such as instability, authoritarianism, domestic violence, institutional decline, national disintegration—all of which occur in the real world of politics. The "institution-building" concept can be applied to the analysis of political systems of any sort, not just modern ones. "Institutionalization is the process by which organizations and procedures acquire value and stability. The level of institutionalization of any political system can be defined by the adaptability, complexity, autonomy and coherence."[7] This implies that those political systems (such as the United States and the Soviet Union) which have high levels of both mobilization and institutionalization are modern, developed, civic polities; primitive polities have low levels of both.[8] On the other hand, there are instances when a country may still be very backward in terms of modernization but may be politically highly developed. Thus India's stable, effective, and democratic government during the first fifteen years of independence rested on its two organizations: The Congress Party and the Indian Civil Service. Lucian Pye, among others, also stresses the importance of organizations. "The ultimate test of development is the capacity of people to establish and maintain large, complex, but flexible organizational forms."[9]

The stress on organization and institutionalization of the political system leads some writers, perhaps, to a slight overestimation of the strictly "organizational" systems of which the Soviet is becoming a model. Since political stability and order constitute the main variables in their analysis of different political systems, their "admiration" for the organizational genius of Lenin becomes quite natural. Both the Soviet and the Chinese predilection with "organization," while neglecting popular consensus, legitimacy, and freedoms of the individual, is sufficient to classify them as different from the political systems of Western Europe and Northern America and also from some isolated individual systems in Asia and Africa. The ignorance of political freedoms and the admiration of political order characterize large synthetic states or parochial systems. If "the art of associating together" cannot be achieved by consensus, then the reasons for preserving such a political community seem questionable. The history of nation-building (through a slow process of amalgamating different tribal and ethnic groups) and the parallel process of empire building seem to have influenced political development and political modernization. Societies that have not achieved a sufficient degree of national identity before the universal recognition of man as an important, if not the most important, factor of the political process, have missed the golden opportunity to build a nation. As J. S. Mill puts it "if the era of aspiration to free government arrives before this fusion has been effected, the opportunity for effecting it has gone by. . . "[10] Joseph R. Strayer is even more explicit, saying that "building a nation-state is a slow and complicated affair, and most of the political entities created in the past fifty years are never going to complete this process."[11]

To put this issue in the framework of political modernization as indicated above, the political communities which have not amalgamated the significant ethnic groups and nationalities, as the case seems to be with the Soviet Union, Yugoslavia, India, and others, will find it difficult to develop in the direction of political modernization and to accept the modernity not merely in Huntington's sense—that is, the ability to rule[12]—but also in Christian Bay's sense, "the maximization of every man's and woman's freedom—psychological, social, and political—[as] the only proper first-priority aim for the joint human efforts that we call political."[13]

Some scholars consider the achievement of the "national unity" as a background condition of modernization, as a first step of political development toward democracy. Thus, according to Dankward Rustow "in the democracy-to-be" the vast majority of the citizens must have no doubts as to which political community they belong to. "In order that rulers and policies may freely change, the boundaries must endure, the composition of the citizenry be continuous."[14] "National unity" according to Rustow "must precede all the other phases of democratization," but otherwise its timing is irrelevant, "nor does it matter by what means national unity has been established."[15] In a sense this is just a reiteration of what J. S. Mill meant by saying that "free institutions are next to impossible in a country made up of different nationalities."[16] Zbigniew Brzezinski, writing of present political development in the Soviet Union and the nationality problems, implies that the nationality question "acts as one of the major sources of restraint inhibiting the Soviet political elite and other relevant groups from embarking on a road of constitutional as well as broader political reform. . ."[17] Brzezinski does not believe that in the Soviet Union the process of political modernization in the Western democratic sense has taken place, or that this will necessarily happen in the foreseeable future. Although it is not entirely clear or empirically evident that multi-ethnicity and democratic government are incompatible, in general there seems to be an agreement that the multi-ethnic societies can survive and continue to do so only under some sort of autocratic regime. "An autocratic state," Sir Ernest Barker has said, "might in the past be multi-national, uniting by the one will of the autocrat a number of nations that were merely social groups. A democratic state which is multi-national will fall asunder into as many democracies as there are nationalities, dissolved by the very fact of will which should be the basis of its life."[18]

The history of the disintegration of the multi-national states and empires has proved the point. When Lord Acton once claimed that "those states are substantially the most perfect which, like the British and Austrian Empires, include various distinct nationalities without oppressing them," he did not experience the decline of both these Empires and therefore merely assumes that they would survive because they were democratic. However, history has proved quite the opposite. And the survival of the Russian Empire has proved that the preservation of different nationalities within its borders was possible only under some sort of autocratic political system. The episode of democratic system in Russia from March to October 1917, accompanied by factual disintegration of the Russian Empire, vividly demonstrates this point.[19]

Of course, most opponents of the nationality principle, such as Lord Acton, E. H. Carr, Kedourie and others, blame not only the disintegration of the large state formations, which produces chaos, but all wars and conflicts among states on nationalism and the nationality principle.[20] Thus, Acton claimed that the principle of "nationality does not aim either at liberty or prosperity, both of which it sacrifices to the imperative necessity of making the nation the mould and measure of the state. Its course will be marked with material as well as moral ruin in order that a new invention may prevail over the works of God and the interest of mankind."[21] This is, of course, easier to claim than to prove. Although the degree of liberty and prosperity is not easy to measure, it seems as if these attributes are to be found more often in the nation-states than in the empires, at least if we think of liberty and prosperity for many and not only for a few (individuals as well as nationalities). On the other hand, there were and still are ethnic and religious groups who, by the "purification" or homogenization of the nation-states have become more like strangers than they were in the previous, more universalistic empires with very low emphasis on one's ethnicity.[22] But on the whole the disintegration of multi-national empires seems to have liberated a large number of nationalities and lifted them to the level of equality among other nations, at least in a theoretical sense. To say, as E. H. Carr does, that there was much more national tolerance in the old Austrian Empire than later in Poland and Yugoslavia among Serbs, Croats, Slovenes and Poles, Ukrainians and Lithuanians, is merely to point out that both Poles and Serbs in Yugoslavia have abused the principle of nationality, applying it to themselves but refusing it to others. But to nullify the validity of the nationality principle only because it did not work well or that it has already been eliminated in the Soviet Union is again merely to prove the same point—namely, that the refusal of a nationality's claims to its own existence can be done relatively successfully only in a totalitarian or authoritarian political system. Neither is there any proof that, as Carr claims, the "great multi-national units" have a better chance to promote the "well-being of the individual man and woman" than the nation-states.[23]

It seems to me that Carr and other critics of the principle of nationalities are confusing some basic issues relevant to the nationality principle and the problem of freedom of man and his well-being. Firstly, their position is totally normative, considering big nations and empires as good, but considering the desire of smaller nations to create their own states as bad and retrograde. Secondly, they seem to use the concept of freedom as a prerogative only of the state but not of its parts. In fact, this concept of freedom does not apply to a man in a group—freedom to form a separate ethnic entity. This sort of reasoning is characteristic of a man emphasizing the importance of bigness; big business, big nation, big empire.

Some writers, like Herbert Spencer, Lord Acton, Karl Marx, Ferdinand Lassalle, Dostoievsky, R. A. Fadieev, and V. I. Lenin, seem to promote the virtue of bigness. Thus, Herbert Spencer implied that "without large aggregates of men there cannot be a developed industrial state" and that "we everywhere find that union of small societies by a conquering society is a step in civilization." He, of course, admits that "by force alone were small nomadic hordes welded into large tribes; by force alone have large tribes been welded into small nations; by force alone have small nations been welded into large nations."[24] This evolutionary doctrine which, in fact, supported the idea of "killing-off of inferior races and inferior individuals" is evident, though only implicit, in the writings of both Acton and Carr.[25] Even J. S. Mill, who invented the phrase that "it is in general a necessary condition of free institutions that the boundaries of governments should coincide in the main with those of nationalities," was of the opinion that small nationalities should remain within the orbit of powerful nations for the sake of civilization.[26] Karl Marx in a certain sense resembles Herbert Spencer, particularly in his total cynicism as regards the "unhistorical" Slavic nationalities. According to Marx, "scattered remnants of numerous nations, whose nationality and political vitality had long been extinguished, and who in consequence had been obliged, for almost a thousand years, to follow in the wake of a mightier nation, their conqueror [German nation] . . . had tried to profit by the universal confusion of 1848, in order to restore their political *status quo* of A.D. 800." This, according to Marx, was an anachronism and "treachery against the European Revolution" and the spread of the civilization whose bearer was the German nation.[27] Even according to Engels, the absorption

into one great state of "all those tiny, shrivelled, weak little nations" benefited
the progress and also "enabled them to participate in the historical development,"
for without violence, "without iron unscrupulousness nothing is achieved in
history."[28]

The Russian nationalists from Fadieev to Lenin and Stalin tended to
emphasize the necessity of bigness in their own frame of reference. Thus, a Tsarist
Major General, Rostislav Fadieev wrote in 1869 that "in the present state of Europe
there is no room for a heap of small nations; disposing of their own small armies,
declaring war, making peace and alliances—each in its own person . . . "[29] The solution of nationality problems of Slavs he saw in the creation of a union with a Tsar
of Russia at its head.

MARXIST-LENINIST SYNDROME

It seems clear that the real thrust of the Russian Community Party was
basically directed toward two ends: political integration and industrial modernization. The integrative aspects of its function seem to be primary, for it implied the
preservation of the territorial unity inherited from the Tsarist regime. This priority
was stressed by the new Russian elite, the Bolsheviks, at the very beginning of their
drive for political power. One may say that this aspect of the Bolshevik Revolution
was most important, second only to the actual seizure of power from the old elite.

When Lenin took the platform on the issue of the nationalities of Russia he
admitted two facts: first, that the Russian empire was multi-national, and the
Russians were in fact a minority (43 percent in 1897), and secondly, that Russia
was "a prison of nationalities," a colonial power, imposing its rule upon non-
Russian nationalities by military conquest, and keeping these nationalities in slav-
ery, exploiting them economically, suppressing their culture, attempting to Russify
them by force, in other words making impossible coexistence between Russian and
non-Russian nationalities.

He concluded therefore that a continuation of the policy of Russian chauvinism
would inevitably lead to: (a) reactionary trends within the Russian nation, because,
paraphrasing Engels, the nation that enslaves other nations cannot be free; (b) disintegration, because the subjugated nationalities in the long run could not be kept
within the Russian state, could not be integrated. In view of all this, Lenin demanded
that the Bolshevik party adopt the slogan "complete equality and right to self-
determination for all the nations oppressed by the Great Russians," because otherwise the nationalities would separate. However, Lenin did not intend to promote
the disintegration of the Russian empire; quite the contrary. "We do not advocate
preserving small nations at all costs; *other conditions* being equal, we are decidedly
for centralisation and are opposed to the petty-bourgeois ideal for federal relationships."[30] In 1915 Lenin made a final verdict on the nationality principle, and clarified his and the Party's position on the question of self-determination: " . . . the
freedom of secession of oppressed nations, not because we dream of economic dis-
memberment and of the ideal of small states, but on the contrary, because we want
large states and drawing together, even merging, but on a genuinely democratic basis
which is unthinkable without the freedom of secession." And arguing with Stepan-
ian, the Armenian Bolshevik, Lenin stressed that "the right to self-determination is
an exception from our general premise of centralism. This exception is absolutely

necessary in view of the Black-Hundred Great Russian nationalism. . . But an exception must not be interpreted expansively. There is and there must be nothing, absolutely nothing, apart from the *right* to *secession*."[31] In a later phase even this "abstract" right was reinterpreted as meaning the right "towards self-determination" not of nations and nationalities but of "the proletariat within every nation."[32]

It is unsafe to assume that Lenin believed in the magic of his "abstract" right of nationalities as a unique device, as a panacea, to bring the ethnically and culturally heterogeneous society into a unitary state. As if by irony the Soviet leadership after half a century of integrating effort had to admit that "the obliteration of national distinctions, and especially of language distinctions, is a considerably longer process than the obliteration of class distinctions."[33] This admission proves the endurance and vitality of national consciousness under the most unfavorable circumstances. This indicates that the twin assumptions of Marxian analysis that (1) "national differences and antagonisms between peoples are daily more and more vanishing, owing to the development of the bourgeoisie, to freedom of commerce, to the world market, to uniformity in the mode of production and in the condition of life corresponding thereto . . . (2) That the supremacy of the proletariat will cause them to vanish still faster . . . or . . . in proportion as the antagonism between classes within the nation vanishes, the hostility of one nation to another will come to an end"[34] have been unfounded. The First Secretary of the CPSU, Khrushchev, had to warn the enthusiastic integralists that, according to Lenin, "even after communism has been built in the main, it will be premature to proclaim a fusion of nations, . . . that state and national distinctions will exist long after socialism triumphs in all countries."[35]

Some analyses of the principle of nationality and nationalism distinguish two basically contradictory tendencies inherent in the age of nationalism: the one acquisitive, integrative, imperial, autocratic, and the other disintegrative, pluralist, defensive, democratic. Nationalism is a functional device of these two tendencies, conducive to the maintenance of the preferred system. It is not our purpose at this time to emphasize the normative, value-laden aspect of nationalism, very often hastily qualified as a diabolic social force. Nationalism in this sense is many-faceted and is equally used as an integrative and as a disintegrative force. It should be mentioned here that Marxism, personified by its classics, has provided the spiritual support of the integrative forces within the Russian Communist movement. Whether what Marx has said with regard to nationality could be attributed to his "scientific" approach formulated in dialectical materialism or to some other more mundane motives, is less clear. Marx, it should be stressed, recognized the right to independent existence only for the strong historical nations. The small unhistorical nationalities, "these dying nationalities, the Bohemians (Czechs), Carinthians (Slovenians)" should yield to the force of history, and sacrifice themselves for, and benefit from, the civilization which according to Hegel or even Marx had embodied itself in Germany. The difference was merely that Hegel saw it in the national spirit, while Marx's position is only a quasi-materialistic retouching of Hegel, for they both regarded the Slavs as "agricultural people" whose role they reduced to stateless vegetation.[36] Although their position towards the Polish nation was more favorable, it was full of contradictions. "The Poles did nothing else in history but brave, impetuous acts of foolishness," Engels wrote in his letter to Marx in 1851. "Everything possible must be taken away from the Poles in the western part, their fortresses must be occupied by the Germans under the pretext of defence, in particular Poznan, they must be kept busy, sent under fire, their lands must be taken away, they must be fed with the prospects of the capture of Riga and Odessa, and if it were possible to rouse the Russians, an alliance with them should be made, and the Poles compelled to surrender."[37]

Although Lenin never approached the smaller nationalities in this Marxian manner, some elements of it were clearly apparent, especially in assigning the historic mission to the Russian proletariat which, after the failure of communist movements in the West, have inherited the role of the vanguard of the new social order, of the new civilization. Stalin at the height of his power, more explicitly than Lenin, ascribed to the Russian nation the leading role in building the new civilization. If Lenin loved the Russian language, if he was "full of national pride because the Great-Russian nation, *too*, has created a revolutionary class, because it, *too*, has proved capable of providing mankind with great models of the struggle for freedom and socialism," Stalin in a typical nationalist hysteria magnified the Russian people as "the most outstanding nation of all of the nations which reside in the Soviet Union. . . . It is the leading people, because it has a clear mind, firm character, and endurance."[38]

Elevating the Russian nation to the top of the hierarchy of nations in the Soviet Union is a far cry from identifying the Soviet Union with the Russian nation and implicitly assuming the abolition of the non-Russian nations. No responsible party or any other political or literate citizen of the Soviet Union has been explicit on this issue. Unfortunately, there are leaders within the party hierarchy and elsewhere who are inclined towards the idea of one indivisible Russian state and nation, but this tendency has not been officially sanctioned. The articulation of the Russian national interest and the gradual linkage of Russian and Soviet patriotism has been observed from the mid-thirties. One of its methods was the purging of the "class" interpretation of the old Russian imperial expansionism, personified by the historian Pokrovsky, according to which Russian expansion in the borderlands was conducted neither in the name of civilization nor by peaceful means.[39] However, this school was accused of being anti-Marxist and anti-Russian and was replaced by a genuine traditional Russian interpretation. Territorial expansion and the conquest of other national states were now regarded as "progressive" or, as a prominent contemporary Party official maintains, during the period of the personality cult of Stalin, "almost all wars waged by Tsarist Russia were regarded as just and progressive."[40] However, he approaches the issue in a slightly retouched Stalinist spirit. He declares that the "dialectic of history is such that despite the reactionary aims and methods of Tsarism the annexation of the peoples to Russia, the uniting of their power with the power of the Russian people in the final analysis led to the liberation of all peoples of the Tsarist Russian Empire, and the creation of hitherto unknown socialistic community of the nationalities, inhabiting our Motherland." By articulating the "progressive character of a uniting of the peoples with Russia in the broad historical perspective, the historian contributed to the strengthening of friendship of the peoples of our country, and the further rapprochement [sblizheniiu] of the nations of the Soviet Union."[41]

One would in vain search for more manifest statements in support of a theory of the withering away of non-Russians. For, as Professor Armstrong indicates, more explicit stress on the Soviet national interest being identical with the Russian interest becomes hazardous. "The major difficulty encountering the program of raising loyalty to the regime on appeals to the national spirit of the Russians arose from the fact that the numerous other nationalities were not only unattracted to Russian nationalism in its traditional form but were usually alienated by it. Consequently, special methods were required to 'adapt' the new line to the non-Russian nationalities, and them to it."[42]

The emphasis on Russian patriotism had to be ideologically motivated, and the best way to support it is by referring to the already idolatrized *pontifex maximus* Lenin. The references to Lenin have been more or less codified and they can justify anything. Not without grounds, the education of the Soviet man in the spirit of the "revolutionary patriotic traditions," the love of "Rodina" (Patrie), and the "feeling of the national pride" all are justified by quotations from Lenin.[43] All the adulation in praise of Russia is the logical consequence of this tendency.[44]

The post-Stalin era briefly interrupted the "Russian" emphasis in the integrative process of the Soviet society. Among other things, it opened the gates to power for some nationalities, such as Ukrainians and Belorussians—gates which were previously closed to them. As Professor Arpaturian indicates, the Ukraine, the second largest nation, was, since 1953, "formalized as the second-ranking nation, or *secundus inter pares*."[45] However, "the interest of the Great Russians continues to predominate as the chief input into the Soviet system."[46]

The integrative process of multi-ethnic Soviet society has been approached very cautiously, that is to say dialectically. The Party has adopted many-faceted methods to implement its policy of national unification. On the one side the nations, nationalities, and ethnic groups are allowed to "flourish and their sovereignty is strengthened"; on the other, they "will draw still closer together." In the economic sphere, in the spheres of culture, "all the Soviet nations will develop," but at the same time "ideological unity of the nations and nationalities . . . and a rapprochement of their cultures will continue." On the one hand, it is stressed that "the obliteration of national distinctions, and especially language distinctions, is a considerably longer process than the obliteration of class distinctions," while on the other the cultures of the socialist nations will "draw closer together" and "an international culture common to all Soviet nations is developing." In the matter of "the socialist content of the cultures of the peoples of the USSR, the Party will *promote their further mutual enrichment and rapprochement*, the consolidation of their international basis, and thereby the formation of the future single world-wide communist society."[47]

There are two important elements of the nationality policy of the Party which are most controversial and which constitute an integral part of the policy, but which have been carefully avoided. One is the tendency towards the new "Soviet nation," the other is the defining of the place of the Russian nation. If there is a programatic plan for assimilating non-Russian nationalities within the Russian nation, it is rather an implicit one. Referring to the "free development of the languages of the peoples of the USSR, and the complete freedom for every citizen of the USSR to speak, and to bring up and educate his children, in any language, ruling out all privileges, restrictions or compulsions in the use of this or that language" the Program stressed the "progressive" tendency of the "voluntary study of Russian in addition to the native language."[48] The interpretation of this stipulation depends on the inclination of the writer. Some Soviet writers see in it the appropriate vehicle for maintaining a pluralism of nationalities, while others see in it the method by which the nationalities will be eliminated.

During the drafting of the Program of the Party in 1961, two extreme tendencies were displayed. One group advocated the codification of nationality differences, suggesting a struggle against nationalism on two fronts: against Great Russian chauvinism and against local bourgeois nationalism. They proposed to include in the Party Program the formula "the right of nations to self-determination," to return to the "korenizatsia" (nationalization) of the apparatus in the Republics. This faction argued that within the confines of the USSR only "rapprochement" in a sense meaning just a mobilization of nationalities was possible, while "fusion" or integration would take place only in the distant future. Others considered even the maintenance of nationality-statehood and the state borders between Republic superfluous. They suggested the abolition of national Republics, the formation of a single Soviet government, and the adoption of the Russian language as the only official language in the country. Some of them considered the recording of the nationality of Soviet citizens in the passports and censuses as a harmful symbol, exacerbating nationalistic feelings. Docent Baglikov, from the Academy of the Social Sciences at the Central Committee, is one of more articulate proponents of this trend, among others, pointing to the "objective fact of the wide usage of the Russian language."[49]

If this interpretation is credited, the position of the Party leadership is clearly in favor of the Russification of the nationalities. The fusion (*slianie*) in fact means the strengthening of Russian elements in Soviet society, at the cost of non-Russian nationalities. The process of their denationalization is labeled as a "progressive," objective process, while the rejection of Russification is regarded as a "reactionary" and subjective tendency, as "bourgeois nationalism."[50]

From this, it follows that the *slianie* of nationalism is confined to the merging of non-Russian nationalities with the Russian nation. The other perspective, more global or at least extended to the socialist bloc, has never been, to my knowledge, explicitly or even implicitly stated by the Party. The prospect of, for example, the fusion of the "socialist Chinese nation" with the "socialist Russian nation" has never been seriously contemplated. As I have already mentioned, Stalin and other Soviet theoreticians have developed the theory of regional languages, thus theoretically providing for coexistence between these two languages and cultures rather than for their merger.

STRUCTURAL FRAMEWORK OF THE SOLUTION
OF NATIONAL PROBLEMS

The "state of its own" is usually considered as one of the essential attributes of a nation. In fact, there are very few nations without their own state of one kind or another—a state to some degree sovereign and independent. As has already been indicated, the creation of nation-states has been the primary tendency of our epoch. From the various definitions of a nation-state I chose, for this particular purpose, a Weberian definition reformulated by Ernst B. Haas, for whom the "nation" is "a socially mobilized body of individuals, believing themselves to be united by some set of characteristics that differentiate them (in their own minds) from 'outsiders' and striving to create or maintain their own state." "Nationalism" is the body of beliefs held by these people searching for "uniqueness and autonomy." A "national ideology" is a body of values and beliefs advocated by some creative minority in an effort to call into being a new nation. If it succeeds, it will build a nation and create a nationalism; if it fails, it "will be a historical curiosity."[51]

In spite of its emphasis on state building, the Haas definition is not as value-laden as that of Lassalle or Marx, for whom some nations were predestined to "repose like motionless ruins outside history" (Lassalle), or who thought that these *geschichtslose Nationen* "these dying nationalities, the Bohemians, Carinthians, Dalmatians, etc.," should be delighted by the prospect of being "absorbed by their stronger neighbours" (Marx).[52] From this it also follows that a nation can assert itself only through its own state, administered, at least symbolically, by its own government, in its own name. It was in this sense that the principle of the right to self-determination of nations was meant by Lenin. In one of his essays on the nationality question he stressed that the right to self-determination, from the historical-economic point of view, cannot have any other meaning than "the political self-determination, state independence and the formation of a national state."[53] On the other hand, Lenin explicitly adhered to the idea of larger state formations in which many other nationalities would be included. In the beginning he worked against even the federal principle, against autonomy in political spheres. The preservation of the single Party organization for the whole Soviet Union must be interpreted as the mechanism to balance formal autonomy in state affairs. Whether Lenin's preference for the larger states implied the identification of this state with the Russian state can be only surmised, for he never committed himself explicitly to such a program. Implicitly, however, it can be argued that he did enjoin the preservation of one state formation within the borders of the old Russia.

The anomaly of the Soviet theory of nation and state lies in the fact that it has permitted differentiated statehood, to accommodate the variety of national formations. Hence Stalin was against the inclusion of the "demand of one's own state" in the definition of nation, for, as he put it, one should be obliged to maintain that the Ukrainians "ceased to be a nation after they have united their Ukrainian Soviet Republic with other Soviet Republics within the Union of the Soviet Socialist Republics." This, he maintained, did not occur, for "entering into the USSR, Ukrainians did not lose their national-statehood." What happened was just a change of its form; an independent Ukrainian Republic was transformed into the "Union Republic."[54] A recent Soviet writer, Korolev, concludes that the state will play an enormous role in the life of the nation, particularly the socialist nation. He disagrees with some Soviet legal theoreticians, who claim that the "mutual assimilation of the nations in fact is denationalizing the national-territorial autonomies and even the Union Republics, moving the Soviet society to the point at which the full state-legal fusion of nations will become a matter of the foreseeable future."[55] As Korolev points out, the ambiguity of Semenov's theses derived from the conclusion that the "fusion of nations was a condition for the withering away of the state." Instead Korolev claims that the national differences will remain long after the withering away of states. He holds that the definite disappearance of national differences will occur first under the conditions of the fully developed Communist society.[56]

Within the framework of the Constitution of the USSR there is a plurality of statehood, divided into three levels. At the top there is the *Soviet Union*, superior in its sovereignty to any other form of state. At the next level there are the fifteen states of the *Union Republics*, representing the highest form of national statehood within the framework of the Soviet federation. The Russian Soviet Republic is one of these fifteen, with all the attributes reserved for the nationality forming the Union

Republic. The Russian nation, similar to other nations with Union Republic status, has its own national territory, its own state, its own constitution, its own government, its own language. It is guaranteed the right to withdraw from the Soviet Union, its territory cannot be altered without its consent. The Russian Union Republic may, according to Section 18a of the Soviet Constitution, "enter into direct relations with foreign states and conclude agreements and exchange diplomatic and consular representatives with them."[57]

The third level of national statehood comprises the *Autonomous Republics*, which are parts of Union Republics. The Autonomous Republics are states in a very narrow sense, with very few attributes of the independent state. They are to be considered, rather, as the national form of cultural autonomy. The Autonomous Provinces and National Regions are the lowest level of local national-cultural autonomy, which are not even formally classified as state formations.[58]

Within the limited confines of the concept "own state," as the essential variable of the nation, it can be argued that the Soviet Union is the highest form, excelling the state-like attributes of the fifteen most "sovereign" nations in the USSR, including the Russian. Constitutionally, the Soviet state and the Russian state are not identical; rather, they exist and indeed function as separate entities. The Soviet Union can be classified as a "nation" only in a legal sense, where "nationality" and "citizenship" are synonymous.[59]

The statehood of the Union Republics, constitutionally, is only one grade below the statehood of the USSR, and because the former possesses, in addition to this limited statehood, a nationality in the ethnic sense, it can by no means be theoretically ruled out or declared as non-existent. The major nationalities within the limits of the USSR do possess states of their own, although the character and degree of "own," the degree of sovereignty, is *sui generis*. On the other hand, one must agree with Aspaturian when he points out the important multidimensional function of the Soviet State. It functions as (a) the Russian national state, (b) the national state of individual non-Russian nations, and (c) as one single state entity for all of the nations combined.[60] One aspect should be stressed in this connection—namely, that the interaction and balance between these functions is neither smooth nor well-defined. And as Aspaturian himself indicates, the Soviet model, together with other "bi-national" and "multinational" states, represents deviations from the standard norm; and in almost all such states, national conflicts are chronic since the national interest of more than one nation by a single state is extremely difficult to articulate.[61]

The contention of my essay is that, in view of the power configuration of two opposing forces, the integralist (represented by the Russians or Russified non-Russians) and nationalist (particularly vital among the major nationalities), the new synthesis is more imaginary than real. As the struggle during the formation of the USSR in the early twenties and the rise of Russian patriotism and chauvinism during the War indicate, Russian nationalism provides the greatest obstacle to the creation of a "new" nation. The Russian national, cultural, military, and technical heritage for too long has had a powerful impact upon Soviet society, or, as Professor Aspaturian indicates, "the interest of the Great Russians continues to predominate as the chief national input into the Soviet system,"[62] and therefore will not easily be integrated into some new national body.

Whether the Soviet leadership will succeed in their intention of solving the problem of the nationalities by integrating the nationalities within the new Soviet framework or an old Russian one is relevant from the point of view of the stability and modernization of that political entity, for a nationally heterogeneous society cannot be expected even to approach the process of political modernization without endangering its existence as a single political entity. And if modernity means, among other things, the subsystem autonomy and the differentiation of roles, the nationality problem, it seems to me, has weakened the Soviet Union's chances of becoming democratic.

The development of the Soviet multinational structure has many optional courses. Whether it will proceed towards the disintegration of the Soviet Union into independent national states, or the creation of a genuine "new" configuration between the dominant Russian and inferior non-Russian parts of Soviet society on the basis of a broad national autonomy or perhaps absorption of nationalities by the Russian nation is difficult to foresee. The recent history of the emancipation of colonial peoples has demonstrated that the mono-national state has become a "normal," most frequent, pattern of the organization of mankind, while multinational, or supra-national entities have become rather a rarity. It has also been proven that neither integration of different nationalities into larger political units, nor their disintegration into smaller parts has been resolved voluntarily.[63] Perhaps in the Soviet case we may witness the perpetuation of the struggle between the two tendencies. It does not follow that because the rest of mankind is marching toward disintegration this "unstable synthesis" may not prove to possess durability, for, as Joseph Schumpeter put it: "though it does require genius of the first order to build up . . . [an Empire] it does not require genius to run it . . . The Russian century once started may run its course almost by itself."[64]

However, the ability of the Soviet Union to survive does not yet prove that it has changed its multinational character, that it has completed the process of nation-building and thereby integration and political stability. After all, under certain circumstances an unstable equilibrium may turn out to be more vital than a stable one, if for no other reason than that of keeping the guardians constantly alert. On the other hand, a semblance of stability may prove to be nothing more than a semblance, for, as Machiavelli observed, "the great majority of mankind are satisfied with appearances, as though they were realities, and are often more influenced by the things that seem than by those that are."

NOTES

[1] Gunnar Myrdal, *Asian Drama* I (New York: Pantheon Books, 1968), p. 64.

[2] A. de Tocqueville, *Democracy in America*, II Phillips Bradley, ed. (New York, 1955), p. 118.

[3] Allen Kassof, "The Administered Society: Totalitarianism without Terror," *World Politics*, XVI, 4 (July 1964), pp. 558-75.

[4] T. H. Rigby, "Traditional, Marked, and Organizational Societies and the U.S.S.R.," *World Politics*, XVI, 4 (July 1964), pp. 539-57.

[5] Perhaps best formulated in Friedrich, Carl J., and Zbigniew K. Brzezinski, *Totalitarian Dictatorship and Autocracy*, 2nd ed. (New York: Frederick A. Praeger, 1966).

[6] Talcott Parsons, *Essays in Sociological Theory* (New York: Free Press, 1964), p. 412.

[7] S. P. Huntington, "Political Development and Political Decay," *World Politics*, XVII, 3 (1965), quoted in Claude E. Welch, Jr., ed., *Political Modernization* (Belmont, Calif.: Wadsworth Publishing Company, 1971), pp. 244-54.

[8] *Ibid.*, p. 257.

[9] Lucian Pye, *Politics, Personality and Nation-Building* (New Haven: Yale University Press, 1963), p. 51.

[10] John Stuart Mill, *Considerations on Representative Government* (Chicago: Henry Regnery Company, 1962), pp. 311-18.

[11] Joseph R. Strayer, "The Historical Experience of Nation Building in Europe," in *Nation-Building*, ed. by Karl W. Deutsch and William Foltz (New York: Atherton Press, 1966), p. 25.

[12] S. P. Huntington, *Political Order in Changing Societies* (New Haven: Yale University Press, 1969), p. 8.

[13] Christian Bay, *The Structure of Freedom* (New York: Atheneum, 1965), p. 390.

[14] D. A. Rustow, "Transition to Democracy," in *Comparative Politics*, 2 (April 1970), pp. 337-63, quoted in R. C. Macridis and B. E. Brown, eds., *Comparative Politics*, 4th ed. (Homewood, Ill.: The Dorsey Press, 1972), p. 465.

[15] *Ibid.*

[16] J. S. Mill, *Considerations on Representative Government* (Chicago: Gateway Edition, 1962), p. 309. Montesquieu has also written on this matter, saying that "a large empire presupposes a despotic authority in him who governs" (in *Esprit des Lois*, Book 8, chapter 19). This was the position accepted by Empress Catherine II, who contended that the size of her domain required the absolutist rule. [See John S. Reshetar, *The Soviet Policy* (New York: Dodd and Mead, 1971), p. 42, note 7.]

[17] Zbigniew Brzezinski, "Political Implications of Soviet Nationality Policy," in Edward Allworth, ed., *Soviet Nationality Problems* (New York: Columbia University Press, 1971), p. 76.

[18] Sir Ernest Barker, *National Character*, 3rd ed., 1939, pp. 16-17, cited in A. Cobban, *The Nation State and National Self-Determination* (New York: Collins, 1969), p. 128.

[19] See especially R. Pipes, *The Formation of the Soviet Union*, rev. ed. (Cambridge, Mass.: Harvard University Press, 1964). Even the Slovaks of Czechoslovakia achieved their autonomy from the "liberal" regime of Dubcek rather than the totalitarian one of Novotny.

[20] See, for example, Lord Acton, "Nationality," in *Essays on Freedom and Power* (New York, N.Y.): Meridian Books, 1957; E. H. Carr, *Nationalism and After* (London: Macmillan, 1945), pp. 66 ff.; Elie Kedourie, *Nationalism* (London: Hutchinson University Library, 1960), pp. 138-40.

[21] Lord Acton, *op. cit.*, p. 169. He admits however that nationality theory "has an important mission in the world and marks . . . the end of two forces, which are the worst enemies of civil freedom—the absolute monarchy and the revolution" (*op. cit.*, p. 170).

[22] This development has been only marginally approached by Hannah Arendt in *The Origins of Totalitarianism* (New York: The World Publishing Co., 1966), Ch. II.

[23] See E. H. Carr, *Nationalism and After*, pp. 64-67.

[24] Herbert Spencer, *On Social Evolution, Selected Writings*, ed. and with an introduction by J. D. Y. Peel (Chicago: The University of Chicago Press, 1972), pp. 169-70.

[25] Lord Acton, *op. cit.*; E. H. Carr, *op. cit.*; and E. H. Carr, *Twenty Years' Crisis* (New York: Harper and Row, 1946).

[26] J. S. Mill, *op. cit.*, pp. 316-17.

[27] Karl Marx, "Restoration of Order—Dret and Chamber" in *New York Tribune*, April 24, 1852. Quoted from *Germany: Revolution and Counter-Revolution*, ed. by Eleanor Marx (New York: International Publishers, 1969), pp. 85-86.

[28] In *Neue Rheinische Zeitung*, January 13 and February 15 and 16, 1849, quoted in J. Borys, *The Russian Communist Party and the Sovietization of Ukraine* (Stockholm, 1960), p. 13. Ferdinand Lassalle also spoke against the rights of existence for small nationalities (see Borys, *op. cit.*, pp. 13-14).

[29] R. A. Fadieev, "What Should Be the Policy of Russia?" in *Readings in Russian Foreign Policy*, ed. by R. A. Goldwin (New York: Oxford University Press, 1959), p. 71.

[30] V. I. Lenin, "On the National Pride of the Great Russians," in V. I. Lenin, *Selected Works*, I (Moscow: Progress Publishers, 1967), pp. 664-67.

[31] *Leninskii sbornik*, III (Moscow-Leningrad, 1925), pp. 470-73, quoted in J. Borys, *op. cit.*, p. 33.

[32] V. I. Lenin, *Sochinenia*, 4th ed. (Moscow, 1941-50), Vol. 6, p. 294.

[33] J. F. Triska, ed., *Soviet Communism: Programs and Rules* (San Francisco: Chandler Publishing Co., 1962), p. 107.

[34] "The Communist Manifesto," in Marx and Engels, *Basic Writings on Politics and Philosophy*, L. S. Feuver, ed. (New York: Doubleday Anchor, 1959), p. 26.

[35] *Documents of the 22nd Congress of the CPSU*, II (New York: Crosscurrents Press, 1961), p. 118.

[36] Borys, *op. cit.*, p. 16.

[37] *Ibid.*, p. 16, note 55.

[38] Quoted in E. R. Goodman, *The Soviet Design for a World State* (New York, 1960), p. 52.

[39] N. Pokrovsky, Diplomatiia i vojny Tsarskoi Rossii . . Moskow, 1924, quoted in J. Borys, "Camouflaged Russian Imperialism," in *Dagens Nyheter* (Stockholm, March 16, 1961). Pokrovsky's theses were widespread among Soviet historians

[see, for example, E. Steinberg, *Ocherki istorii Turkmenii* (Moscow, 1934].

[40] B. Ponomarev, "Istoricheskuiu nauku i obrazovanie na uroven zadach kommunisticheskogo stroitelstva," *Kommunist* (Moscow, 1963), No. 1, pp. 21-22.

[41] *Ibid.*

[42] J. Armstrong, *The Politics of Totalitarianism* (New York: Random House, 1961), p. 83.

[43] Ponomarev, *op. cit.*, p. 21.

[44] I would like to mention just one typical example:
"Our dear Russia knows
That in summer heat and snow
We shall cherish our native land
From the Kuriles to the Carpathians" (The official march published in *Sovetskii voin*, 1966, No. 16, p. 49.)

[45] Vernon V. Aspaturian, *The Soviet Union in the World Communist System* (Stanford, Calif.: Hoover Institution, 1966), p. 47.

[46] *Ibid.*, p. 46.

[47] Triska, *op. cit.*, pp. 107-109.

[48] *Ibid.*, p. 109.

[49] B. T. Baglikov, "Razrabotka i zashshita V. I. Leninym programmy Kommunisticheskoi Partii po natsionalnomu voprosu," *Lektsii po istorii KPSS . . . 1961/62 g.* (Moscow, 1963), pp. 183-91.

[50] It is significant that Russian nationalism is never accused of being "bourgeois nationalism," but is termed "great-power chauvinism."

[51] E. B. Haas, *Beyond the Nation-State. Functionalism and International Organization* (Stanford, Calif.: Stanford University Press, 1968), pp. 165 ff. Haas cites Max Weber: "A nation is a community of sentiment which would adequately manifest itself in a state of its own . . . " [from *Max Weber: Essays in Sociology*, ed. by H. H. Gerth and C. Wright Mills (New York: Galaxy, 1958), p. 176].

[52] Quoted in Borys, *op. cit.*, pp. 11-14.

[53] V. I. Lenin, "The Right of Nations to Self-Determination," in *Selected Works*, I, p. 605.

[54] Stalin, *Soch.*, Vol. 11, pp. 334-35.

[55] A. I. Korolev, "Gosudarstvo i natsia," *Vestnik Leningradskogo Universiteta. Ekonomika, Filosofia-Pravo.* Vypusk 3, September 1968.

[56] *Ibid.* Semenov suggests that in the Soviet Union nations may survive without having their own national states. They will remain in spite of the withering away of the state (in *Voprosy istorii*, 1966, No. 7, p. 81; also V. I. Koslov, "Nekotorye problemy teorii natsii," *Voprosy istorii*, 1967, No. 1, p. 93).

[57] For some reasons only Ukrainian and Belorussian Republics have assumed a limited function in international relations. They are both members of the United Nations.

[58] In Soviet political literature they do figure as national state formations (see, for example, A. I. Korolev, *op. cit.*).

[59] The creation of the Soviet Union was a departure from the old concept of a Russian National state.

[60] Aspaturian, *op. cit.*, p. 49.

[61] *Ibid.*, p. 50.

[62] *Ibid.*, p. 46.

[63] This point was stressed by Bertrand Russell when he said that "there are innumerable instances of small States growing into great empires by conquest, but hardly any of voluntary federation" [*Power* (New York: Norton, 1969), pp. 124-25].

[64] J. A. Schumpeter, *Capitalism, Socialism and Democracy* (New York, 1962), p. 402, note 33.

PART II

WINDS OF CHANGE:
MODERNIZATION AND LIBERALIZATION
AFTER STALIN'S DEATH

THE RUSSIAN CIVIL LIBERTIES FERMENT SINCE THE DEATH OF STALIN

Peter Vanneman
University of Arkansas
Fayetteville, Arkansas

Taking the long view, the Russian civil liberties ferment may provide a catalyst for a significant transformation of the "Russian-Soviet" political culture—a transformation required for the continuing modernization of advanced Communist Party—State systems.[1] This process is embryonic and subject to arrest, and to predict its ultimate matured form would be to indulge in mere futurology; but its potential impact upon the polity demands an attempt to develop a dynamic perspective on the growth and evolution of the Russian civil liberties ferment.

On paper the civil liberties and human rights guaranteed by the Soviet Constitution—promulgated at the inception of the "Great Terror"—may be the most extensive in the world. This dichotomy between extensive legal guarantees and the widespread employment of extra-legal sanctions has always given rise to concern among some elements of Soviet society; however, one should not ignore the fact that even in Stalin's day there remained a sphere of law as well as a sphere of unlaw. The mainstream of the extraordinarily intricate, interlocking, and overlapping currents of the Russian civil liberties ferment is the common tendency to articulate demands that the regime adhere to the rule of law. As one well-known dissident summarized it:

> Although the Democratic Movement is in its formative period
> and has no clearly defined program, all of its supporters assume at
> least one common aim: the rule of law, founded on respect for the
> basic rights of man.[2]

These demands appear to have served as a catalyst, aggregating political forces, motivated to further narrow the sphere of unlaw in the Soviet polity. The rule of law itself is a complex, many-faceted concept, but within the mainstream of the civil liberties ferment its core tenet is restraint on the arbitrary quality of rule, which has always characterized Russian-Soviet political culture.

After Stalin's death, the Soviet power elite itself moved to extend the sphere of law, primarily by gainsaying terror as an instrument of rule, which unleashed many disparate demands from the intermediate strata of society. This ferment below lacked form, organization, or a unifying cause; however, over time, the vacillations of a fractious power elite appear to have provided an opportunity for the metamorphosis of this mere ferment into a genuine movement—admittedly still somewhat amorphous—within the Soviet "middle class," focusing on the central theme of the rule of law in its broadest sense, the rational, non-arbitrary application of published legal norms.

THE CIVIL LIBERTIES MOVEMENT WITHIN THE SOCIOECONOMIC STRUCTURE OF THE POLITY

The Civil Liberties Movement, which gradually emerged as a loosely organized political force from the ferment which culminated in the Siniavsky-Daniel Trial in 1966, comprises an identifiably small portion of the Soviet "middle class," although related articulated demands in other contexts imply more widespread, but latent, support for some of the Movement's objectives. This "middle class," from which the Movement emanated, has been variously described: more broadly, as the "intelligentsia" or "persons engaged in mental labor," an intermediate stratum (*sloi*) of approximately twenty million persons; or, more narrowly, as "those professionally engaged in highly qualified mental labor, requiring specialized secondary or higher education," approximately 15,700,000 persons.[3] The dissident Andrei Amalrik describes them as a class of "specialists":

> Its members have gained for themselves and their families a standard of living that is relatively high by Soviet standards—regular good food, attractive clothes, a nicely furnished cooperative apartment, sometimes even a car; and, of course, available entertainment. They pursue professions that assure them a position of respect in society. . . . They possess the ability to assess more or less accurately their own position in society as a whole.
>
> This group includes people in liberal professions, such as writers or actors, those occupied in academic-administrative work, the managerial group in the economic field and so on. They are, as I have said, a "class of specialists." Obviously, this class is beginning to become conscious of its unity and to make its presence felt.[4]

Briefly put, the "middle class" incorporates the institutional and functional elites of the USSR, minus the power elite. Below this stratum in the socioeconomic order are the relatively politically passive masses of peasants and workers. Sitting at the pinnacle of power in the Soviet polity is the power elite: the heads of the Party-State apparatus—the Politburo, Secretariat, Council of Ministers, Central Committee and Ministers. While the efforts of the Civil Liberties Movement to "go to the people" have been minimal, their attempts to influence the power elite have been multifarious and unrelenting. The process by which the Movement emerged from the "middle class" and the nature of its influence with, and access to, the elite form the central themes of this analysis.

DISSENT AS PURSUIT OF
PROFESSIONAL MILIEU GOALS (1953-1964)

Stalin's death left divided leadership factions struggling for paramountcy and seeking support within the emerging Soviet "middle class" by facilitating, to some degree, what Arnold Wolfers, in a different context, has termed "milieu goals."[5] The more liberal writers and artists, economists, industrial managers, jurists, scientists, and even military officers, among others, who sought to create an environment in which they could more adequately perform their profession, were encouraged to do so; and each group responded, developing what appears over time to be individual dialogues between the elite and each individual group of specialists. These separate dialogues concerned the nature and scope of their respective milieu goals; there seems to have been little coordination of effort among them—each dealt separately with the leadership to further its own group interests with varying success at varying times. Only the specter of a Stalinist reaction eventually galvanized the more liberal elements within some groups of specialists into those concerted efforts now identified as the Russian Civil Liberties Movement; that prospect elicited the combined exercise of the full panoply of influence techniques, developed from years of individual group bartering with the leadership. A brief review of some of the major individual dialogues of the groups from which the Movement draws its chief support (overt and latent) facilitates an appreciation of the evolutionary process which culminated in the crystallization of the Movement from 1965 to 1970. From the cultural intelligentsia: liberal writers (the most prominent), artists, and musicians; and from the technical intelligentsia: liberal scientists, engineers, and technicians, the Movement derived its most overt support. From liberal economists, industrial managers, and jurists, one might venture, perhaps, to imply latent support for some tenets of the Movement from the nature and content of their respective milieu goals, as well as specific articulations in certain issue contexts.[6]

CULTURAL DISSENTERS:
LIBERAL WRITERS IN THE VANGUARD

The first important dialogue between the leadership and reformist intermediate actors after Stalin's death began when, at its plenum in October 1953, the Board of the Writers' Union called for a candid discussion of literary matters. A vigorous debate ensued in the press, with liberal writers demanding complete freedom from censorship, and with Khrushchev, in 1957, stressing that the obligations of writers to the collective should not be completely neglected—a comparatively moderate stance. Although the poet Boris Pasternak was vilified in 1958, a year later Khrushchev urged writers to write as they please, provided that they help in the "building of communism." Going further in his own familiar zig-zag pattern, he forced the Party Presidium to accept publication in 1962 of Solzhenitsyn's *One Day in the Life of Ivan Denisovich* and of Yevtushenko's poem "Stalin's Heirs," as part of his struggle with more conservative factions of the power elite.[7] Liberal writers were permitted to occupy key positions in the Writers' Union and to edit official literary journals such as *Novy Mir*. Their essential milieu goal was, of course, literary freedom—freedom from arbitrary, dogmatic interference in their creative activity by the Party-State bureaucracy. Khrushchev's support and interest did not necessitate their seeking support among other elements of the middle class. In fact, somewhat ironically, it was Khrushchev himself who has been quoted as suggesting the linkage between their milieu goals and those of the scientific and economic intelligentsia, between freedom of expression and economic and scientific progress:

> I favor greater freedom of expression since the level we have achieved in economy and technology demands this. But some of my colleagues in the Presidium think we must be cautious. Obviously we shall have to wait a while before going ahead any further.[8]

Although voiced to a Western diplomat, Khrushchev's comment foreshadowed a central tenet of the Civil Liberties Movement's later appeals to the power elite: the intimate and necessary connection between economic and scientific progress, and freedom of expression. However, the statement also reflected the tenuousness of his moderate position toward the writers; and as his grip on power ebbed away, he turned categorically against the liberal elements of the cultural intelligentsia.

THE ECONOMIC INTELLIGENTSIA:
ECONOMISTS AND MANAGERS

Malenkov's speech at Stalin's funeral and his famous 1953 speech to the Supreme Soviet stressed higher relative rates of investment in consumer goods, which launched intermittent public and private debates over economic policy not yet terminated. Economists and industrial managers espoused a multitude of proposals in a continuing dialogue with the leadership and among themselves. The regime sought higher productivity; economists and managers argued for varying degrees of professional autonomy. The milieu goals of the more liberal elements of the economic intelligentsia were a more rational, more predictable, and less dogmatic economy and society, which, by inherently limiting the arbitrary interference of the Party-State apparatus, would facilitate their specialized functions of planning and managing, and thus enhance the probability of fulfilling the leadership's demands for greater productivity. This argument was occasionally spiced with assertions that greater professional autonomy was for the good of the country—an embryonic and somewhat chauvinistic national-interest stance. Although identifiable participation of the economic intelligentsia in the Civil Liberties Movement remains negligible, articulations such as those above, as we shall see, suggest significant latent support, not easily dismissed in view of their undisputed access to the leadership.

THE TECHNICAL INTELLIGENTSIA:
SCIENTISTS, ENGINEERS, TECHNICIANS

The space and arms races, in particular, won for the technical intelligentsia a relatively privileged status, and also access to the highest councils of authority. By

1954, the leadership had gone so far as to criticize conservative scientists for attempting to stifle creative discussion. Following Khrushchev's 1956 de-Stalinization speech, an Academy of Sciences resolution encouraged scientific debate and free discussion:

> It is necessary to develop more widely criticism and the creative
> free discussion of scientific problems, to eliminate more boldly the
> defects which are retarding development of science, and to raise
> significantly the role of the scientific community.[9]

Thus the essential milieu goal of scientists, freedom from the imposition of dogmatic scientific theories by the leadership, was partially won early in the post-Stalin era, except in biology, where a pseudo-scientific school led by Lysenko held out, with Khrushchev's apparent support, which galvanized some scientists to oppose the official line. Three hundred scientists signed a petition, which effected Lysenko's removal from the Presidency of the Academy of Agricultural Sciences in 1955, but Khrushchev apparently resuscitated him to buttress his agricultural policies throughout his primacy.[10] Lysenko remained a living symbol of arbitrary regime interference with the milieu goals of scientists. It is also symbolic that the rationale for the ultimate demise of his authority in 1965, after Khrushchev's fall, extended beyond scientific grounds to impugning the inefficient, uneconomic nature of his theories; thus officially, if indirectly, linking the lack of both scientific and economic progress with dogmatic suppression of creative freedom.[11]

JURISTS: THE PROFESSION OF THE LAW

The funeral orations for Stalin promised greater attention to constitutional rights of "all the Soviet people," but apparently did not touch off debates among jurists or between the regime and jurists until 1954, when the leadership urged legal reform, and 1956, when the Procurator-General suggested limited steps in the direction of the rule of law, such as wider publication and easier access to legal acts.[12] The legal profession in the Soviet Union, which can be divided into several sub-groups along functional lines, possesses no easily identifiable, all-encompassing milieu goals, except a negative one, which is opposition to terror as the essence of unlaw. An organic legal tradition has never fully developed in Russian or Soviet history, which tends to retard the jurists' influence, as does the stricture against forming an association of jurists. Nevertheless, the legal profession has actively participated in effecting the comprehensive legal reforms of the fifties and sixties and the debates surrounding them. Although jurists are found on all sides of the various debates[13] (including service as spokesmen for the most conservative elements of the power elite), in general, they tend to support two cardinal tenets of the rule of law—rationality and predictability of laws, and procedural safeguards for the accused. Even the role of the Procurator as prosecutor is mitigated by his dual function as guardian of the accused's rights, especially in the early stages of investigation.

In contrast, the power elite tends to view law as an instrument of control, facilitating its rule, rather than as an institutional restraint and limit on its power. While the early Bolsheviks argued that law, as a bourgeois remnant, would wither away, Stalin soon appreciated its utility as a vehicle for repression and propaganda;

however, although some of the leadership still clings to elements of this perspective, there appears a growing sophistication about law, emphasizing its stabilizing and legitimizing functions, and its long-range utility as an instrument of socialization, rather than of repression and mobilization. Despite this more positive view of law, the regime has been consistently more cool toward establishing procedural safeguards for the accused—a core tenet of Western notions of rule of law, which finds the communal traditions of Russia and the Soviet Union very infertile soil, indeed—than toward general rationalization of the legal system. The priority of the communal or Party-State interests over those of the individual threads most official Soviet discussions of civil liberties and human rights. Thus the section of the Soviet Constitution guaranteeing civil liberties, in its preamble, stresses the duties and obligations of Soviet citizens as well as their rights. Soviet jurisprudence consistently maintains that the dignity of man, sought by civil libertarians, rests first on the fulfillment of one's duties to the state, and second, on guaranteed economic rights, such as the right (and duty) to work, which are conceived to be equally as important as the political rights generally given priority in Western notions of civil liberties.

"Socialist Legality," the official Soviet position on law, maintains that, in theory, the Party remains the representative and voice of the will of the people and thus the voice of that communal body, the sovereign state, and therefore the ultimate arbiter of its interests vis-à-vis the individual. In theory, instead of institutional and procedural safeguards, Socialist Legality relies on the psychological safeguard of correctly trained ideological consciousness. This is often the loophole through which arbitrariness raises its head in an essentially legal manner, which may, nevertheless, do violence to the principles of rule of law. The regime, of course, also resorts to an assortment of extra-legal and illegal devices, which are well known; but it is important to realize that by employing the instrument of "correct ideological consciousness" as the ultimate criterion for construing legislation, the regime can "legally" subvert the rule of law through the device of arbitrary interpretation.

Nevertheless, the jurists have a vested interest inherent in the nature of their profession in employing legal means, as well as in a rational, orderly, legal and political system, free from a multiplicity of arbitrary interferences in the name of Socialist Legality by the administrators of the Party-State apparatus. All of this suggests at least some latent support for the Civil Liberties Movement despite negligible evidence of overt acts in its behalf. In this context, it is perhaps even more noteworthy, in assessing the potential of the Movement, to recall that facets of the official line—Socialist Legality—are congruent with some articulated demands of the Movement.

AFTER THE FALL: A NEW DICHOTOMY

For an instant from October 1964 to September 1965, the world glimpsed the image of a new dichotomy between progressive elements of the power elite and the liberal specialists on one side, and their more conservative counterparts on the other, instead of the old image of a relatively united elite alternately encouraging and repressing the liberal specialists. The extraordinary spectacle of the Party organ, *Pravda*, reprimanding the government organ, *Izvestia*, for counterposing intellectuality to party-mindedness had been preceded by another *Pravda* editorial, echoing Khrushchev's comment on the relationship between free expression and scientific and economic progress. Rumiantsev, the editor, argued that it was necessary "to learn how to open the road to everything talented and useful created by Soviet scientists and figures in culture and literature." And going further, he asserted that "genuine creation is possible only in an environment of search, experiment, and free expression and collision of opinions. . . . "[14] In short, progressive factions of the power elite in effect encouraged the aggregative process among the more liberal specialists in the middle class, by seeking their support, reiterating the intimate connections between their milieu goals, and associating these goals with the viability of the regime in order to buttress their claims to power.

FROM FERMENT TO MOVEMENT:
THE PROTEST PHASE

Since this new dichotomy threatened a cornerstone of the polity, Party unity and primacy, elements of the power elite decided to stage a trial of two liberal writers as a low-level warning designed to curb the mounting demands of the middle class. The crude conduct of the trial of Andrei Siniavsky and Yuli Daniel conjured up the specter of re-Stalinization and the loss of hard-won milieu goals, which initiated a series of overt protests and demonstrations almost unheard-of in Soviet history. The regime attempted to mitigate its errors initially, but quickly resorted to persecuting the demonstrators, which elicited new demonstrations and protests. The central theme of these protests from 1965 to 1968 was the demand that the regime adhere to the rule of law in trying the demonstrators, a demand which revealed three fundamental emphases: the proceduralist, the constitutionalist, and the rationalist, none of which can be identified with any particular group, but each apparently carrying different weight with the elite. The proceduralists, whose most eloquent spokesman is the scientist and legal specialist Valery Chalidze, focus on specific procedural guarantees usually associated with the rule of law, but denied most of the prosecuted dissidents. For example, the trials were heard either *in camera* or before hand-picked audiences. Or in some cases the law was *ex post facto*. Or the allegedly violated law was so vague as to provide an inadequate guide to acceptable behavior. The constitutionalists focus on apparent contradictions between the law allegedly violated and the Soviet Constitution, while the rationalists stress the fundamental arbitrariness of the whole mechanism, derived from the lack of clear standards by which one may judge the legality of his acts—a core tenet of the rule of law. While there is much overlapping and interlocking in these positions, the rationalist emphasis appears to have emerged into the mainstream as a result of its instrumentality and appeal to the elite.

FROM FERMENT TO MOVEMENT:
THE PROGRAMMATIC PHASE (1968-70)

By 1968 three forces had exercised an aggregative impact upon that form of dissent which once focused primarily on the disparate milieu goals of specialists: first the impetus of the brief involvement in the power struggle, second the fear of re-Stalinization, and third the umbrella-like theme of rule of law. By sucking the specialists into the vortex of the power struggle, the power elite itself had played a catalytic role in aggregating the Movement, which is often ignored. Both Khrushchev and *Pravda* had associated their milieu goals and related them to modernization. Both fear and the simple theme of rule of law, which retains the political advantage of meaning many things to many people, served to further crystallize the ferment into a loosely structured "Movement," which, nevertheless, encompassed extraordinary diversity in its ideology and tactics.

It is impossible to measure the extent of the support for the Movement. Andrei Amalrik estimates that over one thousand persons signed all the statements and letters, from the Siniavsky-Daniel trial to the arrest of Piotr Grigorenko in 1969, which demanded adherence to the law. For the Ginzburg-Galanskov trial, 738 persons signed the various protests. Of course, this kind of overt support entails enormous risks; thus, one can surmise without any real gauge other than the articulations, discussed previously, that significant latent support covering a vast array of activities also existed. The locus of this support in the middle class is suggested by Amalrik's occupational breakdown of the 738 protestors, described above: 45% were academics, 22% engaged in the arts, 13% were engineers and technical specialists, 9% publishing-house employees, teachers, doctors, and lawyers, 6% workers, and 5% students.[15]

While the tactic of employing open letters protesting violation of the rule of law with either a proceduralist, a constitutionalist, or a rationalist bent continued, the year 1968 ushered in a new array of tactics and messages. From mere protest, the Movement shifted to new organizational forms, designed to disseminate a bewildering variety of ideological appeals and programs, most of which would allegedly strengthen civil liberties. Yuri Glazov, a former Orientalist from Moscow University who fled to the West in 1971, listed eight explicit ideologies reflected in the new programs: neo-communist, constitutionalists, neo-Slavists, Christian-socialists, liberals, Christian Democrats, civil rights advocates, and Jewish activities.[16] Amalrik lists six ideologies competing with the official Marx-Leninism in Soviet society, which he claims have penetrated circles close to the pinnacle of power: official nationalism, neo-Slavophilism, Christian ideology, liberal ideology, genuine Marx-Leninism, and conformist reformist ideology.[17]

In general, the new programmatic documents reflecting these diverse ideologies struck three poses—reformist, oppositionist, and an occasional revolutionary. The reformists project the image of a pressure group lobbying for a variety of changes in the system, while accepting its essential form. The oppositionists seek to create an organized "party of opposition" in the classic sense, ready to replace the present regime, an innovation which would represent a substantial transformation of the system. The revolutionists reject the whole communist system and are quite few in number.

FROM FERMENT TO MOVEMENT:
ORGANIZATIONAL FORMS

In 1968 and 1969 two organizational forms emerged, which focused primarily on civil liberties—making them widely known, at least among the middle class, and facilitating their observance. In a very narrow sense one might define them as the Civil Liberties Movement, as distinct from the Democratic Movement, since their essential focus is securing civil liberties, rather than disseminating programs and ideologies that might also protect such liberties, if implemented. One form was the regular underground journal, *The Chronicle of Current Events*, which appeared in the traditional Russian form for circumventing censorship, the individually typed manuscript, called *samizdat*. Probably edited primarily by the technical intelligentsia, the *Chronicle* provided scrupulously objective accounts of the regime's illegal persecutions of the Movement, thus fostering a certain *esprit de corps* among the otherwise fluid currents of the Movement. The *Chronicle* made no serious appeals to the masses, nor did it seriously associate (although it did sympathize) with militant nationalist or religious movements. It calmly recounted the regime's violations of the rights guaranteed in the Soviet Constitution and the UN Declaration on Human Rights, in a tone characterized by moderation and rationality. The *Chronicle* clearly mirrors the Movement's essential unanimity on the importance of rule of law in promoting civil rights and democratization.[18] In 1971 another hitherto unknown underground journal of a more programmatic nature, *Political Diary*, circulated once a month in *samizdat* since 1964 (over 70 issues), surfaced in the West. Its contents reflected access to the highest levels in the polity. The appearance of these two journals on a regular basis over an extended period suggests significant latent support among elements of the power elite.[19]

The activities of the second organizational form, the Action Group for the Defense of Civil Rights, led by several leading scientists, represented a response to the intensifying repressions conjured up by the specter of the Czechoslovakian Spring. It resorted to a myriad of tactics aimed at forcing the authorities to adhere to the rule of law, such as vigils outside courtrooms and appeals to the UN Commission on Human Rights and to the World Conference of Communist Parties in Moscow. The Action Group went so far as to exclude members of any political party from its membership, and probably was tolerated only because of the international prominence of its central figure, the eminent physicist Andrei Sakharov. In the wave of 1972 repressions, a CPSU Central Committee decision apparently ordered suppression of the *Chronicle*, and the Action Group was somewhat emasculated by the exile of Valery Chalidze, another physicist and its leading legal specialist, whose citizenship was withdrawn while he was on a permitted lecture tour of America.

CIVIL LIBERTIES AND NATIONAL POWER: NATIONALISM AND RATIONALISM

As a result of their instrumentality and access to the regime, the increasingly active participation of liberal elements of the scientific and technical intelligentsia constitutes, perhaps, the most significant aspect of the civil liberties ferment. Between 1950 and 1966 the number of specialists engaged in scientific and technical activity in the USSR jumped from 714,000 to 2,741,000.[20] It is well known that technical competence is widespread among the power elite, and there is evidence that among the younger members of the CPSU Central Committee technical and scientific backgrounds predominate.[21] In Moscow, the seat of power, 164 scientific institutions employ 70,196 persons.[22] The backbone of the *Chronicle* and the Action Group was apparently scientists. Gradually from the liberal elements in this community emanated a new programmatic twist aimed at this multiplying group of specialists in the middle class and among the power elite, and perhaps at the more modernized elements of the military. The central theme was that national power and security depended on modernization; and modernization of an advanced state like the USSR required a rational economy and society, and maximum opportunity for creative freedom of expression. In short, it linked civil liberties and the rule of law with economic efficiency and military power. Without reforms in this direction, the USSR can expect to lag behind capitalist countries in the second industrial revolution and to gradually revert to the status of a second-rate provincial power, the liberal technical intelligentsia argued. The program eschewed militant demands associated with dissident nationality groups as well as direct appeals to the masses in favor of gradual reforms under the aegis of the CPSU.

THE MEDVEDEV AFFAIR: THE MOVEMENT DISPLAYS ITS INFLUENCE TECHNIQUES

Almost at the moment that the scientific-technical intelligentsia's leading spokesmen were presenting this nationalistic-rational appeal to the heads of the Party-State apparatus in 1970, Zhores Medvedev, a prominent member of their community, was confined to a mental hospital, the most morally repugnant of the regime's extra-legal instruments of political repression, an act which elicited the full panoply of somewhat sophisticated influence techniques developed in almost two decades of dialogue with the power elite. Most importantly, representatives of the Movement negotiated directly with members of the power elite to obtain Medvedev's release. To stress their loyalty to Marx-Leninism, they enlisted Old Bolsheviks to petition the authorities. The story of Medvedev's confinement was leaked to the world press to enlist the support of world public opinion. The Movement's legal specialists were consulted to determine the legality of the procedures employed in the confinement. And finally, another channel of access to the leadership, the Academy of Sciences, was enlisted in his behalf—reversing the transmission belt, so to speak. Medvedev's ultimate conditional release symbolized both the extent and limits of the Movement's influence, as well as the refined nature of the Movement's tactics that had evolved since the death of Stalin.[23]

REPRESSION INTENSIFIES (1972-73)

Since the Czech crisis of 1968, repressive measures against Soviet dissent had intensified, and by 1972 the arrest of the hitherto untouchable Piotr Yakir, son of a general executed by Stalin, the exile of Valery Chalidze, and the initiation of repressive measures against the *Chronicle* signalled even harsher times; however, that repression has always remained selective. Thus simultaneously Zhores Medvedev was granted permission to attend a British University. As his brother Roy put it: "In the eyes of the authorities even dissident intellectuals are divided into some kind of hierarchy with various categories—a table of ranks."[24]

CONCLUSION

The civil liberties ferment since the death of Stalin has disseminated among the power elite and the burgeoning middle class (while largely ignoring the masses) the opinion that modernization—which it intimately relates to national military power and security—of an advanced Communist Party-State requires a rule of law and freedom of expression. A broader spectrum of the Soviet middle class already accepts the general need for greater rationality and predictability to facilitate modernization, which would necessitate, at least, some amelioration of the arbitrary quality of rule permeating the Soviet polity. Of course, rationality by its nature entails some of the very same conditions as freedom and legal order. Articulations by elements of the power elite have reflected an appreciation of the importance of creative expression to economic and scientific progress in a post-industrial society. In this atmosphere, despite intermittent, selective repressions, the Civil Liberties Movement may serve over the long run as a catalyst for a gradual narrowing of the sphere of unlaw. It is, perhaps, premature to administer extreme unction to this "Movement" in a polity characterized by latent political activity which often smolders like a swampfire, even for a generation.

NOTES

[1] The term "catalyst" as employed herein emphasizes that the sustained energy required for a transformation of the political culture in the Soviet polity must emanate from above, from the power elite, although over time the ferment may spark a continuing series of minor reforms facilitating it. For a detailed analysis of the gradual transformation of legal institutions, see Peter Vanneman, *The Supreme Soviet: Politics and the Legislative Process in the Soviet Political System* (Beverly Hills, Calif.: Sage Series on Comparative Legislature, 1973).

[2] Andrei Amalrik, *Will the Soviet Union Survive Until 1984?* (New York: Perennial, 1962), p. 13.

[3] H. Gordon Skilling and Franklyn Griffiths, *Interest Groups in Soviet Politics* (Princeton: Princeton University Press, 1971), p. 380.

[4] Amalrik, *op. cit.*, p. 17.

[5] Arnold Wolfers, *Discord and Collaboration* (Baltimore: Johns Hopkins University Press, 1962), p. 73.

[6] The following discussion owes much to the excellent works in Skilling, *op. cit.*

[7] Michael Tatu, *Power in the Kremlin* (New York: Viking, 1968), pp. 246-49.

[8] *Ibid.*, pp. 305-306.

[9] *Vestnik Akademii Nauk*, 1956, No. 6, p. 49.

[10] Z. A. Medvedev, *The Rise and Fall of T. D. Lysenko* (New York: Columbia University Press, 1969), pp. 137-38.

[11] *Vestnik Adademii Nauk*, 1965, No. 11.

[12] A. J. C. Campbell, "The Legal Scene," *Survey*, July 1964, pp. 56-57.

[13] For more information on the impact of legal reforms, see Peter Vanneman, "The Hierarchy of Laws in the Soviet Communist Party-State System," *The International Lawyer*, December 1973.

[14] *Pravda*, September 9, 1965, and February 21, 1965.

[15] Amalrik, *op. cit.*, p. 15; Peter Reddaway estimates 2,000. See *Uncensored Russia* (New York: American Heritage, 1972), p. 23.

[16] *Rheinischer Merkur*, July 7, 1972.

[17] Amalrik, *op. cit.*, p. 39.

[18] Reddaway, *op. cit.*, contains translations of the *Chronicle*.

[19] *New York Times*, September 5, 1971, Section IV, p. 5.

[20] *Science Policy in the U.S.S.R.* (OECD Study: 1969), p. 679.

[21] George Fischer, *The Soviet System and Modern Society* (New York: 1968), pp. 125-134. Also, see A. Sakharov, V. Turchin, R. Medvedev, "Appeal of Soviet Scientists to Party-Government Leaders of the U.S.S.R.," translated and reprinted in *Survey*, Summer 1970, p. 169.

[22] V. Yagodkin, *Kommunist*, No. 11, July 1972.

[23] Z. A. and R. A. Medvedev, *A Question of Madness* (New York: Vintage, 1971).

[24] Medvedev, *op. cit.*, p. 49.

KHRUSHCHEV'S LIBERALIZATION AND THE RISE OF DISSENT IN THE USSR

Oleh S. Fedyshyn
Richmond College
of the City University of N.Y.

THE WEIGHT OF RUSSIA'S PAST

It is neither an exaggeration nor an indulgence in anti-Russian invective to describe Russia's past as a history of despotism and spiritual oppression of the individual. Along with this central theme in Russia's past, one can discern another important historic line—that of continued individual and collective opposition to political control and spiritual oppression which can be observed in that country's life, including its cultural, educational, and religious spheres. More often than not these manifestations of dissent and opposition were forced to assume muted, underground forms. At certain times there was a mere handful of lonely, courageous individuals waging a seemingly hopeless struggle for social justice and political freedom; at other times there existed impressive movements with widespread popular support and enjoying the sympathy of even certain segments of the Establishment.

A study of Russia's past further reveals another interesting pattern which is especially noticeable in the modern period: a repressive despotic tsar, or a period of intensified oppression, is followed by a "despotic reformer," or a period of at least partial easement of the usual suppression of civil and political rights. Thus, the rule of Alexander I followed the hysterical and dark days of his half-deranged father, Emperor Paul. The reign of Alexander I, in turn, was followed by the arch-reactionary rule of his younger brother, Nicholas I. In the sixties and seventies we have the age of great reforms of Alexander II, which was followed by the return to reaction in the reign of the last two Romanovs.

This pattern of spiritual oppression and dissident reaction to it, as well as the alternation between a repressive despotic ruler and a despotic reformer, seems to have continued also during the Soviet period. Thus, with certain obvious qualifications, Lenin's rule may be described as that of a despotic reformer. Then, spiritual oppression and cynical manipulation and dehumanization of man assumed unprecedentedly intense and violent forms under Stalin, and by the same token dissent and opposition to them produced new and more tragic manifestations as well. The mass defections of Soviet citizens during World War II are without parallel in history, and the same may be said of Stalin's purges of the late thirties and the deportations and repressions in the wake of the USSR's victory over Nazi Germany in 1945.

THE NATURE AND SCOPE OF
KHRUSHCHEV'S LIBERALIZATION

To continue the application of Russia's historical patterns to the Soviet period, the Khrushchevian interlude may well be referred to as the period of great reforms which, as was the case in the reign of Alexander II, gave impetus to the further rise of dissent in the country. True to Russia's historical pattern, the post-Khrushchev decade resembles very much the reactionary rule of the last two Romanovs. However, the crudeness of Soviet authorities and the obscurantism of their censors in the late nineteen sixties and seventies make us feel as if we lived back in the dark days of Nicholas I, when Chaadaev was declared insane and placed under house arrest, and Shevchenko was exiled as a common soldier to the Aral Sea area with express orders that he be prevented from doing any writing there.

No one can predict with any certainty how long this post-Khrushchev reaction will last. One thing is clear, however, and that is that Khrushchev's liberalization did leave a lasting mark on the Soviet society, even though it is not always so evident on the surface. It is equally clear that foreign comrades find it more and more difficult to brush aside the concern that their followers expressed recently over the treatment of Sakharov, Solzhenitsyn, and other Soviet dissenters.[1] It is in the light of such a lasting humanizing influence at home and abroad that Khrushchev's liberalization can really be properly appreciated.

It may be appropriate at this point to define the meaning of the term "liberalization" as used in this study. Even in reference to Western experience, with which most of us are well acquainted, the meaning of the term "liberal" is quite vague. In the Soviet context of the post-Stalin era, liberalization meant first of all doing away with the worst abuses of Stalinism and providing the peoples of the USSR with a new hope and purpose. Of course, the type of liberalization that took place under Khrushchev could not impress anyone who approached it from the perspective of constitutional government or democratic pluralism. From the perspective of the Stalinist nightmare, however, Khrushchevian liberalization even to the simplest of Soviet citizens meant that people no longer had to fear sudden and arbitrary arrest, that they were in general treated much better by the authorities, and that they could expect further improvements in their material and spiritual life in the future.[2] As for the educated elites, both within and outside the Party, the fruits of Khrushchevian liberalization were the following:

1. The rise of a more humane and responsible regime genuinely concerned about people's welfare trying to give a fuller and a more realistic expression to their needs and aspirations.
2. Increased influence of various groups and special interests in the governmental decision-making process.
3. Liberalization of the Soviet law and justice and the beginning of the development of a new constitutionalism promising greater freedom and equality for all.

4.   A new political climate more conducive to the development of a freer cultural, intellectual, and scientific life in the country, especially in the non-Russian areas, where Stalinist lawlessness was so much more pervasive and rampant.

It must be noted here that Khrushchev faced many problems as he moved slowly and cautiously away from the worst practices of Stalinism. Like Russia's earlier autocratic reformers, for example the first two Alexanders, Khrushchev too was faced with the classical dilemmas of enlightened despots: How to enact necessary reforms without jeopardizing the despotic controls? How to free creative powers of the people—in the economic, scientific, and cultural spheres—without weakening or even losing the monopoly of political power? How to revive initiative without encouraging too much independence, which may result in insubordination? How to ensure loyalty and cooperation in a more open and liberal society free of Stalinist terror and intimidation?

To these difficult dilemmas one should add Khrushchev's unenviable but, at the same time, from his point of view, unavoidable task of exposing and denouncing Stalin's crimes.[3] This task was all the more difficult because, as everyone knew, Khrushchev was the late dictator's protege and close associate; as a compromise choice of the Party bureaucracy for the top position in the country, he could not possibly agree to any basic changes in the system of which he himself was a product and which he was expected to strengthen and maintain. Unlike his predecessors among the tsarist despotic reformers, however, Khrushchev had to cope with all kinds of internal and external pressures and challenges, and his dilemma was felt and shared by literally millions of communists at home and abroad.[4]

FROM SEMIDESTALINIZATION TO SEMICONSENSUS

It is not surprising, therefore, that it took Khrushchev three long years to deliver his dramatic denunciation of Stalin's crimes, which he did at the Twentieth Party Congress in February 1956. Still, even this historic address, which came to be known as Khrushchev's secret speech, was delivered behind closed doors to a highly select body of communist representatives, and like most of the writings of the later dissenters was never formally published in the USSR. As was so often the case with the underground documents and other writings of the sixties and early seventies, this speech was discussed, praised, criticized, and even quoted, but never officially and explicitly acknowledged as authentic, nor made public. However, unlike the dissenters of the post-Khrushchev period, many of whom were persecuted for the publication of their writings abroad, Khrushchev was never reproached for the appearance of his secret speech in the Western press.

Khrushchev's secret speech, of course, was neither the beginning nor the end of destalinization. A number of quiet but highly significant early steps were taken by Stalin's successors, very much on Khrushchev's initiative, such as political amnesty and various economic concessions designed to reassure the general public. Many more measures were ordered after February 1956, aiming at the establishment of a new, more humane and liberal political climate in the country, then still in the deep shadow of apathy and fear produced by Stalinist terror and bureaucratic obscurantism and inefficiency.

Khrushchev's secret speech was clearly the high point in this painful but necessary process of self-criticism and re-examination of the past in order to build a more promising and impressive future. It will very likely remain one of the most important documents of the twentieth century and one of the most unique and dramatic denunciations of individual despotism of all times. This document is also quite unusual in that it was presented by the man who himself was directly involved in the crimes that he was now exposing, so that it may also be viewed as an extraordinary political confession.

Even though it was not intended as such, the secret speech may be regarded as one of the key writings in the literature of Soviet dissent, and Khrushchev's place in the history of his country will not only be that of a great reformer but that of one of the important dissenters of the post-Stalin period as well. This latter designation is especially appropriate in light of the retreat from his liberal and more flexible positions on the part of his successors in the late sixties and early seventies.

However, Khrushchev's programs and policies were more convincing than his words. One of the most astute West European Communist students of the Khrushchev period, Giuseppe Boffa, is quite right in arguing that domestic considerations were by far more significant in Khrushchev's destalinization efforts than any foreign policy concerns or outside pressures.[5] It was Khrushchev who, often against the stiff opposition of his conservative rivals, approved the publication of the early thaw works, thus preparing the ground for other liberalization measures and producing a more favorable political atmosphere for the historic Twentieth Party Congress.[6] Even earlier, and this was most fundamental in the creation of a new, more liberal climate in the country, Khrushchev dismantled the Stalinist concentration camp empire by freeing millions of its inmates and placed the greatly reduced secret police apparatus under the control of the Party.[7]

Although all these liberalization measures were welcomed abroad as heralds of a new atmosphere in Soviet life, their significance at home could hardly be overemphasized. Khrushchev and his supporters in the Presidium openly and solemnly promised to return to "Leninist norms" in Party life and in the treatment of non-Russian nationalities, and also to restore "socialist legality" in the realm of Soviet law and justice.

This last promise was, of course, most basic to all other reforms and changes and may well be viewed as the foundation of Khrushchev's liberalization as well as the indispensable guarantee for its continuation in the future. However simplistic and nonprofessional Khrushchev's populist views on law and justice may have been,[8] the authoritative foreign students in this field agree that he was both serious and sincere in his determination to make the Soviet system of law more rational and humane. It was Khrushchev who encouraged extensive legal debates which, in spite of certain doubts and zigzags on his part, in the words of one such American expert, produced "hundreds, indeed thousands, of needed reforms."[9]

It is easy to point out the incompleteness and the inadequacies of legal reforms under Khrushchev, but it is less clear to what extent he himself can be blamed for these failures.[10] From the perspective of a wholesale abandonment by his successors of even the modest and limited legal guarantees of the Khrushchev period, which took place in the late sixties and early seventies, his legal reforms look impressive indeed. It is even more important to keep in mind the positive impact that the promise of reestablishing "socialist legality," made shortly after Stalin's death, produced on those who experienced directly the worst practices of Stalinist "legal system." One can mention here police tribunals sentencing to as much as five years individuals accused of "socially dangerous" behavior, or deprivation of the right to legal counsel for those accused of terrorist acts.[11]

FROM LOYAL OPPOSITION TO OPEN DISSENT

The promise to return to "socialist legality" went a long way in reassuring the scientific and intellectual community of the country, whose support Khrushchev needed for his overall modernization drive. However, liberalization of the Soviet system of justice, the rehabilitations, and open admissions of legal violations of the past, also provided the encouragement—especially among the individuals of the younger generation—for their demands for further explanations and concessions, thus laying the basis for an impressive and determined dissent movement of the late sixties and early seventies when Khrushchev was no longer at the helm. Legal claims and arguments were used by many of these dissenters with considerable skill and sophistication. True, most of them have by now been silenced—through arrests, placement in psychiatric clinics, banishment to the West, or "voluntary" renunciation of their views as a result of various pressures or inducements—and at the time of the writing of this study (mid-1973) only Solzhenitsyn and Sakharov can still speak their minds.

These silenced and denounced dissenters have produced an impressive body of literature on Soviet law and various constitutional questions, providing a solid basis for further reforms and improvements in this area. These writings have been suppressed as effectively as the legal safeguards and constitutional guarantees promised in the early and more hopeful Khrushchev era were abandoned or watered down. But too much had been promised, conceded, denounced and even implemented for the hopes and drams of that period to be so easily forgotten. Nor could Khrushchev's motives behind his legal reforms and other domestic changes have failed to leave a deep and lasting imprint on today's generation. Again, as was the case with his secret speech and certain earlier measures of the immediate post-Stalin period, Khrushchev's liberalization of the late fifties and early sixties had its roots in internal pressures, and it aimed at increasing domestic support and cooperation. Similarly, more flexible and liberal relations within the communist camp were more closely linked to these domestic developments than to the influence of the improved relations with the West.

What Khrushchev tried to accomplish by these bold and daring moves and policies at home (and they were invariably viewed by his Stalinist opponents as dangerous and irresponsible) was to restore a feeling of confidence in the Party and the new Soviet leadership, to replace terror and fear by more subtle political controls and economic incentives (made more palatable by the promise to restore certain legal safeguards), and by allowing a carefully rationed amount of free discussion and criticism—which sometimes virtually verged on dissent—to develop a semblance of consensus and popular support which Khrushchev came to view as basic prerequisites for the modernization of the country.

Khrushchev's simplistic and unmarxian explanation of wholesale violations of "socialist legality" under Stalin, which he blamed on the late dictator and his secret police chief Beria alone, and his steadfast refusal to admit any defects or weaknesses in the Soviet system of government and justice, should not obscure his wish to break with the Stalinist heritage completely and irrevocably, nor should they belittle the achievements of his liberalization. Of course, Khrushchev had his doubts and frustrations and on several occasions appeared on the verge of abandoning his destalinization efforts. Perhaps even more significant than any of his doubts were challenges and pressures within the Party ruling circles, where Khrushchev was never as firmly in command as it appeared at the time. Michel Tatu, one of the most impressive Western students of that period, shows rather convincingly the limitations of Khrushchev's power and influence in the decade of his rule in the USSR.[12]

Khrushchev came probably closest to abandoning his destalinization drive in late 1962 and early 1963,[13] but there was never a possibility of his returning to Stalinism. He may not always have fully appreciated all the implications and consequences of his new course, but he was determined to go on with the liberalization of the general political climate in the country, even though he never proposed the weakening of the Party's monopoly of power. However crude his ideas on liberalization may have been, and whatever inconsistencies may have accompanied this process of bringing more rationality and humanity to Soviet life, Khrushchev did have certain choices before launching some of his programs, and he did not always elect to do what seemed easiest and most popular. Many of his economic policies and certain of his legal reforms as well as destalinization measures were in this category. Moreover, some careful students of this period concluded that Khrushchev had a strong and lasting commitment to destalinization and that he wished to carry this campaign further.[14]

It may be worth noting that this destalinization drive, one of the basic prerequisites for his liberalization, was not something that Khrushchev wished to limit to his secret pronouncements. He not only tolerated, but often encouraged the deeper probing into the tragedy of Stalinist terror, thus keeping the manifestations of ferment and dissent within the confines of "the loyal opposition" for which his liberalization seemed to have made a tacit provision. His handling of Solzhenitsyn, Yevtushenko, or Voznesensky is a good example of this flexible arrangement.

Still, the process of destalinization remained carefully controlled throughout Khrushchev's rule, and it is certain that a number of liberal Soviet writers and intellectuals would have preferred a much more thorough and comprehensive critique of the Stalinist aberration. It was, however, much more convenient for such distinguished foreign comrades as the late Palmiro Togliatti to call for further revelations and rehabilitations. In spite of all this, it still remains true that Khrushchev took destalinization more seriously than just about any other high-ranking Soviet official and most foreign communist leaders. At the same time, however, it was on Khrushchev's orders that Boris Pasternak was denounced and vilified in a well-orchestrated campaign after he received the Nobel prize for his *Doctor Zhivago*, and a young Soviet poet, Josif Brodsky, was banished to the subarctic region. Even more ominous was the involuntary confinement, in February 1964, of General Grigorenko in a psychiatric clinic in order to prevent him from continuing his repeated public demands for further revelations of the Stalinist past and for rehabilitation of its innocent victims, especially the Crimean Tatars.[15] Still, these were isolated cases, and it is possible that these were concessions that he was forced to make under the pressure of his conservative detractors.[16]

As disturbing as all these instances of persecution of individual Soviet intellectuals were, Khrushchev did create the atmosphere in which hundreds, even thousands, of similar intellectuals could come to their defense. Even more important was the new legal climate and the widespread feeling, which Khrushchev did so much to foster, that the days of Stalin's lawlessness were over once and for all. Moreover, while forcing Brodsky out of Leningrad and branding him as a "social parasite," Khrushchev permitted scores of poets to read their verses to thousands of eager listeners in sports arenas and public squares and allowed many of these young literary stars to go abroad at government expense.[17] Similarly, Grigorenko's confinement in a mental institution (and I do not mean to suggest here that somehow this most inhuman treatment could be defended) was "balanced" by the freeing and dispatching to Rome, after 18 years of sojourn in Siberian prison camps, of the Ukrainian Catholic prelate Archbishop Josyf Slipyi in 1963.[18]

Indeed, one could not simply conceive of the dissident movement of the sixties and seventies without Khrushchev's flexibility and liberalization. By allowing some criticism and literature of protest to be published legally in the Soviet Union—even though many of these works appeared after long delays and in limited editions—Khrushchev succeeded in retaining the loyalty and cooperation of most of the writers, artists, and scholars. He also refrained from prosecuting those who published abroad, and condoned the circulation of typed versions of works that could not be published officially. Khrushchev read some of these works himself and often approved their publication (*e.g., Terkin in the Other World* by Tvardovsky, Solzhenitsyn's *One Day in the Life of Ivan Denisovich*, or Yevtushenko's *Stalin's Heirs*).

It may be interesting to note that virtually all the dissenters of the late sixties and early seventies were fairly happy members of the Soviet Establishment under Khrushchev. Most of them were loyal and cooperative Soviet citizens who were confident that under his leadership further improvements and progress would be possible. After all, it was under Khrushchev that Soviet humor made its reappearance, poetry again became the property of the masses, and social criticism, human compassion, and love for the weak and meek could again be expressed, even though in cautious Aesopian language, from the Soviet stage.

Last but not least, it was Khrushchev who tried to bridge the widening generation gap by meeting Soviet youth halfway in an attempt to win it over. To accomplish this and also to pave the way for the restoration of "socialist legality"—however simplistically Khrushchev may have understood it—he ordered rehabilitation of many of Stalin's innocent victims. This particular aspect of Khrushchev's liberalization, according to a noted West European communist student of the period, became the "central theme" in the endless and excited talks that he had with his Soviet friends. Said he: "By the end of that year [1955] . . . everybody talked about it all the time."[19]

These rehabilitations, however, which were viewed initially as the best guarantee for the future and were so eagerly, even gratefully, followed by the concerned Soviet citizens, later on contributed significantly to the growth of ferment in Khrushchev's days which, under the leadership of less flexible men who succeeded him in 1964, soon turned into active and open dissent. In this sensitive area of rehabilitations, too, Khrushchev's well-meaning yet so incomplete and ambivalent efforts produced mixed and unexpected results. Not every innocent victim of Stalinist purges was rehabilitated, and too often no explanation was given as to why a given individual was destroyed. Equally disappointing were cases where a liquidated writer or intellectual was rehabilitated but his works were not. And no one was permitted to speak of those corrupt individuals who knowingly acted as false witnesses, nor the countless Stalinist prosecutors who ordered the destruction of so many innocent

Soviet citizens and who continued to hold responsible positions in various governmental agencies. As one may expect, these inconsistencies in the painful process of rehabilitation were especially glaring in the non-Russian Soviet republics, where such Stalinist excesses had been even more widespread and damaging than in Russia.

Thus, while trying to bridge the generation gap—and this was an old problem in Russia which Khrushchev understood better than most in the post-Stalin period—he unwittingly encouraged the Soviet sons not only to glorify the deeds but also to denounce the crimes of their fathers. Speaking of the Soviet youth of the post-Stalin period, a noted American student of modern Russia observed:

> They are not just opposed to their Stalinist parents (often referred to now as "the ancestors"), but are in many ways seeking renewed links with their grandparents. They are, in short, rediscovering some of the culture which was just reaching new richness in both the political and artistic spheres at the time of the Stalinist blight.[20]

Even though this quotation refers to the Soviet youth in general, this denunciation of Stalinist devastation is even more appropriate for the non-Russian areas where the Stalinist axe was wielded with the ferocity and abandon of a madman. Moreover, the sons of these unhappy lands have also come to realize that their fathers as well as grandfathers were more often the executed than the Stalinist executioners; and they also remember who sent to the distant Siberia their even more remote forefathers in the past.[21]

It was above all this human factor, which played such an important role in Khrushchev's destalinization and liberalization, that also contributed to the rise of ferment in his days and later on gave expression to a more outspoken and even more deeply felt dissent and opposition of the post-Khrushchev period. Thus, in spite of the defeats, humiliations and betrayals that have plagued the thinning ranks of these heroic dissenters in the early seventies, they are somehow carrying on, and there are good grounds to believe that the movement will not be crushed dead. For Khrushchev's "sense of personal outrage, a sense of humiliation lived through and resented, a genuine need for self-assertion and self-authentication,"[22]—a feeling that characterized his statements and comments on Stalin—did not disappear with his ouster and his death. This "personal Khrushchevian element"[23] is as much a key to the understanding of his liberalism as the echo of this old Russian sentiment in the stout hearts of the Sakharovs, Morozes, Grigorenkos, and Solzhenitsyns is the best hope for the future of this tortured land and its neighbors.

NOTES

[1] See, for example, the following dispatches in the *New York Times*: Theodore Shabad, "Soviet Dissidents and Confession," September 7, 1973; Theodore Shabad, "Critical Soviet Problem: Critics," September 14, 1973; and Paul Hofmann, "Soviet Curbs Troubling Italian Red Leaders," September 14, 1973.

[2] Khrushchev's popularity, especially in the fifties, cannot be disputed by anyone. As for Khrushchev's reformism and liberalism, one of the most impressive earlier

works suggesting that they played an important role in his policies was Carl A. Linden's *Khrushchev and the Soviet Leadership: 1957-1964* (Baltimore: The Johns Hopkins Press, 1966).

[3] Giuseppe Boffa, *Inside the Khrushchev Era* (New York: Marzani & Munsell, Publishers, 1959), p. 42. The author, an Italian communist journalist, quotes Anastas Mikoyan, who then stood very close to Khrushchev, as stating: "Many things we didn't know ourselves but only discovered at the time. How could we then have kept quiet, when anyone could have blamed us someday for hiding the truth?"

[4] *Ibid.*, especially chaps. 2 and 3. This source is very helpful in reconstructing the atmosphere prevailing in communist circles of the Soviet Union in 1955 and 1956.

[5] *Ibid.*, pp. 41-42. See also Michel Tatu, *Power in the Kremlin: From Khrushchev to Kosygin* (New York: The Viking Press, 1970), pp. 141-48. Tatu, perhaps the foremost Western authority on the Khrushchev period, also emphasized domestic factors behind Khrushchev's destalinization, stressing its use in the struggle against his opponents in the Central Committee.

[6] One of the most useful works on Khrushchev's "literary policies," even though it concentrates on the later period, is Priscilla Johnson and Leopold Labedz, eds., *Khrushchev and the Arts; The Politics of Soviet Culture, 1962-1964* (Cambridge, Mass.: The MIT Press, 1965).

[7] A good earlier work on the Soviet concentration camp empire is David J. Dallin and Boris I. Nicolaevsky, *Forced Labor in Soviet Russia* (New Haven: Yale University Press, 1947); see also Robert Conquest, *The Soviet Police System* (New York: F. A. Praeger, Publishers, 1968).

[8] John N. Hazard, "Soviet Law and Justice," in John W. Strong, eds., *The Soviet Union under Brezhnev and Kosygin* (New York: Van Nostrand Reinhold, 1971), pp. 93-114.

[9] Harold Berman, "The Law and the Soviet Citizen," in D. Richard Little, ed., *Liberalization in the USSR: Facade or Reality?* (Lexington, Mass.: Heath, 1968), p. 67.

[10] Hazard, *op. cit.*, p. 97.

[11] For further details see *ibid.*, p. 96.

[12] Carl A. Linden (*op. cit.*) was among the first students of Khrushchev to suggest the precariousness of his position in the last years of his rule. See also Tatu, *op. cit.*, Part II, chap. 3 and *passim.*

[13] Tatu, *op. cit.*, pp. 312-319. According to Tatu it was not until mid-1963 that Khrushchev could resume his destalinization drive, which he was forced to suspend in early February of that year (*ibid.*, pp. 312-358).

[14] William Hyland and Richard W. Shryock, *The Fall of Khrushchev* (New York: Funk & Wagnalls, 1968), p. 105; see also Linden, *op. cit.*, especially chap. 10.

[15] For further details see the letter from Z. Grigorenko, the General's wife, to Brezhnev, dated January 25, 1968, in P. Litvinov and P. Reddaway, eds., *The Trial of Four* (New York: The Viking Press, 1972), p. 240 and p. 274.

[16]Tatu repeatedly suggests this in his excellent *Power in the Kremlin, passim.*

[17]The best discussion of Khrushchev's relations with Soviet writers, poets, and artists is available in Johnson and Labedz, *op. cit.*

[18]The delicate talks that resulted in the freeing of Archbishop Slipyi were conducted by Norman Cousins, who went to Moscow on Khrushchev's invitation as a special representative of Pope John XXIII. For further details see Norman Counsins, "The Improbable Triumvirate: Khrushchev, Kennedy, and Pope John," *Saturday Review* (October 30, 1971), pp. 27-31.

[19]Boffa, *op. cit.*, p. 25. Between March 1953 and November 1957 four amnesty decrees were issued by the Soviet government (see, for example, *Pravda* of March 28, 1953, and November 2, 1957), and at the Twentieth Party Congress Khrushchev announced that in the three-year period following Stalin's death, the Supreme Court of the USSR rehabilitated a total of 7,679 individuals, mostly posthumously. Boris I. Nicolaevsky, ed., *The Crimes of the Stalin Era; Special Report to the 20th Congress of the Communist Party of the Soviet Union by Nikita S. Khrushchev* (New York: The New Leader, 1956), p. 32.

[20]James H. Billington, *The Icon and the Axe* (New York: Knopf, 1966), pp. 587-588.

[21]One of the most impressive works on this problem is that of a Soviet Ukrainian writer and critic, Ivan Dzyuba, *Internationalism or Russification? A Study in the Soviet Nationalities Problem* (London: Weidenfeldt & Nicolson, 1968).

[22]Abraham Brumberg, "Editor's 'Commentaries,' " in Abraham Brumberg, ed., *In Quest of Justice; Protest and Dissent in the Soviet Union Today* (New York: F. A. Praeger, Publishers, 1970), p. 18.

[23]*Ibid.*

RUSSIAN DISSENTERS AND
THE NATIONALITY QUESTION*

Yaroslav Bilinsky
University of Delaware
Newark, Delaware

> The largest colonial state maintaining
> around the Russian national core the largest
> number of peoples is the Soviet Union . . . The
> self-determination of the nations of the Soviet
> Union should be secured . . .
>
> *Program of the Democratic
> Movement of the Soviet Union*
> (1969), Article 5, Paragraphs 3
> and 5.

> Our slogan is Russia One and Indivisible.
>
> *The Nation Speaks—The Mani-
> festo of Russian Patriots* (1970),
> Section 3.

Ethnic diversity is a "stubborn fact" which has refused to wither away, much like the state in the Soviet Union—and despite the politics of the Soviet state. Zbigniew Brzezinski writes: "Nationality problems are critically important in the evaluation of domestic Soviet reality today. . . "[1] This phenomenon is not limited to the USSR but is a worldwide occurrence. Walker Connor has found that out of a total of 132 contemporary states, less than one tenth are essentially homogeneous from an ethnic viewpoint.[2]

---

*I would like to thank the Prolog Research Corporation of New York City and the staffs of the Library of Congress and the New York City Library for help with source materials. The article is based on a paper that was presented to and discussed at the 12th annual meeting of the Southern Conference of Slavic Studies, at the University of South Carolina, Columbia, S.C., October 12-13, 1973. This is a revised version.

Even more significant is the fact that modernization does not, as a rule, diminish ethnic diversity.[3] The main reason for this may be that essentially nationalism "is psychological, a matter of attitude rather than of fact."[4] Sir Isaiah Berlin defines nationalism—whether in the newly established states or among the minorities of the older nations—essentially as

> an automatic psychological accompaniment of liberation from foreign rule—a natural reaction, on Schiller's "bent twig" theory, against oppression or humiliation of a society that possesses national characteristics.[5]

Most interestingly, Sir Isaiah links contemporary nationalism to the beginning worldwide revolt against the apostles of untrammeled human—but seldom humane—reason in both capitalist and communist states. Far from being a relic of the past, it is, in his words, "a worldwide response to a *profound and natural* need on the part of newly liberated slaves—the 'decolonized' . . . "[6] I might add that it also inspires those who are still colonized, but who have come to resent their status more and more.

In this study I propose to sketch and briefly analyze the views that Russian dissenters have expressed concerning the nationality question in the Soviet Union, in their underground publications (*samizdat*). Because of the very nature of the material, I cannot claim to have exhausted the subject, only to have been reasonably complete.[7] The attitudes of the non-Russian nationalists (the emigrating Soviet Jews, for example; the Estonians, Latvians, and others) are beyond the scope of my work. At the same time it must be admitted that not all of the dissenters I have selected need to be ethnic Russians by descent (Amalrik is; but Grigorenko, for example, was born in a village in the Ukraine). The sample I have considered includes some bona fide Russian nationalists but it also comprises Moscow-based dissenters who think in all-Union terms as opposed to the republican oppositionists. Should I have called my study "All-Union Dissenters and the Nationality Question"? Only a specialist conversant with official Soviet terminology would have grasped the meaning on the second or third try. The term "All-Russian" would have been welcomed only by historians. "Russian dissenters" is an ambiguous and not very elegant concept, but it seems to be backed by popular usage. At the least, the attentive reader has been warned.

I. THE GENUINE MARXIST-LENINISTS

Andrei Amalrik, a professional historian and a well-known figure among the dissenters, has dubbed the main political opposition since about 1968 the "Democratic Movement."[8] In order to avoid confusion with an anonymous group that calls itself the "Democratic Movement of the Soviet Union," and that may or may not be identical to Amalrik's "Democratic Movement," we should avoid the latter term with reference to all the democratic dissenters. But Amalrik's categorization of "ideologies" or sub-groupings within the broad movement can be accepted with only slight modifications. For my purposes I am going to distinguish between those who regard themselves as (1) genuine Marxists-Leninists (the late Kosterin; Grigorenko, Roy Medvedev); (2) the moderate liberals (of the *Political Diary* and of the

Chronicle of Current Events; also the group around the Committee of Human Rights, most notably Academician Sakharov and Dr. Chalidze); (3) the more radical liberals (the anonymous members of the "Democratic Movement of the Soviet Union"); (4) Amalrik, who stands in a category by himself (I would call him a disillusioned Russian patriot); (5) Alexander Solzhenitsyn and Igor Shafarevich, who seem to incline toward neo-Slavophilism; (6) the other neo-Slavophiles (the group around the *samizdat* journal *Veche—The Council*, whose first editor was Osipov); and, finally, (7) the extreme Russian nationalists (the authors of *Slovo natsii—The Nation Speaks*).[9]

The fate of the Crimean Tatars who had been politically rehabilitated but who were not allowed to return to the Crimea presents a clearcut moral case. Both the late Russian writer Aleksei Kosterin and the better known Major General Pyotr Grigorenko have effectively championed their case. But unlike Grigorenko, Kosterin tries to come to grips with the entire nationality problem, not only its most luminous facet, that of the return of the deported Crimean Tatars. In his polemics with official spokesmen he writes, in the letter to the *Literary Gazette*:

> Yes, in the first years of the Revolution, in the 1920's thanks to the decisive and uncompromising application of the Leninist nationality policy, the struggle with local nationalism and even more with (Russian) great-power chauvinism, we had achieved that *all the peoples of the Russian Empire entered the U.S.S.R. really of their own free will.* But the subsequent practice of Stalin and of his followers through its Russian great-power nationalism (*velikoderzhavnost'iu*) has deepened local nationalism, has created centrifugal forces and thus weakened (*razshatyvaiut'*) the foundations of the U.S.S.R. that had been created and cemented by the powerful force of the voluntary union, a union in which there would not have been conceivable that one nation would do violence to another.[10]

An unkind critic might remark that on the general nationality question Kosterin's thought had not advanced beyond Lenin's ideas of 1922 or Khrushchev's of 1956. But this is precisely the point: outside of the glaring injustice perpetrated on the Crimean Tatars, which Kosterin would remedy forthwith, he remains a genuine Leninist in his thinking, one who tries to square the circle of conflicting Russian and non-Russian demands by a return to the 1920's, painted in roseate hues.

A similar Leninist approach was taken in 1968 by the historian Roy A. Medvedev, the brother of Zhores. In his big history of Stalinism (at least to judge by its English version) Roy Medvedev barely touches on the nationality question.[11] He also treats it gingerly in his 1969 protest to the editor of *Kommunist*: he mentions the execution under Stalin of high government officials, including those from Union Republics; the genocidal deportations of entire nationalities; and anti-Semitism.[12] It is in his 1970 pamphlet "The Middle East Conflict and the Jewish Question in the U.S.S.R." that Medvedev directly shows his attitude on the Jewish question and indirectly on the nationality problem as such.[13]

Basically, Roy Medvedev favors voluntary assimilation, especially in the case of Jews, which corresponds to the superficially plausible solution advocated by Lenin. The core of the nationality (the Ukrainians in the Ukraine, Georgians in Georgia, etc.) should be able to cultivate their national cultures, but as soon as they

leave their titular republics they ought to assimilate (e.g., he specifically opposes
Dziuba's demand that Ukrainians outside the Ukraine should be taught in
Ukrainian). The Jews, who have a national home not inside the USSR, but outside
(in Israel), are in a different position. He would allow Soviet Jews who want to cultivate their Jewishness inside the Soviet state to do so, while those who insist on
emigrating to Israel should be allowed to emigrate. But his obvious sympathy rests
with the "progressive" Jews, Armenians, etc., who have assimilated themselves to
the Russians. Being a practical and consistent man, he argues that no barriers be put
against their quest of merging in the Russian sea: specifically, the notorious Point 5
in Soviet personnel questionnaires and Point 3 in internal passports relating to
nationality should be abolished.[14] From the assimilationist Leninist viewpoint this
makes sense; but an outside observer would do well not to take his profession of the
voluntary nature of assimilation too seriously—since the 1930's the regime has
stacked the cards rather obviously in favor of assimilation, except in the case of Jews.

II. THE MODERATE LIBERALS

There are few materials on individual nationalities in the *Political Diary* (a
lengthy sympathetic study of the problem of Crimean Tatars,[15] an account of the
Volga Germans' meeting with the then President Mikoyan,[16] an annoyed and
slightly malicious report on the zeal of Ukrainian nationalists in the summer of
1965).[17] *The Diary*, which is mildly critical of the government, does not contain
any analysis of the nationality question as a whole, but it is difficult to judge since
only 11 out of the total of 70-odd issues had reached the West. The more outspoken
Chronicle of Current Events has refrained from editorializing on the nationality
question in any way, but its coverage of ethnically motivated resistance has been
extensive and sympathetic. By implication this is a testimony to the significance of
the problem.[18]

To turn to individuals who have openly signed their names: the well-known
historian Pyotr I. Yakir in early 1969 did mention the plight of the Crimean Tatars
and other deported nations.[19] More significant, given the author's eminent position
both in Soviet society and within the dissident movement, are the views of Academician Andrei D. Sakharov and his immediate collaborators.

Sakharov's views on the nationality question have shown an interesting progress over time. In his 10,000-word treatise of June 1968 (*Progress, Coexistence,
and Intellectual Freedom*) he mentions in passing Stalin's anti-Semitism and
Ukrainophobia, current anti-Semitism in personnel practices, and the continuing
disgraceful treatment of the Crimean Tatars. His solution: " . . . [A] ll departures
from Leninist principles [must be] acknowledged and analyzed and firm steps . . .
taken to correct mistakes."[20] But he does not provide any such analysis himself,
evidently considering it a secondary problem. On March 19, 1970, in his appeal to
Brezhnev and others (co-signed by physicist V. F. Turchin and Roy A. Medvedev),
Sakharov again demands the restoration of all rights to nations forcibly resettled
under Stalin, and the abolition of registration of nationality in passports and
questionnaires (as suggested by Medvedev perhaps?).[21]

November 4, 1970, A. D. Sakharov, together with A. N. Tverdokhlebov and
Valerii N. Chalidze, as full members, and A. S. Volpin and B. I. Tsukerman as
advisory members ("experts") established the Committee for Human Rights.[22]

Shortly thereafter in his report to the Committee Chalidze stressed the necessity to let the Crimean Tatars return home.[23] Later, both Chalidze and Sakharov defended the right of sentenced Soviet Jews to emigrate.[24] It is in his memorandum of 5 March 1971, together with its postscript of June 1972, that Sakharov comes to grips with the nationality question as a whole. "One must point out the increasingly acute nationalities problem . . . ," he writes in 1971 (in the 1972 postscript he accuses the government of "a deliberate aggravation of the nationalities problems").[25] Not unexpectedly, he calls for the repatriation of the Tatars and others and for allowing the emigration of Jews (Urgent Problem No. 3).[26] He also protests against legal discrimination.[27] But new and most interesting is his suggestion that the right of secession of the national republics be legally clarified and that people not be prosecuted for raising that question, but that open discussion of the issue be allowed. He writes:

> In my opinion, a juridical settlement of the problem and the passing of
> a law guaranteeing the right to secession would be of great internal
> and international significance as a confirmation of the anti-imperialist
> and anti-chauvinist nature of our policies. *The number of republics
> tending towards secession is, to all appearances, very small, and these
> tendencies would doubtless become even weaker with time as a
> result of the future democratization of the USSR.*[28]

He also assures his readers that even if any republic would peacefully secede from the USSR it "would maintain intact its ties with the socialist commonwealth of nations."[29]

Implicitly, Sakharov remains opposed to secession, but he is intellectually honest enough to allow the freedom of discussing that possibility. His hope is that "future democratization of the U.S.S.R." would make the dissolution of the USSR unnecessary, but *in extremis* he would let one or two republics go (the Baltic states? the Ukraine??). Though reluctantly, Sakharov in 1971 appears to have accepted the demand of the "Democratic Movement of the Soviet Union" for national self-determination.

III. THE RADICAL LIBERALS

The "Democratic Movement of the Soviet Union" allegedly comprises as many as 270,000 members, including 20,000 active leaders.[30] One may be skeptical about this claim, but one cannot fail to be impressed by the Movement's articulate writings. Its Program contains the fullest discussion of the nationality question so far, six out of a total of thirty-nine pages.

The authors of the Democratic Movement's Program, who merely sign themselves "The Democrats of Russia, the Ukraine, and the Baltic States," unlike the late Kosterin, proceed on the assumption that "the Soviet Union is a *forcible* union of peoples around the Great Russian national core."[31] At great length the Program describes both Russian and Soviet imperialism, from Ivan III through Stalin;[32] it then turns to a concise analysis of the present situation. As far as the Soviet peoples are concerned, the Soviet Constitution is a sham: it serves neither their interests nor the interests of their irredenta outside the USSR. Peoples have been deported, subjected to anti-Semitic and anti-nationalist persecutions. The more developed republics are being economically exploited. The central government artificially induces ethnic migrations, building up foreign colonies in the union-republics. The non-Russian peoples do not enjoy cultural autonomy outside of their titular republics; nor are there any Yiddish schools anywhere. The Russian chauvinists, who form but an insignificant minority of the Russian people, are violently opposed to any concessions to the peoples of the USSR.[33] The two key statements of the program are:

> 19. The Russian progressive intelligentsia understand and render themselves account of (the fact) that without a freedom of nations there cannot be individual freedom nor full genuine democratization of society.

> 20. The national-liberation movement of the peoples of the U.S.S.R. shall (*dolzhno*) act in full solidarity with and complement, the Russian (movement) for political freedoms, for the democratization of society.[34]

K. Volny (a pseudonym) put it even more clearly:

> Nationalist movements among the peoples of the USSR are natural and valuable allies of the democrats, for democracy is the best condition for genuine self-determination and the basis of the free organization of one's own national way of life. Hence the internationalism of the movement.[35]

Very noteworthy also are the seven detailed goals of the "Democratic Movement" in the nationality question, as follows:

1. The political self-determination of nations by means of an all-national balloting (referendum) with the participation of a supervisory commission of the UN.
2. The offer of cultural or economic autonomy to nations who have chosen not to secede from the Union of Democratic Republics.
3. The solution of territorial questions only with the help of an arbitrating commission of the UN.
4. The restitution of all moral, cultural, territorial and material losses of the nationalities incurred under the great-power hegemony.
5. The right of each small people to restrict the number of foreigners according to a norm acceptable for its ethnic existence.
6. Noninterference of the Union of Democratic Republics in the domestic affairs of the nations that had seceded.
7. Friendship, cooperation and mutual respect of the seceded nations and the Union of Democratic Republics within the framework of the UN.[36]

IV. AMALRIK—THE DISILLUSIONED RUSSIAN PATRIOT

The author of *Will the Soviet Union Survive Until 1984?* does not easily fit any of the dissenters' categories: part-historian, part-visionary, he is in a class by himself. His prognoses are as radical as the goals of the "Democratic Movement," but he shows a healthy skepticism concerning not only the justice of the opposition of the common man, but also the efficacy of the rational ideas of the middle class. Like the Slavophiles, of whom later, Amalrik probes the psyche of the Russian, but unlike them he is not enamored of what he sees. He predicts that the Soviet Union will drift into a long-drawn-out war with the People's Republic of China. Under prolonged stress, first the East European communist countries will break loose, then some of the Union Republics (the Baltic area, the Caucasus, and the Ukraine will experience intensified anti-Russian nationalism, then Central Asia and the regions along the Volga).[37] Most likely, according to Amalrik, "[t] he unavoidable 'deimperialization' will take place in an extremely painful way," with the power passing into the hands of extremist elements.[38] But Amalrik does not rule out a peaceful transition (incidentally, as desired by the "Democratic Movement of the Soviet Union").

Amalrik has been accused of lack of Russian patriotism. Actually, he does not gloat over the prospect of the disintegration of the Soviet Empire during a long and murderous war: he regards it as a painful but necessary step in the development of Russian freedoms. Like the late historian George Fedotov, Amalrik may be a disillusioned, tough-minded, anti-imperialist Russian patriot of democratic persuasion, and his warning against liberals who would sweep the pesky nationality question under the rug of a beautiful Western-type constitution ought—in my opinion—to be taken quite seriously.[39]

V. SOLZHENITSYN'S CALL FOR RUSSIAN MORAL REGENERATION AND THE CONQUEST OF THE "NORTH-EAST"

It would have been completely unnatural if the anti-imperial strictures of Amalrik and the "Democratic Movement" had not been answered by Russians, especially given the fact that the *Chronicle of Current Events* was sympathetic to the non-Russian cause. Though the political views of Alexander Solzhenitsyn and his associates overlap with those of the neo-Slavophiles, Solzhenitsyn's moral stature is such as to warrant separate treatment. In his *Letter to the Soviet Leaders* of 5 September 1973 Solzhenitsyn called upon his countrymen "not to be governed by considerations of political giantism, nor concern themselves with the fortunes of other hemispheres" but "to encourage the *inner*, the moral, the healthy development of the people."[40] For inspiration he would turn to authoritarian, Orthodox rather than to any liberal-democratic, secularist periods in Russian history and—most concretely—he would fully develop Siberia and the Russian North (his "North-East"). What implications has this for the nationality question?

In the first version of the *Letter*, as it apparently had been submitted to Brezhnev, Solzhenitsyn was prepared to pay the price for the shift of attention to the North-East by gradually relinquishing Russian control over Eastern Europe and Western and Southern parts of the USSR. In his words:

Of course, such a shift must mean sooner or later lifting our trustee-
ship from Eastern Europe, *the Baltic republics, Transcaucasia,
Central Asia and possibly even from parts of the present Ukraine.*
Nor can there be any question of our forcibly keeping any peripheral
nation within the borders of our country.[41]

For some unexplained reason, in editing the *Letter* for publication in the West,
Solzhenitsyn eliminated any specific references to the secession of parts of the
USSR itself. The second version reads:

Of course, a switch of this kind would oblige us sooner or later to
withdraw our protective surveillance of Eastern Europe. Nor can
there be any question of any peripheral nation being forcibly kept
within the bounds of our country.[42]

Apart from the tantalizing but smaller question of how Solzhenitsyn would propose
to divide the present Ukraine, there is the major problem why he has toned down
his passage on non-Russian peoples to the somewhat perfunctorily general declaration that there can be no "question of any peripheral nation being forcibly kept within the bounds of our country." Short of a direct explanation by the *Letter*'s author
himself, the analyst is reduced to speculation.[43]

Insofar as Solzhenitsyn approves the views of Igor Shafarevich, who has
extensively written on the nationality question in a book co-authored by
Solzhenitsyn,[44] the answer may be that as a Russian patriot Solzhenitsyn has
become increasingly offended at the tendency of non-Russian nationalists to blame
the Russian people for the existence and excesses of what both of them consider to
be the *Communist Soviet* Empire. While criticizing the "typically Russian . . .
inability to see the line that divides us from other nations, the lack of inner conviction in their right to exist within their own national identity"[45] and while
rejecting *Veche*'s encomiums of the Tsarist general Skobelev[46] (see below)
Shafarevich believes that the old Russian Empire, shorn of "socialist ideology,"
should be preserved.[47] Unlike Sakharov, Shafarevich also holds that as a rule—
"unless all spiritual links between the nations are broken"—plebiscites should not
be used to determine secession: for even a majority in the disputed area is but a
minority in "the state as a whole."[48] This proposition means, of course, that the
numerous Russians would always be able to veto the secession of any smaller
republics. This may also contradict Solzhenitsyn's promise to let the peripheral
nations decide their own fate.

VI. OTHER NEO-SLAVOPHILES

Earlier in 1971, Amalrik and the Democrats were implicitly challenged
by the new Russian patriotic and neo-Slavophile journal *Veche—The Council*. *Veche*
does not enter into political issues, but the direction of its thought has been well
caught by an anonymous collection of epigrams:

Russia is hated, it is covered with accusations, ruin is predicted for
it . . . [by Amalrik?-Y.B.]. But the main thing is that Russia

fails to be understood. All judgments regarding her are human conjectures.

Russia is the greatest sufferer, slandered, and crucified.

Russia will be resurrected contrary to everything and all! . . .

Russia can be only believed in![49]

It is not difficult to imagine how the author of these epigrams would regard the proposal to solve the nationality question through genuine self-determination, secession or cultural autonomy! Its editor, V. N. Osipov, has been described by a leading member of the Democratic Movement in Russia, recently arrived in the West, as a "right-wing nationalist, but a sincere religious believer and a truth-seeking individual."[50] But his journal has published a highly laudatory article on the Tsarist Russian General Skobelev, who conquered Central Asia,[51] and has also serialized a glorification of the Slavophiles by Russian architect M. Antonov.[52] Antonov is an admirer of Tsar Nicolas I; he also happens to be a close associate of fellow-architect A. Fetisov, who venerates both Stalin and Hitler and who considers that Sinyavsky and Daniel should have been shot.[53] Fetisov, in short, is a Russian Fascist, and Antonov, though perhaps not Osipov, is not far removed.

VII. EXTREME RUSSIAN NATIONALISTS

"The Manifesto of Russian Patriots," entitled *Slovo natsii* (*Nation Speaks*), racist—and anti-democratic—as it may be,[54] is most interesting from our point of view because it engages in lengthy and bitter polemics with the preceding "Program of the Democratic Movement," particularly on the nationality question. The extreme Russian patriots poke fun at the Democrats' desideratum that the newly seceded nations should not settle their historical accounts. They envisage Congo-like regimes on the periphery of Russia: they may err on the side of pessimism, but the Democrats' injunction does sound like a pious wish.[55] A lengthy section (4 out of 23 pages), proportionately even longer than in the Democratic Program, is exclusively devoted to the nationality question. It is, in fact, a direct, polemical reply to the corresponding Section in that Program.

The extreme Russian nationalists admit that the nationality question is important. It is to be found not only in the developing countries, but also in such highly developed countries as England, Canada, and Belgium. They take sharp issue with the thesis that Imperial Russia had been an economically, socially and culturally backward country that had overcome its internal dissension by outward expansion. Only a strong Tsardom could have successfully fought the many enemies of Russia. The liquidation of the Kazan Khanate was a historical inevitability, the conquest of Central Asia a progressive phenomenon. The *Nation Speaks* points out that by not having a Russian Communist Party, the Russians play a disproportionately small role in Party politics, unlike the Communist Party of the Ukraine.[56]

An eventual secession of the non-Russian republics is depicted as a *reductio ad absurdum*. In earlier times the Ukrainians and Byelorussians had been regarded only as parts of the Russian people; the Byelorussians still do not feel that they belong to any artificial Byelorussian nation. The nationalist movement in the Ukraine is strong; but the Ukrainian nationalists had better take heed. If and when the question of the separation of the Ukraine will be raised, so will be the question of a revision of Ukrainian frontiers. Entire provinces such as the Crimea, the Kharkov, Donetsk, Lugansk and Zaporozhye oblasts have an overwhelming Russian population; another string of important provinces has a largely Russified population. The Ukrainians might be left with a few rural central and western provinces; and the western provinces will be claimed by Poland! The Russian patriots also reject any Rumanian claims to Bessarabia, which is simply described as "our territory." Kazakhstan and Kirghizia have also been largely settled by Russians. Logically, *Slovo natsii* rejects any attempt to impose restrictions on Russian immigration (one of the most original proposals of the Democratic Program). It asks rhetorically, "Since when have we become foreigners on our land?"[57]

Not unexpectedly, the "Russian Patriots" reject accusations of economic exploitation (by means of a single example: Russia has been a welcome balance factor in Transcaucasia; otherwise the Georgians would have exploited everybody around!); and of anti-Semitism (the Jews are a privileged nation monopolizing Soviet science and culture). They serve notice that they are in favor of a one and indivisible Russia and that they will not spend any money on cultural services to small ethnic groups with their "non-existing cultures." For good measure, the would-be separatists are warned that only under Russian rule will they find greatness! Small nations become the laughing stock of mankind: they either slide into the bourgeois morass of the Swedish type, or degenerate into "a state of permanent anarchy, as in the Arab countries."[58]

VIII. CONCLUSIONS

This study shows that the strands of the Russian political opposition in the Soviet Union do not yield a single pattern with respect to the nationality question. There are those (the *Veche* and *Slovo natsii* groups) who are quite satisfied with the current Russian hegemony and those who call for real self-determination of the non-Russian nations (the drafters of the Program of the Democratic Movement of the Soviet Union, perhaps Sakharov of 1971-72). In between are the genuine Marxists-Leninists (Kosterin, Grigorenko, Roy Medvedev), the moderate liberals (Sakharov before 1971, Chalidze, Yakir), Amalrik, Solzhenitsyn and Shafarevich. There are those who are exclusively concerned with the obvious plight of the Crimean Tatars and those who look beyond. A very important split among the liberals and democrats is between those who advocate individual, human rights first and group, nationality rights second (Sakharov, Chalidze), and those who see nationality rights as being of equal importance (Democratic Movement). Emphasis on controversial nationality rights (self-determination, for example), might well push the regime in a conservative direction and make the attainment of individual rights more difficult.[59] But it is an open question whether a regime that is not prepared to yield on group rights will yield much to individuals. In a deeper sense, as pointed out above by Walker Connor and Sir Isaiah Berlin, since nationalism is essentially a psychological phenomenon, nationality rights and individual rights are closely interwoven. The views of at least one prominent dissenter have changed over time. Also, judging by a sarcastic reference in *Slovo natsii*, some of the Russian Democrats may not be Russian by descent.[60]

How strong and how representative are all these groups? Public disagreements in *samizdat* itself would indicate that some dissenters at least are skeptical about the optimistic claims of fellow-oppositionists. The *Democratic Movement*, for example, has been accused by the *Chronicle of Current Events* of misrepresenting the desirable as the already achieved.[61] In a very revealing autobiographical sketch Yuri Glazov has admitted that dissenters themselves do not know what to expect from their colleagues and friends: some would sign protest petitions despite any reasonable expectations, others on whom one had relied would find pretexts not to sign.[62] Amalrik and some Western authors are skeptical about the probable impact of at least the democratic, liberal dissenters: they may be rejected not only by the popular masses but also by the pseudo-intelligentsia of obedient state bureaucrats, not to speak of leading politicians.[63] On the other hand, to judge by the Iakovlev affair, the regime now seems to favor the Russian nationalista and neo-Slavophiles.[64] But our evidence does not suffice to show how representative those latter groups are of the Russian political opposition and of the Russian people as a whole. Intuitively I feel that they may be more representative than the Democratic Movement.

The most remarkable final conclusion is that whether they be on the left, in the center, or on the right; whether eagerly or reluctantly; whether integrally or piecemeal—in the late 1960's and early 1970's the Russian dissenters have grappled with the nationality question in the Soviet Union. Chances are that they will continue to do so for many more years: the problem is increasingly becoming more acute rather than attenuated.

NOTES

[1] Zbigniew Brzezinski, "Political Implications of Soviet Nationality Problems," in Edward Allworth, ed., *Soviet Nationality Problems* (New York: Columbia University Press, 1971), p. 72.

[2] Walker Connor, "Nation-Building or Nation Destroying?," *World Politics*, XXIV, 3 (April 1972), p. 320.

[3] *Ibid.*, pp. 321 ff., 328. For a good discussion of the term modernization, see Gunnar Myrdal, *Asian Drama: An Inquiry into the Poverty of Nations* (New York: The Twentieth Century Fund, 1968), Vol. 1, pp. 57-69; and John H. Kautsky, *The Political Consequences of Modernization* (New York: John Wiley, 1972), pp. 19-22. I would incline toward Myrdal's broader concept.

[4] Connor, "Nation-Building or Nation-Destroying?," p. 337.

[5] [Sir] Isaiah Berlin, "The Bent Twig: A Note on Nationalism," *Foreign Affairs*, 51, 1 (October 1972), p. 22.

[6] Berlin, "The Bent Twig," pp. 24 ff.; quotation on p. 30, emphasis added.

[7] I have, for example, systematically combed Vols. 1-13, 20-22 of Radio Liberty's *Sobranie dokumentov samizdata* (the other volumes were not available at the time of writing). I have read 32 issues of *Chronicle of Current Events*.

[8] Andrei Amalrik, *Will the Soviet Union Survive Until 1984?* (New York: Harper & Row, 1970), pp. 9-10. It had been written in April-June 1969.

[9] For Amalrik's breakdown see *ibid.*, p. 39.

[10] See *Sobranie dokumentov samizdata* (Munich: Radio Liberty, n.d.), Vol. 2, AS No. 114, pp. 10-11; emphasis added. Letter was written in mid-1968. Source henceforth abbreviated *S.d.s.*

[11] Roy A. Medvedev (David Joravsky and Georges Haupt, eds.), *Let History Judge: The Origins and Consequences of Stalinism* (New York: Alfred A. Knopf, 1971), pp. 203-207, 491-497. The original was finished in 1968.

[12] Roy Medvedev, *Faut-il réhabiliter Staline?* (Paris: Seuil, 1969), pp. 43, 44.

[13] Document AS No. 496 (47 pp.), in *S.d.s.*, Vol. 7. Long excerpt translated as Roy Medvedev, *"Samizdat*: Jews in the USSR: Document: Soviet Union," *Survey*, 79, 2 (Spring 1971), pp. 185-200.

[14] See either *S.d.s.*, Vol. 7, AS No. 496, pp. 28-36; or *"Samizdat*: Jews . . . ," pp. 195 ff.

[15] *Politicheskii Dnevnik*, No. 67 (April 1970), in *S.d.s.*, Vol. 20, AS No. 1011.

[16] *Politicheskii Dnevnik*, No. 9 (June 1965), in *S.d.s.*, Vol. 20, AS No. 1002.

[17] *Ibid.*

[18] See *Khronika tekushchikh sobytii*, Nos. 1-27 *passim* in *S.d.s.*, Vols. 10A and 10B. See also the analysis by D. Pospielovsky, *"Two Years" of the Chronicle of Current Events: A Review and Summary of Eleven Issues of the Samizdat Journal*. Radio Liberty Research Paper No. 37, 1970, pp. 29-32. Issues 28-31 and 32 of the *Chronicle* were published in 1974 by Khronika Press in New York.

[19] In his letter to the editor of *Kommunist* of 2 March 1969; translated as "Stalin: A Plea for a Criminal Investigation," *Survey*, 70/71 (Winter-Spring 1969), p. 266.

[20] Andrei D. Sakharov, *Progress, Coexistence and Intellectual Freedom* (New York: Norton, 1968), pp. 54, 65-66. Quotation on p. 66.

[21] A. D. Sakharov, V. F. Turchin, and R. A. Medvedev, "Appeal of Soviet Scientists to the Party-Government Leaders of the USSR," *Survey*, 76 (Summer 1970), p. 167 (points 8 and 14).

[22] See Valerii N. Chalidze, comp., *Obshchestvennye problemy*, No. 8 (November-December 1970), in *S.d.s.*, Vol. 9, AS No. 660.

[23] Chalidze, "Vazhnye aspekty problemy prav cheloveka v Sovetskom Soiuze: doklad Komitetu Prav Cheloveka," 10 December 1970, in *S.d.s.*, Vol. 9, AS No. 661, pp. 6-7.

[24] Sakharov, "On Freedom to Leave the Country," 20 February 1971, mentioned in Sakharov, "Memorandum," *Survey*, 18, 3 (Summer 1972), p. 233; "Obrashchenie V. Chalidze, podderzhanoe A. Sakharovym i A. Tverdokhlebovym v Prezidium VS SSSR o presledovanii evreev-repatriantov v SSSR," 20 May 1971, in *S.d.s.*, Vol. 9, AS No. 625.

[25] Sakharov, "Memorandum," pp. 225, 233.

[26] *Ibid.*, p. 224. In his critique of the Solzhenitsyn *Letter*, Sakharov went further and called for "a democratic solution of the problem of free departure from the USSR and return—for Russians, Germans, Jews, Ukrainians, Lithuanians,

Turkic peoples, Armenians and all others." See *The Times*, April 16, 1974, p. 7.

[27] "Memorandum," p. 229.

[28] *Ibid.*, p. 230; emphasis added.

[29] *Ibid.* It should also be noted that in a later work Sakharov briefly confirmed "the right of Soviet republics to secede and the right to discuss the question of secession." See A. D. Sakharov, *My Country and the World* (New York: Vintage Books, 1975), p. 102. The 1975 book contains relatively many sympathetic references to non-Russian nationalists (pp. 24, 27-28, 34, 36, 38, 42-43, 55, 89, 97).

[30] "Ocherk K. Vol'nogo 'Intelligentsia i demokraticheskoe dvizhenie'," *S.d.s.*, Vol. 8, AS No. 607, p. 36; excerpts translated in *Survey*, 17, 3 (Summer 1971), pp. 180-190, specific reference on p. 185.

[31] "Programma Demokraticheskogo Dvizheniia Sovetskogo Soiuza," (SSSR, 1969 god), *S.d.s.*, Vol. 5, AS No. 340, p. 24 (point No. 1).

[32] *Ibid.*, pp. 24-26 (points Nos. 2-10).

[33] *Ibid.*, pp. 26-28 (points Nos. 11-17).

[34] *Ibid.*, p. 28.

[35] "Ocherk K. Vol'nogo 'Intelligentsia . . .'," p. 35; translated in *Survey*, 17, 3 (Summer 1971), p. 185.

[36] "Programma Demokraticheskogo Dvizheniia . . . ," pp. 28-29.

[37] Amalrik, *Will the Soviet Union Survive Until 1984?*, p. 63.

[38] *Ibid.*, p. 64.

[39] See his critique of Miliukov reported by his American Friend Anatole Shub, " 'Will the USSR Survive . . . ?'—A Personal Comment," *Survey*, 74-75 (Spring 1970), p. 89. Also, *ibid.*, pp. 93-94.

[40] As first published in the *Sunday Times*, March 3, 1974, p. 36 f; emphasis in original.

[41] As cited by Theodore Shabad, "Solzhenitsyn Asks Kremlin to Abandon Communism and Split Up Soviet Union," *The New York Times*, March 3, 1974, p. 26 b; emphasis added.

[42] *Sunday Times*, March 3, 1974, p. 35 b.

[43] I have tried to obtain such an explanation, without success so far.

[44] Igor Shaferevich, "Separation or Reconciliation? The Nationalities Question in the USSR," in Alexander Solzhenitsyn *et alii, From Under the Rubble* (Boston, Mass.: Little, Brown, 1975), pp. 88-104. Shafarevich, a mathematician, had also been a member of the Human Rights Committee headed by Sakharov.

[45] Shafarevich, "Separation or . . . ," p. 102.

[46] *Ibid.*, p. 101.

[47] See, for example, *ibid.*, p. 99 (emphasis in original): "Has history not taught us at least this, that it is hardly the height of political wisdom to throw away centuries-old alliances like useless trash, and that it is necessary to begin, not by razing to the ground, but rather by *changing* and *improving*?"

[48] *Ibid.*, p. 103, approvingly referring to V. A. Maklakov, a Russian Constitutional Democrat.

[49] As cited by Dimitry Pospielovsky, "The Resurgence of Russian Nationalism in *Samizdat*," *Survey*, 19, 1 (Winter 1973), pp. 68-69.

[50] Pospielovsky, "The Resurgence . . . ," p. 56n. In September 1975 a Soviet court in Vladimir sentenced Osipov to eight years of strict regime labor camp (*The New York Times*, September 28, 1975, p. 9).

[51] "General M. D. Skobelev kak polkovodets i gosudarstvennyi deiatel'," *Veche*, No. 2 (19 May 1971), in *S.d.s.*, Vol. 21, AS No. 1020, pp. 48-66.

[52] M. Antonov, "Uchenie slavianofilov—vysshyi vzlet narodnogo samosoznaniia Rossii v doleninskii period," *Veche*, Nos. 1 (January 1971) and 2, in *S.d.s.*, Vol. 21; AS No. 1013, pp. 13-44; AS No. 1020, pp. 4-27.

[53] Pospielovsky, "The Resurgence . . . ," pp. 65 and 65n.

[54] "What are the basic characteristics of the nation? First, the racial type." See "Slovo natsii" (1970), *S.d.s.*, Vol. 8, AS No. 590, p. 8.

[55] "Slovo natsii," p. 7; cf. with "Programma Demokraticheskogo Dvizheniia Sovetskogo Soiuza (henceforth "Programma D.D.S.S.")," *S.d.s.*, Vol. 5, AS No. 340, p. 12.

[56] "Slovo natsii," pp. 15-16; cf. with "Programma D.D.S.S.," pp. 24-28.

[57] "Slovo natsii," pp. 16-17; last quotation on p. 17. Cf. "Programma D.D.S.S.," 28-29. N.B.: According to the 1970 census Russians did *not* constitute the absolute majority in any Ukrainian oblast, except in the Crimea. See *Radians'ka Ukraina*, 25 April 1971, p. 2 or *Digest of the Soviet Ukrainian Press*, 15, 6 (June 1971), 17-23.

[58] "Slovo natsii," pp. 17-19. The entire section on nationalities has been translated in "A Word to the Nation," *Survey*, 17, 3 (Summer 1971), pp. 195-198.

[59] Brzezinski, "Political Implications of Soviet Nationality Problems," pp. 76-77.

[60] Setting up a foreigners' immigration quota by Russians would reduce the number of "Russian democrats." "Slovo natsii," p. 17.

[61] *Khronika tekushchikh sobytii*, No. 14 (30 June 1970), in *S.d.s.*, Vol. 10A, AS No. 407, p. 38, and Vol. 10B, No. 25 (20 May 1972), p. 41 (AS No. 1130).

[62] Yuri Glazov, "*Samizdat*: Background to Dissent," *Survey*, 19, 1 (Winter 1973), p. 83.

[63] Amalrik, *Will the Soviet Union Survive Until 1984?*, pp. 16-21, 31-37; Lewis S. Feuer, "The Intelligentsia in Opposition," *Problems of Communism*, 19, 6 (November-December 1970), 7, 12 ff.; Pietro Sormani, "Dissidence in Moscow," *Survey*, 17, 2 (Spring 1971), 17 ff.

[64] In November 1972 Doctor of Historical Sciences and acting chief of the ideological department of the Party's Central Committee A. Iakovlev wrote a huge article more critical of Russian than of non-Russian nationalism ("Protiv antiistorizma," *Literaturnaia Gazeta*, 15 November 1972, pp. 4-5). In May 1973

he was demoted to Soviet Ambassador to Canada—see Robert G. Kaiser, *Washington Post*, 6 May 1973, A3. The sentencing of Osipov for Russian nationalism (see note 50 above) would seem to contradict this, except that non-Russian nationalists still outnumber Russian nationalists in Soviet labor camps.

THE SOCIAL STRUCTURE OF THE
MAJOR NATIONS OF THE USSR AS AN INDICATOR
OF THE SOVIET NATIONALITY POLICY

Borys Lewytskyj
Munich, West Germany

DIE SOZIALSTRUKTUR DER HAUPTNATIONEN DER
SOWJETUNION ALS INDIKATOR FÜR DIE
NATIONALITÄTENPOLITIK DER UDSSR

Der Begriff "Sozialstruktur" wird unterschiedlich definiert und verschieden weit gefasst. So versteht man darunter einmal die grobe Einteilung in Klassen oder Schichten, zum anderen aber auch die detaillierte Aufgliederung in Berufsgruppen und untermediäre Schichten. Sowjetische Autoren, Gesellschaftswissenschaftler wie Parteiideologen benutzten vor allem den weiter gefassten Strukturbegriff. Erst im letzten Jahrzehnt konstruierte man nicht mehr nur das Verschwinden der Ausbeuterklassen und das Anwachsen der Klassen der "Arbeiter" und "Angestellten," sondern begann allmählich zu differenzieren und Gruppen innerhalb der Arbeiter, Angestellten und Kolchosniki zu untersuchen.

Bei der Erforschung dieser bisher vernachlässigten Problematik fühlte man sich—wie üblich—gehalten, nach verbindlichen Aussagen Lenins zu suchen. Wie die bisher veröffentlichten grösseren Arbeiten zeigen, lieferten diese Schürfarbeiten doch kaum einen Ansatz für eine Bestandsaufnahme und Deutung der inzwischen eingetretenen sozialen Veränderungen. Es zeigte sich nämlich wieder einmal, dass Lenin nur gewaltsam als Prophet nutzbar zu machen ist, obwohl er eine treffende Analyse der Gesellschaft seiner Zeit geliefert hatte. Diese Gesellschaft vom Anfang des zwanzigsten Jahrhunderts gibt aber weder Raster noch Kategorien her, um die heutige differenzierte Industriegesellschaft zu erfassen.[1]

Worauf Statistiker, empirische Sozialforscher und Demographen stiessen, als sie sich vor etwa 15 Jahren an das Problem herantasteten, das war zunächst ein eklatanter Mangel an statistischem Material, an aussagekräftigen Daten. Damals häuften sich die Klagen über das lückenhafte und manipulierte Zahlenmaterial, was sicher mit dazu beitrug, dass sich inzwischen die Erhebungsmethoden wesentlich verbessert haben.

Ein zweites—wohl noch entscheidenderes—Problem war politischer Natur. Während bestimmte Behörden und Wissenschaftler vor allem ein Bild der Sozialstruktur der *gesamten sowjetischen Gesellschaft* wünschten, verlangten andere Wissenschaftler, neben diesen Globaldaten solle auch die *Sozialstruktur der einzelnen Nationen* erfasst werden.

Die Auseinandersetzung zwischen den Anhängern beider Standpunkte verschärfte sich im Zusammenhang mit der Diskussion über die Nationalitätenpolitik ganz allgemein, so wie sie an der Wende zwischen fünfziger und sechziger Jahren aufgeflammt war. Damals wurde die "wirtschaftliche Einheit" aller sowjetischen Nationen als ein Annäherungsfaktor immer wieder beschworen, während über die inhaltliche Auslegung dieses Annäherungsfaktors unterschiedliche Auffassungen bestanden. Die Anhänger der "Verschmelzungstheorie" interpretierten die ökonomische Einheit vor allem als einheitliche Eigentumsform und Wirtschaftsleitung, die daraus folgenden engen wirtschaftlichen Wechselbeziehungen als Gemeinsamkeit wirtschaftlicher Interessen und Ziele im gesamtstaatlichen Masstab. Die Anhänger einer auf "internationalistischen" Prinzipien—so wie sie von der offiziellen sowjetischen Propaganda selbst immer wieder beschworen werden—beruhenden Deutung kritisierten diese Theorie als einseitig und unzulänglich. Sie verwiesen darauf, dass die ökonomische Einheit der sowjetischen Völker nicht nur eine wechselseitige Annäherung bringe, sondern—das wichtigste--auch die *Arbeitsteilung innerhalb der einzelnen Nationen beschleunige.*[2]

Diese Auseinandersetzung über Einheit und Einheitlichkeit der sowjetischen Wirtschaft beeinflusste unmittelbar die Richtung der Erforschung der Sozialstruktur. Das Problem der Arbeitsteilung innerhalb einer "sozialistischen Nation" und damit zusammenhängend das Problem des Wandels der Sozialstruktur wurden aus der Fragestellung "Was ist eine sozialistische Nation eigentlich" ganz herausgelöst. Die Folge davon war, dass die Erforschung der Sozialstruktur der einzelnen Nationen und Völkerschaften der UdSSR vernachlässigt wurde, während die Sozialstruktur der gesamten sowjetischen Gesellschaft in den Mittelpunkt des Interesses rückte. Diese Beschränkung ist besonders in den letzten Jahren deutlich hervorgetreten, die feierliche Proklamation des Entstehens des "sovetskij narod" als einer "neuen historischen Menschengemeinschaft" gab den Wissenschaftlern eine unmissverständliche Anweisung, wie sie künftig das Problem anzugehen haben.

Bei der Untersuchung der gesamtsowjetischen Sozialstruktur sprechen sowjetische Autoren gewöhnlich von drei Entwicklungsphasen. Sie bezeichnen die erste als "Übergangsphase vom Kapitalismus zum Sozialismus" und datieren sie von 1917-1937; parallel zur Vernichtung der "Ausbeuterklassen" und des Klassenfeindes habe sich die "sozialistische" Wirtschafts- und Gesellschaftsordnung etabliert. Die nächste Phase des "Übergangs" wird von 1937 bis zum Ende der fünfziger Jahre angesetzt und z.B. von S. L. Senjavskij folgendermassen charakterisiert:

In diesen Jahren festigten sich noch mehr die soziopolitischen Grundlagen unserer Gesellschaft—das Bündnis der Arbeiterklasse mit der Kolchosbauernschaft und der sozialistischen Intelligenz. In dieser Zeit konnten sich jedoch im Zusammenhang mit der Vervollkommnung der sozialistischen Ungestaltungen die Tendenzen zur Bewegung hin zur klassenlosen, sozial homogenen kommunistischen Gesellschaft noch nicht in weitem Masse entfalten.[3]

In diesen Zeitraum fiel auch die Notwendigkeit, die Sozialstruktur der neu hinzugekommenen Republiken des Baltikums, eines Teils Moldawiens, der Westukraine und Westbelorusslands anzugleichen.

Die dritte Phase wird als die des "entfalteten Sozialismus" bezeichnet, in der sich eine weitere fortschrittliche Entwicklung der Sozialstruktur abzeichne:

> In dieser heutigen Etappe ist die Haupttendenz des Wandels der Sozialstruktur der sowjetischen Gesellschaft die weitere Annäherung der Klassen und sozialen Schichten in Richtung grösserer sozialer Homogenität auf der Grundlage der stürmischen Entwicklung der Produktivkräfte, die sich unter der wachsenden Einwirkung der wissenschaftlich-technischen Revolution und der weiteren Vervollkommnung der Produktionsverhältnisse vollzieht.[4]

Im folgenden soll die Sozialstruktur der Hauptnationen anhand jüngster verfügbarer Daten dargestellt werden. Eine solche Untersuchung wird es uns ermöglichen, die Unterschiede zu analysieren, die zwischen den Ergebnissen einer gesamtsowjetischen Betrachtung und denen einer Analyse nach nationalen Kriterien auftreten. Daran ist dann auch zu prüfen, ob die Proklamierung der nationalen Gleichberechtigung und des Aufblühens der Nationen der Wirklichkeit entspricht, ob sich nicht im Gegensatz zu diesem Anspruch ein erhebliches soziales Gefälle abzeichnet. Hier, bei der Untersuchung der Sozialstruktur, kann die sowjetische Nationalitätenpolitik auf ihren wahren Gehalt hin überprüft werden: positive bzw. negative Veränderungen sind unmittelbare Folge der bewusst und planmässig betriebenen Politik der Partei- und Staatsführung, in deren Dienst ja die Tätigkeit all ihrer mächtigen Hebel und Apparate gestellt ist.

Vorauszuschicken ist allerdings, dass eine solche Untersuchung erheblichen Schwierigkeiten begegnet, denn die sowjetischen Statistiken wurden zwar in bezug auf Grossgruppen etwas auskunftsfreudiger, nicht jedoch dort, wo es um soziale Schichten innerhalb der einzelnen Nationen geht, über einzelne Berufsgruppen ist unter dieser Fragestellung häufig gar nichts zu erfahren. Trotz dieser Schwierigkeiten genügt das vorliegende Material, um die Grundtendenz der Wandlungsprozesse und die gegenwärtigen Hauptmerkmale der Sozialstruktur herauszuarbeiten.

ZU DEN WICHTIGSTEN VORAUSSETZUNGEN SOZIALER VERÄNDERUNGEN

Unter den spezifischen vom zaristischen Russland ererbten Bedingungen mussten im Sowjetstaat die schlichtesten Voraussetzungen für Fortschritt jeder Art zunächst mühsam geschaffen werden. Ein wichtiges Hindernis war der Analphabetismus der Bevölkerung; bei der Volkszählung von 1926 waren erst mehr als 56 % der Bevölkerung zwischen 9 und 49 Jahren alphabetisiert, auf dem Lande war es gerade die Hälfte dieser Altersgruppe. Die zaristische Nationalitätenpolitik hatte inweiten Landstrichen verhindert, dass Schulen in nationalen Sprachen bzw. Schulen überhaupt errichtet wurden. Die sofort nach der Oktoberrevolution ausgerufene "Kulturrevolution" und die "Likbez"–(Beseitigung des Analphabetismus) Kampagne brachten hier in relativ kurzer Zeit beachtliche Verbesserungen. Es gelang, der weitgehend abgestumpften Landbevölkerung einen gewissen Bildungsenthusiasmus zu vermitteln. Träger der Bildungskampagne in den nationalen Gebieten war vor allem die einheimische Intelligenz, einschliesslich klerikaler Kreise. Die heutige Propagandabemühung, die Kulturrevolution rückwirkend zu einem "Geschenk des grossen russischen Bruders an die nichtrussischen Völker" umzudeuten, widerspricht weitgehend den Tatsachen, und zwar allein schon deshalb, weil die Russen einmal selbst einen erklecklichen Anteil von Analphabeten zählten und zum anderen auch die Sprache der "Beschenkten" gar nicht beherrschten. Deren Alphabetisierung jedoch musste zwangsläufig in ihrer Muttersprache erfolgen. Der Alphabetisierungskampagne waren bis 1939 bereits sehr grosse Erfolge beschieden, die Alphabetisierungsquote in der Altersgruppe 9-19 Jahre lage zwischen 93,4 % in Georgien und 77,7 % in Turkmenien. Gleichzeitig wurde sehr rasch ein Netz von Schulen verschiedenster Typen aufgebaut. 1939 hatten von je Tausend Personen im Alter von über 10 Jahren Hoch- und mittlere (abgeschlossene wie nichtabgeschlossene) Bildung: in der Georgischen SSR 165, Ukrainischen SSR 120, RSFSR 109, Usbekischen SSR 55 und Tadshikischen SSR 40. Die Förderung des Bildungswesens war in den dreissiger Jahren in allen Republiken zu beobachten und hätte auch verhindern können, dass das Bildungsgefälle zum Hindernis für einen Kurs nationaler Gleichberechtigung bei der weiteren Entwicklung der Sowjetunion wurde.

URBANISIERUNG ALS ENTWICKLUNGSFAKTOR

Der Trend zur Urbanisierung in den Unionsrepubliken ist aus nachstehender Tabelle ersichtlich.

Tabelle 1

Stadtbevölkerung

Republik	Stadtbevölkerung insg. (in Mill.)				in % zur Gesamtbev. der Republik			
	1913	1940	1965	1971	1913	1940	1965	1971
RSFSR	15,7	37,9	74,7	84,4	17	34	59	64
Ukrainische SSR	6,8	14,0	23,3	27,0	19	34	51	56
Belorussische SSR	0,9	1,9	3,3	4,2	14	21	39	46
Usbekische SSR	1,0	1,6	3,7	4,6	24	25	36	37
Kasachische SSR	0,5	1,8	5,7	6,9	10	30	47	52
Georgische SSR	0,6	1,1	2,0	2,3	26	31	46	48
Aserbaidsh. SSR	0,5	1,2	2,3	2,6	24	37	50	51
Litauische SSR	0,3	0,6	1,3	1,6	13	23	45	53
Moldau SSR	0,2	0,3	0,9	1,2	13	13	28	33
Lettische SSR	0,9	0,6	1,3	1,5	38	35	60	64
Kirgisische SSR	0,1	0,3	0,9	1,1	12	22	37	38
Tadshikische SSR	0,09	0,2	0,9	1,1	9	19	36	38
Armenische SSR	0,1	0,3	1,2	1,5	10	28	56	61
Turkmenische SSR	0,1	0,4	0,9	1,1	11	35	48	48
Estnische SSR	0,1	0,3	0,8	0,9	19	34	63	66

Quelle: "Narodnoe chozjajstvo SSSR 1922-1972," S. 499 ff.

Mehr als 50 % Stadtbevölkerung zählten 1971 acht Unionsrepubliken, wobei die Estnische SSR mit 66 % an der Spitze steht, gefolgt von der RSFSR und der Lettischen SSR mit 64 %, der Armenischen SSR mit 61 %, der Ukrainischen SSR mit 56 %, der Litauischen SSR mit 53, der Kasachischen mit 52 und der Aserbeidshanischen mit 51 %.

Neben dem natürlichen Bevölkerungszuwachs wird die Zunahme der Stadtbevölkerung in der Sowjetunion aus drei weiteren Quellen gespeist: die erste ist—ein weltweites Phänomen—die Abwanderung der Landbewohner in die Städte. Die zweite liesse sich als "administrativ" charakterisieren, indem bestimmte, bisher als "ländliche" Siedlungen definierte Orte nun als "städtische" geführt werden. Die Kriterien für eine solche Umbenennung sind recht uneinheitlich, einmal geht man von der wirtschaftlichen Abhängigkeit und Quasi-Zugehörigkeit zu einer grösseren Industriestadt aus, in anderen Fällen geschieht es nach der Ansiedlung von Industriebetrieben. Daneben spielen auch verschiedene andere Kriterien eine Rolle, die hier im einzelnen nicht aufzuzählen sind. Der Anteil der Einwohner von Städten mit weniger als 10 Tsd. Bewohnern ist relativ hoch, 1970 betrug er 11,9 % der Gesamtbevölkerung der UdSSR.[5]

In den nichtrussischen Republiken ist eine der wichtigsten Urbanisierungsquellen eine dritte: *die Immigration von ausserhalb der Republik.* Im Vielvölkerstaat Sowjetunion—zur Hälfte vom früheren Kolonialvolk der Russen bewohnt—stehen deren Beziehungen zur zweiten Bevölkerungshälfte zwangsläufig im Mittelpunkt aller Probleme der Wechselbeziehungen zwischen den einzelnen Völkern, ja sozusagen im Zentrum von deren Entwicklung. Lässt man die Migration der Russen in Republiken ausserhalb der RSFSR ausser acht, dann vernachlässigt man den entscheidenden Faktor sozialen Wandels in der gesamten Sowjetunion. Die nachstehende Tabelle zeigt den Anteil und die Anzahl der Russen in den nichtrussischen Unionsrepubliken.

Tabelle 2

Russen ausserhalb der RSFSR

Republik	1926 in Taus.	in %	1959 in Taus.	in %	1970 in Taus.	in %
Ukrainische SSR	2.530	8,8	7.091	16,9	9.126	19,4
Belorussische SSR	384	7,7	659	8,1	938	10,4
Usbekische SSR	243	5,5	1.091	13,5	1.473	12,5
Kasachische SSR	1.280	20,0	3.974	42,7	5.522	42,4
Georgische SSR	96	3,6	408	10,1	397	8,5
Aserbaidshan. SSR	221	9,5	501	13,6	510	10,0
Litauische SSR	-	-	231	8,5	268	8,6
Moldau SSR	49	8,5	293	10,2	414	11,6
Lettische SSR	-	-	556	26,6	705	29,8
Kirgisische SSR	116	11,7	624	30,2	856	29,2
Tadshikische SSR	1	0,7	263	13,3	344	11,9

Tabelle 2 (cont'd)

Republik	1926 in Taus.	in %	1959 in Taus.	in %	1970 in Taus.	in %
Armenische SSR	20	2,2	56	3,2	66	2,7
Turkmenische SSR	75	8,2	263	17,3	313	14,5
Estnische SSR	-	-	240	20,1	335	24,7

Quellen: für 1926: A. M. Jegiazarjan "Ob osnovnych tendencijach razvitija socialistiĉeskich nacij SSSR" (Über die Haupttendenzen der Entwicklung der sozialistischen Nationen der UdSSR), S. 88 ff; für 1959: "Itogi vsesojuznoj perepisi naselenija 1959 goda" (Ergebnisse der Volkszählung von 1959) nach Republiken; für 1970: "Narodnoe chozjajstvo SSSR 1922-1972," S. 516 ff.

Ausserhalb der RSFSR lebten 1926 5,0 Mill. Russen, 1970 waren es—die baltischen Republiken ausgenommen—19,959 Mill., also fast viermal soviel. In der Zeit zwischen den Volkszählungen von 1959 und 1970 stieg die Anzahl der ausserhalb der RSFSR lebenden Russen von 16,25 Mill. auf 21,267 Mill., also um etwas mehr als ein Drittel. Die folgende Tabelle zeigt ein weiteres entscheidendes Merkmal der russischen Migrationspolitik: die Russen siedeln vorzugsweise in den Städten der Gastrepubliken.

Tabelle 3

Anteil der Russen an der Stadtbevölkerung der Unionsrepubliken (ohne RSFSR) (Stand v. 1959 und 1970)

Russen ausserhalb d. RSFSR insg.	1959 (in Taus.)	1970
	16.250	21.267
davon i.d.Städten	12,085	17.054

	Absol. Zahl d.Russen i. d. Städten d.Republik (i.Taus.)		Ihr Anteil in % a.d. Gesamtzahl d.Russen i. d.Republik		Anteil d. Russen in % a.d.gesamten Stadtbevölk. d.Republik	
	1959	1970	1959	1970	1959	1970
Ukrainische SSR	5.726	7.712	80,7	84,5	29,9	30,0
Belorussische SSR	480	768	72,8	81,9	19,4	19,3
Usbekische SSR	913	1.312	83,7	87,7	33,5	30,4
Kasachische SSR	2.343	3.818	58,9	69,4	57,6	58,0
Georgische SSR	322	328	78,8	82,6	18,7	14,6
Aserbaidshanische SSR	439	470	87,6	92,1	24,8	18,3

Tabelle 3 (cont'd)

	Absol. Zahl d.Russen i. d.Städten d.Republik (i. Taus.)		Ihr Anteil in % a.d. Gesamtzahl d.Russen i. d.Republik		Anteil d. Russen in % a.d.gesamten Stadtbevölk. d.Republik	
	1959	1970	1959	1970	1959	1970
Litauische SSR	178	227	77,0	85,0	17,0	14,5
Moldau SSR	195	319	66,5	77,0	30,3	28,2
Lettische SSR	405	561	72,8	79,6	34,5	38,0
Kirgisische SSR	360	564	57,6	65,9	51,7	51,4
Tadshikische SSR	228	322	86,6	93,9	35,3	30,0
Armenische SSR	40	52	71,4	78,8	4,5	3,5
Turkmenische SSR	248	299	94,2	95,5	35,3	30,0
Estnische SSR	208	298	86,6	89,2	30,8	34,0

Quelle: "Itogi vsesojuznoj perepisi naselenija 1959 goda," nach Republiken (unter der Rubrik 'Stadtbevölkerung') und eigenen Berechnungen und "Itogi vsesojuznoj perepisi naselenija 1970 goda," Bd.4,

Die Angaben für 1970 bestätigen einen verstärkten Zustrom der Russen in die Städte der Unionsrepubliken, besonders in der Ukraine, in Mittelasien und im baltischen Raum. In den 11 Jahren zwischen den beiden letzten Zählungen übersiedelten z.B. nach Mittelasien und Kasachstan, 1,5 Mill. Russen, mehr als eine Million in die Ukraine, ca. 200 Tausend nach Belorussland und 250 Tausend in die beltischen Republiken.[6]

Während 1959 80,7% aller Russen in der Ukraine in den Städten lebten, waren es 1970 bereits 84,5%. In Mittelasien entsprechend 66% und 74,3%, in den baltischen Republiken 78% und 83%. Besonders ungünstig ist die Situation für die Hauptnationen der mittelasiastischen Republiken. 1959 betrug der Anteil der Russen an der Stadtbevölkerung 46,3% mit und 36,7% ohne Kasachstan, der Anteil der Hauptnationen dagegen nur 25,6% mit und 32,5% ohne Kasachstan. 1970 machten die Russen dort 45% mit und 33,2% ohne Kasachstan und die Hauptnationen 28,0% mit und 37,5! ohne Kasachstan aus.

Wie die detaillierten Angaben zur Sozialstruktur zeigen werden, ist dieser hohe Anteil von Russen und der anhaltende Zustrom ein Indiz für Praktiken, die dem proklamierten Internationalismus der sowjetischen Nationalitätenpolitik strikt zuwiderlaufen.

DIE SOZIALSTRUKTUR DER REPUBLIKEN UND HAUPTNATIONEN

Sowjetische Analysen untersuchen in letzter Zeit fast nur noch die gesamtsowjetische Sozialstruktur, wobei Daten über die grossen sozialen Gruppen— Arbeiter, Angestellte und Kolchosbauern—als gesamtstaatliches Phänomen global ausgewiesen werden. Dies ist als statistische Manipulation zu werten,mit der zu verschleiern versucht wird, welches Gefälle sich beim näheren Hinsehen zwischen der Sozialstruktur der einzelnen Republiken und Nationen enthüllt. Hier ist ausdrücklich davor zu warnen, dieser euphemistischen Darstellungsweise zu folgen, und die nationalen bzw. regionalen Unterschiede zu ignorieren.

Die beiden nachstehenden Tabellen zeigen, dass 1939 wie auch noch 1959 in der Russischen SFSR der höchste Grad von Identität zwischen der Sozialstruktur der Hauptnation und der der Republik zu beobachten war. Für 1959 fallen beide noch am wenigsten bei der Estnischen SSR auseinander.

Betrachtet man die "Arbeiter"—im sowjetischen Selbstverständnis als die "führende Kraft" und "fortschrittlichste Klasse" der Sowjetunion wie auch natürlich der Republiken apostrophiert—, so ist vorauszuschicken, dass hierbei einen sehr hohen Anteil die Sowchosarbeiter darstellen.

Entscheidende Aussagekraft kommt daher den Angaben über die Industriearbeiter zu, deren Anteil leider nur für die Hauptnationen bekannt ist.

Den höchsten Anteil von Industriearbeitern weisen die Russen in ihrer Republik auf, gefolgt von Letten, Esten und Armeniern, während die Ukraine—die ein sehr hohes Industriepotential hat—nur 15 % ihrer nationalen Bevölkerung als Industriearbeiter ausweisen kann. Besonders niedrig ist der Anteil der Industriearbeiter unter den mittelasiatischen Hauptnationen und bei den Moldawiern.

Für die Gruppe der "Angestellten" wies die Volkszählung von 1959 aus, dass etwa ein Viertel von ihnen auf dem Lande lebt. Doch wie unsere Tabelle zeigt, klafft auch hier der Anteil bei den Hauptnationen und den Republiken auseinander, die RSFSR und die Russen wieder ausgenommen. Ein besonders starkes Abweichen ist wiederum für Mittelasien und für die Moldaurepublik zu beobachten. Die auf dem Lande dominierende Hauptnation kann sich in der Gruppe der "Angestellten" nicht entsprechend im Gesamtrepubliksmassstab durchsetzen, da offensichtlich in den Städten mit ihrem hohen russischen Bevölkerungsanteil eine sehr starke Überfremdung gerade des Verwaltungs—, gehobenen Dienstleistungs- und vor allem Managementbereiches in den Anteilswerten so stark durchschlägt.

Ein Vergleich mit den Daten für 1926 bestätigt zudem, dass die einheimische Bevölkerung vom volkswirtschaftlichen Wachstum und von Modernisierungsmassnahmen praktisch ausgeschlossen blieb, dass die Vorteile der Entwicklungspolitik vor allem von den Eingewanderten getragen wurden. Am Fortschritt und Wohlstand der Städte partizipierte die einheimische Bevölkerung am wenigsten. Diese Tabelle hält praktisch die Ausgangslage vom zaristischen Russland fest.

Tabelle 4

Soziale Struktur der Bevölkerung der Unionsrepubliken und Ihrer Hauptnationen (in %)

Stand von 1959

	Gesamtbevölkerung				Hauptnation				
	Arbeiter und Angest.	Arbeiter	Ange-stellte	Kolchos-bauern u.a.	Arbeiter und Angest.	Arbeiter	Indu-strie-arbeiter	Ange-stellte	Kolchos-bauern u.a.
UdSSR	68	48	20	32	-	-	-	-	-
RSFSR	76	54	22	24	76	54	23	22	24
Ukrainische SSR	58	41	17	42	47	34	15	13	53
Belorussische SSR	51	35	16	49	43	31	11	12	57
Usbekische SSR	57	40	17	43	35	27	4	8	65
Kasachische SSR	79	58	21	21	60	44	6	16	40
Georgische SSR	56	32	24	44	45	22	10	23	35
Aserbaidsh. SSR	57	35	22	43	39	24	8	15	51
Litauische SSR	56	40	16	44	48	34	12	14	52
Moldau SSR	32	21	11	68	17	13	4	4	83
Lettische	73	51	22	27	65	46	19	19	35
Kirgisische SSR	58	40	18	42	30	22	4	8	70
Tadshikische SSR	46	30	16	54	26	18	4	8	74
Armenische SSR	62	40	22	38	60	38	17	22	40
Turkmenische SSR	57	37	21	42	31	22	5	9	69
Estnische SSR	79	55	24	21	73	51	19	22	27

Ju.V. Arutjunjan "Social'naja struktura sel'skogo naselenija SSSR" (Soziale Struktur der Landbevölkerung der UdSSR), S. 84.

Tabelle 5

Soziale Struktur der Bevölkerung der UDSSR
(in %)

Stand von 1939

Republik	Gesamtbevölkerung					Hauptnation				
	Arbeiter und Angest.	Arbeiter	Ange-stellte	Kolch.-bauern	and. soz. Gruppen	Arbeiter und Angest.	Arbeiter	Ange-stellte	Kolch.-bauern	andere soziale Gruppen
UdSSR	50,2	32,5	17,7	47,2	2,6	–	–	–	–	–
RSFSR	53,6	35,0	18,6	43,9	2,5	56,9	38,2	18,7	38,5	4,7
Ukrainische SSR	49,8	32,6	17,2	48,7	1,5	42,4	29,3	13,1	54,6	3,0
Belorussische SSR	36,4	21,9	14,5	57,2	6,4	31,5	20,7	10,8	60,4	8,1
Usbekische SSR	32,2	19,3	12,9	64,9	2,9	16,5	11,1	5,4	79,6	3,9
Kasachische SSR	51,2	33,8	17,4	47,5	1,3	33,6	25,6	8,0	60,8	5,6
Georgische SSR	36,7	19,5	17,2	52,7	10,6	29,4	12,4	17,0	58,2	12,4
Aserbaidsh. SSR	41,7	25,1	16,6	54,2	4,1	21,7	12,2	9,5	70,1	8,2
Litauische SSR	–	–	–	–	–	–	–	–	–	–
Moldau SSR	–	–	–	–	–	–	–	–	–	–
Lettische SSR	–	–	–	–	–	–	–	–	–	–
Kirgisische SSR	33,7	21,3	12,4	62,2	4,1	12,1	7,5	4,6	83,8	4,1
Tadshikische SSR	23,1	12,9	10,2	72,5	4,4	14,4	8,7	5,7	79,2	6,4
Armenische SSR	32,2	17,6	14,6	64,1	3,7	41,3	21,5	19,7	52,5	6,2
Turkmenische SSR	40,6	25,2	15,4	56,3	3,1	17,7	11,7	6,1	77,2	5,1
Estnische SSR	–	–	–	–	–	–	–	–	–	–

"Istorija SSSR" Nr. 4/1972, S. 6.

Tabelle 6

Nationale Zusammensetzung der Arbeiter und Angestellten der Unionsrepubliken

(Stand von 1926)

Republik	Gesamtbevölkerung (in Taus.)	Anteil in %	Arbeiter (in Taus.)	Anteil in %	Angestellte (in Taus.)	Anteil in %
Ukrainische SSR	29.018,2	100,0	1.071,9	100,0	750,1	100,0
Ukrainer	28.218,8	80,0	585,7	54,6	388,2	51,7
Russen	2.677,2	9,2	312,6	29,2	187,6	25,0
Belorussische SSR	4.983,2	100,0	121,9	100,0	99,7	100,0
Belorussen	4.017,3	80,6	71,8	58,9	50,9	51,0
Russen	383,8	7,7	16,2	13,3	16,3	16,4
Armenische SSR	880,5	100,0	28,3	100,0	16,5	100,0
Armenier	743,6	84,5	22,9	80,9	15,2	92,2
Russen	19,5	2,2	0,4	1,4	0,6	3,4
Aserbaidshanische SSR	2.314,6	100,0	149,2	100,0	71,0	100,0
Aserbaidshaner	1.438,0	62,1	63,5	42,6	17,2	24,3
Russen	220,5	9,5	33,6	22,5	28,9	40,8
Georgische SSR	2.666,5	100,0	67,2	100,0	74,5	100,0
Georgier	1.788,2	67,1	35,5	52,8	43,5	58,5
Russen	96,1	3,6	7,8	11,6	12,1	16,2
Usbekische SSR	5.272,8	100,0	136,9	100,0	73,9	100,0
Usbeken	3.475,2	65,9	69,0	50,4	16,4	22,2
Russen	246,5	4,7	24,0	17,5	38,1	51,6
Turkmenische SSR	1.000,9	100,0	25,9	100,0	17,9	100,0
Turkmenen	719,8	71,9	6,9	26,6	1,4	8,1
Russen	75,4	7,3	9,1	35,1	11,5	64,2

"Istorija SSSR" Nr. 6/1972, S. 139.

Die letzte grosse soziale Gruppe, die "Kolchosbauern," machen nur bei fünf Hauptnationen weniger als 50 % der nationalen Erwerbebevölkerung aus: bei Russen, Kasachen, Letten, Armeniern und Esten. Eine besonders herausragende "Kolchosnation" sind danach die Moldawier mit mehr als vier Fünfteln, gefolgt von Tadshiken, Kirgisen und Turkmenen mit etwa drei Vierteln, und den Usbeken mit zwei Dritteln der Bevölkerung. Besonders bemerkenswert ist in diesem Zusammenhang der hohe Anteil von Kolchosbauern unter den Ukrainern, der erheblich über dem entsprechenden Anteil der Republik liegt (53 % gegenüber 42 %).

Diese Tabelle ist insofern präziser als die von Arutjunjan ausgearbeitete, als sie nicht "gesellschaftliche Gruppen," sondern nur die in der Volkswirtschaft Tätigen berücksichtigt. Für die Sozialstruktur der Hauptnationen ist sie aufschlussreich insoweit, als—Kasachstan ausgenommen—die Russen an der Landbevölkerung der Unionsrepubliken nur einen geringen Prozentsatz stellen. Aus der Rubrik "Anteil der in der Landwirtschaft beschäftigten Arbeiter auf dem Lande an der Gesamtzahl der Arbeiter" lässt sich ein allgemeines Bild gewinnen, das noch schlechter ausfällt, als das über die "gesellschaftlichen Gruppen" vermittelte. So gehen in den gesamtsowjetischen Durchschnitt von 11 % für den Anteil der in der Landwirtschaft beschäftigten Arbeiter an der Gesamtzahl der Arbeiter so unterschiedliche Werte ein wie 5,3 % für die Aserbaidshanische SSR, 19,0 % für die Belorussische SSR und 32,0 % für die Usbekische SSR. Diese Zahl hängt natürlich direkt damit zusammen, einen wie grossen Anteil die Sowchosen in der Landwirtschaft der jeweiligen Republik haben. Zu den in Tabelle 4 angeführten Kolchosniki müssen also die Landwirtschaftsarbeiter hinzugerechnet werden, um ein Bild von der agrarischen bzw. "modernen" Struktur einer Volkswirtschaft zu geben.

Die Daten über die Angestellten sind insofern sehr aufschlussreich, als sie in einigen Republiken einen sehr hohen Anteil der auf dem Lande tätigen Angestellten abenso wie der in der Landwirtschaft beschäftigten Angestellten ausweisen. Das bedeutet aber, dass die Gesamtgruppe der Angestellten nach dem Kriterium der nationalen Zusammensetzung entsprechend korrigiert gesehen werden muss: der Anteil der Hauptnationen an den auf dem Lande tätigen Angestellten ist—nach der deutlichen Gewohnheit der Russen, überwiegend in Städten zu siedeln—als sehr viel höher anzusetzen als in den Städten. Der Anteil der Hauptnationen unter den Angestellten in Städten muss demnach also entsprechend niedriger sein.

Tabelle 7

Anteil der Arbeiter und Angestellten auf dem Lande an der Gesamtzahl der Arbeiter und Angestellten nach Unionsrepubliken

(Stand 1959)

Republik	Anteil d. Arbeiter auf dem Lande a.d. Gesamtz.d.Arbeiter in der Republik	Anteil d.in der Landwirtsch. besch. Arbeiter a.d.Ge-samtzahl d.Arbeiter	Anteil d.Angest. auf dem Lande a.d. Gesamtz.d.Angest. in der Republik	Anteil d.in der Landwirtsch. besch. Angest.a.d.Gesamt-zahl d. Angest.
Udssr	32,6	11,0	27,0	2,5
RSFSR	31,3	9,6	26,0	2,3
Ukrainische SSR	28,6	7,4	25,5	1,8
Belorussische SSR	48,0	19,0	35,0	2,6
Usbekische SSR	49,2	32,0	34,3	5,0
Kasachische SSR	46,0	27,7	38,5	7,5
Georgische SSR	25,4	8,7	9,4	1,8
Aserbaidshanische SSR	19,2	5,3	22,5	1,5
Litauische SSR	38,4	14,5	24,6	3,3
Moldau SSR	41,8	11,0	40,5	1,1
Lettische SSR	31,0	12,7	18,4	2,8
Kirgisische SSR	46,1	20,6	40,7	4,5
Tadshikische SSR	31,7	13,0	33,0	2,3
Armenische SSR	26,7	11,7	23,4	1,8
Turkmenische SSR	20,8	6,7	20,1	1,6
Estnische SSR	32,3	14,4	20,9	3,6

Berechnet nach Tabelle 33 der "Itogi ..." für die UdSSR und die Unionsrepubliken.

ANTEIL DER SPEZIALISTEN DER HAUPTNATIONEN

Wie die nachstehende Tabelle zeigt, entspricht auch bei den Spezialisten mit Hoch- und mittlerer Fachschulbildung der Anteil der einzelnen Nationen nicht ihrem Bevölkerungsanteil.

Table 8

Zahl und Anteil der in der Volkswirtschaft beschäftigten Spezialisten mit Hoch- und mittlerer Fachschulbildung nach den Hauptnationen der Unionsrepubliken

(Stand: November 1970)

	Ant.a.d. gesamt- bev. in %	Spezialisten (in Taus.)			
		mit Hoch- schul- bildung	Ant. in %	mit mittl. Fachschul- bildung	Ant. in %
Gesamtzahl der in der Volkswirtschaft be- schäftigten Spezialisten		6.852,6		9.988,1	
darunter:					
Russen	53,3	4.033,6	58,9	6.425,9	64,3
Ukrainer	16,8	1.031,2	15,0	1.613,7	16,1
Belorussen	3,7	204,1	3,0	337,7	3,4
Usbeken	3,8	139,6	2,0	131,5	1,3
Kasachen	2,1	96,8	1,4	104,9	1,0
Georgier	1,3	149,3	2,2	110,4	1,1
Aserbaidshaner	1,8	98,2	1,4	107,4	1,1
Litauer	1,1	66,8	1,0	103,3	1,0
Moldauier	1,1	32,7	0,5	45,4	0,5
Letten	0,5	43,2	0,6	62,6	0,6
Kirgisen	0,5	24,0	0,3	22,2	0,2
Tadshiken	0,8	29,6	0,4	26,8	0,3
Armenier	1,4	128,1	1,9	102,1	1,0
Turkmenen	0,6	26,0	0,4	21,8	0,2
Esten	0,4	35,7	0,5	49,5	0,5

"Narodnoe obrazovanie, nauka i kultura v SSSR," S. 240 und "Vestnik statistiki" No. 5/1971, S. 22.

Bei den Russen ist ein deutliches Übergewicht zu spüren, vor allem bei den Beschäftigten mit mittlerer Fachschulbildung. Deren Bedeutung liegt vor allem darin, dass hier die gesamte für die Industrialisierung und für eine Industriegesellschaft erforderliche Schicht von Technikern, Meistern und qualifizierten Facharbeitern, Laboranten u.a. erfasst ist. Obwohl ihre Ausbildung kürzer und auch weniger kostspielig als die der Hochschulabsolventen ist, darf man ihre Wichtigkeit also nicht unterschätzen. Eine sehr starke Diskrepanz ist für die mittelasiatischen Nationen festzustellen. Angaben über die nationale Zusammensetzung der Beschäftigten mit Hoch- und mittlerer Fachschulbildung *in den Republiken* werden von der sowjetischen Statistik nicht geliefert. Doch selbst wenn man annimmt, dass alle Spezialisten einer bestimmten Qualifikation in der Republik selbst tätig sind, deren Hauptnation sie angehören—was ziemlich unwahrscheinlich ist—so ergäbe sich, dass sie in den fünf mittelasiastischen Unionsrepubliken zusammengenommen immer noch nicht mehr als 44,7 % aller dort tätigen Hochschul- und 32,4 % aller dort tätigen Fachschulabsolventen ausmachen.

Die nachstehende Tabelle gibt einen Überblick über die landwirtschaftlichen Spezialisten und ihren Einsatz in ihrer Republik bzw. in der UdSSR überhaupt.

Tabelle 9

Landwirtschaftliche Spezialisten
(in % zur Gesamtzahl der in der Landwirtschaft Beschäftigten)

Stand v. 1959

Nationalität	Spezialisten insges.	darunter			
		Leiter u.Spezialisten		Mechanisatoren	
		i.d.Unions- republ.	in der UdSSR	i.d.Unions- republ.	in der UdSSR
Russen	15,7	3,6	4,5	10,6	11,2
Ukrainer	10,6	2,7	2,9	7,0	7,7
Belorussen	7,6	2,3	2,5	4,3	5,1
Usbeken	6,5	2,2	2,2	4,3	4,3
Kasachen	13,1	6,5	5,9	7,9	7,2
Georgier	5,4	3,9	3,9	1,5	1,5
Aserbaidshaner	6,5	3,5	3,3	3,3	3,2
Litauer	8,1	3,2	3,3	4,7	4,8
Moldauier	5,5	1,1	1,2	4,2	4,3
Letten	11,5	4,7	5,2	6,2	6,3
Kirgisen	5,3	2,4	2,3	3,2	3,0
Tadshiken	4,5	1,9	2,0	2,2	2,5
Armenier	7,0	3,8	3,8	3,3	3,2
Turkmenen	7,1	1,9	2,8	2,9	4,3
Esten	12,1	5,3	5,5	6,4	6,6

Ju.V. Arutjunjan "Social'naja struktura sel'skogo naselenija SSSR," S. 85.

Arutjunjan, der Tabelle berechnet und zusammengestellt hat, führt zu diesem
Punkt aus:

> Eine besonders aktive Rolle übernahm bei der Entwicklung der
> Landwirtschaft des Landes das zahlenstärkste Volk—die Russen.
> So sind z.B. in der Landwirtschaft Kasachstans 1959 280 Tsd.
> Russen tätig gewesen, von ihnen 28 % Mechanisatoren, während
> nur 8 % der Kasachen als solche Tätig waren. In der Landwirtschaft
> Kirgisiens waren 43 Tsd. Russen tätig, der Anteil der Mechanisa-
> toren betrug dabei 15 % (unter den Kirgisen 5,5 %). Von den in
> der Landwirtschaft Moldawiens beschäftigten 27 Tsd. Russen
> waren 9 % Mechanisatoren (dagegen unter den Moldawiern
> 4 %). In anderen Republiken waren weniger Russen in der Land-
> wirtschaft tätig, doch lag bei ihnen der Anteil qualifizierter
> Kräfte stets (im Vergleich zur örtlichen Bevölkerung) höher.[7]

Arutjunjan bemüht sich, die Ergebnisse seiner Untersuchungen mit der Parteilinie
in Einklang zu bringen und erklärt den hohen Anteil von Russen unter den
Landwirtschaftsspezialisten in den nichtrussischen Republiken als "besonders
aktive Rolle bei der Entwicklung," also als Ergebnis ihrer Entwicklungshelfertätig-
keit. Den durchweg niedrigen Anteil unter der einheimischen Bevölkerung
erklärt er vorsichtshalber nicht. Das wäre wohl auch schwer zu erklären, denn die
Ausbildung eines Landwirtschaftsexperten ist eine nicht allzu kostenund
zeitraubende Angelegenheit. Diese Diskrepanz dürfte sich inzwischen weiter
verschärft haben, da ein Teil der Posten landwirtschaftlicher Spezialisten zu
Nomenklatura-Posten gemacht wurden.

NATIONALE ZUGEHÖRIGKEIT DER WISSENSCHAFTLER

Von sehr grosser Bedeutung für eine moderne Industrie-Nation sind
Ausbildungsstand und Anzahl ihrer wissenschaftlichen Kader. Die nachstehende
Tabelle zeigt deren nationale Zusammensetzung in Zehnjahresabständen seit 1950
unter Berücksichtigung der hochqualifizierten Doktoren und Kandidaten der
Wissenschaften.

Tabelle 10

**Wissenschaftliche Kader, Doktoren und
Kandidaten der Wissenschaften nach Nationen**

	1950			1960			1970		
	Zahl d. wissenschaftl. Kader	davon		Zahl d. wissenschaftl. Kader	davon		Zahl d. wissenschaftl. Kader	davon	
		Dr.d. Wiss.	Kand.d. Wiss.		Dr.d. Wiss.	Kand.d. Wiss.		Dr.d. Wiss.	Kand.d. Wiss.
Insgesamt	100,0	100,0	100,0	100,0	100,0	100,0	100,0	100,0	100,0
Russen	60,9	59,8	57,3	64,8	58,8	60,3	65,9	55,0	59,0
Ukrainer	9,0	5,0	8,2	10,0	7,0	9,9	10,8	9,5	11,4
Belorussen	1,7	1,1	1,5	1,8	1,4	1,9	2,0	1,7	2,1
Usbeken	0,5	0,3	0,5	1,0	0,7	0,8	1,3	1,1	1,7
Kasachen	0,4	0,2	0,4	0,6	0,4	0,6	0,8	0,7	1,0
Georgier	2,6	3,6	3,5	2,3	3,4	3,1	2,0	4,2	2,5
Aserbaidshaner	1,2	0,9	1,2	1,4	1,5	1,7	1,4	2,6	2,1
Litauer	0,7	0,4	0,2	0,8	0,4	0,7	0,9	0,7	1,1
Moldauier	0,08	0,02	0,07	0,1	0,09	0,1	0,3	0,1	0,3
Letten	0,9	0,7	0,4	0,7	0,5	0,5	0,6	0,5	0,8
Kirgisen	0,06	0,01	0,03	0,1	0,05	0,5	0,2	0,1	0,3
Tadshiken	0,1	0,06	0,07	0,2	0,5	0,2	0,2	0,2	0,3
Armenier	2,3	3,0	2,8	2,2	3,5	2,8	2,2	3,8	2,5
Turkmenen	0,08	0,07	0,08	0,2	0,1	0,2	0,2	0,1	0,3
Esten	0,8	0,8	0,4	0,8	0,7	0,6	0,5	0,6	0,7

Eigene Berechnung nach "Narodnoe obrazovanie, nauka i kultura v SSSR," S. 270 f.

Tabelle 11
Nationale Zusammensetzung der Aspiranten

(Stand 1970)

Gesamtzahl der Aspiranten	99.427	

davon:

Russen	59.517	59,8 %
Ukrainer	12.248	12,3 %
Belorussen	2.540	0,2 %
Usbeken	2.493	0,2 %
Kasachen	1.780	1,8 %
Georgier	1.846	1,8 %
Aserbaidshaner	2.036	2,0 %
Litauer	1.195	1,2 %
Moldauier	619	0,6 %
Letten	700	0,7 %
Kirgisen	452	0,5 %
Tadshiken	489	0,5 %
Armenier	2.292	2,3 %
Turkmenen	480	0,5 %
Esten	657	0,7 %

"Narodnoe obrazovanie, nauka i kultura v SSSR," S. 278.

Was den Anteil an Wissenschaftlern betrifft, so sind die nichtrussischen Republiken ebenso wie die nichtrussischen Nationen benachteiligt.

Tabelle 12
Wissenschaftliche Kader auf je 10.000 der Bevölkerung

(Stand 1970)
UdSSR = 38

Republiken		Hauptnationen	
RSFSR	59	Russen	47
Ukrainische SSR	27	Ukrainer	24
Belorussische SSR	24	Belorussen	20
Usbekische SSR	21	Usbeken	13

Tabelle 12 (cont'd)

Republiken		Hauptnationen	
Kasachische SSR	20	Kasachen	14
Georgische SSR	43	Georgier	56
Aserbaidsh. SSR	33	Aserbaidshaner	29
Litauische SSR	28	Litauer	30
Moldawische SSR	15	Moldawier	9
Lettische SSR	37	Letten	41
Kirgisische SSR	20	Kirgisen	13
Tadshikische SSR	17	Tadshiken	11
Armenische SSR	51	Armenier	56
Turkmenische SSR	16	Turkmenen	12
Estnische SSR	34	Esten	47

Berechnet nach "Vestnik statistiki" No. 5/1971 und "Narodnoe obrazovanie, nauka i kul'tura v SSSR," S. 270 f.

Bei den Republiken liegen nur drei—RSFSR, Armenien und Georgien—über dem Unionsdurchschnitt von 38 je zehntausend der Bevölkerung, bei den Nationen sind es Russen, Georgier, Armenier, Letten und Esten. Die Ukraine liegt als Republik an 8., nach der Nation der Wissenschaftler an 9. Stelle, was ihre volkswirtschaftliche und kulturelle Bedeutung in keiner Weise spiegelt.

ERGEBNISSE UND ZUSAMMENFASSUNG

Die notwendig gedrängte Darstellung dieser Arbeit zwang dazu, nur die wichtigsten Schwerpunkte herauszugreifen. Allerdings ist es nur in sehr beschränktem Ausmass möglich, darüber hinaus weitere Vertiefungen und Differenzierungen vorzunehmen, denn die sowjetische Statistik ist wie gesagt in puncto Angaben über die Sozialstruktur der Nationen sehr sparsam, ja geradezu verschämt.

Als ein erstes Ergebnis ist festzuhalten, dass sich *ein erhebliches Gefälle* zwischen Nationen und Republiken beobachten lässt. Sicherlich hängt die Veränderung der Sozialstruktur von verschiedenen Faktoren ab; hier sei nur an volkswirtschaftliche und demographische erinnert, doch genügen sie nicht, um das innerhalb der Sowjetunion erkennbare Gefälle zu erklären. Der wichtigste Faktor dafür, dass sich verschiedene Gebiete und ihre Bewohner unterschiedlich rasch und intensiv modernisieren und fortentwickeln, ist darin zu suchen, dass der traditionelle Zuzug von Russen in die Republiken ausserhalb der RSFSR zunahm, dass sie ihre Position unter der städtischen Bevölkerung stetig ausbauen und ihren Einfluss auf die Gestaltung des öffentlichen Lebens in den Republiken praktisch unumschränkt ausüben können. Typisch für diese Migrationsprozesse ist ja, dass sie sich gerade auf die Grossstädte und Ballungszentren richten, die für die Republiken von lebenswichtiger und zukunftsträchtiger Bedeutung sind. So gilt für die Ukraine, dass die Russen im Industriezentrum Donezbecken dominieren, während sie in Mittelasien in den

Hauptstädten eine vorherrschende Rolle spielen. 1970 war ihr Anteil an der Bevölkerung von Taschkent, der Hauptstadt der Usbekischen SSR, 40,8 %, der der Usbeken dagegen nur 37,1 %; in Alma-Ata, der Hauptstadt Kasachstans, stellten die Russen sogar 70,3 %, die Kasachen nur kümmerliche 12,1 %.

Für die Wirtschaft wie für die Sozialstruktur und ihre Veränderungen ist auch bedeutsam, dass alle Republiken, die als bevorzugtes Ziel russischer Wanderungsbewegungen gelten, selbst einen erheblichen Arbeitskräfteüberschuss aufweisen. Ukrainische Experten berechneten, dass die Hoch- und mittleren Fachschulen der Republik durchaus in der Lage sind, die erforderliche Anzahl von Experten auszubilden. Dennoch wird hier unverdrossen weiter die bekannte koloniale Praxis—in der Sowjetunion als "Internationalisierung" euphemistisch modernisiert—gepflegt, die Absolventen der ukrainischen Hoch- und mittleren Fachschulen zur Arbeit ausserhalb ihrer Republik abzukommandieren. Hier setzt dann ein circulus vitiosus ein, denn die ausserhalb ihrer Republik tätigen Experten finden am Ort ihres Einsatzes weder Schulen noch andere kulturelle Einrichtungen ihrer Nation vor, ein Zustand, wie er schon im zaristischen Russland gang und gäbe war.

Die weitere "Modernisierung" der Sozialstruktur der einheimischen Bevölkerung in den nichtrussischen Republiken ist auf diesem Hintergrund sehr pessimistisch zu prognostizieren. Dies hängt u.a. damit zusammen, dass die sowjetische Führung inzwischen das einheitliche "sowjetische Volk" (sovetskij narod) aus der Taufe gehoben hat, das alle die hier aufgezeigten Unterschiede endgültig in sich aufhebt. So ist man einigermassen verblüfft, wenn man Breshnew auf der feierlichen Sitzung anlässlich des 50-jährigen Bestehens der Sowjetunion verkünden hörte:

> Heute, wo die Aufgabe der Angleichung des Niveaus der wirtschaftlichen Entwicklung der nationalen Republiken bei uns im wesentlichen gelöst ist, haben wir die Möglichkeit, an Wirtschaftsfragen vor allem unter dem Aspekt gesamtstaatlichen Interesses, der Erhöhung der Efizienz der gesamten Volkswirtschaft der UdSSR heranzugehen.[8]

Diese Manipulation lässt sich nur dadurch erklären, dass die sowjetische Führung nicht im geringsten daran denkt, den nichtrussischen Republiken die erforderlichen Mittel zur Verfügung zu stellen, damit die bewussten Vernachlässigungen und Ungerechtigkeiten wieder ausgeglichen werden können. Das "sowjetische Volk" als homogene Einheit und geschlossener Organismus erübrigt ja sozusagen den Ausgleich im einzelnen Fall einer Vernachlässigung, da sich das Gefälle immer wieder im ganzheitlich gesehenen Durchschnitt ausgleicht. Die statistischen wie auch alle sonstigen Angaben über die Nationen vermeiden eine wirklichkeitsgetreue Darstellung der Lage unter den nichtrussischen Völkern, wobei man noch am liebsten im Vergleich zu 1913 und mit den Vergrösserungen um ein Vielfaches operiert. Wohl weniger das schlechte Gewissen bremst hier, als vielmehr die Angst, dass diese Politik beim Namen genannt werden könnte—Spätkolonialismus; denn diese Politik hat ja nichts mehr mit "proletarischem Internationalismus" und mit der Gleichberechtigung aller Völker und Rassen zu tun. Ihre Auswirkungen auf die Sozialstruktur haben dies deutlich gezeigt.[9]

QUELLEN

[1] Von den vielen hierzu erschienenen Büchern und Artikeln, die den Aspekt "Lenin und die Sozialstruktur" behandeln, seien hier nur folgende genannt: *V. I. Lenin i nekotorye voprosy izmenenija soical'noj struktury sovetskogo obŝĉestva v perechodnyj period* (W. I. Lenin und einige Probleme der Veränderung der Sozialstruktur der sowjetischen Gesellschaft in der Übergangsperiode) im Verlag der Moskauer Staatsuniversität 1973; *V. I. Lenin pro rozvytok soical'no-klasovoj struktury radjan'skoho suspil'stva* (V. I. Lenin über die Entwicklung der sozialen und der Klassenstruktur der sowjetischen Gesellschaft) im Verlag der Charkower Universität, 1970; *Problemy izmenenija social'noj struktury sovetskogo obŝĉestva* (Probleme der Veränderung der Sozialstruktur der Sowjetgesellschaft), herausgegeben vom Institut für Philosophie der Akademie der Wissenschaften der UdSSR, Moskau 1968; *Sovetskoe obŝĉestvo: problemy izmeninija social'noj struktury* (Die Sowjetgesellschaft: Probleme der Veränderung der Sozialstruktur), Verlag "Znanie," Moskau, 1973.

[2] Siehe z.B. A. M. Egiazarjan *Ob osnovnych tendencijach razvitija socialisticeskich nacij SSSR* (Über die Hauptentwicklungstendenzen der sozialistischen Nationen der UdSSR), Erevan 1965, S. 105 und S. B. Batyrov *Formirovanie i razvitie socialisticeskich nacij v SSSR* (Bildung und Entwicklung der sozialistischen Nationen in der UdSSR), Moskau 1965, S. 183.

[3] S. L. Senjavskij *Izmeninija v social'noj strukture sovetskogo obŝĉestva (1937-1970 gg)* (Veränderungen in der Sozialstruktur der sowjetischen Gesellschaft) in "Voprosy istorii" No. 4/1973, S. 4.

[4] ebd.

[5] "Vestnik statistiki" No. 4/1972, S. 20.

[6] S. I. Bruk "Etnodemograficeskie processy v SSSR (Po materialam perepisi 1970 goda)" in *Sovetskaja etnografija* No. 4/1971, S. 28 f.

[7] Ju. V. Arutjunjan *Social'naja struktura sel'skogo naselenija SSSR* (Die Sozialstruktur der Landbevölkerung der UdSSR), Moskau 1971, S. 86.

[8] *Pravda*, vom 22.12.1972.

[9] Die Gesamtanalyse, sowie die einzelnen zitierten Quellen, beziehen sich auf die Lage bis 1973.

PART III

FERMENT AND DISSENT IN THE WESTERN PART OF THE USSR

MODERNIZATION AND NATIONAL IDENTITY IN THE BALTIC REPUBLICS: UNEVEN AND MULTI-DIRECTIONAL CHANGE IN THE COMPONENTS OF MODERNIZATION

Thomas Remeikis
Calumet College
East Chicago, Indiana

THE APPARENT PARADOX OF MODERNIZATION AND NATIONALISM

Both the Marxist model and the developmental model of social change expounded by some Western scientists are essentially teleological, assuming that modernization leads to changes of a definite kind in the economic as well as in the social, cultural, and political spheres—changes that are mutually interdependent and consistent in terms of the content or direction of change in the various components of society. It is predicted that modernization leads to integration, development of loyalties to the center, the breakdown of parochialism and nationalism. Yet it is widely conceded that the integration of the Soviet state in terms of the dominant identification with the community has not taken place or has progressed relatively slowly compared to the other dimensions of integration—control over means of violence and ability to affect allocation of resources.[1] National identity, even outright nationalism in the Soviet state, continues to show undiminished vitality.

The Baltic republics of Lithuania, Latvia, and Estonia are notable examples of this apparent paradox of advanced modernization and advanced cultural identity and nationalism. According to a host of indicators, the Baltic republics are the most developed in the Soviet Union and approach the developmental levels of many Western countries. Yet the rationalizing, universalizing, and secularizing forces of modernization have failed to eradicate localism, provincialism, nationalism and to create a higher level of integration (psychologically) within the Soviet state. The fundamental problem of this study is to explain this apparent contradiction in the case of the Baltic republics.

The approach to resolving the problem posed must involve a model that does away with the teleological thrusts of Marxist and Western theories of development. While modernization involves change not only in the economic system, but also in social, cultural, and political systems, the changes in the various components of modernization may be uneven in rates of change and multidirectional in content.[2] From the point of view of systemic integration—i.e., the development of supranational loyalties and the whittling away of sub-system commitments—under certain circumstances the modernization process may be dysfunctional. Deutsch and Scott have noted that "economic and social change does not automatically create loyalties and institutions, but, at best, gives one opportunities for their creation . . ."[3] The question to be considered in this study is to what extent the socio-economic changes brought about by industrialization and its concomitant forces have affected national identity and socio-political integrity of the Baltic nations and the rate and direction that these changes are taking. First, the degree and direction of socio-economic development will be considered, then the rate and direction of change in the concomitant components of the general process of change in society—national identity, political groups, and leadership—will be analyzed.

SOCIO-ECONOMIC CHANGE IN THE BALTIC REPUBLICS

According to numerous indicators (see Table 1), after World War II the Baltic republics were developed at a faster rate than the rest of the Soviet Union. Whatever the political and economic reasons for such Moscow policy may have been,[5] the Baltic republics today are the most developed area of the Soviet Union. In many respects the Baltic republics are economically leading republics of the Soviet Union and compare favorably with many developed Western countries. The non-Balts in the Soviet Union often refer to them as their "foreign countries," where the standard of living (and of nationalism) is at the height. Within a quarter of a century the primarily agrarian economies were transformed into advanced industrial ones. This industrial revolution obviously affected profoundly the social and cultural systems of these societies, secularizing and rationalizing attitudes and behavior patterns. However, the rate, direction, and level of economic change were different for the three republics, leading to different social, cultural, and economic consequences.

The rate of development of the Baltic republics varied significantly. As can be seen from the rates of growth of industrial production, from the very start Latvia and Estonia were developed at about twice the rate for the entire Soviet Union. Intense industrialization in Lithuania began in the late 1950's and continues at above union-average to the present day. The relatively late start of intense industrialization in Lithuania is due at least in part to the intense resistance to sovietization and a devastating guerilla war, which was not subdued until approximately the end of the Stalin era.[6] The weaker industrial base in Lithuania than in Latvia and Estonia may also have influenced the priorities of Soviet planners, with a larger share of investment funds initially going to the more developed republics. Because of its lower level of industrialization, Lithuania is scheduled to increase industrial production up to 49 percent during the ninth five-year plan, one of the highest rates of development, while in Estonia and Latvia industrial production is to be increased up to 39 and 38 percent, respectively.[7] The scheduled rates of industrial production are likely to equalize industrial development in the Baltic republics. In the perspective plans of development, a much slower rate of development is foreseen and can be expected.

Table 1

Economic Development of the Baltic Republics and the USSR[4]

INDICATOR AND YEAR		LITHUANIA	LATVIA	ESTONIA	USSR
1) Rates of growth of industrial production, 1940 = 100	1945	40	47	73	92
	1950	191	303	343	173
	1960	1030	1099	1150	524
	1970	2808	2403	2557	1097
2) % of population workers and employees	1940	6.1	13.9	16.7	17.5
	1950	12.8	23.3	23.5	22.7
	1960	24.5	34.3	37.5	29.2
	1970	37.3	43.7	45.2	37.3
3) Per capita gross national output in rubles, current prices	1960	1,342	1,971	1,834	1,431
	1965	2,071	2,612	2,679	1,831
	1969	2,841	3,339	3,471	2,450
4) Per capita industrial output, in rubles, current prices	1965	1,166	1,735	1,731	1,160
	1969	1,595	2,225	2,233	1,093
5) Per capita national income, in rubles, current prices	1960	646	937	810	682
	1965	929	1,188	1,153	843
	1969	1,241	1,457	1,495	1,093
6) Per capita agricultural output, in rubles, at 1965 prices	1965	491	444	491	309
	1969	570	449	501	329
7) % of gross national output from industry/agriculture, at current prices	1965	53.3/27.6	66.4/18.6	64.6/19.2	68.0/11.7
	1969	56.1/25.7	66.6/16.8	64.3/17.6	64.9/15.0
8) % of total industrial capital funds in	1971				
a) Electrical & heat energy		20.2	18.5	30.5	15.9
b) Fuel production		2.0	2.4	12.7	13.2
c) Machine construction & metal working		20.3	19.2	11.3	20.1
d) Light industry		10.0	10.1	7.6	4.5
e) Food industry		20.6	21.2	20.1	8.5
f) Chemical industry		7.5	7.9	3.5	—

The levels of development are evident in Table 1. Latvia is the most industrialized and productive republic in the Soviet Union, closely followed by Estonia, while Lithuania already is surpassing union averages on many indicators and is quickly catching up with the other Baltic republics. In terms of per capita national income, in 1969 Latvia, Estonia, and Lithuania ranked first, second, and third, respectively, in the Soviet Union. In 1969 the Baltic republics, with only 2.8 percent of the population, contributed almost 10 percent of the gross national product of the USSR.

The structures of Baltic economies were affected by the changing priorities of development. The lower industrial base and later start of intense industrialization in Lithuania meant that Lithuanian economy was influenced to a greater degree by the policies of the Khrushchev era. A slightly greater concern with development of consumer-oriented industries and a degree of decentralization in economic management under Khrushchev allowed Lithuania to develop its economy more consistently with the labor and natural resources profile of the republic than was the case in Latvia and Estonia. In 1969 Latvia derived 66.1 percent of its gross national output from industry, while in Lithuania the equivalent contribution was only 56.1 percent. In Lithuania over a quarter of the gross national output is derived from agriculture. The greater importance of agriculture in Lithuania is likely to persist for some time. Lithuania ranks first among the union republics in terms of agricultural production per capita and per 100 ha of arable land. In 1959 per capita agricultural production in Lithuania was 570 rubles, 449 rubles in Latvia, 501 rubles in Estonia, and 329 rubles in the Soviet Union (at 1965 prices).

The structure of Baltic industry differs from that of the Soviet Union as a whole. Light industry and food industry are vastly more important in the Baltic republics than in the Soviet Union as a whole. Energy production, machine construction, and metal-working industries are particularly developed. In Estonia fuel industry (principally shale oil) has a significant role, having almost 13 percent of the fixed capital funds (the respective figures for Lithuania and Latvia are 2.0 and 2.4). On a per capita basis, Estonia ranks first in the production of electrical energy, mineral fertilizer, paper, cotton fabrics, fish, and butter.[8]

Latvian industry diverges from Estonian and Lithuanian industry in the degree of development of heavy industry. Without any iron or coal deposits, in 1971 Latvia produced 445,000 tons of steel. In the Soviet Union Latvia also produces 24 percent of all electric railroad passenger cars and 18 percent of trolley buses. In 1971 Latvia produced 250,000 mini-buses. Latvia also produces about 24 percent of radio sets, and 60 percent of the telephones.[9] In 1970 32.1 percent of industrial workers were in machine construction and metal-working industry, 22.9 percent in light industry, and 13.0 percent in food industry.

In 1970 32.7 percent of the Lithuanian industrial workers worked in machine construction and metal-working industry, 24.8 percent in light industry, and 13.0 percent in food industry. Lithuania has a rapidly growing chemical industry, including a giant oil refinery under construction in Mažeikiai. Lithuania produces about 12 percent of metal cutting lathes and ranks fourth in the Soviet Union. On per capita basis, Lithuania ranks fifth in the production of electrical energy, third in production of mineral fertilizer, second in wool fabrics, first in meat, and third in fish.[10]

The relative standard of living in the Baltic republics can be judged from retail turnover in state and cooperative commerce, including restaurants. In 1970 Estonia, Latvia, and Lithuania ranked first, second, and fourth among the union republics in per capita retail turnover, ranging from 900 rubles in Estonia to about 650 rubles in the RSFSR and Lithuania (as compared to about 600 rubles for the Soviet Union as a whole).

With modernization came numerous social changes, including urbanization, growing secularization, declining birth rates, increased population mobility, and rising educational levels. Some of these changes are suggested in Table 2. On all suggested dimensions Latvia and Estonia were more advanced than Lithuania in 1940. This differential has persisted to the present day. Today Latvia and Estonia are the most urbanized, educated, and secularized republics of the Soviet Union. On many dimensions of social change Lithuania is still below the union averages, but is catching up rapidly.

Differential social change in the Baltic republics led to significantly different consequences. Consider, for example, birth rates: modernization brought about declining birth rates, with the rate approaching zero population growth in Estonia and Latvia, but with a still substantial birth rate, about the average for the Soviet Union, present in Lithuania. Birth rate was relatively high in Catholic and traditional Lithuania, while in Protestant and more advanced Latvia and Estonia birth rates were already low in pre-war years. The significant result of this demographic situation is that labor resources in the highly developed Latvia and Estonia are among the scarcest in the USSR and are still quite adequate in Lithuania. The low birth rate, combined with the breakneck speed of development in Latvia and Estonia, resulted in labor shortage and massive immigration from other republics. The fact that Latvia and Estonia have the highest standard of living in the Soviet Union also contributed to a high rate of immigration.

Immigration in Lithuania was to a great extent politically rather than economically induced and so far has remained minimal for several reasons. Intense industrialization started here later and substantial labor reserves were available in the countryside. Mechanization of agriculture and a relatively high birth rate can keep labor demand and supply in balance for some time in the future. In addition, Lithuania has tried, with some success, to decentralize industrial development, thus utilizing more effectively rural labor reserves. Nevertheless, given the intense rate of development, a labor shortage could develop in the near future and, given the high standard of living, immigration could become significant. It remains to be seen to what extent the republic managers will be able to accomplish optimal utilization of internal resources and to take other measures to contain immigration.

Although in 1940 Latvia and Estonia were more advanced than the Soviet Union, according to many social and economic indicators, and Lithuania was not far behind, Moscow's policies changed rather drastically the direction and rate of development after Soviet takeover of the Baltic states. Intense industrialization was prescribed at the expense of development of the agrarian sector, which was the pre-eminent and basic economic factor in the pre-Soviet period. Such drastic reorientation of economic development at the expense of the bulk of the populations could not help but be resisted and had to be imposed forcefully from Moscow. Thus, the industrial revolution was accompanied by a social and political upheaval. A period of intense resistance, even violent guerilla warfare, followed the reabsorption into the Soviet Union of the formerly independent states. Extensive political suppression, liquidation of all pre-war institutions, and the imposition of the Soviet system was carried out largely by force and personnel sent from Moscow. The ruthless socio-political revolution that accompanied modernization of the economies left an

Table 2

Some Objective Indicators of Social Change in the Baltic Republics and the USSR[11]

INDICATOR AND YEAR		LITHUANIA	LATVIA	ESTONIA	USSR
1) % of population urban	1940	23	35	34	33
	1959	39	56	56	48
	1970	50	62	65	--
2) Natural increase of population per 1000 population	1940	10.0	3.6	-0.9	13.2
	1960	14.7	6.7	6.1	17.8
	1970	8.7	3.3	4.7	9.2
3) % of total population increase mechanical *1951-1970	1959-1970	12.2	58.3	54.1*	--
4) % of population literate	1939	76.7	92.7	98.6	87.4
	1970	99.7	99.8	99.8	99.7
5) Number of people with higher education per 1000 population (10 yrs. and older)	1959	16	25	25	23
	1960	35	46	47	42
6) Number of people among 1000 of working population with some secondary education	1959	250	502	448	433
	1970	496	661	660	653
Rank in the USSR		15	6	7	--

indelible mark on at least the older generations, which to this day expresses itself in a hostile anti-Russian attitude and nationalistic protests. Loyalty to the center still rests mainly on the coercive sanctions of the center, even though the structure of Baltic societies is now consistent with the structure of Soviet society in general.

THE IMPACT OF MODERNIZATION ON NATIONAL IDENTITY

The Marxist model of development, as well as the teleological versions of development theory of the West, have predicted that in the course of modernization there occurs not only economic, but also socio-cultural integration of territorial states, composed of diverse elements. In the course of development the multinational state should be transformed into a new monolithic community. The Soviet version of Marxism also maintains that while the breakdown of national distinctions is an inevitable and spontaneous process, it can be advanced through human intervention. For this reason the Communist Party, through a variety of policies, seeks to advance "the growing together" and the eventual merger of nations, for the time being tolerating their "flowering." The Soviet policies designed to advance the development of the "Soviet people" are not the subject of this study. Rather, the question is to what extent have modernization and overt de-nationalization policies succeeded in breaking down ethnic loyalties and creating a higher loyalty to the Soviet state.

Unfortunately, direct psychological data are not available on changes in attitudes and national identity among the Baltic peoples. The status of national identity must be inferred from a variety of objective indicators, some of which are presented in Table 3 (page 122).

Unlike many other nationalities in the Soviet Union, the Baltic nations had a well-developed national identity by the time they were absorbed into the Soviet state in June of 1940. National renaissance occurred in the course of the second half of the nineteenth century, culminating in the establishment of their own nation-states in 1918. The two decades of national independence were marked by an intensive cultural and political development, leaving an indelible mark on the consciousness of the Baltic nations. The Soviet Union had to use ruthless suppression measures to control the nationally and politically conscious populations. Only in the late 1950's could something approaching normalcy and degree of acquiescence to a Soviet rule be noted among the Baltic nations. Even so, in view of recent manifestations of dissent, one has to raise the question whether the acquiescence is approaching a genuine acceptance of the political system or is a mere toleration of it in the absence of realistic alternatives. The recent historical experiences of the Baltic nations thus obviously constitute a significant factor in the maintenance of their identity. It is plausible that the forceful incorporation of these nations into the Soviet state and the political violence attending this process reenforced the already strong national identities, at least with the immediate generations.

In certain respects the process of modernization reenforced and strengthened national identity. While modernization has affected values, the trend toward secularization is quite apparent; at the same time, it seems to have sharpened the study and understanding of the nation's uniqueness and commitment to maintaining cultural distinctiveness in face of the threatening leveling and denationalization. Cultural distinctiveness is to be maintained not through revival and veneration of ancient cultural patterns, but by synthesizing the old with the new in a distinctive pattern. These appear to be at least the hopes of the intelligentsia, even if it might be difficult or impossible to attain this in reality.[12] However, as long as such goals persist, there will be an intense resistance to the universalizing and leveling policies of the center.

For illustrative purposes let us consider one component of the modernization process—i.e., education and its actual and potential impact on national identity. Despite the intense efforts of the educational system to change loyalties, in fact it seems to operate dysfunctionally. Education is in the national language and is universally accessible. The Baltic republics alone have an eleven-year primary and secondary education. No doubt the additional year contributes to a deeper appreciation of national subjects—history, language, literature. In Lithuania 84 percent of all students in primary and secondary schools are taught in Lithuanian.[13] In Estonia 73 percent of all general education schools use Estonian.[14] Thus, in Lithuania and Estonia schools in the language of titular nationality are disproportionate to the native populations. Precise data are not available on Latvia, but it is reasonably certain that all Latvians in Latvia can attend Latvian-language schools if they so desire. The situation in Latvia is somewhat different from that in Lithuania and Estonia in that possibly most schools in Latvia are bilingual—that is, with classes

in Latvian and Russian.[15] Nevertheless, in all three republics national subjects—
language, literature, history, culture—are taught in the national language. The educational level is rising rapidly. Latvia ranks first among the Soviet republics in the
number of people with incomplete and complete secondary and higher education,
Estonia ranks fourth, while Lithuania is still catching up with most of the republics (according to 1970 data).[16] Knowledge of national culture and past has never
been as widely available or consumed as it is today.

Table 3

Some Objective Indicators of National Identity among the Baltic Nations[17]

INDICATOR AND YEAR		LITHUANIA	LATVIA	ESTONIA
1) % of population from titular nationality	1959	79.3	62.0	74.6
	1970	80.1	56.8	68.2
2) % of titular nationality in republic using own language	1959	99.2	98.4	99.3
	1970	99.5	98.1	99.2
% of titular nationality fluent in Russian	1970	35.9	45.2	29.0
3) % of books published in the language of the titular nationality	1961	80.4	51.7	75.9
	1971	71.7	48.8	63.6
4) % of students in higher education from titular nationality	1960	88.4	64.0	82.4
	1970	84.0	47.1	72.1
5) % of scientific workers from the titular nationality	1960	82.0	73.2	82.6
	1970	85.5	62.2	91.7
6) Rate of ethnic intermarriage per 1000 registered marriages	1959	59	158	100

Yet the record is not an unmixed one, and various perceptible trends in the long run may begin to modify significantly national identity and distinctiveness.

So far there is no clear evidence of a linguistic assimilation trend. About 99 percent in each Baltic nation consider the national language as the mother tongue. At the same time, however, fluency in Russian is substantial and rising. Over 45 percent of highly educated Latvians are fluent in Russian, and about a third of the Lithuanians; a little less than 30 percent of the Estonians know Russian. With rising educational level the knowledge of Russian also increases. The Russian language is indeed becoming a universal medium of communication in the Soviet state. As long as bilingualism or multi-lingualism is not the official policy, development of national languages, especially in the technological sphere, may begin to suffer. A point may be reached where the bulk of communications will be in the Russian language. Indeed, this is exactly the complaint of the Latvian communists in the letter to foreign communist parties. They cite in particular the preemption of Latvian by the Russian language in an increasing number of social and official functions.[18]

What will be the impact of the growing knowledge and use of the "common medium of communication" on the vitality of the national culture and national identity in general? A recent study of the use of Russian language among Latvians by the Soviet sociologist A. I. Kholmogorov, provides a possible answer.[19] According to Kholomogorov, 78 percent of the Latvian respondents had knowledge of Russian. Its use and function varied among various occupational and age groups. For example, he found that 70 percent of the professionals in the arts and teachers, 58 percent of engineers and technicians, and only 25 percent of field and livestock hands used Russian on the job. Significantly, however, the use of Russian in cultural and social spheres (reading of books, television and radio, etc.) was also high. Thus, 46 percent of the field and livestock hands, 58 percent of the engineers and technicians, 43 percent of the teachers, 60 percent of government employees, and 64 percent of school children and students used the Russian language in cultural and social spheres. Only in the family and household environment was the use of Russian minimal—7.4 percent average for all Latvians. The mother tongue is thus becoming "a kitchen language" and is gradually being pushed out of social and cultural spheres of life. Although no strictly comparable data for Estonia and Lithuania are available, it is reasonably certain that the impact of the growing knowledge and use of Russian is generally in the same direction as in Latvia.

At a somewhat slower pace than modernization in general, creeping bilingualism and the resulting increase in the use of Russian is detrimental to the functionality of the mother tongue, especially in the context of a very complex technological civilization. The intelligentsia in the Baltic republics is acutely aware of this possibility, and efforts are being made to negate such trends (such as, for example, attempts to develop technological terminology and dictionaries, to rid the languages of loan words, and to perfect the usage of the national language). It remains to be seen whether such efforts will be sufficient to withstand the universalizing forces of centrally controlled mass communications, integrated economy, and complex technology.

The greatest threat to national identity in the Baltic context comes not from the content of political socialization or linguistic policies, but rather from the

physical conglomeration of diverse nationalities. The Baltic region is one of positive
in-migration despite the fact that it is a labor shortage area and at the same time
adjacent to a labor shortage area.[20] Between 1959 and 1970 the mechanical increase
of population in the Baltic republics was about 300,000. The immigration was of
principally non-Balt nationality. At the present time, the immigration appears to be
mainly economically motivated, although it may be argued that Moscow, by resist-
ing artificial barriers to population movement, is also playing a political game.
Although there is a considerable movement of people in both directions, there is
also a high degree of permanence; most of the non-Balts in the Baltic republics are
relatively permanent settlers. Thus in 1969, 9,464 Russians left Latvian cities and
12,566 arrived in Latvian cities, producing a net gain of 3,102 for the year.[21]
However, according to one Soviet study, conducted around 1965, over 70 percent
of the Russians in Latvia have been there for over ten years.[22] The positive balance
of the in-migration is sufficiently large and permanent to affect the ethnic composition of the Baltic republics.

Latvia and Estonia, with the highest standard of living in the Soviet Union and
with available jobs, are especially attracting large numbers of immigrants (see
Table 2, page 120). Mechanical population growth in these republics is higher than
natural increase, which, combined with the low birth rates of Latvians and Estonians, is rapidly shrinking the proportion of the titular nationality. Between 1959
and 1970 Latvians decreased from 62.0 percent to 56.8 percent of the population,
while the Estonians declined from 74.6 percent to 68.2 percent. At the moment
there are no indications that Moscow would permit artificial barriers to immigration. The rate of development scheduled for Latvia and Estonia for the 1971-1975
plan is among the lowest in the Soviet Union, but it is still beyond the labor
reserves of these republics. Finally, neither the birth rate nor the age structure
promises substantial increases in Latvian and Estonian populations. Immigration
thus seriously threatens the titular nationalities; without some dramatic reversal the
Latvians may already become a minority nationality by the end of this decade, while
the Estonians may come close to such a status.

The Lithuanians alone managed to improve their proportion from 79.3 percent in 1959 to 80.1 percent in 1970. This is due to the lower industrial development, higher birth rate, lower standard of living, some assimilation of the Polish
minority, and certain efforts of the Lithuanian ruling elite. However, the future here
is by no means certain. The above average rates of industrial development, relatively high standard of living, increasingly tight labor market in Lithuania may
increase immigration.

In the long run, increasing ethnic heterogeneity cannot help but have a profound impact on the cultural, social, and political life of a republic. The potential
of denationalization as a result of the conglomeration of nationalities so far has been
moderated by the degree of ethnic heterogeneity and the geographical distribution
of ethnic groups. At some point the increasing heterogeneity will result in a preemption of cultural patterns of the native population by those of the immigrants;
in the case of the Soviet Union, normally the Russian culture replaces the local
culture. A possible example is cited by the 17 Latvian communists who recently
have protested the Russification of Latvia. Among other things, they noted the
following:

The arrivals' demands for increased Russian language radio and television programming have been met. Currently one radio station and one television station broadcast programs only in Russian, while the other broadcast programs bilingually. Thus, approximately two thirds of radio and television broadcasts are in Russian.[23]

The Russians in Lithuania constitute a very small minority (8.6 percent of the population in 1970) and their cultural impact so far has been quite circumscribed. In Estonia the Russian minority is already 24 percent of the population and is likely to generate strong pressures against the relative Estonian hegemony in the cultural life of the republic.

The geographical distribution of ethnic groups within the republics also has differential impact on the cultural life of the republics.[24] First of all, the Slavic inhabitants of the Baltic republics are overwhelmingly urban. In 1970, 85 percent of the Russians in Lithuania were urban inhabitants. Their largest concentration at that time was in Vilnius, where they comprised 24.5 percent of the population (a slight drop since 1959). The Lithuanian population in Vilnius increased from 33.6 percent in 1959 to 42.8 percent in 1970. About 60 percent of the Russians were concentrated in the three largest cities of Vilnius, Kaunas, and Klaipeda. Because the bulk of urban population growth resulted from migration from the Lithuanian village, all cities over 10,000 population increased their Lithuanian percentage, which is below 70 percent only in exceptional cases.

In Estonia 85 percent of the non-Estonian population was urban in 1959. In 1970 about 35 percent of the non-Estonian population lived in Tallinn. Tallinn was increasingly internationalized as the Estonian proportion dropped from 60.2 percent to 55.7 percent between 1959 and 1970. Outside Tallinn a large concentration of non-Estonian population will be found in the shale oil fields, especially the northeastern urban regions of Narva and Kohtla-Jarve.

Unlike in Lithuania and Estonia, non-Latvians are in the majority in the largest cities of Latvia, including the capital city of Riga, where close to a third of the population of Latvia lives (in contrast, only 11.9 percent of the 1970 population of Lithuania lived in Vilnius and 26 percent of the population in Estonia lived in Tallinn). Already in 1959 Riga, Daugavpils, and Rezekne had non-Latvian majorities, while Liepaja and Jelgava came close to that status. Although data of the 1970 census on distribution of ethnic groups were not available, it is reasonable to assume that at best the situation did not change and at worst non-Latvians increased their proportion in the largest cities as a result of intensive immigration. In 1959, 41.5 percent of the population of Riga were Russians and 43.8 percent Latvians. By 1970 the balance probably shifted in favor of the Russians. Heavy Russian concentration is also found in the Eastern cities and districts of Latgalia along the border with Russia. Already in 1959 the Russians constituted more than 40 percent of the population in this area, while in a number of districts and cities the Russians were in the majority (Daugavpils, Rezekne, Ludza, Zilupe, Kraslava, Krustpils).

The cultural consequences of the geographic distribution of ethnic groups are readily apparent. The cities, especially the capital, set the tone for the cultural life of a nation. To the extent that the capital is internationalized, to that extent the cultural life of the indigenous nationality is likely to suffer. Today the Latvian capital city of Riga is under a biological if not a cultural Russian hegemony. A similar situation prevails in other major cities of Latvia. The purely Latvian element remains dominant in rural areas outside Latgalia. As far as the survival of national identity is concerned, by its size and ethnic composition Riga constitutes a serious problem to the Latvian nation. In contrast, Tallinn is an essentially Estonian city because the Estonians are still in the majority and predominate among the ruling elite and intelligentsia of the republic. In Vilnius the Lithuanians still constitute a minority, but they are the dominant group, consisting of the cultural and political intelligentsia.

One measure of the denationalizing effect of conglomeration of nationalities is the rate of ethnic intermarriage.[25] In all three republics intermarriage is still the exception rather than the rule. It is evident that the social distance between ethnic groups remains great. Actual intermarriage is significantly rarer than statistical probability of uniform ethnic mix predicts. For example, in 1968 actual percentage of Estonian-Russian intermarriage was 6.2, while the predicted percent was 33.7.[26] The social interaction among ethnic groups appears to be minimal. The immigrant group has its own community, it is usually concentrated geographically, and it has its own social and cultural life. Still, there is a relationship between the rate of intermarriage and the proportion of the population of various ethnic groups. Intermarriage is most frequent in Latvia, least frequent in Lithuania. However, for the time being intermarriage seems to offer no serious threat to the survival of the Baltic nations.

The long-term impact on cultural life of the Baltic republics by increasing ethnic conglomeration is suggested also by a number of other indicators (see Table 3, page 122). The percentage of books published in the languages of the Baltic nations is declining, Latvia having the lowest percentage of 48.8 (1971). The trend toward publication in the Russian language is especially notable in the area of scientific, technical, and political literature. The intelligentsia, which determines the cultural life of a country, is also seriously affected. Thus, the percentage of Latvian students in Latvia has dropped to 47.1 in 1970, while it is still higher in Lithuania and Estonia than the proportion of the respective national groups. Similarly, in 1970 the proportion of scientific workers of Latvian nationality was down to 66.9, while it remained extremely high in Lithuania and Estonia. Thus, the universities and scientific establishments are extremely internationalized in Latvia, while they still remain strongholds of titular nationalities in Estonia and Lithuania. In Latvia cultural life is on the verge of becoming multi-national.

At the moment all the Baltic nations are highly developed culturally and possess strong national identities. However, a number of notable long-run trends are beginning to affect the integrity of Baltic nations. The Latvian nation is in a particularly difficult situation, the Estonian nation so far has remained dominant in its own country but is threatened by an intense immigration from other parts of the Soviet Union, and Lithuania, the least developed of the three, is in the best position demographically. However, a continued intense development of the economy could produce the same trends in Lithuania as in Latvia and Estonia. Cognizant of the impact of large numbers of aliens, the Lithuanian ruling circles have resisted closer association with Kalinin Oblast (East Prussia), to at least parts of which Lithuania has some ethnic and historical claims, because of the predominantly Russian population of the Oblast. The Lithuanian and Estonian party leaders have opposed any federation or regionalization of the Baltic area. However, the possibility remains that in the course of rewriting the Soviet Constitution or the proposed economic regionalization, ethnic identity of the various republics, including

Lithuania, will be affected. Thus, while in the short run the Baltic nations will continue to prosper culturally and maintain identity, in the long view prospects for national survival are not that promising. Only the development of genuine federalism, with substantial autonomy for the republics, at least in the cultural sphere, can reverse the pessimistic prognosis.

POLICY ORIENTATIONS OF THE RULING BALTIC ELITES

Despite the formally centralized political and administrative system of the Soviet Union, a number of circumstances—ideological, legal, political, and sociological—permit a limited deviation or a modification of central directives, deviations which, in the long run, may be functional for the maintenance of a degree of sub-system autonomy, the preservation of ethnic and regional heterogeneity, and the evolution of a more decentralized system or even a genuine federalism. These conditions of sub-system autonomy and capabilities for its acquisition, maintenance, or advancement are unequally present and are utilized with different effectiveness by elites in the various republics.

Not all autonomist tendencies are nationalistic in nature; it might be more appropriate to refer to them as "republic orientation," as distinguished from "union or centralist orientation." Two types of decentralist tendencies are readily apparent. First, some policies could be defined as *nationalistic*—i.e., they seek to maintain or enhance national identity and a degree of exclusiveness. Other decentralist tendencies are *bureaucratic* in nature. The latter are universal characteristics of bureaucratic empires, where the provincial elites aspire to expand their sphere of competence and to enhance their role in decision-making. In the Soviet context such bureaucratic tendencies can be called nationalistic only in terms of their consequences, but not necessarily in terms of motives of the elites supporting such a course. In actuality behind every centrifugal policy will be found nationalistic and bureaucratic motives. Different people support such policies for different reasons.

To a greater or lesser degree every republic party organization contains centralist and decentralist factions. An attempt to determine the relative balance of these factions in the Communist Parties of the Baltic republics is necessary as part of the overall assessment of the degree to which political integration has occurred and a political community on the union level has emerged. This will also suggest some of the reasons for the kind and intensity of nationalist unrest in the Baltic republics.

Among the significant factors that might reenforce autonomist orientation is the ethnic composition of the ruling elite. The responsiveness of the republic party organization to popular sentiments depends in part on the ethnic and political background of the leadership group. While ethnic background alone is not a decisive factor, the greater the ethnic purity of the party organization and its leadership, the greater the potential for policies aimed at advancing national interests. Similarly, the greater the control of the titular nationality over the institutions of the republic, the greater the capability of advancing national or republic interests within the existing limits for deviation.

The changing ethnic structure of the Baltic Communist Parties is suggested in Table 4. On mass membership level, the communists of titular nationality are underrepresented in all three parties. However, a trend of increasing the proportion of communists of the titular nationality is evident in the Communist Party of Lithuania (CPLi) and the Communist Party of Estonia (CPE), while possibly an opposite trend may be present in the Communist Party of Latvia (CPLa). A distinct majority of the CPLi are Lithuanians, the Estonians constitute a slight majority in the CPE, while the Latvians are in an obvious minority in the CPLa. The increasing proportion of Lithuanians in the CPLi is especially dramatic. After the war the

Table 4

Ethnic Structure of the Communist Parties of the Baltic Republics[23]

INDICATOR AND YEAR		LITHUANIA	LATVIA	ESTONIA
1) Number of party members and candidates	1946	8,060	10,987	7,138
	1961	60,551	72,519	37,848
	1973	131,539	133,938	77,430
% of adult population in CP (CPSU - 9.0%)	1971	5.5	7.2	8.4
2) % of republic party membership from titular nationality		31.8 (1945)	68.9 (1946)*	100.0+ (1946)*
		44.7 (1959)	43.0 (1961)*	51.9 (1966)
		67.1 (1970)	42.5 (1965)*	52.3 (1970)
		69.1 (1973)*	42.9 (1973)*	55.2 (1973)
3) % of Central Committee members and candidates from titular nationality	1952	56	65 (1956)	64
	1960	75	61	74
	1971	78	62	78
% of Politbureau and Secretariat from titular nationality	1971	87	68	73

*Calculations are adjusted to the proportion of titular nationality residing in its own republic.

Lithuanians comprised less than a third of the CPLi membership. Thousands of communists from other parts of the Soviet Union were sent in to help pacify nationalist revolt and carry out sovietization. Only in the middle 1950's did Lithuanians begin joining the Party in greater numbers. There evidently was a realization that active resistance is futile and there is no alternative to the Soviet regime. Party membership gradually became respectable and justified by national interests. At the same time, throughout the post-Stalin years, especially in the 1950's, intense promotion of national cadres to leading positions was carried out, often at the expense of non-Lithuanian personnel. This Lithuanianization of the institutions of the republic proceeded so far that Moscow took notice and in 1959 a purge had to be carried out to placate the Kremlin. Nevertheless, this was a relatively minor purge, involving the Rector of the University of Vilnius and a small number of other educators for alleged nationalist deviation in cadre policies.[28]

The CPE started with a very large Estonian base. In 1946 there were more Estonians in the CPSU than the number of members in the CPE. The rapid post-war development as well as the imposition of Soviet institutions in Estonia resulted in a rapid growth of the republic organization and an influx of non-Estonian communists. It is very likely that in the 1950's Estonians constituted only a minority of the CPE. By 1960 a recovery occurred and a slight trend of growing proportion of Estonian communists is in evidence today. The CPLa also started with a larger Latvian base than the CPLi. As in the case of Estonia, intense development and sovietization resulted in massive influx of non-native communists, changing the ethnic balance against native communists. The proportion of Latvians in the CPLa today stands at about 40 percent.

Unlike the mass membership, in all three parties the titular nationality is over-represented on the politbureaus, secretariats and apparati, while approaching their proportion in the population on the central committees. The top of the hierarchy of the CPLi is the most national, while the hierarchy of the CPLa is the least nationally homogeneous. Thus, other things being equal, the leadership of the CPLi is potentially the most nationally oriented, while that of CPLa the least nationally oriented. At least part of the explanation why Estonia and Lithuania so far have remained ethnically and culturally stronger than Latvia is the fact that the social, cultural, economic, and political institutions are controlled largely by members of the titular nationality. To the extent that Baltic communists have retained their ethnic identity, to that extent they are sensitive to the policies affecting national interests. All available evidence indicates that the intelligentsia and the bulk of communists of the titular nationality are ardent adherents of their national heritage. Obviously, the capabilities of such nationally oriented communists to safeguard national interests depends in part on the degree of control over republic institutions.

The ethnic background of the ruling elite is only one variable that influences their behavior. The political past and prevailing views of the leading party faction influences the degree to which advancement of national interests will be undertaken. In this respect the leadership groups of the Baltic republics are quite different. A brief discussion of the leading factions of Baltic party organizations and some of their policies is in order.

Historical evidence suggests that all three Baltic parties expected greater autonomy—a sort of "Outer Mongolia" status—than they actually got in 1940 and subsequently, when the Soviet Union annexed the Baltic States. National communists were purged in the Soviet Union and later after the annexation in Estonia and Latvia. In place of the purged national communists, Latvian and Estonian communists reared in Russia were placed in leading positions. Only the original underground communist leaders of Lithuania managed to survive in top positions to this day.

Two possible reasons for the survival of old underground Lithuanian communists in positions of leadership may be advanced.[29] First of all, the top Lithuanian communist, Antanas Sniečkus, was fairly accurate in judging the political demands of the Kremlin and the limits of permissible deviation. Sniečkus and his associates always tried to execute faithfully the explicit commands from above. Secondly, the Lithuanian communists had no chance even to begin expressing their demands for autonomy because the CPLi was too weak to exercise control functions in a nation which was in an almost total resistance. Until the 1950's Lithuania was ruled through a special bureau of the CPSU in Moscow, for a while headed by M. Suslov. Still, Sniečkus cannot be considered as an absolute Moscowite; he has on occasion opposed virtually openly the policies of Moscow (for example, opposition to Khrushchev's agricultural policy for Lithuania).

The CPLi has been headed by the same man—Antanas Sniečkus—since the 1930's. He has served as First Secretary of the CPLi since its inclusion into the CPSU in 1940, weathering all the political storms in the Kremlin. This Lithuanian-grown communist, with his colleagues from the pre-war underground days, managed to maintain Moscow's confidence to this day. Under his leadership the CPLi has become increasingly Lithuanian in membership and leadership. Through seniority and experience he has acquired excellent knowledge of Kremlin politics and influential supporters (including probably M. Suslov, possibly Kosygin). He is the dean of republic party secretaries in the Soviet Union. He has created an effective political machine in Lithuania and successfully protected it from purges. Sniečkus and his lieutenants were sufficiently entrenched to weather the intense nationalist and religious unrest of the past few years, including the dramatic self-immolations in national protest and riots that followed in the late spring of 1972.[30]

In the context of Kremlin politics Sniečkus is a moderate. He is both a Moscowite and a champion of his fief. He carefully listens to the directives from Moscow, but at the same time tolerates and even supports demands from below. Sniečkus carefully balances central and republic interests, doing enough to satisfy Moscow and the local autonomists. In a sense he has interposed himself between Moscow and the Lithuanian nation, keeping the demands from the top and the bottom in reasonable bounds.

Among the policies advanced by the Lithuanian ruling elites the following can be considered as beneficial to the republic: retention of eleven-year secondary education; moderation of the rate and direction of industrial development, fairly consistent with the resource profile of the republic; containment of immigration through a variety of measures, including the development of national cadres and decentralization of industry in the republic; vigorous development and advancement of national cadres; and a relatively effective promotion of national culture.

Although there is a small faction of hard-liners and Stalinists, the bulk of the CPLi and its leaders are united in respect to the advancement of national and republic interests. At the moment this leading faction is concerned that another nationalist manifestation might call Moscow's hand and sweep away the gains of the last two decades. However, even without the repetition of a nationalist protest, the future of CPLi leadership is by no means certain, for soon Sniečkus's age, if nothing else, will dictate a replacement. The orientation of the new leadership could very well be contrary to that of the current leadership. The possibility of continuing Sniečkus's line of carefully balancing republic and union interests will depend on the political situation in the Kremlin and the Kremlin's definition of the situation in Lithuania.

The CPLa has been subject to much greater control by Moscow or by Moscow-oriented leaders than CPLi or CPE.[31] Since 1959 the dominant group in the CPLa has been the Russian-reared Latvian communists, whose principal association with Latvia was the nationality of their parents. Because of the advanced industrialization of Latvia prior to World War I, communism was a significant force there. Latvian bolsheviks played a key role in the Russian Revolution and many remained in Russia after the establishment of independent Latvia in 1918. These Latvians in Russia and their descendants were sent to Latvia in 1940 and after 1945 to help rule an antagonistic population. These foreign-born Latvians, in alliance with non-Latvian communists, form the ruling clique in the CPLa, which is notably internationalist, centralist, and Stalinist in orientation.

The representatives of the native Latvian communists, who probably constitute the majority of Latvian communists and who have a strong republic if not nationalist orientation, briefly managed to attain numerous positions of power in Latvia. Included in this group were Deputy Premier E. Berklavs; Chairman of the Latvian SSR Supreme Soviet, K. Ozolins; First Secretary of Riga party organization, Straujums; CPLa secretaries Bisenieks and Krumins; and many others. They eventually were supported by the majority of the Central Committee of the CPLa. From the charges against the representatives of this group it appears that some time between the de-Stalinization speech of Khrushchev and his ultimate triumph against opposition the Latvian national communists attempted to oppose various policies that were denationalizing Latvia. They attempted to shift industrial development away from heavy industry to one more consistent with the needs and resources of the republic, to gain greater control over economic planning and administration, to stem immigration, and to advance Latvian cultural development. In 1959, under the direct supervision of Khrushchev, who traveled to Riga, this autonomist faction was purged from positions of responsibility. They were replaced largely by Russianized Latvians.

Under the rule of the Moscowite faction Latvia is subjected to intense internationalization. Over a decade after the abortive attempt of national communists to stem denationalization, the situation became so alarming that in 1971 17 communists, all native Latvian revolutionaries, wrote an open letter to the Communist Parties of Romania, Yugoslavia, France, Austria, Spain, and other countries, addressing it also to the French communist intellectuals Aragon and Garaudy, denouncing the genocidal policies of Moscow and their thorough application by the Latvian Moscowites. They described the current leadership of the Latvian regime as composed of Russian Latvians, who know very little or no Latvian, and other foreigners.[32] That this is not merely a nationalistic rhetoric is indicated by the actual policies of the current Latvian regime. The national communists, including the 17 authors of the cited protest letter, are concerned that current economic policies are denationalizing Latvia and are advocating a drastically reduced rate of industrial development as an answer to immigration (caused in part by labor shortage in Latvia). Among those calling for less capital investment is P. Strautmanis, a native

Latvian on the Politbureau (who reportedly is in trouble for that).[33] In 1971 and 1972 First Secretary Voss wrote articles in Moscow's *Pravda* attacking such views. On March 20, 1971, Voss wrote:

> We cannot overlook the localistic tendencies and national narrow-mindedness that can still be encountered in the views and attitudes of some people. Such people, sometimes not realizing that communist construction is inconceivable without the closest political, economic and cultural cooperation and fraternal mutual assistance of all the peoples of the USSR, think, for example, that it would not be worthwhile to build certain major industrial, power-engineering and other facilities in our republic. Why? Because, so they say, the number of non-Latvian population in the Latvian republic would increase in this connection, and the republic's nationalities composition would become mixed. The republic's party organization, following Lenin's teaching and the CPSU's general line and relying on the people's support, has always resolutely opposed such sentiments and continues to do so. Our unchanging course is aimed at the all-round strengthening of fraternal friendship, comprehensive cooperation and mutual assistance among the peoples of the USSR.[34]

A year later, on March 12, 1972, Voss reaffirmed in no uncertain terms the policy of continued integration of nationalities in the Latvian republic.[35] It is fairly certain that the current leadership is not going to take effective measures to preserve the Latvian nation. And if immigration continues, the prospect that national communists might attain positions of leadership is not very promising.

Another circumstance that has brought about a greater presence of central authority in Latvia is the key position of Riga, which serves as the headquarters of the Baltic Military Region and is a locus of many federal and inter-republic offices. It is no coincidence that the 1959 purges were initiated by the Soviet military.

Until 1949 the leadership of the CPE were native Estonians.[36] However, as in the case of the CPLa, there was a group of Estonian communists who grew up or spent the inter-war years in Russia. When Estonia was incorporated into the Soviet Union, many of these communists were sent there. The national communists were purged as early as 1950 and replaced with Russia's Estonians. Included in this group are the First Secretary J. Kǎbin; the former Chairman of the Presidium of the Supreme Soviet, A. Mǘǘrisepp; the former Chairman of the Council of Ministers, Klauson; and the present Chairman of the Presidium of the Supreme Soviet, Vader.

Three circumstances possibly explain why the Estonian leadership in its orientations evolved in a direction contrary to that taken by the Latvians. First of all, the infusion of non-Estonian elements into Estonia was somewhat smaller, and Estonia and the CPE remained ethnically more homogeneous than Latvia or the CPLa. Second, Estonia, like Lithuania, was peripheral to the Soviet administrative and military center in the Baltic area. Third, Russian Estonians became increasingly Estonianized and committed to the defense of republic interests. As one scholar of the CPE observed,

After more than twenty years back in Estonia, it would be surprising if the "Yestonians" (i.e., the Russian-born Estonians) were not reintegrated into the national framework. We have pointed out a few psychological and practical reasons why such a mental and spiritual homecoming may be expected. It is not just Kåbin relearning his ancestral language and Muurisepp trying to secure greater administrative autonomy. There are people in Estonia who think that there is a tacit understanding between Kåbin and the more nationalistically minded communists: Kåbin barks at nationalism more than he bites, and the nationalist wing no longer tries to unseat him.[37]

The degree of autonomist tendencies in the CPE is suggested by an interest in the proposal that Estonia be granted a satellite, or People's Democracy, status. We can infer this from private and open attacks on such idea. On two reported occasions top Estonian communists, including A. Vader, the Chairman of the Presidium of the Supreme Soviet, denounced the idea of a ploy of "bourgeois emigrants" in their anti-Soviet propaganda, seeking to persuade Estonians that Estonia should leave the Soviet Union.[38]

The CPE's ability to balance national and all-union interests may be on the decline. Foreign influence in the top leadership of the CPE has grown in the last few years. The leadership, as elected in 1971, contained five Russians in top positions. There are now two Russian secretaries—the Second Secretary K. Lebedev, who replaced the Estonian A. Vader (who in turn was kicked upstairs to serve as Chairman of the Presidium of the Estonian Supreme Soviet), and Secretary F. Usanjov. In addition, three Central Committee Departments are now headed by Russians. This strengthening of Russian control in Estonia may reflect the growing percentage of non-Estonian population in general and/or may be viewed as a preemptive move to contain nationalism. Obviously, as in Latvia, the concern with immigration is resulting not only in heightened nationalistic reaction (as a self-protective reaction), but also in proposals to deal with it. The Plenum of the CPE, called in March of 1972, was in part a response to such pressures from below or even from the top. Reportedly, the Plenum dealt with "inter-ethnic indoctrination of the working people in the light of decisions of the 24th Congress of the Soviet Communist Party."[39] However, in contrast to the Latvian attack cited earlier, Kåbin in his report did not attack internal nationalism; according to one report, his "speech almost sounded like that of a defense attorney, against unspecified charges of nationalism."[40]

A new generation of leaders is bound to emerge in the near future in all the Baltic republics. The new generation of communists is better educated, is less ideologically committed, and very likely has stronger national attachments than did the older generation of revolutionaries, war communists, and immediate postwar communists, who had to be strong internationalists (i.e., Moscowites). There are no indications that the outlook of the new generation of communists is centralist, internationalist, or Stalinist. No doubt, there is at least a minority of such home-grown communists in each republic, and Moscow may very well decide to promote them to the top positions. In the future the possibility of leadership with strong republic orientation thus cannot be taken for granted in any of the Baltic republics.

The brief comparison of the ethnic structure and policy orientations of the Baltic Communist Parties indicates that in terms of potential and actual degree of republic orientation the CPLi has the strongest ethnic basis and has the most successful record of advancing national and republic interests, while the CPLa at the moment displays the weakest ethnic basis and republic orientation. The CPE is somewhere between the CPLi and the CPLa, but much closer to the CPLi on the dimensions of comparison used here. The leadership of the CPLi and the CPE are ideological and national moderates, while the members of the Latvian top command display Stalinist traits and are hard-liners on the nationality question. These different orientations of Baltic Communist Parties had a significant impact on national identity, reinforcing it in Lithuania and Estonia and seriously threatening it in Latvia.

SOME CONCLUDING REFLECTIONS

This study has considered only one of several possible relationships emanating from the ongoing processes of modernization—i.e., the impact of modernization on national identity and system loyalty. It is evident that the impact is not even and is by no means unidirectional. There are leveling or integrating forces at work, as there are differentiating trends. The most serious threat to the survival of national identity comes from the physical conglomeration and dispersal of ethnic groups, particularly in the case of Latvia and, to a lesser extent, Estonia. Current nationalism in the Baltic republics stems from a deeper psychological commitment to the nation (brought about in part by modernization) and/or from a perception of a threat to national existence (by deliberate policies of denationalization advanced by the center) among the nationally committed.

Modernization has produced other trends that are by no means functional for the current Soviet system. For example, the human rights movement in the Soviet Union is a reflection of the increasing citizen competence that comes with modernization. The increasing complexity of social and economic life has also imposed constraints on the use of coercion. The Soviet citizen is beginning to be a participant citizen in a very real sense. In such a situation the loyalty to the system depends upon a high degree of satisfaction of citizen expectations.

The expectations of the Baltic peoples are intensely expressed in demands for respect of human rights. Consider, for example, the recent unrest in the Baltic republics. Recently the *Chronicle* (No. 25, 1972) reported that an underground organization, "The Estonian National Front," demanded in its underground journal *Eesti Demokraat* self-determination for Estonia. A few years earlier "numerous representatives of the technical intelligentsia of Estonia," in answer to Sakharov's memorandum on co-existence, called for much broader reforms than Sakharov envisioned, including political freedom and self-determination for the nationalities. The open letter of the 17 Latvian communists protested the denationalization of Latvia. A young Lithuanian, Romas Kalanta, committed self-immolation during a national protest in which crowds of young people raised the slogan of independence. Recently the Catholics of Lithuania have become very vociferous in their demands for religious freedom, while the Baltic Jews have been among the leaders in the struggle for the right to emigrate. This national and religious protest is also a protest against the violations of basic human rights—national equality, self-determination, respect for national character, religious freedom, freedom of movement, and general democratic freedoms. Thus, the national protest is merged with the general protest against the violations of human rights, both movements reenforcing each other and both in part emanating from factors brought about by the modernization of society.

NOTES

[1] Amitai Etzioni, *Political Unification: A Comparative Study of Leaders and Forces* (New York: Holt, Rinehart, and Winston, 1965), p. 4.

[2] These guidelines are derived from Samuel P. Huntington, "The Change to Change: Modernization, Development, and Politics," *Comparative Politics* (April 1971), 283-322.

[3] Karl W. Deutsch and William J. Foltz, *Nation-Building* (New York: Atherton Press, 1966), p. 13.

[4] Unless otherwise indicated, all economic statistics of this section, including those in Table 1, are derived from the official statistical yearbooks, published by the Central Statistical Administration under the Council of Ministers of the USSR and the Councils of Ministers of Union Republics. The following yearbooks were used: *Narodnoe khoziaistvo SSSR 1965 g.* (Moskva, 1966) (hereafter referred as *Narkhoz, year*); *Narkhoz SSSR, 1970* (Moskva, 1971); *Promishlennost' SSSR* (Moskva, 1964); *Narkhoz Estonskoi SSR, 1969* (Tallin, 1970); *Narkhoz Estonskoi SSR, 1970* (Tallin, 1971); *Narkhoz Latviiskoi SSR, 1970* (Riga, 1972); *Lietuvos TSR Ekonomika ir Kultūra 1970 metais* (Vilnius, 1971); *Promislennost' Litovskoi SSR* (Vilnius, 1973).

[5] For an analysis of Soviet reasons for developing the Baltic republics rapidly, see Benedict V. Maciuika, "The Role of the Baltic Republics in the Economy of the USSR," *Journal of Baltic Studies*, III, 1 (Spring 1972), 18-22.

[6] For the post-war history of Lithuania, see V. Stanley Vardys, ed., *Lithuania under the Soviets: Portrait of a Nation 1940-1965* (New York: Praeger Publishers, 1965), especially the chapter on "The Partisan Movement in Postwar Lithuania"; also K. V. Tauras, *Guerrilla Warfare on the Amber Coast* (New York: Voyages Press, 1962).

[7] *TSKP XXIV Suvažiavimo Medžiaga* (Vilnius, 1971), pp. 259-263.

[8] *Liaudies Ūkis*, No. 2 (1972), 60-61.

[9] *Ibid.*

[10] *Ibid.*

[11] Sources for Table 1: 1) *Narkhoz SSSR, 1970.* 2) *Narkhoz SSSR, 1970*, pp. 50-51. 3) *Narkhoz Estonskoi SSR, 1970*, p. 19; *Tiesa*, June 4, 1970; Gundar J. King and Juris Dreifelds, "Demographic Changes in Latvia," in Arvids Ziedonis et al., *Problems of Mininations: Baltic Perspectives* (San Jose, Calif.: Association for the Advancement of Baltic Studies, 1973), p. 134. 4) *Narodnoe obrazovanie, nauka i kultura v SSSR* (Moskva, 1971), pp. 21-22.

[12] Private conversations with representatives of Soviet intelligentsia.

[13] *Kietuvos TSR Ekonomika ir Kultūra 1970 Metais*, p. 333.

[14] *Eesti Kommunist*, No. 11 (1972), as cited in *Baltic Events*, April 1973, p. 8.

[15] This is a claim of 17 Latvian communists, who in 1971 wrote a letter to foreign communist parties, denouncing russification of Latvia. Text was first printed in *Dagens Nyheter*, January 29, 1973. The text used here is an English translation obtained privately and will be cited as Letter of Seventeen Latvian Communists.

[16] *Narkhoz Estonskoi SSR*, 1970, p. 32.

[17] Sources for Table 3: 1) and 2) *Narkhoz SSSR, 1970*, pp. 15-21; *Lietuvos TSR Ekonomika ir Kultūra 1970 Metais*, p. 33; *Narkhoz Latviiskoi SSR*, 1970, p. 11; *Narkhoz Estonskoi SSR*, 1970, p. 29. 3) *Pechat' SSSR v 1961 godu* (Moskva, 1962), pp. 129, 140, 169; *Pechat' SSSR v 1971 godu* (Moskva, 1972), pp. 96-97. 4) *Narodnoe obrazovanie*, pp. 270-271, 260-269; calculations adjusted to percentage of titular nationality residing in its own republic. 6) A. I. Kholmogorov, *Internatsional 'nye cherty sovetskikh natsii* (na materialakh konkretno-socsiologicheskikh issledovanii v Pribaltike) (Moscow: "Mysl' " Publishing House, 1970), as translated in *Soviet Sociology*, XI, 3-4 (Winter-Spring 1972-73), p. 279.

[18] Letter of Seventeen Latvian Communists.

[19] Kholmogorov, *op. cit.*, pp. 310-311; some comparative data on the knowledge of Russian in the Lithuanian village is provided by S. Šimkus, "Internacionalinis auklėjimas ir kalbų mokymasis Tarybų Lietuvos kaime," *Komunistas*, 2 (1972), 42-48.

[20] See the following Soviet studies on population mobility: V. I. Perevedentsev, *Narodonaseleniye i Ekonomika* (Moscow, 1967), as translated in *Soviet Geography*, X, 4 (April 1969), 192-208; V. I. Perevedentsev, *Migratsiia naseleniia i trudovye problemy Sibiri* (Novosibirsk: "Nauka," 1966), as translated in *Soviet Sociology*, VII, 3 (Winter 1968-69).

[21] *Vestnik Statistiki*, 3 (1971), 79-81.

[22] Kholmogorov, *op. cit.*, p. 249.

[23] Letter of Seventeen Latvian Communists.

[24] Besides the census data for 1959 and 1970, the following studies of demographic trends and distribution of ethnic groups in the Baltic republics are the basis for this discussion: the special articles on population by Tõnu Parming, Arnold Purre, Andrivs Namsons, and Benedictas Mačiuika in *Acta Baltica* XI (1971), 21-116; Tõnu Parming, "Population Changes in Estonia, 1935-1970," paper presented to the Second Conference on Baltic Studies, San Jose State College, San Jose, Calif., November, 1970; Juris Dreifelds, "Characteristics and Trends of Two Demographic Variables in the Latvian SSR," *Bulletin of Baltic Studies*, No. 8 (Winter 1971), 10-17.

[25] For a detailed study of ethnic intermarriage in Latvia and to some extent in other republics, see Kholmogorov, *op. cit.*, pp. 277-294. He reaches the conclusion that "the principal tendency in the development of marital and family relationships in the Latvian SSR is the steady increase in mixed marriages."

[26] As calculated by Yaroslav Bilinsky, "The Background of Contemporary Politics in the Baltic Republics and the Ukraine: Comparisons and Contrasts," in Ziedonis, *op. cit.*, p. 106.

[27] Sources for Table 4: The data in 1) and 2) are derived from party statistics published in *Partinaya zhizn'*, No. 1 (January 1962), 44-54 and No. 10 (May 1965), 8-17; *Kommunist Estonii*, No. 12 (December 1967), 19-33; *Komunistas*, No. 9 (September 1973), 6-12. Data for 3) are based on the surnames of members of central party organs, as announced after republic party congresses. As a consequence, the data are subject to error and should be considered as a very general indicator. For the list of members of party central organs, see: *Tiesa*, August 27, 1952, March 4, 1960, and March 5, 1970; *Sovetskaya Latviya*, January 20, 1956, February 18, 1960, and February 27, 1971; *Rahva Hääl*, September 20, 1952, and *Sovetskaya Estonia*, February 19, 1960, February 20, 1971.

[28] For a detailed study of recruitment and promotion of national cadres in Lithuania, see Thomas Remeikis, "Berücksichtigung der nationalen und verwaltungsmässigen Interesen der Unionsrepublik, dargestellt um Beispiel Litauens," *Acta Baltica*, X (1970), 121-156; on the purge, see *Komunistas*, No. 8 (August 1959), 2.

[29] The discussion of the CPLi and its leadership is based on the following studies: Thomas Remeikis, *Communist Party of Lithuania: A Historical and Political Study*, unpublished Ph.D. dissertation in political science, University of Illinois, 1963; also the cited article by Remeikis in *Acta Baltica*, X (1970).

[30] The recent national and religious protest in Lithuania has been widely reported in the world press. *Khronika tekushtshikh sobytii* has a running account of events in Lithuania. Also revealing is the underground chronicle of the Lithuanian Catholic Church—*Lietuvos Katalikų Bažnyčios Kronika*, six issues of which have appeared since 1971. For a survey and documents of national and religious protest in Lithuania, see *The Violations of Human Rights in Soviet Occupied Lithuania: A Report for 1972*, prepared by the Lithuanian American Community, Delran, N.J.: 1973; also "Self-Immolations and National Protest in Lithuania," *Lituanus* XVIII, 4 (Winter 1972), 58-72.

[31] The following sources were used in the discussion of the CPLa and the policy orientations of its leaders: Gundar Julian King, *Economic Policies in Occupied Latvia: A Manpower Management Study* (Tacoma, Wash.: Pacific Lutheran University Press, 1965); Andris Trapans, "A Note on Latvian Communist Party Membership, 1941-1961," *The Baltic Review*, No. 26 (April 1963), 17-30; "Arvids Ianovich Pelshe: Political Profile," *The Baltic Review*, No. 27 (June 1964), 43-46; Vilis Hazners, "Key Officials of Occupied Latvia," a manuscript, dated September 27, 1966.

[32] Letter of Seventeen Latvian Communists.

[33] As reported in *Estonian Events*, February 1972, p. 1.

[34] *Pravda*, March 20, 1971.

[35] *Pravda*, March 12, 1972.

[36] The best available study of the CPE is by Rein Taagepera, "Nationalism in the Estonian Communist Party," *Bulletin, Institute for the Study of the USSR*,

XVII, 1 (January 1970), 3-15. Also extremely useful are the various reports on Estonia (and lately on Latvia) in *Baltic Events* (previously *Estonian Events*), a bi-monthly newsletter published by Rein Taagepera at the University of California (Irvine) and Juris Dreifelds at the University of Toronto.

[37]Taagepera, *op. cit.*, p. 10.

[38] As reported in *Estonian Events*, August 1972, p. 6; see also *Estonian Events* for December 1969, p. 4.

[39] As reported in *New York Times*, March 13, 1972, p. 5.

[40]*Estonian Events*, April 1972, p. 2.

BELORUSSIA: MODERNIZATION, HUMAN RIGHTS, NATIONALISM*

Stephan M. Horak
Eastern Illinois University
Charleston, Illinois

The recent intellectual dissent movement within the USSR fostered renewed interest in Soviet studies among Western scholars and also generated a larger interest in non-Russian peoples. Although East European experts in the Western world are well acquainted with the Soviet system, the specific case of the Belorussian SSR holds many unknown factors that diminish the clarity of the picture. The essence of the problem can be seen by the very fact that only two works on the subject were available in English by 1973,[1] and that such a respectable journal as *Slavic Review*, in its thirty-one published volumes, contains only one article.[2] Apart from Soviet publications, including *Bielaruskaia savietskaia entsyklapedyia* (a twelve-volume set to be completed by 1974), there are two journals, *Belorussian Review* and *The Journal of Belorussian Studies*, and a bulletin, *Facts of Byelorussia*,[3] which provide minimal information on a Republic that has over nine million people.

Only recently has it been reported that an underground *samizdat, Listok* (Newsletter) began to appear aperiodically in Belorussia,[4] thereby supplementing the Russian language *Chronicle of Current Events* and the *Ukrainian Herald* in Ukrainian. Thus far, little of the material related to Belorussian dissent has reached the West through unofficial channels.

On the other hand, the official Soviet publications in the Russian and Belorussian languages have to be evaluated carefully, especially on such complex issues as human rights and nationalism. They are, however, more dependable in providing some insights as to the modernization of the nation.

Another factor contributing to the researcher's difficulties stems from semantics resulting from the substitution of the meaning of basic political terminology as commonly used within the Marxian and Western definitions. A case in point is the issue of human rights as applied to the national self-determination in general

---

*Reprinted with the kind permission of the *Canadian Slavonic Papers* (Vol. XVI, No. 3, 1974).

and to personal freedom specifically. The "Universal Declaration of Human Rights," as adopted and proclaimed by the General Assembly of the United Nations on 10 December 1948, does not require additional comment or interpretation and is in the Western world generally accepted as written and understood according to the prevailing definition of words used. The Soviet attitude to this quite plainly written document has been based on the premise that its principles were long ago established in the USSR; however, it does not explain the Soviet refusal to vote in support of the Declaration. Using a self-serving vocabulary, *USSR: Questions and Answers* (Moscow, 1965) claims:

> If we compare the Soviet Constitution with the Universal Declaration of Human Rights adopted by the United Nations it is clear that citizens of the USSR have been granted the principal democratic rights and liberties proclaimed by the Declaration. What is more, many of the rights and liberties secured by the Constitution are broader and fuller. And the essential thing is that they are not merely proclaimed, but are guaranteed by the social conditions prevailing in the USSR. (p. 60)

Despite the Soviet claim of adherence to basic human rights and criticism of the *Declaration*[5] of the U.N., the nature of the totalitarian system contradicts the language of many articles and especially of Article 2: "Everyone is entitled to all the rights and freedoms set forth in this Declaration, without distinction of any kind, such as race, colour, sex, language, religion, political or other opinion, national or social origin, property, birth or status."

Marxian totalitarian exclusiveness, promoting class war and the dictatorship of one class and a single philosophy, denies this article in its entirety. Moreover, the Soviet promise to solve once and for all the national question on the basis of unconditional national equality failed to materialize. After fifty years of existence the USSR exposes its inability to implement the promises made in 1917 to numerous nationalities of former tsarist Russia. Emerging from a century of intensive Russification, Belorussians (Beloruthenians or White Ruthenians) entered the twentieth century lacking the features that characterize a modern nation. Stateless, but not without a great past, these people are rooted in a thousand-year-old history that has been marked with political oppression and economic exploitation, first within the Polish Commonwealth following 1569 (Union of Lublin), and later (after Poland's partition) under the tsarist Russian regime.

National awakening began only at the turn of the century and coincided with another powerful ideology, socialism, and with the 1917 socialist revolution in Russia. The meeting of two modern ideas in an area which at that time was the most backward in Europe affected the Belorussian people by deepening their tragedy and, at the same time, stimulating positive achievements. For a while Lenin's attempt to please both the growing number of Belorussian nationalists and the Russian Marxists, who were already in a position of power, had all the prospects of succeeding and of being beneficial to both sides. However, suffering and heavy human losses brought on by World War I, the Civil War, and the Polish-Soviet Russian war had their effect, and the relatively peaceful 1920's turned into the bloody purges of the 1930's, only to be followed by the utter devastation of the Nazi-Soviet war, and new persecution after the second occupation of Belorussia in 1944 by the Soviet army.

There are no exact statistics of the total losses, but what is known, even allow-ing for deliberate exaggerations, is shattering. Mikola Abramčyk, President of the *Rada* of the Byelorussian Democratic Republic, in exile, accuses Moscow of liquidat-ing 500 scientists, 70 poets and writers, 600 journalists, political and social workers, 20,000 intellectuals, professionals, and students, and 3,000,000 peasants and workers.[6]

On the other hand, Soviet sources describe the devastation of Belorussia under the German occupation with equally horrendous numbers. Two hundred and nine towns and settlements are said to have been burned and destroyed, together with 10,000 industrial enterprises. In addition, 2,200,000 inhabitants and war prisoners were exterminated.[7]

In the absence of other supporting factors, both data are to be examined with caution. But with the absence of a normal population increase during a period when other nations almost doubled in numbers, one is inclined to accept the loss of some 2 million lives as a conservative estimate. In terms of numbers, the figure goes as high as 25 percent or, by way of example, equal to the percentage of Jews who perished during the Nazi holocaust compared with all Jews living in Europe, Africa, and North America. Surprisingly enough, the Belorussian tragedy of the twentieth century remains basically unknown in the Western world.

Referring to Stalin and the great purges, an American historian observes: "In the Belorussian and Ukrainian republics, he [Stalin] liquidated not only his political enemies but the nationalists as well."[8] Otherwise, "Not a single man who had labored for the establishment of the Belorussian Home under the Soviets in the 1920's was alive or free in 1939."[9]

This two-dimensional aspect of Belorussia's past and present is epitomized by the observations of T. Ia. Kiselev and Mikola Abramčyk, the first a communist writer, the second a nationalist. Kiselev said,

> The Byelorussian people have traversed a great and glorious path under the leadership of the Communist Party. And under this leadership, marching side by side and hand in hand with the other peoples of the Soviet Union, it will achieve its cherished goal—the building of a real communist society.[10]

A quite different picture of this same period of Belorussian history emerges in the eyes of Abramčyk:

> They opened Byelorussian higher educational establishments and scientific institutes which had been closed by the Russian tsars; but those Byelorussian scientists who attended, believing the sin-cerity of the bolsheviks, were, without exception, arrested and later liquidated. They gave to the Byelorussian peasants the states of the landowners, but subsequently consigned them to a slavery unknown in the history of Byelorussian peasantry.[11]

These contradictory evaluations are also carried into the areas of modernization and nationalism. The consequences of Soviet-style modernization, combined with the deeply-rooted nationalistic desires of the Belorussian society, create a confused and very often invisible, yet continuous, conflict. To measure the degree of conflict with all its potential consequences in an oppressed situation is almost impossible, and the Belorussian case does not represent an exception. But if the assumption that political changes always accompany modernization is historically supportable,[12] then it may be assumed that Belorussia, in addition to the other non-Russian Soviet republics, is not likely to be an exception. The essence of the problem, therefore, seems to revolve around the question: does the process of modernization foster the advance of local nationalism and human rights, or does it contribute to the total and final elimination of the Belorussian national identity, including individual freedom, resulting in a total Russification and a permanent sovietization? The answer may perhaps be found in the application of the socio-historical analysis to the contemporary status of the Belorussian republic.

The BSSR in the realm of the contemporary standard of living and modern computerized technology is to be placed somewhere in the middle of the overall world standard. In areas such as education, literacy, and health service, the BSSR falls into a leading group. At the same time, however, in political, national, and human rights (assuming that these can be measured), the Belorussian people are still at the bottom of the world's scale. Such a discrepancy results from the resolute and systematic imposition of priorities and purposes on the part of the centralistic Soviet regime. Certain deviations from this basic rule, in both time and place, are determined by various factors of internal as well as external origin[13] and are dependent on the empirical political decisions of the ruling clique in Moscow.

Considering all three areas of special concern, the Belorussian situation, as compared with some others, may look like this:

Parabola of Contemporary Societies

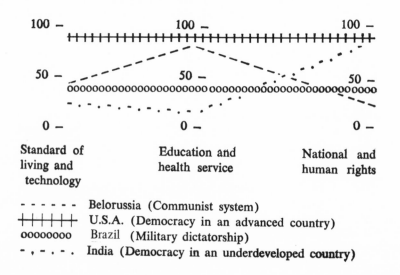

100 –	100 –	100 –
50 –	50 –	50 –
0 –	0 –	0 –
Standard of living and technology	Education and health service	National and human rights

- - - - - - Belorussia (Communist system)
++++++ U.S.A. (Democracy in an advanced country)
ooooooo Brazil (Military dictatorship)
- , - . - . India (Democracy in an underdeveloped country)

The socio-economic foundation of the Republic, which has a population of 9,002,000 and comprises 81 percent of Belorussian nationality (7,290,000), spanning an area of 83,000 square miles, remains agrarian, with 43 percent of the people living in cities.[14] This is reflected in the fact that Belorussia now produces more milk and butter per capita than Britain and Italy, more meat than Britain and Norway, and two and a half times more flax than Belgium. The production of basic agrarian commodities per capita is above the world's average: Grain—966 pounds (1969); Potatoes—3022 pounds; Fruit—158 pounds; Meat—154 pounds; Milk—1184 pounds; Eggs—14 dozen. The gross output of agricultural commodities for 1969 is estimated at 3,377,100 tons.[15]

Industrial production for 1969, while modest by comparison with that of industrial powers, looks impressive for a country of this size: Electricity—12,934,200 kilowats; Oil (crude)—2,760,000 tons; Torph—900,900 tons; Steel—189,600 tons; Fertilizer—4,791,000 tons; Trucks—290,400; Tractors—79,500; Paper—99,700 tons; Radios—426,400; Television sets—544,000; Freezers—150,800; Bicycles—506,900; Watches—2,300.[16]

The translation of the massive Soviet statistics, covering the whole body of economics coupled with the inherent uncertainties as to its accuracy and intended interpretation, reveals several meaningful results. The standard of living can best be assessed through the indicator of the per capita income. In this regard, the BSSR occupied seventh place within the USSR in 1968, or last place among the European Soviet republics, with 836.64 rubles per person. For the USSR as a whole, the income was 1022.17 rubles.[17] This rather modest income for an industrialized society is reflected in the Republic's budget. Statistical data for 1969 of the state budget include 2.8 billion rubles as revenues (income) and 2.7 billion as expenditures, leaving a surplus of 92.2 million rubles not spent in the BSSR and possibly transferred to the general USSR budget.[18]

Another essential insight into the socio-economic structure of the Belorussian society can be gained from the distribution of employment. The 1968 employment figures are: Industry and construction—30.1 percent; agriculture and forestry—41.7; transport—6.5; trade and supply—5.8; health, education, cultural, and social institutions—11.8. As far as the educational aspect of employment is concerned, 200,800 persons with advanced (university) education were employed in the BSSR in 1968.

From this incomplete, yet for our purposes sufficient, review of the current Belorussian economy and technological-industrial base emerges the conception of a society which by Western standards is reaching the first phase in the evolution of a modern industrial nation. The time gap between the most advanced Western countries and Belorussia can be estimated to be between 25 and 50 years, taking into account various aspects of modernization. A more favourable situation prevails in the area of education and health care, suggesting Belorussia's chances of a rapid improvement in the immediate future.

In the past under the tsarist regime, illiteracy was the highest in Eastern Europe; in 1897, 76 percent of all Belorussians were illiterate. National consciousness was almost non-existent, and Belorussian literature did not reappear as an independent branch until the end of the eighteenth and the beginning of the nineteenth centuries. The first newspaper in Belorussian, *Nasha Dolia* ("Our Lot"), before long replaced by *Nasha Niva* ("Our Field"), appeared only in 1906 in Vilna.[19] The two most outstanding literary figures, Janka Kupala (1882-1942) and

Jakub Kolas (1882-1956), acted not only as men of letters and founders of the modern Belorussian literary language, but also as the representatives of revolutionary peasant democracy. The first Belorussian learned society, the Belorussian Academy of Science, was not organized until 1928, and the first university of the Republic in Minsk was established in 1921.

Apart from the nature and purpose of the Soviet educational policy, statistical data indicate that the progress made in the last fifty years is impressive.[20] Illiteracy was eliminated by 1932, and by the first two decades a modern school system encompassed the whole country. As of 1969-70 there were 28 institutions of higher learning with 144,400 students, including those in correspondence courses and in evening classes. Enrollment in technical high schools increased to 250,000, and there are 1.5 million students in elementary schools (grades 1-7) and high schools. The ratio of students per 10,000 people for Belorussia is 153,[21] slightly lower than in the U.S.A. The educational system has 9,500 university and institute instructors, 59 academicians, 56 corresponding members, and 3,102 research fellows employed with the Academy of Science.[22] The Academy publishes 11 scholarly journals. Of that number, however, only six, including *Vestsi A. N. Seryia hramadskikh navuk*, are in the Belorussian language.

Russification of education is not restricted to the Academy alone. In fact, the language of instruction in all institutions of higher learning is Russian with the exception of the Departments of Belorussian literature and language. Out of eight serial publications issued by the state universities, only one monthly, *Viesnik Bielaruskaha Dziarzhaunaha Univiersiteta* (Minsk), is in Belorussian. This journal consists of four series, each of which is published quarterly. Articles cover a variety of subjects including history, philology, philosophy, mathematics, physics, and economics. This single periodical in the Belorussian language is restricted to relatively few copies, in the case of *Viesnik* to 800.

On the level of high schools the situation has deteriorated since Khrushchev's educational reform. In the 1971-72 school year, only 35 percent of the schools conducted instruction in Belorussian. The Republic's 5,529 club-houses, 7,280 libraries, 39 museums, and 5,024 cinemas are thoroughly Russified too.

In the life of East European peoples, national theatres were for centuries the symbol and mainstay of national identity, and in the case of the Belorussian people the national theatre assumed a function of vitalizing historical memories. The theatre experienced a period of expansion in the 1920's and early 30's and directly reflected the degree of national culture. Since the 1950's, however, the Belorussian theatre has been undergoing a process of de-nationalization, stagnation, and typical provincialism.[23] Out of 81 plays staged by 28 national theatres in 1968, only 12 can be classified as Belorussian in topic and language; the rest were written by Russians and reflect the banality of Soviet and Russian national propaganda, contributing nothing to Belorussian national culture.

The extent of national expression is narrowing in the realm of publishing too. There is blatant evidence of a polarity between writing that reflects the national and the individual state on the one hand, and the quantity of Soviet data on the other. Just as the Communist idea of mass education is identical with total indoctrination, Communist publishing is an exclusive domain of the system. Pre-determined planning to Russify eight million people by sovietization and publishing is in operation. What in any other part of the world would be classified as disloyalty and even treason is becoming in Soviet Belorussia a new "virtue."[24]

   The Bibliography of Soviet Belorussian Bibliography[25] reveals that out of 1,935 entries covering all fields of knowledge, 1,540 works are in the Russian language. Under "History" 69 books are in Russian and only 26 in Belorussian, and under "Chemistry," of 103 entries only 7 are in Belorussian. Books published after 1950 maintain a ratio of 10 to 1 in favour of the Russian language. The Belorussian linguistic bibliography,[26] covering a period of 140 years, lists 3,514 works, of which 65 percent are in Russian. According to *Pechat SSSR* (1972), in 1971 there were 2,135 books published in the BSSR in Russian in editions of 1,582,000 copies, and only 419 books with 900,000 copies in Belorussian. Obviously it is not just the 938,000 Russians living in the BSSR who read the annual one and a half million copies of printed titles. The thoroughly Russified publishing system has to be seen as one of the means to keep, for the time being, the Belorussian language on the level of an elevated dialect until it becomes dispensable.
   Additional evidence of the existence of a long-term policy of eliminating a nation can be seen in newspaper and periodical publishing. While the country's 128 newspapers published in Belorussian have a single edition of 1,598,000 copies, the 40 papers in Russian are printed in 2,576,000 copies. From three national daily newspapers, *Zviazda*, *Selskaia gazeta*, and *Sovetskaia Belorussiia*, only one (*Zviazda*) uses the Belorussian language. Out of 29 journals, 17 are in Belorussian and 12 in Russian; those in Russian have doubled since 1963. There is no Belorussian historical journal, and the official publication of the Community Party of the BSSR, *Kommunist Belorussii* is in Russian. From the Belorussian monthlies, apart from the series of the Academy, *Viaselka* and *Polymia* are basically literary journals. Unfortunately, such essential titles as *Promyshlennost Belorussii* and *Zdravokhranenie Belorussii* are in Russian.[27]
   Returning once again to books, additional data make the general picture more nearly complete. During the 53 years of the existence of the USSR, 135,424 *belles-lettres* titles have appeared in the Russian language; in Belorussian there are only 4,401. Although the ratio of Russians to Belorussians within the USSR is about 1 to 12, the ratio of books declines sharply to about 1 to 35—that is, 35 books in Russian to one book in Belorussian. For 1971 the statistics show 3,361 books in Russian and 136 books in Belorussian, a fact which Lenin himself would probably not have dared to approve; it was he who on several occasions condemned Russian chauvinism.[28] In addition to the deluge of Russian language publications within the Republic, a statistically undetermined number of Russian books, journals, and newspapers published in Leningrad and Moscow are distributed in Belorussia. On the other hand, not a single Belorussian publication appears outside of the BSSR. In the final counting, the ratio between Russian and Belorussian material can be estimated at 10 to 1, with all the disadvantages being on the side of the Belorussian language and culture.
   This leads to the question of the political structure that imposes and executes policy in the Republic. Obviously, the centre for making decisions that affect Belorussia is Moscow; the Communist Party is the solemn agent of Moscow's will, and Minsk is a transformer, not an initiator. In this situation, the composition of the implemental apparatus within the BSSR should be considered.
   The Belorussian Communist Party, from its inception in May 1917[29] until the 1930's, was *de facto* a party of the Russian minority in the BSSR. By 1933 70 percent of the Party membership was composed of Russian and Jewish nationals.

Not until 1927 had the Belorussian element within the CP of the BSSR risen from 21 percent in 1922 to 46.7 percent and 60 percent in 1933.[30] No subsequent official figures on CP BSSR members' nationalities have been available except for those of the whole of the Party (CPSU) which has, as of 1967, 424,360 Belorussians ("KPSS v tsifrakh." *Partiinaia zhizn.* No. 19. October 1967. p. 14). Nevertheless, the three waves of purges during the 1930's hit Belorussians in the Party more frequently than the Russians, although during the earlier stages the first secretary, Vasil Sharanhovich, was himself a Belorussian. He was, in fact, the only Belorussian ever to serve in that capacity. The process of de-Belorussianization of the Party can be measured by the fact that at the Seventeenth All-Union Party Congress which assembled in January 1934, only nineteen out of 1,227 delegates were from Belorussia, and only nine were Belorussian nationals.[31]

At the present time (1 January 1970), the Party's membership is said to number 412,873, along with 21,654 candidates. Against the total of the population of the Republic, the membership of the Party constitutes less than 5 percent, thereby remaining elitarian in nature. This fact reflects also the Belorussians' lack of enthusiasm to become *partiichyk.* In the absence of any official information as to the nationality composite of the present membership, the percentage of Belorussians can only be estimated at 60-65 percent.

A somewhat easier problem in this regard, yet one not altogether resolvable, is the determination of the nationality of individuals in the Party's leadership.[32] The first Secretary of the CP BSSR, M. Masherov (Mašerou), is one of those Belorussians, thoroughly Russified, who speak exclusively Russian in public.

Of the eleven members of the Bureau of the Central Committee, four persons have a Belorussian national identity. In the Secretariat, the Second Secretary and two secretaries, A. T. Kuzmin and V. F. Matskevich are Belorussians. Out of 132 members of the CC some 44 persons might not deny Belorussian identity. In all other commissions, committees, and regional offices, the Belorussian element can be estimated at 55 percent. Using A. Inkeles' findings[33] in determining social groups as they exist in the Soviet society and applying them to Belorussia, it is plausible to estimate the Russian element in Belorussian government and social structure as shown on page 147. In the absence of dependable data, data deliberately withheld by Soviet authorities, a marginal deviation of 5 to 10 percent in both directions is possible in all categories as specified above. Therefore, this scheme must be regarded as a very rough approximation, containing many ambiguities resulting from forceful interferences into the social structure such as purges, shifts in policies, deportations, and so on. Nevertheless, this social pyramid basically can be regarded also as a hierarchical arrangement of the ruling Russian minority in the BSSR. It also indicates that Belorussians are exposed to two forms of pressure: the first coming from the implementation of the Marxian dogma as interpreted by the CPSU, and the second one which has its roots in historic Russian colonial-minded nationalism as carried out by Russian bureaucrats posted in non-Russian republics and areas.

The scissors of power in this particular case affect people who have had little chance to pass through all stages of national rebirth and who, at the same time, have been subjected to numerous purges. Terror and police state methods have curtailed and continue to curtail attempts to go beyond the officially outlined borders for national manifestation. Those who cross the lines risk either prison or Siberian camps.

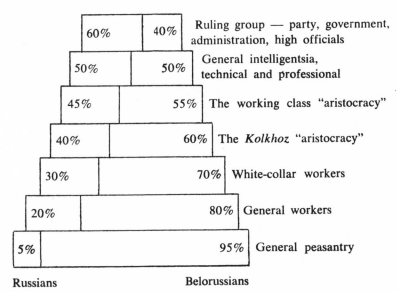

60%	40%	Ruling group — party, government, administration, high officials
50%	50%	General intelligentsia, technical and professional
45%	55%	The working class "aristocracy"
40%	60%	The *Kolkhoz* "aristocracy"
30%	70%	White-collar workers
20%	80%	General workers
5%	95%	General peasantry

Russians   Belorussians

(Other nationalities are about equally distributed between these two nationalities.)

Simultaneously, an enormous apparatus of propaganda works continually to maintain the status quo on Moscow's terms. For instance, during the 1969-70 school year, 480,000 persons participated in political courses. In 1969 more than 500,000 lectures indoctrinated the people of the Republic. On the occasion of Lenin's centennial, 30,000 agitators criss-crossed the country. In one year, 1968, 68 thousand lectures were given on the subject of Marxism and the Communist Party.[34] According to S. Pavlov, Director of the Propaganda and Agitation Section of the CC of CPB, over 240,000 persons attended special schools supervised by the Party and Komsomol in 1972.[35] During the 1972-73 school year, more than 750,000 persons were enrolled in all sectors of the system of Marxist-Leninist education of Communists and members of the Komsomol. Taking all forms of mass propaganda into account, 1.5 million people are reached by these means (*"Polymia,"* No. 12, 1972, p. 20). The extent of brain-washing, not always properly understood in the West, can convince even a slave that his oppressor is right. In this socio-political environment, where 99 percent of the population has not read the *U.N. Declaration of Human Rights* or G. Mazzini's writings, the ideals of national self-determination and personal freedom are seen as "utopias of the past." Officially, Belorussians are told in the Russian language that "The Great October socialist revolution once and for all has dealt with national oppression, liberated the Belorussian people from foreign capitalistic exploitation, created conditions which enabled them to resolve the question of national socialist statehood, to develop cultural and economic progress."[36]

Soviet economic achievements have been stressed before, and it is true that the Belorussian peasant today is physically and materially better off than his grandfather. Education, medical service, and technological advancement in all branches of national life have moved forward considerably. However, in addition to the restrictions typical of a totalitarian system, Belorussian people cannot freely use their own language on all levels in their own Republic. Lacking utilization in such areas as Party, government, diplomacy, church, army, transportation, communication, internal security, and international exposition, the Belorussian language can be considered as a modern language only to a limited degree. There is a real danger that Belorussian is becoming a language of family entertainment, of writers and poets,[37] and of lower educational institutions. Should the present trend continue for another half century, it will become once again a language of mere folkloristic importance and application. The present Soviet policy regarding non-Russian nations aims unmistakably at the transformation of nations as they are distinguished by historical, cultural, and linguistic differentiations, into societies set apart by geographical identity (like "Siberians"), speaking the language of the ruling master nation—Russian.

The absence in Belorussia of a noteworthy opposition, such as the well-established dissent movements in the Ukraine, the Baltic republics, among the Jewish minority, and even in Central Asia,[38] indicates the weakness of the national forces, which have suffered losses since the second World War. Only against this background may one understand the Belorussian restraint in challenging the system in the fashion of Alexander Solzhenitsyn, Andrei Sakharov, Andrei Amalrik, Viacheslav Chornovil, Ivan Kandyba, Lev Lukianenko, Valentyn Moroz, as well as numerous other Russians, Ukrainians, and Jews. However, the silence of nationalism in Belorussia is not absolute. Already it has been interrupted by Vasil Bykau, whose speech at a closed session of the 1966 Fifth Congress of Belorussian writers at Minsk is now available in the West.[39] He reasons that "undoubtedly it requires not only talent but courage to write the truth; but it also needs courage to accept the truth in its fullness and complexity."[40] While still basically loyal to the system, he assures the reader that he and his generation are aware of the truth and the absence of truth in Belorussia.

The restless voices of the 1960's, so typical of the whole of Soviet society, were by no means limited to Russians, Ukrainians, Jews, and Balts. National dissenters were present and active in Belorussia too. The sudden increase of official Soviet propaganda against growing nationalistic manifestations has only come about because of the alarming symptoms. The policy of silencing events on the highest level of the media either failed or became counter-productive. Therefore, a campaign from above had to be initiated, as in the past, with the expectation that the identification of the sources of troubles would discourage the spread of nationalistic sentiments. Implementation of accusations, supplemented by realities or even by the possibility of a new wave of terror, has been considered valid because of its past merit.

Otherwise, the system, perhaps for the first time in decades, is on the defensive, testifying not only to the existence of acute grievances but also to the limits of the system. Writing in *Polymia* "About some features and peculiarities of national relations in conditions of developed Socialism,"[41] Masherov complains:

> Our ideological adversaries, including those fierce nationalist repro-
> bates who are active in the imperialist backyards, shed many
> crocodile tears because the rapprochement, mutual influence,
> and international character of socialist nations' cultures lead
> allegedly to their "unification" and "levelling" and are conductive

to the "imperishment of national content." Ideologues and servants of the bourgeoisie clamor about "Russification" and linguistic "assimilation" taking place in the Soviet Union. However, this outcry is in no way motivated by a concern for the lot of the socialist nations but solely by the desire to distort the essence of the pro- cesses which are taking place in life and to sow in our land the poison seeds of national distrust which were eradicated a long time ago.

Masherov refers to Belorussians living in the Western world as the only source of dissatisfaction with the Russification of Belorussia; this is a dubious argument, since their number is rather small and their influence upon world opinion is mini- mal. Hence, the more reasonable conclusion seems to come from the growing dis- approval of the Soviet policy in the BSSR by the Belorussian people themselves.

The reference to "imperialist backyards" is a warning to Belorussian dissenters of how they can possibly be accused should the regime choose to use force.

Belorussian émigrés were singled out for special attention in Ilia Roshkov's article "*Diversiia slovom*" (Subversion by word) in *Neman*,[42] a Russian-language organ of the Writers' Union of Belorussia. Roshkov, a Russian national, attacking *bieburnacy* (Soviet term meaning "Bielorussian bourgeois nationalists"), blames them for joining Western "Sovietologists"

> [in] reviling of the Belorussian people with all their might .... In the field of slander and falsification they have indeed refined their dirty blood-stained hands. ... The "well-wishers" from among the nationalistic rabble make believe they don't notice the immense successes in the realm of politics, economics, and culture attained by the Belorussian people during the years of Soviet power.

A. Malashko, in his Russian book *Militant Nationalism as an Ideology and Policy of Imperialism*,[43] enlightens his readers on how to distinguish the national and international and how to recognize "a chauvinist and provocateur behind the mask of peoples' defender." During the years 1971-1972, the number of books and articles in various journals accusing nationalists of numerous crimes and of anti- Soviet propaganda increased substantially.[44]

Recently the regime's nervousness and uncertainty as to the size and scope of the nationalistic sentiments among the people reached as high as the First Secretary of the CP BSSR. In February 1972, at the conference of instructors of social studies in Minsk, Masherov imposed upon them an additional task:

> Special attention should be paid to the question of struggle against *recydyvy* (relapses) of nationalism and nationalistic views. Today, the national question is one of the acute elements of the ideological- political struggle between socialism and capitalism. The instigators of anti-Communist propaganda increasingly count on nationalism and make attempts to use its pernicious weeds in ideological subver- sion directed against socialism.[45]

Not since Lenin's death has the Soviet regime admitted the existence of Rus- sian nationalism, but other nationalities of the Soviet Union, including Belorussians, have been continuously reminded of and reprimanded for nationalistic deviations.

Kommunist Belorussii (No. 8, 1966) admonished the Belorussians in its Russian language editorial:

One must not close his eyes to the fact that certain of our people sometimes fall under the influence of bourgeois propaganda and become bearers of nationalist and chauvinist tendencies. This is why the very first obligation of Party organizations is to conduct an uncompromising struggle against manifestations and remnants of any form of nationalism and chauvinism, against tendencies toward national limitation and exclusiveness.

In the light of such an intensive campaign against the nationalist challenge to the system, there is no point of arguing about its absence, even though statistical data and documentary support are not always available to the researcher.

Oppression does not eliminate nationalism; it never did, and the Belorussia of the past, as a case in point, is no exception. On the other hand, it is advisable to consider all facets of life within the Soviet Union and weigh them against such factors as time and the ability to resist under adverse circumstances, including the impact of a concentrated propaganda, before accepting an *ad hoc* resolution. Only time and additional evidence of growing national determination and individual desire for a larger margin of freedom will test the tenacity of the Belorussian nation as an independent entity. Until that time Belorussia must be classified as a society advancing into the technological age with restricted experiences in national freedom and personal liberties.[46]

The Belorussian people paid exorbitant prices for socialist promises, for their right to become a republic after centuries of oppression, and, above all, for speedy modernization within the USSR. Indeed, progress in almost all areas has been achieved, particularly in technological and educational matters. These gains, however, were balanced and even outweighed by the absence of political freedom, by the restriction of national culture and, last but not least, by the forceful Russification of a nation that only a few decades earlier had had such high hopes. Yet, the future, particularly the political future of the Belorussians, is not altogether predetermined by the Moscow pattern. John H. Kautsky, together with numerous other Western scholars of various fields, correctly depicts growing internal contradictions in the industrialized societies, including communist regimented structures.[47] This, in turn, offers some leeway for an unpredictable course of events, rejecting any pessimistic hypotheses and conclusions of the moment. For instance, under Nicholas I and Alexander III, the Belorussian nation did not even "exist" for administrative purposes; 150 years later, however, there are still 7 million people whose national awareness is intensely stronger than their forefathers' a century ago.

Having preserved natural vitality as exhibited by Olga Korbut, the girl who astonished the whole world at the Munich Olympiade,[48] literary creativeness as shown by V. Rich,[49] and the habit of hard work as illustrated in various statistics, this nation still reads Janka Kupala's famous lines:

Arise from out our people, native seer
Proclaim your burning, thunderous prophesies.
With wisdom witchcraft from our nation clear
Which foes have cast on her for centuries.[50]

NOTES

[1] Nicholas P. Vakar, *Belorussia: The Making of a Nation. A Case Study* (Cambridge: Harvard University Press, 1956); Ivan S. Lubachko, *Belorussia under Soviet Rule, 1917-1957* (Lexington: The University Press of Kentucky, 1972). Surprisingly enough there is only one book on Belorussia in German: Eugen von Engelhardt, *Weissruthenen: Volk und Land* (Berlin, 1943).

[2] Nicholas P. Vakar, "The Name "White Russia,' " *American Slavic and East European Review*, VIII (1949), p. 3.

[3] *Belorussian Review* published with the Institute for the Study of the USSR (Munich, 1956); *The Journal of Byelorussian Studies* is published by the Anglo-Byelorussian Society (London, 1965–); *Facts on Byelorussia*, ed. by Jan Zaprudnik (New York, 1972–).

[4] *Homin Ukrainy* (Toronto, Ont.) 21 October 1972. According to the article, it became known only from information brought by emigrants to Israel.

[5] *Pravda*, 13 December 1948; *Bolshaia sovetskaia entsyklopediia*, Vol. 9; *Mezhdunarodnaia zhizn*, No. 12 (1955).

[6] Mikola Abramčyk, *I Accuse the Kremlin of Genocide of My Nation* (Toronto: Byelorussian Alliance in Canada, 1950), p. 1.

[7] T. Y. Kiselev, *Byelorussia*. In: *The Fifteen Soviet Socialist Republics Today and Tomorrow* (London: Crosscurrent Press, 1960), p. 9.

[8] Lubacko, *Belorussia*, p. 124.

[9] Vakar, *Belorussia*, p. 150.

[10] Kiselev, *Byelorussia*, p. 24.

[11] Abramčyk, *I Accuse*, p. 6.

[12] As proven by John H. Kautsky in his study, *The Political Consequences of Modernization* (New York: John Wiley and Sons, 1972).

[13] In the case of the Soviet nationalities policy it suffices to mention the fate of Jews, so well publicized in the Western world, in contrast to the almost unknown forceful Russification of the BSSR as reflected in Soviet statistics. The percentage of Russians in the BSSR increased from 8.2 percent in 1959 to 10.4 percent in 1970, a net increase of 42.1 percent.

[14] Statistical data available in: *Belorusskaia SSR za 50 let. Statisticheskii sbornik* (Belorussian SSR in 50 years: Statistical Collection) (Minsk, 1968); *Belorusskaia SSR v tsifrakh v 1969 godu* (Belorussian SSR in figures in 1969) (Minsk, 1970).

[15] *Belorusskaia SSR*, pp. 104, 130, 140.

[16] *Ibid.*, p. 104.

[17] Data on income obtained from: Hans-Juergen Wagener, *Regional Output Levels in the Soviet Union* (New York: Radio Liberty Committee, 1971) Radio Liberty Research Paper, No. 41 (1971).

[18] *Belorusskaia SSR v tsifrakh*, p. 21.

[19] A short history of Belorussian literature and language in: *Belorussia*. Printed by Human Relations Area Files, Inc. (New Haven, Conn.: HRAF, 1955). Also in Vakar, pp. 75-92.

[20] Soviet version of this aspect of Belorussia in: S. Z. Ieshin, *Razvitie kultury v BSSR za gody Sovetskoi vlasti* (Cultural progress of the BSSR during years of the Soviet regime) (Minsk, 1970).

[21] *Belorusskaia SSR v tsifrakh*, p. 301.

[22] *Ezhegodnik Bolshoi sovetskoi entsiklopedii* (1971), p. 125; K. P. Buslau, "Ab vynikakh raboty Instytutau Addzialennia hramadskikh navuk AN BSSR za 1971 hod," *Vestsi Akadiemii navuk BSSR. Seryia hramadskikh navuk*. No. 3 (1972), pp. 5-12.

[23] On the fate of the Belorussian theatre: Vladimir Seduro, *The Byelorussian Theater and Drama*. Foreword by Ernest J. Simmons (New York: Research Program of the USSR, 1955). The 1953 repertoire of the Belorussian theatres reveals the following distribution: Communist propaganda—60 percent; Russian plays (drama, opera, musicals)—20 percent; national Belorussian—15 percent and Western classic—5 percent (Seduro, *The Byelorussian Theatre*, pp. 483-502).

[24] No one, with the exception of a Belorussian by nationality, a member of the Academy of Sciences of the BSSR writing in an official of this institution, pleads in favour of Russification of his own nation. It is not merely a wishful intention of academician Martsinkevich but by now a very real possibility supported by facts and statistics. F. S. Martsinkevich, "Iekanamichne razvitstse Belarusi u sastave Soiuza SSR." *Vestsi Akademii navuk BSSR, Serya hramadskikh navuk*, No. 6 (1972), p. 16.

[25] A. J. Zbralevich and S. V. Fedulova, eds., *Bibliografiia Belorusskoi sovetskoi bibliografii, 1922-1961. Ukazatel bibliograficheskikh materialov izdanykh v Belorusskoi SSR* (Minsk: Akamiia navuk Belorusskoi SSR, 1963).

[26] *Belaruskae movoznaustva: Bibliahrafichny ukazalnik, 1825-1965 hh.* (Minsk: Akademiia navuk BSSR, 1967).

[27] *Pechat SSSR v 1971 godu*, p. 59.

[28] The reader will find more on this aspect of Soviet policy in: Nicholas P. Vakar, "Soviet Nationality Policy: The Case History of Belorussia," *Problems of Communism*. No. 5 (1954); N. Nedasek, *Ocherki istorii bolshevizma v Belorussii*. I. *Bolshevizm na putiakh k ustanovleniiu kontrolia nad Belorussiei* (From the History of Bolshevism in Belorussia. I. The Development of Bolshevik Control over Belorussia. Munich: Institute for the Study of the History and Culture of the USSR, 1954); Anton A. Adamovich, "Academic Freedom in the Study of Byelorussian Literature in the USSR," *Academic Freedom under the Soviet Rule: A Symposium* (Munich: The Institute for the Study of the USSR, 1954); A. Stankevich, "Natsionalnaia politika Kremlia v Belorussii," *IV Konferentsiia Instituta po izucheniiu istorii i kultury SSSR* (Munich: Institute for the Study of the USSR, 1954); William Forwood, "Nationalities in the Soviet Union," In: George Schöpflin, ed., *The Soviet Union and Eastern Europe: A Handbook* (New York: Praeger Publishers, 1970), pp. 199-208.

[29] Richard Pipes, *The Formation of the Soviet Union: Communism and Nationalism, 1917-1923*. Rev. ed. (New York: Atheneum, 1968), p. 74; Lubachko, *Belorussia*, pp. 15-16.

[30] John S. Reshetar and K. Luther, *Aspects of Nationality Problem in the USSR* (Alabama: Air University, Human Resources Research Institute, 1954), pp. 33, 66.

[31] Lubachko, *Belorussia*, p. 116.

[32] A guarded estimation can be made on hand of the following sources: *Directory of Soviet Officials*. Vol. II. (U.S. Dept. of State, 1961); Edward L. Crowley, *et al.*, eds., *Prominent Personalities in the USSR* (Metuchen, N.J.: The Scarecrow, 1968).

[33] Alex Inkeles, "Social Stratification in the Soviet Union," *Class, Status and Power*. R. Benedix and S. M. Lipset, eds., pp. 610-11.

[34] *Kommunist*, No. 3 (1970), pp. 20-21; Ieshin, *Razvitie kultury v BSSR*, pp. 149-51.

[35] "Kommunist Belorussii," No. 9 (1972), pp. 11-13.

[36] *Belorusskaia SSR za 50 let*, p. 5.

[37] On the fate of Belorussian literature under the Soviet regime see: Anthony Adamovich, *Opposition to Sovietization in Belorussian Literature: 1917-1957* (New York: Scarecrow Press, 1958).

[38] As discussed in Edward Allworth, ed., *The Nationality Question in Soviet Central Asia* (New York: Praeger Publishers, 1973).

[39] Michael Glenny, "Writing in Byelorussia," *Partisan Review*. Rutgers University XXXIV, 2 (1972), pp. 255, 259-263; *Facts on Byelorussia*, I, 6 (1972), pp. 44-47.

[40] Glenny, p. 259.

[41] The article was originally published in *Kommunist* (October 1972) and then reprinted in *Kommunist Belorussii* (No. 12, 1972), and in *Polymia* (No. 12, 1972).

[42] Neman, No. 10 (Minsk, 1972).

[43] *Voinstvuiushchii natsionalizm—ideologiia i politika imperializma* (Minsk, 1971).

[44] Few titles: I. Hurski, *Chuzhy khleb* (Minsk, 1971); S. Z. Pochanin, *V grozovom vosemnadtsatom* (Minsk, 1969); L. Proksha, comp., *Na zadvorkakh: artykuly, fieltony, pamflety* (Minsk, 1970); G. Shmygov, "XXIII siezd KPSS ob usilenii borby s ideologicheskimi diversiiami imperializma," *Kommunist Belorussii*, No. 2, 1967.

[45] *Nastaunitskaia Hazieta*, 5 February 1972.

[46] On this aspect of Soviet experience see Alex Inkeles, "Models and Issues in the Analysis of Soviet Society," *Survey*, No. 60 (1966), pp. 3-17.

[47] Kautsky, *The Political Consequences*. Especially chapter: "A Postscript on Communism."

[48] The performance of the Belorussian athletes in Olympiads since World War II is not only impressive but also a source of Belorussian pride. To them belong more than fifty medals. See Michail Supanieu, "Lik u nashu korysc," *Maladosc* (Minsk) No. 9, 1968; R. Siarhieienka, "Paslaslouie da Alimpiiady," *Zviazda* (Minsk) 30 October 1968; Report of the performance of Belorussian athletes in Munich in *Zviazda*, 15 September 1972.

[49] Vera Rich, comp. & trans., *Like Water, Like Fire.* UNESCO Collection of Representative Works. European Series. (London, 1971). The anthology contains 222 poems by 41 Belorussian poets from 1828 to the present day.

[50] From *Facts on Belorussia*, vol. I, No. 3 (1972), p. 18.

RELIGION IN THE SOVIET UKRAINE:
A POLITICAL PROBLEM OF MODERNIZING SOCIETY

Vasyl Markus
Loyola University
Chicago, Illinois

Soviet experience in development and the results achieved over the course of half a century are generally rationalized as a process of modernization common to other developing nations. Some authors would rather attribute the aberrations and adverse effects of Soviet socio-economic and political systems to the phenomenon of rapid development than to the intrinsic nature of totalitarian ideology or politics. Hence there is a tendency to view Soviet policies (economic, cultural, social) as functions of a general trend in the twentieth century world to bring about fundamental changes in society commensurate to the expectations of its various segments.[1]

Yet the same authors hasten to acknowledge some fundamental differences between the Soviet and other models of modernization. "The evolution of Soviet politics has encompassed significant deviations from what elsewhere are usually considered the characteristics of modernization."[2]

If modernization had to mean economic development, industrialization, urbanization, and resulting bureaucratization of political and production systems, combined with the spread of mass education, then, certainly, the Soviet Union is eligible for that status. If, on the other hand, "the central significance of the total development process is in its capacity to widen human choice and alternatives,"[3] then the USSR, like most other communist-ruled Party-States, represents a conspicuous failure in its quest of a modern society. The cultural and religious policies, among other aspects of political development, do evidence this conclusion.

Other manifestations that accompany modern political development and that are generally observed by students of the problem are nationalism and secularization. In both respects the Soviet model deviates from the common concept of modernization. As a substitute to the overdue Marxian internationalism (which, theoretically, might be the answer to modernization), there emerged an extreme form of Russian nationalism at the expense of the nationalisms of developing non-Russian peoples in the USSR.

The Soviet brand of secularism happens to be only the cloak for the elimination of other value systems, primarily religious, by instituting monopolistic ideology as the only orthodoxy in all spiritual matters. The secularized Soviet state and society resemble in a number of ways their tsarist predecessor. They even exceed the latter in the quasi-religious features of their ideology. "Secularization" here, in substance, is a misnomer: old religions and churches are replaced by the new pseudo-religion.

The vicissitudes of Soviet religious and national policies in the particular case of one nationality, the Ukraine, will prove not only such inconsistencies but also the "dialectical" approach of policy-makers to this problem.

RATIONALE FOR THE LIQUIDATION OF UKRAINIAN CHURCHES AFTER 1945

The story of the forced liquidation nearly three decades ago of two national churches in the Ukraine, the Ukrainian Catholic (Uniate) and the Ukrainian Orthodox Autocephalous, is relatively well documented.[4] It will suffice to state here the underlying causes and justifications as presented by the Soviet government and the Russian Orthodox Church (R.O.C.) authorities for their actions in 1946 and 1949.[5]

The following observations will illustrate these policies:

1. The Ukrainian Catholic Church (also known as the Greek Catholic or Uniate Church), a semi-autonomous body within the Catholic Church and one of the several Eastern Rite Catholic Churches, constituted in the newly incorporated territories a Western-oriented community, supervised by an outside authority—i.e., the Holy See. In the Western Ukraine this Church numbered close to four million faithful in 1945, as well as over three thousand priests who were educated in the Ukrainian national spirit and molded under Western influences. As such, it could have become a stronghold of nationalism in the Soviet Ukraine, potentially threatening the Soviet Russian rule.

2. The Ukrainian Autocephalous Church (U.A.O.C.), a national orthodox body in the Ukraine, revived in 1942 against the centralized R.O.C., was also instrumental in the promotion of anti-Russian Ukrainian nationalism in the German-occupied Ukraine during World War II. As such, it was denounced by Moscow as counter-revolutionary, and labeled as a "creature of Petlurites."[6] The continuation of this Church after 1945 could have been a threat to the new Soviet policy of promoting Russian nationalism, initiated during World War II. Again, the "bourgeois nationalist" character of this Church provoked its suppression.

3. Consequently, both national churches of the Ukraine were considered to be "anti-people and alien bodies" in the life of the Ukrainian nation and its history. "Instead of Church unity, it brought us divisions, hostility and hatred. It has suppressed religious and national self-consciousness of our people," as Filaret, the present Metropolit of Kiev, characterized the effects of the Union of Brest (the act in 1596 when part of the Ukrainians were united with Rome, hence the Uniate

Church).[7] Concerning the attitude of the R.O.C. to the Ukrainian Autocephalous Church, now existing only in the Western world, it is noteworthy that the new Patriarch of Moscow, Pimen, recently addressed à *propos* a lengthy message to the Ecumenical Patriarch of Constantinople warning him against any contacts with that "schismatic" and "chauvinistic" church.[8]

4.   Reconciled since 1943 with the Kremlin, the Russian Orthodox Church expected compensation for its loyalty and patriotism during the war. There was nothing more logical than to reward the R.O.C. with the Uniates (Ukrainian Catholics), as well as to penalize the Ukrainian Orthodox who, through their Autocephaly, denounced allegiance to Moscow. Nothing else could have better served the interests and ambitions of the traditionalist and nationalist Russian Church, as well as those of a rising totalitarian world power, than the dissolution of these two disruptive religious bodies claiming allegiance to the counter-revolutionary Ukrainian nationalism.

5.   The precarious existence of these two churches under German occupation presented the Russians with a convenient opportunity to suppress them for allegedly being pro-German, with a collaborationist hierarchy and clergy. With the painful experience of their church in the 1930's added to such labels,[9] the bishops of the U.A.O.C. fled into exile before the Soviet troops reoccupied the Ukraine in 1944. The same accusations were raised against all the Ukrainian Catholic bishops who were arrested in 1945 and tried secretly in 1946 for their alleged collaboration with the Nazis; a similar fate befell a large number of priests, nuns and laymen. Siberian concentration camps became the new missionary territories of these modern confessors of faith.

After this major operation—i.e., the formal dissolution by the government of one of the two national churches of the Ukraine (Ukrainian Catholic), and the *de facto* elimination of the other (Ukrainian Autocephalous Orthodox), Soviet policy-makers returned to the business of religion as usual.

States with monolithic structure, autocratic government and a wide range of community imperatives face a particular problem. This problem stems from the fact that productivity and role integration become primary concerns of the government, with the result that all social life becomes politicized in the same degree. . . Monopolistic authority needs to replace older beliefs about other forms of allegiance. New political forms are developed that have the effect of providing for the continuity, meaning and purpose of an individual's action. The result is a political doctrine that is in effect a political religion.[10]

Professor Apter's observation, although made in a more general context, perfectly applies to the Soviet conditions. Despite the support and relatively privileged position granted by the C.P.S.U. to the Russian Orthodox Church in a specific historical situation, the entire Party apparatus continues its anti-religious policy. Simultaneously, it fosters a new pseudo-religion in the form of Marxist ideology manifested in quasi-religious practices and rituals. If the R.O.C. has obtained an extended existence, this was due to its instrumental role in the elimination of other politically more harmful religious groups.

Also, the prospective role of that Church in future foreign-political combinations contributed to its being unearthed from its previous state of almost non-being. Moreover, the regime's changed attitude toward the traditionally established church body in Russia, the R.O.C., could be explained in terms of a need to channel common people's social and psychological frustrations to relatively harmless and controlled outlets.

Neither of the two Ukrainian churches could have performed the roles described above. On the contrary, their eventual toleration might have created new problems and complicated the C.P.S.U.'s delicate task of pacifying Ukrainian nationalists after World War II.

THE R.O.C. IN THE UKRAINE: A REACTIONARY FORCE

The occasional preference for certain reformist denominations and sects as opposed to the conservative church bodies can find an adequate interpretation in ideology. The regime's ideological leanings toward modernity and progressive world outlook and its stress on secularization might be factors in that. An example would be the Soviet policy vis-à-vis the *Living Church* in the 1920's, or the initial, positively neutral attitude toward the Ukrainian Autocephaly, which at the time strongly challenged the old established Russian Orthodoxy in the Ukraine.

However, the shift from official endorsement of reformist dissidence to the old legitimacy evidences other Soviet considerations than the concern for modernity, such as the efficiency of control, the submissiveness of the religious body, the tactics of "keeping hostages," and, not lastly, the availability of an easier target to compromise religion as such.

Wherever a reformist trend has appeared in recent times in the recognized religious groups, it has been viewed with much suspicion. Thus, the modernizing concepts of ecclesiastic organization as they were discussed in the 1960's by some quarters of the R.O.C., or the emergence of Christian socialist ideas among the young faithful and intelligentsia, are approached with apprehension if not with outright hostility.[11]

The modernizing trends in religion are being "unmasked" by official propaganda as the dangerous and insidious tactics of the churchmen. A recent Soviet publication on the Catholic Church exposes the attempts "to adjust and conciliate the dogmas and the church policies with the achievements of contemporary science and civilization of our days."[12] Similar modernizing ideas are being disseminated by certain church spokesmen in the U.S.S.R., states the author. Catholics, in particular, are attempting to present their teachings as being rational and in harmony with science.[13]

With the anti-religious struggle becoming more intricate and arduous under such conditions, the *Agitprop* and other institutions in charge of controlling religion are manifesting a preference for a conservative non-reformist church body.

The R.O.C. in the Ukraine has been such a church body, in contrast to two national denominations: the Ukrainian Catholic, which is Western oriented and in many ways modernized; and the U.A.O.C., which, evolved politically from the national independence movement of 1917-1921, has displayed tendencies toward modernization and reforms.[14] The Russian character of the officially recognized Orthodox Church in the present Ukraine has been continuously criticized by dissident circles. Recently such criticism has been expressed by a priest, H. Budzynskyj (repressed in 1969), with harsh words in the Ukrainian *samizdat*.[15]

THE SOVIET OBJECTIVE:
DENATIONALIZATION OF NATIVE CHURCHES

No other religious body was better equipped to serve the purpose of weakening the national character of the Ukrainian churches than the established traditional institution, the R.O.C. In that endeavour, the interests of both the Church and the regime coincided perfectly. In fact, what the C.P.S.U. and anti-religious agencies were not in a position to accomplish has been entrusted to the Russian Church.

The entire history of the Ukrainian people proves that Christianity, as represented by the two Ukrainian churches, was a nation-building factor. Such was the role of the Orthodox Church of the Ukraine, at least until the end of the eighteenth century when that Church was fully absorbed by the Moscow Patriarchate and when that Church was fully absorbed by the Moscow Patriarchate and then became Russianized. A similar nation-building function was performed by that branch of the Ukrainian Church which recognized the supremacy of Rome in 1596 while preserving its ethnic-cultural heritage and Eastern Rite, common to all Orthodox Churches.[16] If the crucial theme of Ukrainian history since the eighteenth century has been the struggle for national survival, then the Uniate Church in particular played the decisive role in this struggle. Soviet sources themselves testify to this, although indirectly, and through negative arguments.

Religious sociologists and historians in the USSR try to work out a whole theory based on the relationship between the two superstructural phenomena: religion and nationality. They also attempt to place the Uniate Church in this conceptual framework. However, when dialectics prove inadequate, pure political arguments must prevail.

A Soviet author, V. I. Bodnar, assessing the interaction between nationalism and religion, stresses in particular the role of tradition and national customs. He contends that religion (meaning the Church) successfully exploits the national feelings. Similarly, conscious nationalism finds its expression through religious channels, also attracting a certain number of followers among the faithful. A consistent dialectical interpretation of this interaction between nationalism and religion (for example, the former sanctions national exclusiveness and opposes ideas of international cooperation, and the Church attempts to influence mostly older and less educated people attached to traditions) cannot hold as a general rule. The same author remarks that "obviously, the remnants of nationalist psychology are not innate in all religious people, and vice-versa."[17]

Bodnar's main thesis can be validly questioned when he asserts:

The survival of religious feelings, in many respects, is explained by their interaction with the survival of nationalist feelings. The

survival of nationalism, as a rule, appears stronger where the
religiosity of the people is higher.[18]

The modern secular nationalism flatly refutes this categorical statement.

Bodnar argues that the Church often presents its rituals with a regard to preserving national traditions—religious holy-days, funeral rites, separate interment in
cemeteries according to religious affiliation, insistence on marriage between co-
religionists, and all the other traditions that appeal to national sentiments. By
asserting that "the efforts of the Church to conserve a score of rituals and pass them
off as national is a serious obstacle on the way to formation of inter-nationalist and
atheist views," Bodnar seems to disregard the solidarity among co-religionists of
different nationalities (e.g., Catholics, Baptists, and especially smaller sects in the
USSR).

The author designates both nationalism and religion as targets for ideological
struggle, yet in practice he proposes a differentiated approach to those phenomena,
depending on historical and political circumstances—the so-called objective conditions. He admits that, even in an industrialized society, some people may react
emotionally to certain consequences of socioeconomic development (immigration
of alien elements, rapid change in the traditional way of life, etc.), and therefore
seek religious outlets. At the same time, Bodnar cautions that religion, unlike
nationalism, does not always breed merely survivals of nationalism, but sometimes
sound national traditions. (Does Bodnar have in mind the Russian Orthodox
Church?!) Therefore, in political practice, the attitudes to religion and tradition
must be differentiated. Unfortunately, the author does not elaborate on distinctions between the "nationalist" and "sound national traditions," so that the decision
in concrete cases is finally left to the power-holders, who decide arbitrarily in the
light of "objective conditions."[19]

Bodnar further states that religion is often presented to the people mistakenly
"as an important part of national history and natural culture." As a consequence,
those who express an interest in the national past may also develop a sympathetic
attitude toward religion. Certain quarters of the intelligentsia easily develop such an
attitude. "Through the idealization of particular religious aspects in the national
culture, they may end in the defence of religion and church."[20]

Such an error has been discovered in the works of a Carpatho-Ukrainian
writer, Ivan Chendei (former chairman of the regional Writers' Union) who, in his
novels and short stories, idealized old customs, traditions, and the way of life of
the mountain-people (*Verkhovyntsi*). In light of this, Chendei's critics reproached
him because in his novel *Ivan* he held in high esteem "Christian-priestly morality"
as if it were a progressive phenomenon in social life.[21]

Yet Bodnar admits that ignoring national particularities may backfire by reviv-
ing nationalism and religiosity. But again, he does not elaborate on the specific
aspects of national culture and ethnic particularities that could be cultivated. In
fact, he does not cite concrete cases that show how disregarding the national culture can revive nationalist or religious expression. Instead, such instances are rather
drastically voiced by the spokesmen of national dissent in the Ukraine and
elsewhere.

VALENTYN MOROZ:
HERETIC OF THE SOVIET MODERNIZATION MODEL

The most severe indictment of the Soviet design of cultural modernization came from a Soviet Ukrainian citizen, Valentyn Moroz. For his heretical ideas he is now undergoing his second term of imprisonment.[22]

V. Moroz, after his release in 1969, visited a Ukrainian village, Kosmach, in the Carpathian mountains, a "nest" of natural beauty and of original popular culture. He observed the crime of "culture-cide" committed against the entire nation. The village was deprived of its *ikonostasis*[23] under the pretense that it will be preserved in a museum of Kiev. Like hundreds of other artistic objects robbed from churches and stored in the police-controlled warehouses, this artistic treasure never reached any museum. Private "collectors" also were pillaging the Ukrainian countryside of the folkloric and handicraft items. The authorities, on the other hand, were destroying artifacts of religious art (church edifices, road crosses, etc.). They even burned the monastery library in Kiev in 1966.

This situation created the setting and the social-psychological framework for Moroz's defense of national culture. He set up his defense in the most universal way, using the village of Kosmach and the *Hutsul* Church with its iconostasis only as a pretext to reflect on more fundamental issues of culture, human creativity, traditions, progress, development, religion, nationality, etc.

It is generally acknowledged that the spread of education, the literacy of the masses, and the acquisition of technical-professional skills are among the most spectacular achievements of the Soviet regime. Popularization of fine arts, literature, theater, and of other performing arts are further proofs of Soviet cultural progress, particularly among small ethnic groups and nationalities.

At the same time, however, the Soviet pattern of cultural development produced a phenomenon known as mass culture—uniform, stagnant, uninspiring, standardized—which smothers individual creativity. In V. Moroz's words, "A colorless culture is emerging in the Soviet Union." Pointing to the core of the problems, he dramatizes the situation, saying that "instead of the bliss that the Utopians have promised us, there has come anti-intellectualism, withdrawal, de-humanization, and the loss of one's roots."[24]

V. Moroz does not systematically analyze the mass culture in sociological or philosophical terms. In fact, the mass culture has become for him an anti-culture. This inhibiting reality imposes itself upon his life and work and upon the life and work of his fellow intellectuals and of the Ukrainian people. Culture for Moroz is an existential experience—that is, human creativity based primarily on spiritual values. With this in view, the dominance of technology and economics in society is anti-cultural. He observes that "there is an English bank, but there is no English folklore." To the extent that a society relies only on utilitarian achievement and pursues a technical-material progress, it experiences cultural decadence. "People are hypocritically developing technical functions at the expense of the spiritual, and for some reason they call it culture."[25]

Nor is culture the accumulation of formal practical knowledge and its dissemination. Rather, this is what the Soviets term "enlightenment" or, in Western terms, mass culture. For Moroz it is the phenomenon of the "universal malady." In his views, Soviet "enlightenment" occurs when a person deprived of traditions is given formal education.[26]

True culture develops organically; it is rooted in the natural and the historical experience of the people. "High cultural attainments are possible with the continuity of tradition." The culture must develop its own personality spontaneously from its natural sources. "It cannot be built by a five-year plan as might a canal in Stalin's time."[27]

The "planned culture" is void of national roots, traditional values, and deep human desires. New artificial values as dogmatically defined by ideologues and inculcated by practitioners are deforming the true culture still in existence among traditional people. Actually it amounts to the dehumanization and deculturalization of a nation. V. Moroz reaches this conclusion when he observes the forced policy of cultural assimilation, the moving of populations (by uprooting one group and setting it within a culturally alien milieu), and the eradication of traditions, religion, church and folklore, etc. The policy of de-nationalization fostered by the Party amounts, in fact, to the Stalinist program to "atomize human beings," detaching them from their national and natural groups and values.[28] To Moroz's satisfaction, Stalin's plan did not work in the *Hutsul Land* as well as in the village of Kosmach. Here, the "instinct of self-preservation" is still very strong.

Among the traditional values contributing to the culture and human growth are nationalism and religion, especially with regard to the Church, ceremonies, and religious art-symbols of religious consciousness.

The relevance of these symbols is well illustrated in the experience of the people of Kosmach. "Iconostasis is a holy relic to the people in *Hutsul Land*."[29] The villagers fought for its return to Kosmach because of this, and not for any "preservationist" reasons. The people of Kosmach feel that the Church they were defending was not merely an esthetic structure, prayer house, or museum. "Behind it stood a nation, spiritually all that without which man simply becomes a working animal."[30]

The new *Kulturtraeger* are attempting to annihilate these foundations of national culture, either by destroying them directly or by creating cheap substitutes. Moroz condemns the destruction of churches, icons, roadside crosses, and the introduction of new Soviet "rituals," poorly and artificially modelled along traditional customs and ceremonies. These, however, are void of sound, traditional content. Added to this is the official anti-religious struggle and the forced destruction of the socio-economic base of the Ukrainian people with industrialization. All this is deplored by Moroz, who cautions that its catastrophic results have not yet become fully apparent.[31]

On the other hand, referring to *Agitprop*'s efforts to create new secular traditions, Moroz observes:

> You cannot create traditions. They are created by themselves
> through the centuries. . . . You can call everyone to a clubhouse and
> announce some idiotic holiday of Pig-tenders or Milkmaids instead
> of Easter, but it will never become an observed holiday. This will
> create merely another *kolhosp* meeting with another booze party
> to follow. . . [32]

Moroz's concept of traditionalism, which he so zealously defends, does not imply the petrification of the old forms and ways. It is not a rigid conservatism. What he has observed among the *Hutsul* "montagnards" (a tribe in the Carpathian mountains) is the ability "to take on the new without destroying the old." The age-old foundations should not be abolished by progress, otherwise "the spiritual shall be built on fragments starting practically from nothing." The *Hutsuls* have learned through trying experience how to use their "hidden art of national preservation." The new religion, Christianity, did not destroy the ancient rituals, deities and the spiritual outlook of this people. These rituals continued to exist in new religious form and meaning: e.g., the day of St. Ulas coincided with the day of the fox, the feast of St. Fokiy with the day of fire. The ceremony of lowering the cross into the river during the Epiphany is greeted by the *Hutsul* folk with rounds of *trembitas* (shawms) and horns as they used to greet deities in their pagan past.[33]

The same thing happened in the eighteenth century, when the former Ortho-dox Church in the land of the *Hutsuls* fell under Catholic influence and became Uniate. The beliefs of the people were not changed by the switch in allegiance to Rome or by other formalities, such as the reblessing of the Church by the Uniate priests. The main thing was that the Church remained there and continued to be theirs. As a historian, Moroz rightly observes: "The Uniate movement has grown into the spiritual body of the Ukraine and becomes a national symbol."[34]

PLEA FOR RELIGIOUS FREEDOM AND HUMAN RIGHTS

The nature of the present resistance in the Western Ukraine is the defense of the Church and religion as such, regardless of whether it is formally Orthodox or not. The less dependent it is on the political authorities, the more loyalty and attachment it can claim from the people. But, again, the main thing is the Church, the religious feelings of the people, and the traditional manner of gratifying their spiritual needs.

This is the reason why former Uniates defend their presently "Orthodox" Churches against closing, destruction, desecration, etc. The parishioners are sending delegations to the Soviet authorities, writing petitions, going on strike, and even physically defending their churches.[35]

The defense of religious rights, coupled with the national resistance, consti-tutes the core of the modern opposition movement in the Soviet Ukraine. In many respects the difference between the two vanishes. The Church in the Ukraine, particu-larly the one which suffers most from the regime (underground Uniate community), has become a mainstay of national resistance. Therefore, one who embraces the Ukrainian national cause against the Soviet Russian program of denationalization must logically defend the Ukrainian Church and religion.[36]

Also, the cause of persecuted Protestant sects finds support and sympathy among the Soviet dissidents. Evangelical Baptists, *"Initsiativniki,"* Jehovah's Witnesses, and Seventh-Day Adventists must hide their activities; they are legally prohibited and repressed as religious communities just as the Uniate underground Church is.[37] Their plea for recognition is based on the philosophy of human rights, to which the USSR and the Ukrainian Soviet government have solemnly subscribed. Soviet constitutional provisions are also being invoked by those who raise the issue of religious freedom in the USSR. Neither "freedom of conscience," guaranteed by the Soviet Constitution (Article 124), nor "freedom of religious worship" (a some-what restricted notion of it) is respected, particularly in the case of the Ukrainian

Uniates. The principle of the separation of the Church from the state is only declaratory; in fact, the state plays a decisive role in directing and restraining the activity of the churches.

For the implementation of the freedom of conscience in the USSR, the Soviet legislation provides that 20 believers who are 18 years old or over can petition the Soviet authorities to establish a religious association "for the common satisfaction of their religious needs."[38]

This right has been continuously denied to the groups of Uniates in the Western Ukraine who attempted to legalize their Church locally. Numerous cases were registered when the authorities rejected the petitions of 20 believers and the performance of religious rites were prosecuted, despite the sanctions prohibiting such actions as provided in the Soviet Criminal Code.[39]

There is no known instance in the USSR when a person, organization, or a state agency has been prosecuted under this article. Its purely propagandistic value is obvious, as is also the publicized adherence of the USSR, along with her two constituent Republics, to the Universal Declaration of Human Rights. Its Article 18 announces:

> Everyone has the right to freedom of thought, conscience, and religion; the right includes freedom to change his religion or belief, and freedom, either alone or in community with others and in public or private, to manifest his religion or belief in teaching, practice, worship, and observance.[40]

This principle, even more precisely elaborated in the Covenant on Social, Economic and Cultural Rights (the latter not being signed as yet by the USSR), has become a "dead-letter" in the Soviet policy on religious and human rights. The plea of the Lithuanian Catholics to the United Nations concerning the Soviet violations of religious freedom in the spring of 1972 and a series of other representations, including those of the unofficial Soviet Committee of Human Rights, headed by A. Sakharov, did not influence the attitude of the Soviet policy makers.[41]

The problem of human rights remains a purely academic question in official Soviet policy. In reality, however, it continues to be a vulnerable area causing embarrassment in the eyes of international opinion. Moreover, it is a serious stumbling-block in the internal political development and modernization of Soviet society.

NOTES

[1] Such views are advanced by authors like Alfred G. Meyer (*The Soviet Political System: An Interpretation*, 1965) and John H. Kautsky (*Communism and the Politics of Development*, 1968) in their comparative approach to the study of communist political systems. See also: "Symposium on Comparative Politics and Communist Systems," in Frederic J. Fleron, ed., *Communist Studies and the Social Sciences* (Chicago: Rand McNally & Co., 1969).

[2] Roy D. Laird, *The Soviet Paradigm* (New York: The Free Press, 1970), p. 95.

[3] David E. Apter, *Some Conceptual Approaches to the Study of Modernization* (Englewood Cliffs, N.J.: Prentice Hall, 1968), p. 336.

[4] Ivan Hrynioch, "The Destruction of the Ukrainian Catholic Church in the Soviet Union," *Prologue* (New York), IV, 1-2, 5-51; Bohdan R. Bociurkiw, "The Uniate Church in the Soviet Ukraine: A Case Study in Soviet Church Policy," *Canadian Slavonic Papers*, VII, (1965): 89-113. On the fate of the Ukrainian Orthodox Church in the Ukraine after 1945, little has been written. See some information in B. R. Bociurkiw's article, "The Orthodox Church and the Soviet Regime in the Ukraine, 1953-1971," *Canadian Slavonic Papers*, XIV (1972): 2, 191-211. Both authors include a substantial bibliography.

[5] March 8-10, 1946, a "Synod of the Greek Catholic Church," in Lviv, proclaiming the dissolution of that religious body in the province of Galicia, and its incorporation into the R.O.C. In August 1949, at a religious assembly in the city of Mukachiv, Transcarpathia, the Greek Catholic diocese of that Ukrainian region was also absorbed by the R.O.C.

[6] A call name derived from Simon Petlura (1879-1926), leader of the Ukrainian independence movement during the revolution in Russia. In 1921, many sympathizers of Ukrainian independence in the Soviet Ukraine established the Ukrainian Autocephalous Orthodox Church, tolerated by the Soviet regime until 1929, when it was suppressed.

[7] *Pravoslavnyi Visnyk* (Kiev), No. 7 (1971), p. 10.

[8] *Zhurnal Moskovskoi Patriarkhii* (Moscow, 1973).

[9] A similar attitude toward the Autocephalists has been expressed without substantiation by an American author: Harvey Fireside, *Icon and Swastika, the Russian Orthodox Church under Nazi and Soviet Control* (Cambridge: Harvard University Press, 1971).

[10] Apter, *Some Conceptual Approaches to the Study of Modernization*, p. 194.

[11] Cf. reprisals against dissident priests in the R.O.C., Eshliman, Iakunin, and others, as well as the treatment of *Initsiativniki*, a dissident group within the Baptist religious organization. See Michael Bourdeaux, *Patriarch and Prophets; Persecution of the Russian Orthodox Church Today* (New York, 1970) and, by the same author, *Religious Ferment in Russia: Protestant Opposition to Soviet Religious Policy* (London, 1968).

[12] M. B. Mchedlov, *Katolitsizm* (Moscow, 1970), p. 246.

[13] *Ibid.*

[14] The collegiality (*Sobornopravnist'*) and the enhanced role of the laity in the Church administration introduced by the U.A.O.C. sharply contrast with the authoritarian and centralist rule of the R.O.C.

[15] Budzynskyi wrote in one of his pamphlets: "The Orthodox Church does not exist as a whole but as separate churches: Russian, Georgian, Armenian, Polish, Czechoslovak, etc. However, there is no Ukrainian Orthodox Church [in the Soviet Union!—V.M.]. In the Ukraine, the Russian Church is dominant, with all the consequences following thereof. The Ukrainian language is prohibited like in the times of the Romanovs . . . These were not the true Orthodox people who forced others

to accept the Russian religion, but actually the protagonists of the godless sect of a militant atheism. This is an undeniable proof why the Russian Church ceased to be an authentic orthodox church and turned into an atheistic-orthodox one . . . " See *Ukrains'kyi Visnyk*, vol. I (Paris-Baltimore: Smoloskyp, 1971), pp. 69, 71.

[16] See this author's "Religion and Nationality: The Uniates of the Ukraine," in B. R. Bociurkiw and J. Strong, eds., *Religion and Atheism in the U.S.S.R. and Eastern Europe* (London: McMillan, in progress).

[17] V. L. Bodnar, "Osobennosti razvitiia ateizma v protsesse kul'turnoi revoliutsii v natsional'noi respublike" (Peculiarities of Atheist Development in a National Republic) in: *Steizm i sotsialisticheskaia kul'tura* (Atheism and Socialist Culture) (Moscow: 1971), p. 51. As an example of the close relationship between the two, the author cites the situation in areas where the capitalist system was abolished relatively late, such as the Baltic areas and the Western *Oblasti* (regions) of the Ukraine and Byelorussia. The case in point is the phenomenon of the *Pokutnyky* movement, an extremely non-conformist faction among the Uniates.

[18] *Ibid.*, p. 52.

[19] This "differentiated" approach is well illustrated by the way the traditional caroling has been handled in the Ukraine. Since some "secular" carols were found, and because of the regime's interest in promoting new "Soviet rituals," the caroling has been more or less tolerated. However, when the Party discovered a certain genuine interest in the religious relevance of this custom among some youths, as well as the "glorification of the old national folklore," it has been moving drastically against the caroling practice.

[20] V. L. Bodnar, "Osobennosti razvitiia ateizma . . . ," p. 53, quotes here an authority on the literary art and atheist propaganda, A. V. Belov, in: *Voprosy Nauchnogo Ateizma* (The Questions of Scientific Atheism), vol. IX, p. 299.

[21] The protagonist of the novel is a Uniate priest, affectionately attached to his people but forced to conceal his priestly activities.

[22] V. Moroz, a young historian and man of letters (born 1936), taught history at the Pedagogical Institutes of Luts'k and Ivano-Frankivs'k. He was arrested in 1965 and sentenced to five years of hard labor for "anti-Soviet propaganda and agitation." Released in 1969 for good behavior, he continued his dissident activity and wrote in 1970 an essay entitled, "The Chronicle of Resistance," which can be considered one of the strongest apologies for national culture and tradition ever expressed in the Soviet Union. Along with Moroz's other essays ("A Report from Beria Preserve," "Amidst the Snow," "Moses and Dathan"—written in the labor camp), "The Chronicle" reached the West and has been published in Ukrainian and other languages. The quotations used here are from the Australian editions *A Chronicle of Resistance in Ukraine*, translated by Z. Hayuk (Sidney: 1971); originally published by *Smoloskyp* (Baltimore: 1971). For this essay and other literary activities, Moroz was arrested again in June 1970 and sentenced to nine years of hard labor and five years of exile.

[23] An impressive wall of icons separating the altar from the nave in the Eastern Rite churches.

[24] *A Chronicle of Resistance in Ukraine*, p. 22.

[25] *Ibid.*

[26] *Ibid.*, p. 16.

[27] *Ibid.*, pp. 13, 16.

[28] *Ibid.*, p. 15.

[29] *Ibid.*, p. 5.

[30] *Ibid.*, p. 12.

[31] *Ibid.*, p. 20.

[32] *Ibid.*, p. 21.

[33] *Ibid.*, pp. 11-13.

[34] *Ibid.*, p. 4.

[35] Recent facts of religious resistance in the Western Ukraine have been exposed in the underground *Ukrains'kyi Visnyk*, Vol. I, pp. 56-71.

[36] The publication in the *Ukrains'kyi Visnyk* of materials concerning the religious situation provoked critical remarks from some readers. The editors disagreed with this criticism stating: "Religious persecutions, including the wanton liquidation of the Greek Catholic (Uniate) Church by the henchmen of the Beria, were illegal and unconstitutional, and therefore the *Ukrains'kyi Visnyk* will write on them in the same manner as on other similar issues. By the way, the person who collected information for the *Ukrains'kyi Visnyk* about the persecution of Greek Catholics is not a practicing Greek Catholic himself—as far as we can judge, he is an atheist." See *Ukrains'kyi Visnyk*, vol. III. (Paris-Baltimore, 1973).

[37] For information on *Initsiativniki*, see M. Bourdeaux, *Religious Ferment in Russia*.

[38] See Soviet religious legislation in the appendix of Richard H. Marshall, Jr., and others, eds., *Aspects of Religion in the Soviet Union 1917-1967* (Chicago: University of Chicago Press, 1971).

[39] Article 139 of the Criminal Code of the Ukrainian S.S.R. provides: "Obstructing the performance of religious rites, insofar as they do not violate public order, and are not accompanied by infringement of the rights of citizens, shall be punished by correctional labor for a term not exceeding six months or by social censure."

[40] The United Nations General Assembly Resolution 217, 3 GAOR, Doc. A/810.

[41] According to unconfirmed information, the Sakharov group devoted its attention to legal implications of the dissolution of the Uniate Church in the Ukraine; the relative materials are not yet available in the West.

POLITICS, PURGE, AND DISSENT IN THE UKRAINE SINCE THE FALL OF SHELEST*

Yaroslav Bilinsky
University of Delaware
Newark, Delaware

In the last four years official politics in the Ukraine has been dramatically unpredictable. The increasing repression of unofficial dissidents could have been foreseen, but the release of Leonid Pliushch from a so-called insane asylum came as a surprise. Volodymyr Shcherbitsky, who in May 1972 replaced the ousted Peter Shelest as First Secretary of the Communist Party of the Ukraine (henceforth CPU), has proceeded to consolidate his power but without that elegant smoothness that bespeaks complete success.

This paper attempts to probe both official Party politics and unofficial dissent activity in the Ukraine from about the beginning of 1972 through the Republican and All-Union Party Congresses of February-March 1976. My hope is that the paper will not only help to bring the Soviet Ukrainian story up to date,[1] but will help us gain an insight into both Soviet elite politics under Brezhnev and into the particular setting under which human rights—both individual and collective—are being defended in the communist part of the world.

Eleven days before the opening of the 25th Congress of the CPU in Kiev, January 30, 1976, it was announced that Ivan K. Lutak, the Second Secretary of the CPU Central Committee (CC)—i.e., Shcherbitsky's deputy for Party organization and personnel—was released from his duties in Kiev "in connection with his having been elected First Secretary of the Cherkassy Province Committee" (henceforth: *obkom*).[2] Cherkassy is essentially an agricultural province that in January 1954 had been carved out of the neighboring Kiev, Poltava, Kirovohrad, and Vynnytsia Provinces. On January 1, 1972, it had 74,000 Party members.[3]

*Prepared for delivery at the Midwest Slavic Conference, at the University of Illinois at Chicago Circle, May 6-8, 1976. I would like to thank Messrs. Godfrey Baldwin and Stephen Rapawy and their superior, Dr. Murray Feshbach, of the Foreign Demographic Analysis Division, Bureau of Economic Analysis, US Department of Commerce for their kind assistance with special sources and calculations.

(As Second CC Secretary Lutak had supervised the activity of some 2.5 million Communists!) The suddenness of the move apparently caught the Cherkassy *obkom* unprepared: as late as mid-January 1976, at the regularly scheduled pre-Congress Conference, O. M. Andreev had been reelected First *obkom* Secretary.[4] At a new special *obkom* plenum, January 27, 1976, Andreev was released from his position "in connection with retirement on a pension for reasons of health," most likely to vacate a niche for Lutak.[5] It stands to reason that this game of musical chairs had been cleared with the All-Union Party (CPSU) Secretariat in Moscow, most probably with Brezhnev himself. Striking, however, is the transparent clumsiness of this last minute maneuver, indicating perhaps that there had been some opposition to the move in Moscow and that it was not until approximately January 26, 1976, that the opposition was overcome. A parallel to Lutak's demotion may be found in Shelest's abrupt dismissal from the First Secretaryship of the CPU at a Politburo-CC CPSU meeting in Moscow May 19, 1972, of which the Ukrainian CC learned only ex post facto.

Who is Lutak? A Ukrainian by nationality, immediately after World War II Lutak became a Deputy Director of a sugar refinery near Kiev and probably caught the fancy of Podgorny, a well-known "sugar specialist" who was then Deputy People's Commissar of the Food Industry of the Ukraine and eventually became Second (in 1953) and then First Secretary of the CC CPU (in 1957), before he moved on to Moscow in 1963. After serving in a number of fairly responsible Party positions in the Kiev region, in 1954—i.e., under Podgorny's patronage—Lutak was made Chairman of the Cherkassy Oblast Executive Committee and in 1961 First Secretary of the more significant Crimean *obkom*. He may or may not have played a role in the overthrow of Khrushchev (in October 1964 Khrushchev stayed in his summer residence in the Crimea and Lutak was his local host). In January 1967, when Shelest was First Secretary, Lutak was promoted to Agricultural Secretary of the CC CPU (Lutak had graduated from the Kazakh school of agriculture). In June 1969 he was further elevated to Second Secretary.[6]

Lutak was working in the Kiev Oblast Party Organization at a time when Shelest was managing a factory in Kiev. Not long after Lutak took over the Cherkassy Oblast Executive Committee, Shelest became First Secretary of the neighboring and pivotal Kiev *obkom* (in 1957), and thus Lutak's de facto overseer. After Shelest's overthrow, Lutak was kept on as Second Secretary by Shcherbitsky, even though Lutak did not speak during the May 19, 1972, CC CPSU plenum that unseated Shelest, which could be interpreted as a sign of continuing loyalty toward Shelest.[7] I have not been able to find any issues on which Shcherbitsky and Lutak clashed. Lutak was cashiered within a year of reporting on the results of the so-called exchange of Party cards in the Republic's Party organizations.[8] Lutak had formally directed that Party card exchange and presumably made enemies in doing so. Incidentally, the very same technique was used by Brezhnev against fellow CC CPSU Secretaries Podgorny and Titov in 1964-65: the two had formally supervised the restructing of the All-Union Party.

The sudden demotion of Lutak is important from still another point of view. At the 25th CPU Congress the Second Secretaryship was given to I. Z. Sokolov, a graduate of the Kharkov Party Organization and presumably an early protégé of Podgorny. (Podgorny's last regional assignment had been Kharkov, from 1950 to 1953.) Prior to his appointment to Second Secretary, Sokolov had been heading the Kharkov *obkom*. In addition, Sokolov is an ethnic Russian.[9]

To have a member of the non-indigenous nationality—mostly a Russian—in the important position of Second Secretary has now become the rule: after Sokolov's appointment in February 1976 there appears to be only one indigenous Second Secretary left: Aksenov of the Belorussian CP. On the other hand, after the dismissal in December 1958 of the Turkmenian Party Secretary Babaev[10] and the demotion in February 1960 of Latvian Second Party Secretary Kruminsh[11] for advancing the interests of their republics at the expense of central objectives, including—in the Turkmenian case—preference for hiring indigenous officials, it need not be assumed that a Second Secretary belonging to the indigenous nationality would be either willing or able to resist pressures from Moscow to pursue a so-called "Leninist internationalist" personnel policy. Particularly not in the Ukraine, where already April 7, 1970, a certain A. A. Ulanov (presumably a Russian) had been appointed Head of the Organizational Party Work Department of the CC CPU.[12] By November 1972 Ulanov was succeeded by Georgii K. Kriuchkov, whose name sounds Russian, too.[13] But the changeover from Ukrainian Lutak to Russian Sokolov had at the very least a symbolic significance in that even under the Ukrainophobe Stalin since 1949 the Second Secretary had been a Ukrainian (A. I. Kirichenko, admittedly serving under Russian First Secretary Leonid I. Melnikov) and that after Stalin's death, since June 1953, both the First and Second Secretaries have always been Ukrainians. (The latter may have been one of the causes for the rapid increase in membership of the CPU under Khrushchev.) It is possible, of course, that the appointment of Sokolov to be Shcherbitsky's deputy was the result of an intricate balancing maneuver: on the eve of the 25th CPU Congress, the Russian Degtiarëv was removed from the First Secretaryship of the Donetsk *obkom* in favor of presumed Ukrainian Boris V. Kachura.[14] Consequently, at the Congress, Degtiarëv lost his full seat on the CPU Politburo, Kachura gained a candidate seat, while Sokolov, the only Russian left on the Politburo, was promoted from candidate to full membership and given the Second Secretaryship besides. Kharkovite Sokolov appears never to have been as closely identified with the Shcherbitsky-Brezhnev group as O. F. Vatchenko, First Secretary of the Dnipropetrovsk *obkom*. Vatchenko's appointment to the Second Secretaryship would have been a dramatic indication of the victory of Brezhnev's Dnipropetrovsk clan; but, Vatchenko being a Ukrainian, this might have been difficult to reconcile with the current pressures for an "internationalist" (i.e., pro-Russian) personnel policy.

A brief comparison of the last CPU Politburo, elected under Shelest at the 24th CPU Congress in 1971, with Shcherbitsky's Politburo, elected at the 25th CPU Congress, shows the following.[15] In 1976 there were 11 full members (or one more than in 1971), five candidate members (as in 1971), and six Secretaries (as in 1971). The names have changed, however. Among the full members, Shelest, Lutak and Degtiarëv were out, and so were two old administrators: M. O. Sobol[16] and N. T. Kalchenko (the latter a former Prime Minister of the Ukrainian SSR). In their place, in chronological order, stepped I. S. Hrushetsky, M. M. Borysenko, V. O. Solohub, O. P. Botvyn, I. Z. Sokolov, and V. V. Fedorchuk. I. S. Hrushetsky used to be a third-ranking CPU official with some ties to Brezhnev. A candidate Politburo member in 1971, in July 1972 (i.e., at the first CC CPU plenum after Shelest's dismissal) he was promoted to full member and given the (honorific?) post of Chairman of the Presidium of the Ukrainian SSR Supreme Soviet.[17] Borysenko is the Third CC CPU Secretary in charge of agriculture. Solohub has headed the Ukrainian trade unions. Those two were promoted from alternate Politburo members during the second round of advancements in September 1973. Sokolov's promotion has been mentioned already. Fedorchuk, head of the Ukrainian SSR KGB, who according to Soviet émigré sources had been literally foisted on Shelest in July 1970, was elected candidate member of the Politburo in September 1973 and was promoted to full member at the Congress of 1976, apparently as a reward for energetically arresting Ukrainian "bourgeois nationalists."

The catapulting into full membership of O. P. Botvyn is a more interesting case, for Botvyn had not previously served as an alternate. (Four new faces appear among the alternates: V. F. Dobryk, First Secretary of the Lviv *obkom*; B. V. Kachura, the brand-new First Secretary of the Donetsk *obkom*; Ideological CC Secretary V. Iu. Malanchuk, who replaced in that position and among the alternate Politburo members F. D. Ovcharenko in October 1972; and ex-Ukrainian SSR Minister of Agriculture, now Deputy Prime Minister P. L. Pohrebniak.[18] The CC Secretariat remained unchanged except for the appointments of Shcherbitsky, Malanchuk, and Sokolov.) Botvyn's rapid advancement appears to be connected with changes among the First *obkom* Secretaries, and especially with the slow decline of the Donetsk faction in the CPU.

For perspective's sake we may note that between the CPU Congresses of 1971 and 1976 in the 25 Ukrainian *obkoms* and the Kiev City Party Committee, incumbent First Secretaries remained unchanged in twelve committees (Chernihiv, Crimea, Dnipropetrovsk, Kiev Province and Kiev City, Kirovohrad, Odessa, Ternopil, Transcarpathia, Vinnytsia, Zaporizhia, and Zhytomyr),[19] while First Secretaries were changed in all the remaining 14 *obkoms*. But even among the 12 relatively stable organizations, we should note that in May 1975 Kiev Province was emasculated when the Kiev City Organization was removed from its jurisdiction and made directly subordinate to the CC CPU Secretariat.

The changes in the 14 other *obkoms* can be summarized as follows. Two (in the Khmelnytsky and Mykolaïv *obkoms*) took place under Shelest and need not concern us here.[20] Twelve were made by Shcherbitsky. Of these, two (in Ivano-Frankivsk and Rovno) were due to promotions or lateral transfers of the incumbent Secretaries.[21] But 10 occurred with a whiff of suspicion or were frankly punitive in character (Cherkassy, Chernivtsi, Donetsk, Kharkov, Kherson, Lviv, Poltava, Sumy, Volhynia, Voroshilovgrad).[22] Ten out of 26 top regional and city positions is a weighty number, particularly if we consider that the last group includes some of the largest organizations, such as Donetsk, Kharkov, and Voroshilovgrad.

Elsewhere I have already commented on the replacements of the Kharkov, Poltava, and Voroshilovgrad First Secretaries,[23] and I will briefly comment on the advancement of Dobryk to the Lviv post in connection with the Ukrainian *samizdat* materials. Most significant of all the changes between May 1972 and February 1976 are the splitting of the Kiev Province Party Organization, which brought a nice promotion to Votvyn of Kiev City and a demotion to Tsybulko of Kiev Province, and the sacking of Degtiarëv of the Donetsk *obkom*. The three events may be interrelated.

In July 1972, when Shcherbitsky was trying to get his team organized (it was not until then, more than a month after Shelest's overthrow, that Hrushetsky was moved into the Chairmanship of the Ukrainian SSR Supreme Soviet), Volodymyr M. Tsybulko, First Secretary of the united Kiev Province and Kiev City Party Committees, was elected candidate member of the CPU Politburo. Tsybulko, a graduate of the Donetsk Party Organization, from March 1969 to April 1970 had headed the

Organizational Party Work Department before he was given the Kiev post, with its uneasy fluidity in leadership. It was an important assignment: in January 1971 the united Kiev Party Organization was the second largest in the country, after Donetsk; it counted 229,000 members.[24] First Secretary of the Kiev *City* Organization (close to 147,000) from August 1962 to January 1963 and again from December 1964 to date has been A. P. Botvyn. In the mid-1950's Botvyn held a district Secretaryship in Kharkov. Kharkov was Podgorny's home base, and Botvyn presumably enjoyed his support. Botvyn was not taken into Shcherbitsky's Politburo in 1972.[25]

By mid-May 1975, however, Kiev City, then including 177,000 Party members, was directly subordinated to the CC CPU, leaving the rump Kiev Province and Tsybulko with only 77,000 Party members.[26] Trying to justify that decision, Lutak said that the separation would undoubtedly help to "improve the direction of economic and cultural life, both in the republic's capital and in Kiev oblast as a whole," which implicitly was a criticism of Tsybulko.[27] In any case, at the 25th CPU Congress Tsybulko gave a rather cool speech. The reason for this soon became obvious: Tsybulko was dropped from candidate membership in the CPU Politburo, whereas Botvyn became full member, jumping the alternate status.

The undercutting of Tsybulko may really have had wider implications. Tsybulko was a member of a group of Party and State officials from the Donets Basin. Until January-February 1976 the group included V. I. Degtiarëv, First Secretary of the Donets *obkom* and full Politburo (PB) member; A. P. Liashko, Ukrainian SSR Prime Minister and full PB member; Ia. P. Pohrebniak, a CC Secretary and alternate PB member; the Trade Union leader V. A. Solohub, a full PB member; A. A. Tytarenko, industrial CC Secretary and full PB member; and USSR Minister of Ferrous Metallurgy Kazanets. Borys Lewytzkyj may have been right when he wrote that *"their experience and mentality have been moulded by their subordination to all-Union authorities and by the priority of all-Union interests."*[28] But politics makes strange bedfellows: it does appear now that autonomist Shelest was using the support of the strong Donetsk Party group (the Donetsk *Province* alone had 260,000 Party members in 1970, the Voroshilovgrad Province had more than 150,000)[29] against Shcherbitsky's home base, the 179,000-men-strong Dnipropetrovsk contingent, with its sister Province of Zaporizhia (102,000 communists).[30] Behind Shcherbitsky stood, of course, two old graduates of the Dnipropetrovsk Party Organization: Brezhnev and Kirilenko. Degtiarëv's career may have been considerably advanced by Shelest.[31] In any case, Shcherbitsky moved against him carefully, in five stages. Already in January 1974 a relatively obscure district Secretary Boris V. Kachura was eased into the convenient position of Second Donetsk *obkom* Secretary.[32] In December 1975 Degtiarëv was degraded to the obscure job of Chairman of the Ukrainian State Committee for the Supervision of Safe Working Practices in Industry and for Mine Supervision.[33] Only gradually was the extent of criticism against him made public. Finally, in his CC report to the 25th CPU Congress, Shcherbitsky singled out Shelest and Degtiarëv for blunt criticism, perhaps indicating thereby the real link between the two. Degtiarëv was accused of "showing lack of discipline in carrying out the orders of the CC CPSU and CC of the CP of Ukraine in questions relating to the work with cadres."[34] The details have not been spelled out any further, but the accusation already raises one piquant question: it was not only Degtiarëv who slipped up in personnel questions but Botvyn as well. To my knowledge, Botvyn has been publicly criticized for that twice: in May 1975 and again in January 1976.[35] Yet Botvyn was promoted to full PB member. Had Botvyn's transgressions been only minor, or did he have some countervailing virtues which Degtiarëv, an ex-protégé of Shelest, lacked?

In view of Brezhnev's and Suslov's 1972 attempts at "aggressive denationalizing"—to borrow Hodnett's pat term[36]—and in view of Shcherbitsky's rather pointed support, at the April 17, 1973, CC CPU plenum, of the so-called practice of exchange of cadres (i.e., the emigration of educated Ukrainians and the influx of Russians into the Ukrainian republic),[37] it would have been priceless if we could have analyzed any possible differential impact of the so-called exchange of Party cards on the nationality composition (a) of the leadership group of the CPU (the entire Central Committee and the Auditing Commission) and (b) upon the CPU as a whole. Unfortunately, at the level of the republican Party CC and below, the nationality data from the USSR Supreme Soviet become utterly insufficient. Nor have I found any published figures on the nationality composition of the CPU after 1972. Nor, for that matter, have any aggregate figures on the purge been released, except in heavily veiled form.

No figures at all were published after Lutak's report on the completed exchange of Party cards, May 20, 1975.[38] At the 25th CPU Congress Shcherbitsky merely said that in the period between the 1971 and 1976 CPU Congresses, the Party had increased by 247,000 persons, that at present it numbered 2,625,808 communists (including candidate members), and that in the period covered by the report 350,647 persons had been accepted into the Party.[39] The figures are really too good to be true. 2,625,808 minus 247,000 gives us 2,378,808, which is almost exactly the figure given by the *Big Soviet Encyclopedia Yearbook* for CPU membership on January 1, 1971 (2,378,789). The difference between the net admissions and the net increase gives us the number of those who either died or were expelled from the Party (350,647 minus 247,000 equals ca. 103,647). With the help of Messrs. Godfrey Baldwin and Stephen Rapawy of the Foreign Demographic Analysis Division, Bureau of Economic Analysis of the U.S. Department of Commerce, who kindly supplied the author with expected mortality figures, we find that approximately 134,135 CPU members of *those 2,378,789* can be presumed to have died between the Congresses. In other words, there appears to have been no purge in the Ukraine at all, but a mysterious surplus of as many as 30,488. Assuming that our expected mortality calculations are correct, a possible explanation of this surplus would be that there was such a heavy net immigration of Party members into the Ukraine from 1971 through 1975 as to completely offset the expulsions and still leave a surplus of 30,488 CPU members.[40]

The cryptic figures of Shcherbitsky should be contrasted with the somewhat franker statement by Brezhnev at the 25th CPSU Congress. Brezhnev admitted openly that 347,000 had not had their Party cards exchanged—i.e., had been expelled from the Party. At the time of the 1976 Congress, the CPSU numbered about 15,694,000 (or 15,694,187, to be exact). We know that at the preceding Congress there had been exactly 14,455,321 members. According to Brezhnev the number of new admissions was almost 2.6 million. (It was exactly 2,593,824.)[41] The difference between the total admissions and the net increase is about 1.3 million (1,354,958). If 347,000 were openly expelled during the period when Party cards were exchanged (March 1973-February 1975) and 895,915 may be presumed to have died between January 1, 1971, and January 1, 1976, this gives us a total of only 1,242,915. This still leaves us with some 112,043 who presumably have been forced to resign or have otherwise been dismissed in the remainder of the interval between the Congresses, possibly including in this number 44,796 who may have died in the first three months of 1976. Altogether, in the All-Union Party some 414,247 to 459,043 or about 2.9 to 3.2 percent of the total CPSU membership of February 1971 have been purged.[42] According to even more revealing figures from the Azerbaidzhan SSR, a *minimum* of 2.3 percent of the republican Party membership were either openly or secretly purged.[43] But in the Ukraine apparently not a single Party member lost his or her Party card—which is, of course, absurd.

The explanation may lie in a deliberate fudging of the figures by Shcherbitsky: the figures that are usually announced at the Congresses include Party members among military and internal security personnel that are stationed in the republic and that send their delegates to the Congresses; the yearbook figures appear to be net of such personnel. I suspect that Shcherbitsky has taken the gross 1976 figure and compared it to the net 1971 figure. According to his predecessor Shelest, the 1971 (gross) CPU membership figure was 2,534,561, not 2,378,789! This would give us a net increase between 1971 and 1976 not of 247,000 as per Shcherbitsky, but of only 91,247, contrasted with 350,647 new admissions. The deficit of 259,400 can then be explained as follows: the expected deaths number about 142,918, leaving about 116,482 for secret expulsions (4.6 percent of the 1971 gross membership). These figures might be more plausible than the surplus of 30,488 persons. If our hypothesis that the CPU membership figures have been tampered with are correct, this would give us an expulsion rate for the CPU which is considerably higher than the All-Union Party average, by 58.6 or 43.8 percent higher. In general, there seems to be something suspicious about the Ukrainian Party data as presented by the *Soviet Encyclopedia* yearbooks and about those given by Shcherbitsky.

Surveying some of the official Soviet materials after the well-known anonymous denunciation of Shelest's book *Oh, Our Soviet Ukraine!* in April 1973,[44] it is difficult to avoid the impression that instructions have gone out from Moscow for Ukrainians to humiliate themselves in public. Half-way understandable are the public *mea culpas* and recantations of writer Victor Korzh, who in May 1974 retracted the few kind words that he said about the Ukrainian language at the Ukrainian writers' congress in 1966,[45] and especially the declaration of November 6, 1973, by literary critic Ivan Dziuba, who admitted that he had been in error when in 1965 he wrote his classic treatise *Internationalism or Russification?* After all, Dziuba had been arrested in April 1972 and in March 1973 had been sentenced to five years' deprivation of freedom; his recantation brought him a pardon.[46] Exceedingly fulsome praise of the great Russian people has been heard before, under Stalin. But it was under Brezhnev that the Ukrainian writer and Hero of the Soviet Union Yurii Zbanatsky outdid himself in that direction, in May 1975.[47] That the Ukrainian literary historian Shamota castigates two brilliant Ukrainian translators—V. Kochur and M. Lukash—in particular and Ukrainian writers in general for cultivating a slightly archaic, but pure, non-journalistic language, may be par for the course: this has now become his bread and butter.[48] Professional Party ideologist Malanchuk may be depended on to be as orthodox as the moment dictates.[49] But what *communist* purpose is served by bringing out the future second edition of the *Soviet Ukrainian Encyclopedia* in both Ukrainian and Russian, in contrast to the first edition of the 1960's, which was exclusively in Ukrainian (with the last volume on Soviet Ukraine being translated into English)?[50] The further displacement of the Ukrainian language from Ukrainian cities? What is the *communist* point of awarding as many as five of the six 1976 Shevchenko Prizes (i.e., a Ukrainian Republican, not an All-Union literary and artistic, prize) to the late Soviet Russian composer Dmitri Shostakovich and to four main performers of his old opera "Katerina Izmailova"? What has Keskov's adulterous merchant wife from a small provincial Russian town have in common with the Ukraine and with the Ukraine's greatest poet Shevchenko, after whom the prize is named? Is the new line that anything goes so long as it is Russian? For appearance's sake, the sixth prize went to a genuine Ukrainian poet: one out of six![51] If Shostakovich absolutely had to be honored in the Ukraine, the Shevchenko Prize ought to have been given him for his 13th Symphony, including the unadulterated text of Yevtushenko's "Babi Yar"—this at least would have been more appropriate! Or why has Shcherbitsky given his Central Committee report to the 1976 CPU Congress in Kiev *in Russian*, as verified by Radio Liberty monitoring in Munich?

The extent of the increasingly brutal persecution of Ukrainian intellectuals, students, and ordinary workers for such crimes as protesting against the suppression of Ukrainian language and national heritage can, however, best be gauged from Ukrainian *samizdat* and—in a more condensed form—from Leonid Pliushch's interview in *Le Monde*.

The sixth issue of the *Ukrainian Herald* is dated March 1972—that is, it depicts the situation in the Ukraine on the eve of Shelest's overthrow. Seventeen persons are listed who were arrested in the second wave of persecutions in January 1972.[52] Some of the best material in the issue reflects older news items: e.g., the second installment of a detailed rejoinder by Viacheslav Chornovil to government writer or writers "Bohdan Stenchuk" (see in particular the very detailed account of an attempt by Shelest and his Minister of Higher Education M. Iu. Dadenkov in August 1965 to improve the position of the Ukrainian language in higher educational institutions under the Minister's jurisdiction; the attempt failed)[53] or the anonymous and also very detailed study of the Ukrainian language in the elementary and secondary schools of the republican capital Kiev.[54]

The joint seventh and eighth issue of the *Ukrainian Herald* is more interesting and more significant for an understanding of the post-Shelest period. It is dated spring 1974 and has been edited by one Maksym Sahaidak, which may well be a pen-name. The joint seventh and eighth issue differs considerably from its predecessors: besides seven very patriotic poems by Sahaidak and a brief article by him sharply denouncing "Partial Détente" between the United States and the USSR,[55] the bulk of the *Herald* consists of one major analytical study, unsigned, on "Ethnocide of the Ukrainians in the USSR," which is further subdivided into two parts: (1) "Demographic Statistics and the Disclosure of the Colonial Policy of the Muscovite Occupants in the Ukraine," which is mostly based on open sources; and (2) "General Pogrom," which gives some inside information on Soviet policy in the Ukraine after the 1971 CPSU Congress.[56] The tone is sharper than in the preceding issues (note, for example, the reference to the "regime of occupation in the Ukraine" instead of the "Soviet regime in the Ukraine"). Circumstantial evidence would seem to indicate that (a) the latest issue had been written by a different group of dissenters, and (b) the authors might be from the Western Ukraine.

In the first, demographic part of the study the strong socio-economic position of the Russians in the Ukraine is presented as follows: "In the Ukraine in 1970

Russians with a higher education numbered 601 thousand. This is at the same time that only a total of 1,583 thousand inhabitants of the Ukraine have a higher education. Russians have thus more than one third of the total number of persons with a higher education."[57] My own calculations yield a somewhat lower figure for Russians in the Ukraine with higher education (492,950). But even close to one third of the total is still a disproportionate share (in 1970 Russians numbered 19.4 percent of the total population in the Ukraine). The difference between the calculations, incidentally, is due to the Soviet habit of heavily disguising sensitive figures.[58] Following Solzhenitsyn, the *Ukrainian Herald* denounces psychiatric jails as "a new variety of gas chambers."[59] There are a spirited polemic with Shcherbitsky's pro-Russian definition of internationalism[60] and some relatively general remarks on the Russification of schools and colleges in the Ukraine,[61] and Ukrainians giving Russian as their native language in the population census are denounced as having lost psychological bonds with the Ukrainian nation, as having joined the three million strong "corps of janissaries."[62] One of the most original features of the first demographic part is the contrast between the cultural achievements of Ukrainian immigrants in the United States and Canada, and the "spiritual ethnocide" (cultural genocide) being practiced on the Ukrainians in the Soviet Union, particularly on those living outside the boundaries of the Ukrainian SSR.[63]

The second, political part ("General Pogrom") gives some new facts and confirms some old suspicions. The new campaign against Ukrainian dissidents was started almost as early as November 1971. At the November 1971 CC CPSU plenum, First Secretary of the Lviv *obkom* Kutsevol allegedly reported on the work of his Party Organization. A secret decision was taken by the plenum that the work of the Lviv *obkom* in the fields of internationalist and atheistic education was unsatisfactory, whereupon Suslov suggested the dismissal of Kutsevol right then and there. But Shelest managed to save Kutsevol in November 1971. Such a resolution directed against the Lviv *obkom* is not mentioned in the Soviet press, but a reading of the materials of the plenum has convinced me that there may indeed have been a secret point on the agenda concerning ideological policy in Lviv, the center of Western Ukraine.[64]

The *Herald* claims that Shelest has repeatedly been denounced by the new KGB chief Fedorchuk and by Shcherbitsky and Malanchuk, who "in their pursuit of a careerist goal have convinced the Moscow Politburo that Shelest was a national-deviationist."[65] On the other hand, Shelest was defended in Moscow "by a number of Party leaders in the non-Russian republics, particularly in Georgia, Moldavia, and other [republics]."[66] Finally, Shelest was dismissed at a session of the Politburo in Moscow (no date is supplied, alas). He was not allowed to return to the Ukraine and not allowed to take part in the CC CPU plenum in Kiev on May 25, 1972, which "elected" Shcherbitsky his successor.[67] Interesting is the revelation that in 1973 34 instructors at the Higher Party School of the CC CPU, including its president, were purged and that its curriculum was totally revamped.[68] Even more fascinating is an account of Dobryk's speech in December 1973, after he had replaced Kutsevol as First Secretary of the Lviv *obkom*. Dobryk has been educated and has started his Party career in Dnipropetrovsk Province—i.e., in Brezhnev and Shcherbitsky country. He has been characterized by the *Herald* as a zealous Russifier and great friend of the KGB. In his speech Dobryk emphasized that under Shelest serious mistakes had been made both in the "cadre question" (i.e., the placement of officials) and in the internationalist education of toilers. If the CC CPSU had not taken determined steps, within a few years in the Ukraine there might have arisen a situation akin to that in Czechoslovakia in 1968. For good measure he added that Shelest and Shcherbitsky could not get along.[69]

For lack of space I cannot comment here on the long lists of persecuted Ukrainian intellectuals.[70] The more important general points are perhaps as follows. The Soviet Ukrainian press has been fed only semi-abstract pap, concrete information has been secretly channelled only as far down as the leaders [Secretaries?—Y.B.] of Party District Committees.[71] Second, the number of arrests is impossible to estimate accurately since the relatives are forced by the KGB to sign promises that they will not disclose the fate of the suspects, and fellow workers are being fed stories about long trips, etc. Frequently the neighbors in the apartment house do not know for a long time that a fellow resident has been arrested.[72] Thirdly, to cite the *Herald*:

> It is characteristic that the Purge of Party cadres in the Ukraine is *numerically the largest in the USSR*. It can be compared only with the purges of the 1930's. Though, in contrast to the purges of the 1930's it has an even more pronounced anti-Ukrainian character and is proceeding under conditions of strict secrecy: there is imitation of various official transfers, retirement on a pension, release from leadership positions in connection with bad health, struggle with corruption, etc. The true reasons are carefully hidden from wide sections of the community.[73]

This is a strong accusation that is impossible to document, but in the light of our estimates on the number of CPU members who have been purged, it is not an implausible one. In conclusion, the unsigned author of the *Herald* study writes:

> By a whole series of facts we have contradicted the assertions of L. Brezhnev and other Muscovite leaders that the nationality question in the USSR has been solved and that the nationality problem does not exist. The character of the cited facts of the misdeeds helps us to understand that the Soviet regime is a Fascist dictatorship (in the form of Social-Fascism).[74]

The neo-Marxist Ukrainian mathematician Leonid Pliushch was miraculously released from that new variety of gas chamber, the Dnipropetrovsk psychiatric jail, only under pressure of Western public opinion, including efforts by leaders of the French and Italian Communist Parties. His words on the Ukraine carry special weight, since Pliushch had started out not as a Ukrainian nationalist but rather as a cosmopolitan. Only later was he converted to the Ukrainian cause, under the impression of reading Dziuba's *Internationalism or Russification?* Nevertheless, he has remained a spiritual adherent of the a-national, all-Union movement for the defense of human rights led by Academician and Nobel Peace Prize Laureate Sakharov. In an interview with *Le Monde* which he gave shortly before his first press conference in Paris, only three weeks after his release from the Soviet Union, Pliushch said:

[*Question:*] *Is there a nationality problem in the USSR?*

[*Answer:*] It exists and grows in intensity from year to year. Take the Ukraine, for example. The Russification of the republic has reached an intolerable [*insupportable*] degree. In the large cities the national language has almost disappeared.

Pliushch then gave some concrete examples and sketched the developments in the 1920's and 1930's. With reference to the new renaissance of the Ukrainian culture in the 1960's he said: "At present all of this has been completely crushed [*étouffé*]." He continued:

This is why I am for the separation of the Ukraine from Russia. For it is only in an independent Ukraine that the building of socialism and the saving of the Ukrainian culture would be possible.[75]

What general conclusions can be drawn from this special study of Soviet Ukrainian official politics and unofficial dissent after Shelest's fall? There still seems to be some opposition—possibly originating with Podgorny, possibly with somebody else—to Shcherbitsky's or really to Brezhnev's high-handed moves: Lutak was not dislodged until the very last minute, creating much publicity and a minor scandal. But in the long run it does not matter: the Secretariat of the CPU has been purged, so has the Politburo, so have 10 out of 26 Provincial Secretaries, and so has the Ukrainian Party as a whole, though the figures have been nearly hidden. The Ukrainians as such have been humiliated no end and Ukrainian dissidents have been arrested and jailed by the hundreds and thousands: for one Pliushch that has been released there are hundreds and thousands of Morozes who have not. What is the meaning of all this?

Commenting as late as 1974 on post-1966 Soviet Ukrainian Party politics, I thought that a kind of "consociational autocratic" or "consociational oligarchic" solution was still possible: the Russian and the non-Russian elites would mutually cooperate in politics and in economics in order to build a stronger Soviet Union without suppressing the pattern of cultural diversity and without destroying the nationality groups on whose support the non-Russian elites ultimately depended. There would be protective family circles, a lot of infighting, but nobody would try to upset the pluralistic status quo.[76] In 1976 I am no longer sure that this is still in the cards. I am reminded of an article that Zbigniew Brzezinski wrote 20 years ago. Arguing against facile assumptions that a totalitarian regime would liquidate itself in the process of socio-economic development, Professor Brzezinski pointed out that, by committing itself to high domestic and international goals, the regime would maintain at least some of its revolutionary drive, would be able to justify its retention of harsh discipline shorn of irrational terror, and, above all, would persist as a totalitarian government.[77] Brezhnev has certainly not set his sights low. He wants to develop the resources of Western Siberia—with Western capitalist money, preferably; he wants to "solve" the nationality problem; and, according to press reports, he wants to achieve for the Soviet and East European bloc an economic and military superiority over the United States and Western Europe within 12 to 15 years, counting from 1973.[78] The late George H. Sabine has eloquently warned us:

The only condition that submerges the divergent social and economic interests of a modern nation is preparation for war. Accordingly fascism and national socialism were in essence war governments and war economies set up not as expedients to meet a national emergency but as permanent political systems.[79]

The most melancholy and at the same time the most challenging conclusion may be that fundamentally there is no difference between Fascism of the Right— that of Hitler and Mussolini—and Fascism of the so-called Left—that of Stalin and now Brezhnev. The unsigned author of the *Ukrainian Herald* and other non-Russian authors may be right on this.[80] What is the difference, for instance, between the Nazi concept of "das Volk" and Brezhnev's and Suslov's concept of the "single Soviet people"? They are both myths of the twentieth century. In their frantic attempts, however, to make the myth a reality, Brezhnev and Suslov have entered the path of domestic political war, not peace. Will it end there, or will the Fascist logic drive them first to international political war and then to war as such?

NOTES

[1] For relatively recent analyses of Soviet Ukrainian politics see, among others, Michael Browne, ed., *Ferment in the Ukraine: Documents by V. Chornovil, I. Kandyba, L. Lukyanenko, V. Moroz and Others* (London: Macmillan, 1971); Peter J. Potichnyj, ed., *Ukraine in the Seventies* (Oakville, Ont.: Mosaic Press, 1975); Konstantyn Sawczuk, "Opposition in the Ukraine: Seven Versus the Regime," *Survey*, Vol. 20, No. 1 (Winter 1974), pp. 36-46; Robert S. Sullivant, "The Ukrainians," *Problems of Communism*, Vol. 16, No. 5 (September-October 1967), pp. 46-54; Roman Szporluk, "The Ukraine and the Ukrainians," in Zeb Katz, Rosemarie Rogers, and Frederic Harned, eds., *Handbook of Major Soviet Nationalities* (New York: Free Press, 1975), pp. 21-48; Lowell Tillett, "Ukrainian Nationalism and the Fall of Shelest," *Slavic Review*, Vol. 34, No. 4 (December 1975), pp. 752-768. I myself have dealt with these problems successively in *The Second Soviet Republic: The Ukraine after World War II* (New Brunswick, N.J.: Rutgers University Press, 1964); "Assimilation and Ethnic Assertiveness among Ukrainians of the Soviet Union," in Erich Goldhagen, ed., *Ethnic Minorities in the Soviet Union* (New York: Praeger, 1968); "The Communist Party of Ukraine after 1966," in Potichnyj, ed., *op. cit.*, pp. 239-66; and "The Incorporation of Western Ukraine and Its Impact on Politics and Society in Soviet Ukraine," in Roman Szporluk, ed., *The Influence of East Europe and the Soviet West on the USSR* (New York: Praeger, 1976), pp. 180-228.

[2] *Radians'ka Ukraina* (henceforth abbreviated *RU*), January 31, 1976, p. 1.

[3] *Istoriia mist i sil Ukrains'koi RSR*, Vol. 18 (*Cherkas'ka oblast*), pp. 86-87.

[4] *Pravda Ukrainy*, 18 January 1976. See also Christian Deuvel [sic], "Ex-Protégé of Podgorny and Shelest Demoted from Key Post in the Ukraine," *Radio Liberty Research* (henceforth omitted), RL 67/76 (2 February 1976), p. 1.

[5] *Pravda Ukrainy*, 28 January 1976, p. 1. Also Duevel, *loc. cit.*, p. 2.

[6] Besides Duevel, see *Deputaty Verkhovnogo Soveta SSSR, Vos'moi sozyv* (Moscow: Izvestiia, 1970), p. 263 (henceforth cited *Deputaty V.S. SSSR, 1970*) and Grey Hodnett and Val Ogareff, *Leaders of the Soviet Republics, 1955-1972* (Canberra: Department of Political Science, Research School of Social Science, The Australian National University, 1973), p. 347. Lutak's second appointment to the CC CPU Secretariat was in *June* 1969, as stated in the main text.

[7] Bilinsky, "The Communist Party of Ukraine after 1966," in Potichnyj, ed., *op. cit.* (note 39), p. 263. Main source henceforth cited as *Ukraine in the 70's*. See also Grey Hodnett, "Pyotr Efimovich Shelest," in George W. Simmonds, ed., *Soviet Leaders* (New York: Crowell, 1967), p. 99.

[8] *RU*, 22 May 1975, pp. 1-2 or *Digest of the Soviet Ukrainian Press* (henceforth *DSUP*), XIX/7 (July 1975), pp. 1-2.

[9] *RU*, 14 February 1976, p. 1. Ethnic identification and biographical data from *Deputaty Verkhovnogo Soveta SSSR: Dev"iatyi sozyv* (Moscow, 1974). Sokolov's successor in the Kharkov post is former First Secretary of the Kharkov City Party Committee I. I. Sakhnyuk (*RU*, 18 February 1976), p. 1, or *DSUP* XX/4 [April 1974], p. 2. Sakhnyuk's official nationality is not given, but judging by his name is Ukrainian.

[10] See editorial "The Leninist Forms of Party Life Must Be Strictly Observed," *Kommunist Turkmenistana*, No. 2, 1959, as quoted in "Nationalism in the Soviet Muslim Republics," *Central Asian Review*, VII (1959), pp. 341-342. S. Babaev, First Secretary, and N. Durdyeva, CC Secretary for Propaganda were both dismissed 14 December 1958. Though the Second Secretary was F. A. Grishaenkov, according to Hodnett and Ogareff it was Babaev who supervised the Turkmenian Party Organization—see their *Leaders . . .*, p. 319.

[11] Kruminsh was demoted to Latvian SSR Minister of Education on 17 February 1960 (Hodnett and Ogareff, *Leaders . . .*, p. 211), apparently in connection with the "Berklavs affair" of 1959. Kruminsh's involvement in that affair is confirmed by the underground "Latvian Communist Letter of 1971" (see Radio Liberty, *Arkhiv Samizdata*, AS 1042, "Obrashchenie 17 kommunistov Latvii . . . ," p. 9).

[12] See *Deputaty V.S. SSSR, 1970*, p. 474 and Hodnett and Ogareff, *Leaders . . .*, p. 350.

[13] See Central Intelligence Agency, Reference Aid, *Directory of Soviet Officials, Vol. III: Union Republics* (A [CR] 75-18, May 1975), p. 246.

[14] See below.

[15] Cf. *RU*, 21 March 1971, p. 1, with *RU*, 14 February 1976, p. 1.

[16] Sobol, a graduate of the Kharkov Party Organization, had been removed from the Politburo for reasons of retirement already under Shelest, in March 1972. For further discussion, see Bilinsky, "The Communist Party of Ukraine after 1966," *Ukraine in the 70's*, p. 245.

[17] *RU*, 28 July 1972, p. 1, or *DSUP*, XVI/9 (September 1972), pp. 1+9. See also C. Duevel, "Stalemate in Ukrainian Leadership Reshuffle," RL CRED 144/72 (13 June 1972). Hrushetsky's ties to Brezhnev are touched upon by John Dornberg, *Brezhnev: The Masks of Power* (New York: Basic Books, 1974), p. 67.

[18] On Pohrebniak's appointment to succeed retired Kalchenko, see *RU*, 14 February 1976, p. 2, or *DSUP*, XX/3 (March 1976), p. 37. The replacement of Ovcharenko by Malanchuk has been discussed by Bilinsky, *loc. cit.* (note 16), pp. 248, 250, 252-53, and by Jaroslaw Pelenski, "Shelest and His Period in Soviet Ukraine (1963-72): A Revival of Controlled Ukrainian Autonomism," *ibid.*, pp. 293-294.

[19] A good starting point for research would be the comparison of the results of the pre-Congressional *obkom* elections in 1971 with those in 1976. See *DSUP*, XV/3 (March 1971), pp. 1-2, and *DSUP*, XX/2 (February 1976), pp. 22-23.

[20] In the *Khmelnytsky* oblast M. D. Bubnovsky, a veteran Party official, was retired and replaced by T. H. Lisovy in March 1972 (*RU*, 15 March 1972, or *DSUP*, XVI/4 [April 1972], pp. 28-29). From the Mykolaïv *obkom* Ia. P. Pohrebniak was elected a Secretary of the CC CPU (*RU*, 21 March 1971, p. 1). The former Second *obkom* Secretary V. O. Vasliaev took his place—*Istoriia mist i sil Ukrains'koi RSR*, Vol. 15 (1971), p. 72.

[21] Dobryk of *Ivano Frankivsk* was promoted to First Secretary of the Lviv *obkom* in November 1973 (*RU*, 29 November 1973, p. 3, or *DSUP*, XVIII/1 [January 1974], p. 6). Dobryk was succeeded by his Second Secretary, P. F. Bezruk. See also main text, p. 20. I. O. Mozhovy of *Rovno* moved to replace fired Kochubey of the Kherson *obkom*. *RU*, 7 October 1972, or *DSUP*, XVI/11 (November 1972), p. 28. Mozhovy was replaced by T. I. Panasenko.

[22] *Cherkassy:* See main text, p. 2. There had been some criticism of the Cherkassy leadership even under Shelest, at the 31 March 1972 plenum (see *DSUP* of May 1972). *Chernivtski:* V. H. Dykusarov replaced O. S. Hryhorenko in June 1972 [*DSUP*, XVI/7 (July 1972), p. 29]. *Donetsk:* Very sharp critique of Degtiarëv in January and February 1976 (see main text, pp. 10-12 and note 34). *Kharkov:* 15 June 1972 H. H. Vashchenko was relieved of Secretaryship and moved into government position as First Deputy Prime Minister of UkrSSR; was succeeded by his deputy I. Z. Sokolov [*RU*, 16 June 1972, or *DSUP*, XVI/8 (August 1972), pp. 27-28]. *Kherson:* A. S. Kochubey was fired in October 1972; was replaced by Mozhovy from Rovno [*RU*, 6 October 1972, or *DSUP*, XVI/11 (November 1972), p. 28]. *Lviv:* Kutsevol was demoted to Chairman of Committee of Public Control; replaced by Dobryk (see note 21). *Poltava:* O. M. Muzhitsky was "retired" and replaced by F. T. Morhun [*RU*, 27 January 1973, p. 1, or *DSUP*, XVII/3 (March 1973), pp. 1-2]. *Sumy:* O. I. Ishchenko was eased out in April 1975, replaced by I. H. Hrintsev, formerly of the Donetsk *obkom* [*RU*, 24 April 1975, or *DSUP*, XIX/6 (June 1975), p. 1]. *Volhynia:* In August 1973 S. Ia. Zaichenko was removed because of "ill health," was replaced by M. P. Korzh [*RU*, 16 August 1973, or *DSUP*, XVII/10 (October 1973), p. 1]. *Voroshilovgrad:* V. V. Shevchenko was fired in December 1973, replaced by B. T. Honcharenko [*RU*, 15 December 1973, p. 1, or *DSUP*, XVIII/1 (January 1974), p. 5].

[23] Bilinsky, "CPU after 1966," *loc. cit.*, p. 253.

[24] *Istoriia mist i sil Ukr. RSR*, Vol. 14, p. 69.

[25] Hodnett and Ogareff, *Leaders* . . . , p. 349; also *Deputaty V. S. SSSR, 1970*, p. 65.

[26] See "Transforming Kiev into a Model City: From the Plenum of the Kiev City Party Committee," *RU*, 15 May 1975, pp. 1-2, or *DSUP*, XIX/7 (July 1975), p. 2.

[27] "Raising the Initiative and Responsibility of Cadres," *RU*, 13 June 1975, pp. 1+3, or *DSUP*, XIX/7 (July 1975), p. 10.

[28] Borys Lewytzkyj, "The Ruling Party Organs of Ukraine," *Ukraine in the 70's*, p. 273. Emphasis in original.

[29] *Istoriia mist i sil Ukr. RSR*, Vol. 12 (1970), p. 75 (Donetsk) and *ibid.*, Vol. 4 (1968), p. 65 (Voroshilovgrad).

[30] *Ibid.*, Vol. 7 (1969), p. 57 (Dnipropetrovsk) and Vol. 10 (1970), p. 60 (Zaporizhia).

[31] Degtiarëv was promoted to First Secretary of the Donetsk *obkom* immediately after Shelest took over the Ukraine, in July 1963. In March 1966 he was promoted to alternate and in March 1971 to full member of the CPU PB. See C. D., "Dismissal of High-Ranking Protégé of Shelest Strengthens Brezhnev Faction," RL 17/76 (9 January 1976), p. 1.

[32] *Ibid.*, p. 2, citing *Pravda Ukrainy*, 29 January 1974.

[33] *Pravda Ukrainy*, 27 December 1975, and C.D., "Degtyarëv Given Post of Safety Supervisor in the Ukraine."

[34] See *RU*, 11 February 1976, p. 5b. Earlier, more restrained critiques of Degtiarëv in *RU*, 11 January 1976, pp. 1+2.

[35] In Shcherbitsky's speech to the 20 May 1975 CC CPU plenum [See *RU*, 21 May 1975, p. 1, or *DSUP*, XIX/7 (July 1975), p. 3]. Also at the pre-Congress City Party Conference (*RU*, 25 January 1976, p. 2f.).

[36] See Brezhnev's famous speech on the 50th anniversary of the USSR, *Pravda*, 22 December 1972. See also Suslov's "Obshchestvennye nauki–boevoe oruzhie partii v stroitel'stve kommunizma," *Kommunist*, 1972, No. 1 (January), p. 20, as cited by Teresa Rakowska-Harmstone, "Recent Trends in Soviet Nationality Policy," in Norton T. Dodge, ed., *Soviets in Asia* (Mechanicsville, Md.: Cremona Foundation, 1972), p. 12. The term "aggressive denationalizing" has been used by Grey Hodnett in a different but compatible context. See his "What's in a Nation?," *Problems of Communism*, Vol. 16, No. 5 (September-October 1967), p. 6.

[37] V. V. Shcherbitsky, "Pro zavdannia partiinykh orhanizatsii respubliky po dal'shomu polipshenniu roboty z kadramy u svitli rishen' XXIV Z"izdu DPRS," *RU*, 20 April 1973, p. 1, or *DSUP*, XVII/6 (June 1973), p. 15.

[38] See *RU*, 22 May 1975, pp. 1-2; or *DSUP*, XIX/7 (July 1975), pp. 4-6.

[39] *RU*, 11 February 1976, Section IV, p. 4 c + d.

[40] Figures on inmigrations between 1971 and 1975 have not been available, but Frederick A. Leedy in his "Demographic Trends in the U.S.S.R.," U.S. Congress (93rd Congress: 1st Session), Joint Economic Committee, *Soviet Economic Prospects for the Seventies* (Washington: GPO, 1973), p. 455, gives 429,000 as the net inmigration figure for the Ukrainian SSR between the 1959 and 1970 censuses. Between the censuses the Russian population in the republic increased by 2,035,000

(Leedy, p. 436) of whom, according to my own calculations, assuming for Russians an average annual increase rate of 1.1 percent (Leedy, p. 450), some 1,127,000 or 55.4 percent of the total increase was due to net inmigration of Russians into the Ukraine. The in-migrating Russians may be assumed to have relatively high socio-economic status and a high Party rate per population (conversation with Mr. Rapawy, 9 November 1976). If the inmigration, especially of Russians, has continued from 1971 to 1976 there may have been a considerable inmigration of Party members.

The surplus is reached as follows: Expected mortality 134,135 minus actual difference between net admissions and net increase 103,647 = surplus of 30,488. The detailed mortality calculations were made by Mr. Godfrey Baldwin. They are based on the following assumptions: (1) The age-sex structure of the Party membership in the Ukraine and the USSR is identical (23 percent female membership for the period was assumed). Age data for CPSU as of January 1, 1973, from *Partiynaya zhizn'*, 1973, No. 14 (July), p. 19. (Parallel source on CPU, viz., *Komunistychna Partiya Ukrainy: Naochny posibnyk z partiynoho budivnytstva* [Kiev: Politvydav, 1972] was not available to the author.) (2) Furthermore, zero mortality was assumed for the members who joined the Party between 1971 and 1976. These two assumptions also underlay the mortality calculations for the CPSU.

[41] See Brezhnev in *Pravda*, 25 February 1976, p. 7 a + b. The more exact data are derived from a new source, *Partiynaya zhizn'*, 1976, No. 10 (May), pp. 13-22, as summarized in *Current Digest of the Soviet Press*, XXVIII, No. 35 (September 29, 1976), p. 1.

[42] The expected mortality figure is by Mr. Godfrey Baldwin. A non-classified CIA source estimated the total expulsions from the CPSU at 575,000 from 1971 through *1974* only—i.e., considerably higher than I have done. See CIA, Research Aid, *The CPSU under Brezhnev* (April 15, 1976; CI 76 10019U), Part I, p. 6.

[43] At the 1976 Congress of the Azerbaidzhan CP, Aliev gave the following figures: the total of Party members and candidates was 287,823. From 1971 to 1976, 47,502 new Party members had been accepted. 3,658 Party members had been expelled, 1,682 had "lost touch with their Party organizations" and were dropped; 670 candidates were refused admission. See *Bakinskii rabochii*, 29 January 1976, p. 6. Taking the total of the expulsions and quasi-expulsions as a *minimum* figure (no mortality calculations were made) we obtain 6,010 or 2.3 percent of the January 1, 1971, Party figure of 258,549 (see the 1971 *Ezhegodnik Bolshoi Sovetskoi Entsyklopedii*). Unwittingly, perhaps, Aliev gave a good account of the many ways in which Party members could be purged. No such calculations are possible for the purges in Georgia (see Shavarnadze in *Zaria Vostoka*, 23 January 1976, p. 9) and in Armenia (see Demirchian, *Kommunist* [Erevan], 21 January 1976, p. 8).

[44] Editorial, "Pro ser"iozni nedoliky ta pomylky odniiei knyhy," *Komunist Ukrainy*, 1973, No. 4 (April), pp. 77-82. The episode is discussed in Bilinsky, "The CPU after 1966," *Ukraine in the 70's*, p. 250 and by Pelenski, "Shelest . . . ," *ibid.*, pp. 284-285.

[45] Viktor Korzh, "To the Eternally Damned," *RU*, 35 (sic) May 1974, p. 3, or *DSUP*, XVIII/7 (July 1974), pp. 29-30.

[46] Ivan Dziuba, "To the Editorial Office of *Literaturna Ukraina:* A Statement," *Literaturna Ukraina*, 9 November 1973, p. 4, or *DSUP*, XVII/12 (December 1973), pp. 22-24.

[47] Zbanatsky, "A Word about the Great Russian People," *Komunist Ukrainy*, 1975, No. 5 (May), pp. 35-40, or *DSUP*, XIX/11 (November 1975), pp. 25-26.

[48] M. Shamota, "Urgent Questions of Literary Criticism," *Lit.U.*, 8 February 1974, pp. 2-3, or *DSUP*, XVIII/3 (March 1974), pp. 12-14.

[49] V. Iu. Malanchuk, "The Ideological Sources of Literature," *Vitchyzna*, 1973, No. 12 (December), pp. 1-6, or *DSUP*, XVIII/5 (May 1974), pp. 11-15.

[50] "In the CC CPU," *Lit.U.*, 25 November 1975, p. 1, or *DSUP*, XX/1 (January 1976), p. 26. The first edition appeared from 1959-1965 in Ukrainian, 80,000-100,000 copies (the first volumes started out with 100,000 copies). It had 17 volumes. The projected 12-volume edition, to be published from 1977 to 1982, will have 50,000 copies in Ukrainian and 50,000 copies in Russian.

[51] *RU*, 12 March 1976, p. 4.

[52] "Areshty i obshuky," *Ukrains'kyi Visnyk*, VI (Paris-Baltimore: Smoloskyp, 1972), pp. 7-10.

[53] V. Chornovil, "Iak i shcho obstoiuie Bohdan Stenchuk," *ibid.*, pp. 24-30.

[54] N. N., "Pid shovinistychnym presom," *ibid.*, pp. 63-72.

[55] M. Sahaidak, "Chastkove spivrobitnytsvo i sprytna dyplomatiia," *Ukrains'kyi Visnyk*, VII-VIII (Paris-Baltimore-Toronto: Smoloskyp, 1975), pp. 17-32.

[56] "Etnotsyd ukraintsiv v SSSR," *ibid.*, pp. 33-147. The first part runs from pp. 33-111.

[57] *Ibid.*, p. 61.

[58] The underground author has apparently multiplied the *total* number of Russians in the Ukraine by 0.066 (9,126,331 x 0.066 = 602,338). Actually the higher education figures are per 1,000 population *10 years old and over* (66/1000 such Russians in the Ukraine have higher education). For the Ukrainian SSR, *Itogi vsesoiuznoi naselenia 1970 goda*, Vol. IV, p. 377, gives the number of Ukrainians in the Ukr. SSR *11* years and over, but not a comparable figure for Russians in the Ukr. SSR. I have arbitrarily assumed that the age composition of Russians in the Ukraine is equal to that of Russians in the USSR as a whole (figures *ibid.*, p. 360). This gives us an adjustment factor of 18.16 percent, which, applied to the total number of Russians in the Ukraine (*ibid.*, p. 12), results in a new base figure of 9,126,331 - 1,657,342 = *7,468*, which multiplied by 0.066 gives 492,953 or ca.492,950. Even in these calculations I had to disregard the difference of one year's contingent!

[59] *Ukr. Visnyk*, VII-VIII, p. 71.

[60] *Ibid.*, pp. 71-72. The definition was given in a speech at Kiev University, 3 October 1973.

[61] *Ibid.*, pp. 74-78.

[62] *Ibid.*, p. 81.

[63] *Ibid.*, pp. 90-111.

[64] *Ibid.*, p. 113. *Pravda*, 23 and 24 November 1971, p. 1, did not list Kutsevol as a speaker. But in the resolution on the international activity of the CC CPSU there is the following statement: "The plenary session deems it necessary to continue resolutely to combat bourgeois ideology and to instill in Soviet people the spirit of Marxism-Leninism and proletarian internationalism" (*Pravda*, 24 November 1971, p. 1, or *Current Digest of the Soviet Press*, XXIII/47, p. 3). The statement may be routine or it might have been buttressed by a secret resolution in the same vein on the Lviv *obkom*.

[65] *Ukr. Visnyk*, VII-VIII, p. 114.

[66] *Ibid.* The support by soon to be ousted Mzhavanadze of Georgia appears plausible, that of Brezhnev's Moldavian protégé Bodiul does not. But on p. 110, *ibid.*, there is the tantalizing statement that Shelest had reached an agreement with Moldavian Party leaders to open Ukrainian-language schools for Ukrainians in Moldavia. But nothing came of it.

[67] *Ibid.*, p. 115.

[68] *Ibid.*, p. 116.

[69] *Ibid.*, pp. 117-118. See also notes 21 and 22, above. Biographical data in *Deputaty V.S. SSSR, 1970*, p. 133.

[70] *Ukr. Visnyk*, VII-VIII, pp. 125-134.

[71] *Ibid.*, p. 117.

[72] *Ibid.*, p. 125.

[73] *Ibid.*, p. 118.

[74] *Ibid.*, p. 146.

[75] "Une interview de Leonid Pliouchtch," *Le Monde*, 4 February 1976, pp. 1 + 3. Statements on p. 3.

[76] Bilinsky, "The CPU after 1966," *Ukraine in the 70's*, pp. 240-241.

[77] Zbigniew Brzezinski, "Totalitarianism and Rationality," *American Political Science Review*, Vol. 50 (September 1956), pp. 751-763 passim, esp. pp. 762-763.

[78] See John W. Finney, "US Hears of Brezhnev Reassurance to Bloc that [Détante] Accords Are a Tactic," *New York Times*, 17 September 1973, p. 2.

[79] George H. Sabine, *A History of Political Theory* (New York: Holt, 1953; rev. ed.), p. 864.

[80] See, for example, Israel Klejner, *Anekdotychna trahediia* (An Anecdotal Tragedy) (Munich: Suchasnist', 1974), p. 155: "Russia is sliding into fascism." Klejner is a Zionist from the Ukraine who recently emigrated from the USSR.

PART IV

THE SEARCH FOR IDENTITY AMONG
SOME NON-WESTERN SOVIET NATIONALITIES

RELIGION, MODERN NATIONALISM AND
POLITICAL POWER IN SOVIET CENTRAL ASIA*

Michael Rywkin
City College of New York
New York, New York

Central Asian Muslim nationalism, long viewed as marginal in the field of
Soviet affairs, is finally attracting attention. This is due in part to the recent wave of
Jewish migration from the USSR with its inescapable emphasis on the gravity of the
national question in that country. But primarily it is due to several recent developments in the Central Asian region itself.

Most significant of these developments is the 1970 Soviet census, which
reveals the demographic growth potential of the Muslim people contrasted with the
declining Slavic birth rate. Before the end of the century, this may drastically alter
the present internal balance of power between the main national blocs within the
USSR. It is already causing grave concern in Moscow.

Next is the growing international importance of Central Asia's neighbors,
especially China, India and the Muslim Middle East. Because of this, Central Asia
moved from the geopolitical backwaters into a position of strategic importance
during the sixties. Future Central Asian events will no longer be internationally
ignored, as they were during the post-revolutionary Basmachi revolt. Russia of the
1970's no longer enjoys the total freedom of action in that area that it possessed
with Stalin.

Furthermore, a Muslim-based, modern, nationalist spirit is emerging in Soviet
Central Asia. It is an unplanned by-product of Soviet nationality policies and a
direct result of Soviet socio-economic achievements in the area. Moscow is learning
that progress fosters nationalism instead of curtailing it. This nationalism refuses
to be channelled into a national cultural form modelled to house a Russian-
prepared socialist content. On the contrary, it provides a Muslim nationalist
content dressed in a Moscow-made socialist form. To the communist "national in
form, socialist in content" policy, it offers a "socialist in form, nationalist in

---

*Reprinted with the kind permission of the *Canadian Slavonic Papers* (Vol. XVII, Nos. 2 and
3, 1975).

content" alternative. The Islamic tradition, while losing many of its ritualistic aspects, provides the essential ingredients for this new nationalism.

Finally, the impact of increasing jingoism among many conservative Russians, whether Party members or not, triggered by Stalin's "Great Russian" victory speech, has been gaining momentum recently. This in turn activates the self-defense mechanism of non-Russian groups and exacerbates the nationality problem.

THE NATIONAL AND THE RELIGIOUS

Irish or Polish nationalism has been traditionally Catholic, Arab nationalism, Muslim, while World War II Italian or German nationalism, despite its intensity, was rather indifferent to religion. History teaches that "when conflicting nationalities were of different religions, religion often played a large part in the defense mechanism of the weaker nationality."[1] It is therefore quite normal that for the Muslim Turkic peoples of Central Asia, group identity *vis-à-vis* the European, mostly Russian, settlers has been based on feelings of Muslim religious identity.

Moreover, in the eyes of the native Central Asians, there is little difference among most settlers found in the area. Russians, Ukrainians, Byelorussians, Georgians and Armenians, or even wartime immigrants like Poles, Volga Germans and Russian Jews, appear as Europeans who use the Russian language in their social intercourse and have a European way of life. On the other hand, Central Asian Muslims are predominantly Turkic speaking and have their own "oriental" life style, quite different from that of the settlers. Therefore, terms like "outsider," "non-native," Russian, Slavic, European, etc., appear to label similar categories while terms like "native," Muslim, Turkic, Turkestani and Central Asian appear alike, and opposite to the first group. Thus the word "Muslim" does not necessarily indicate religious beliefs, but rather a group identification of Central Asian peoples as opposite to the competing and stronger Slavic group.[2]

Furthermore, Islam is a religious belief very difficult to separate from the national credo. Alexandre Bennigsen, a leading expert on Soviet Islam, explains:

> Islam . . . is a collectivist religion, authoritarian: one whose doctrine is binding on the mass of believers and which tends to deploy its directions and its judgements over the whole field of life, corporate and individual alike. In Islam, no distinction is drawn between the temporal and the spiritual; there is a traditional fusion of the two which endows life, public and private, and all its manifestations, with a sacred character.[3]

The Soviet organ of anti-religious propaganda, *Science and Religion*, admits the close relationship between the national and religious elements among the Muslims and warns that the matter should be delicately handled. "In some customs and traditions the national and the religious are closely interconnected. Their delimitation is a very delicate and complex business."[4]

Another important consideration, according to Maxime Rodinson, the eminent French student of Islam, is that communism and Islam are both movements of militant types, presenting a number of common characteristics: an "utopian" ideology, a "lay" program geared at practical application of ideological principles, a structured organizational setup, often with a charismatic leader, as well as practices, rites and symbols, showing adherence to the movement.[5] Like Islam, communism also presents several characteristics of an established church: its own credo, councils, excommunications, fidelity of adherents, etc. Both Islamic *umma* (community) and communist "international" started, according to Rodinson, as *Vereine* (associations), but *umma* evolved into *Anstalt* (establishment), whose membership is determined by birth, not by association.[6] Obviously, the latter movement tends to be even more exclusive than the former, while both consider control over people's minds crucial to their existence. If one accepts the classical definition that a nationality is "a state of mind corresponding to a political fact,"[7] then in Soviet Central Asia the state of mind of the Muslim population is cemented by feelings of Islamic community, standing in opposition to the political fact of Western, European, Russian, Soviet (used interchangeably) domination. Thus the religious and national feelings of the natives on the one side, and the anti-religious and anti-nationalist actions of Moscow on the other, tend to become not only interrelated, but also interdependent.[8]

However, the Islamic element of the modern Central Asian nationalist spirit is no longer the traditional one. Some religious practices, like that of the long *Ramadan* fast, the required five daily prayers, religious pilgrimages, strict observance of Friday's rest, the customs of religious charity, polygamy, the wearing of veils, women's separate way of life, and many others have either disappeared or are rarely observed. The number of mosques also has been reduced drastically.

The important factors remain: the basic one of belonging to the Muslim community; and those customs which can be practiced under modern living conditions without much hindrance. Among these are circumcision, wearing of local costumes, eating habits, the tradition of *kalym* as reverse dowery (without its old bride-buying implications), the customary way of furnishing one's home, the *chaikhana* (tea house) style of "café life," the strict sexual morals of Muslim women, and finally the rarity of mixed marriages, especially between Muslim girls and European men.[9] This general lack of social interaction between the two communities (European and Muslim) aggravates the situation.

The Soviet authorities, in their unsuccessful attempts to eradicate Muslim traditions, are trying to devise "new customs and rituals" of Soviet character to compete with the traditional ones.[10] One can doubt the value of such an enterprise. As early as 1922, a leading proponent of modern Soviet Islam, the Tatar revolutionary Sultan Galiev, warned that the majority of Muslims view anti-religious propaganda as a political, not a religious, act. Consequently, such propaganda should be conducted by Muslims only, against certain backward religious practices, and never against the socio-political content of Islam.[11] It is the socio-political content of modern Islam that is important, not the old-fashioned traditions attached to it. As explained by a young Turk in 1921: there are three Islams—one of the Koran, the only true one; another of the *ulemas* (Islamic clerics), a legalistic one; and the one of the masses, the one of superstitions.[12] Modern Muslim nationalism, whether in the Arab world or in Central Asia, turns for strength to the first source.

The fact that both communism and Islamic nationalism are exclusive ideologies with strong totalitarian trends does not facilitate their co-existence. Rodinson states that communism has been moving from a non-totalitarian origin to totalitarian grounds, while Islam took the opposite road; but he still considers future coexistence between the two probable, from sheer historical necessity.[13] Others view the differences between the two doctrines as fundamental and not conducive to a Marxist "thesis, anti-thesis, synthesis" conclusion, especially with the Russian chauvinist element present in the communist formula. Original Muslim nationalist-communists like Sultan Galiev, Khodzhaev, Safarov, Hanafi Muzzafar and others failed in their attempts to amalgamate the two ideologies. Such amalgamation could succeed only if communism presented a national Islamic image, not a European-dominated and European-imposed one. Soviet hostility to national communist "deviation" at home precludes, at least for the time being, such a development.

THE NUMBERS AND THE MUSLIM IDENTITY

The balance between the relative importance of the national languages of individual republics and the Russian language seems to favor the latter. Not only is Russian the *lingua franca* for communication between diverse Soviet nationalities, as most of the Soviet writers in this field underscore, but it is also the language of the bureaucratic and military machinery and industrial management. From accounting to train schedules, from technical specifications to copies in triplicate, the Russian language is the one used. Even Lenin thought it would be advantageous (*vygodno*) for non-Russians to learn the language.[14] Learning Russian is equal to acquiring a tool for modernization through modern science, technology and cultural progress.[15]

Among the principal Central Asian nationalities, the proportion of those who declared themselves "fluent in Russian" in the 1970 census varied between one out of ten for the Karakalpaks to almost two out of ten for the Kirgizes (with other groups in between). In Kazakhstan it was four out of ten, as compared to almost five out of ten for the USSR as a whole. This evidence of native progress cannot be construed as proof of linguistic Russification.

This is especially so since the percentage of those declaring their language as one different from their native tongue is insignificant: less than 2 percent in both Kazakhstan and Central Asia. The 1970 census shows a slight decrease in this category for all Central Asian nationalities, with the exception of the Kazakhs.[16] These one or two out of a hundred almost certainly adopted another Central Asian language rather than Russian. Moreover, the circulation of native language newspapers increased sharply throughout the 1960's, while the circulation of locally printed Russian papers remained almost static. Finally, reversing the trend of the 1930's and 1940's, Russian loan words are being purged from local languages. A genuine linguistic de-Russification "has become overt and official."[17] The conclusion is clear: better-educated Muslims do learn Russian as an indispensable tool for their own advancement, but linguistic Russification does not take place and local Turkic languages are undergoing a real revival.

In their expansion into Asia, the Russians, unlike the English, were never confronted with the problem of dealing with overwhelming numbers of subjects. The natives were never numerous and the acquisition of new territories (the Christian areas of Transcaucasia aside) was usually followed by waves of Russian settlers. Among the conquered regions, Central Asia was the most populous, but even there the proportion of Russian (and other Slavic) settlers increased constantly (compare the 1897, 1926, 1939 and 1959 census). By 1959 the proportion of Europeans in Kazakhastan rose to about 65 percent and in Central Asia proper to approximately 25 percent. Pre-World War II deportations of *kulaks*, "socially danger-ous elements," and Koreans, as well as war-connected transplantations of "western-ers" (from Poland and the Baltic states), Volga Germans and other "unreliables" accounted for a large proportion of the Europeans. In addition, some wartime refugees were prevented or dissuaded from returning to the European area of the USSR. The "virgin lands program" in Northern Kazakhstan in the early 1960's was the last large-scale influx of Europeans into the area. In total, one-and-a-half-million Russians and other outsiders were transplanted into Kazakhstan and Central Asia between 1959 and 1970.[18]

According to the 1970 census, the proportion of Europeans fell to about 63 percent in Kazakhstan and to just over 21 percent in Central Asia proper.[19] Immi-gration was unable to balance the decreasing Slavic and the rapidly increasing Mus-lim birth rates. In 1969, for example, the birth rate in the three Slavic republics of the USSR was between 14.2 and 15.9 per 1,000, as compared to 16.8 to 18.1 in Western Europe and the USA, and 30.1 to 34.7 in the Muslim republics of Central Asia! The comparison of net rates of growth is even more ominous for the Slavs: 5.7 for the RSFSR versus 26.8 for the Uzbek Republic.[20] Thus, between 1959 and 1970, the number of Central Asian Muslims grew by 46.3 to 52.9 percent while that of the Slavs by only 9.4 to 14.4 percent.[21] An American expert, Rein Taagepera, explains this situation as follows: in a choice between having children and finally reaching long-desired minimum material standards, the consumer-oriented Russians select the latter. Soviet Muslims, on the other hand, with their different life style and values, choose the former. Moreover, drastic improvement of medical and sanitary conditions in Central Asia contributes to the growth of the indigenous population while housing shortages in urban areas restrict Slavic growth.[22] Solomon Bruk, a leading Soviet demographer, explains the situation in terms of differences in tradi-tions and marital-sexual habits (including community pressures against divorce and childless marriages).[23] Thus, without precisely saying so, Bruk attributes the popu-lation explosion among Soviet Muslims to their own life style, which in turn, comes from their own traditional national-religious heritage.

Projections for 1985 envisage the Muslim population of Central Asia and Kazakhstan increasing from the present 19.6 million to about 35 million and their relative proportion in the area from 55 to 72 percent.[24] It also is considered possible that the Slavic population of the USSR might remain static for many years to come,[25] while the total number of Muslims in the entire USSR could reach 80 to 100 million by the year 2000.

The ethno-demographic projections are closely connected with those of labor resources. Future labor surpluses in Central Asia are envisaged, based on the rapid growth of available manpower in that area: a 1.7 percent yearly increase compared to 0.6 in European Russia.[26] An analysis of the present labor situation in Uzbekistan suggests the main elements contributing to such growth: first, the net population increase; second, the still hesitant but promising shift of Muslim women from domestic occupations to gainful employment; third, the slow but steady movement of Muslim families from the country to the cities; and fourth, the influx of labor from outside the area.[27] Two of the causes originate in the current modernization of Muslim religious tradition and the third in its continuity. None can be analyzed without understanding this tradition. Basing their predic-tions on labor projections for Central Asia, as well as on U.S., British, French, and West German examples, some American students of Central Asian affairs envisage future large-scale movements of unskilled Muslim manpower from Central Asia into European Russia and Siberia, along with the continuous influx of technically qualified Europeans into Central Asia.[28] This is supposed to resemble the influx of Puerto Ricans to New York, of Pakistanis and Jamaicans to London, of Arabs and Portuguese to Paris, and of Turks and Yugoslavs to West Germany. Proponents of such theories base their arguments on articles by V. Perevedentsev, an outspoken Soviet economic demographer.[29] While statistical arguments seem to favor such theories, there are even stronger arguments to the contrary: among them, the reluctance of Central Asian Muslims to leave their own land and way of life and to settle in non-Muslim areas. Additional factors are that living standards in Central Asia are equal to or higher than those in labor-short industrial areas of Russia (which is not the case with the above mentioned Western examples); and that the usual Soviet red tape is weaker in outlying areas than in Russia proper, quite an inducement in itself. As a result, manpower-hungry Siberia exports workers to labor-rich Central Asia, a phenomenon stressed by Perevedentsev.[30] One can either see in this proof of job discrimination against qualified natives of Central Asia or a sign that Central Asian living conditions are more attractive. Soviet economists seem to doubt future prospects for any large-scale Muslim migrations from their homeland and see the solution to Central Asian labor surpluses in correcting manpower imbalances within the area itself.[31] This could include shifting population from farming to industrial areas,[32] and even adjusting existing borders between the union republics of Central Asia to reflect the actual "forms of economic life and economic relations between nationalities."[33] The recent division of the USSR into seven major economic areas, four of which are located in Asia (two in Central Asia and Kazakhstan), seems to indicate that Moscow expects to bring industry to Central Asia, instead of exporting labor from that area.[34]

Some speakers at a 1972 Central Asian conference held at Columbia University insisted that job discrimination against the natives of Central Asia is commonplace. In reality, hiring discrimination against the natives has been limited to two fields only. First, in assigning more reliable Slavs and other Europeans to key Party and state positions (Second Secretaries, heads of Departments of Party organs and special sections, KGB, military command, communications, etc.), and "doubling" key Muslim functionaries with Slavic deputies. Second, in keeping enterprises of all-Union importance under the control of more trusted and also more qualified European technicians. These are obviously important, but the total number of positions not open to native Central Asians is minimal. In the majority of cases, Central Asian Muslims with equal or even lesser qualifications are given priority in their own republics, and this causes a great outcry from European job seekers. Warnings directed from time to time against those Muslims who object to the use of Russian cadres in their own republics are aimed at discouraging those who would like to "Muslimize" the economy as a step towards achieving political control.[35] Similar warnings are directed at those who are said to "show [a] condescending attitude toward the representatives of other nationalities and their culture."[36] Neither case can be viewed as proof of active discrimination against the Muslims in the field of labor practices, but rather should be seen as Moscow's preoccupation with "survivals of nationalism and chauvinism"—i.e., modern Muslim nationalism.

AUTONOMY: "SOCIALIST" IN FORM

Since the time of Stalin, when dealing with Muslim areas Moscow has employed the already mentioned method of staffing specific key positions with Russians and other Slavs, and "doubling" important Muslim functionaries with its own men. This method survived Khrushchev as well and seems to remain the cornerstone of Soviet control mechanism in the area.[37]

A second method of control lies in the division of ministries into three main groups: All-Union (federal) ministries located in Moscow and providing direct administration down to the local levels; Union-Republicans existing in both Moscow and in the local republics and sharing control, albeit unevenly, between the centre and the republics; and republican ministries present only in individual republics. The latter alone represent a meaningful degree of local control. The third method is one of keeping the bulk of heavy industry situated in individual republics under "all-Union jurisdiction," thus removing it from local Party or administrative interference. The fourth method consists of keeping Russians in firm control of the KGB apparatus and armed forces in the republics as well as assigning European draftees to serve in Central Asian republics and vice-versa.

These basic methods of control are not evenly applied throughout the Soviet Union. They are fully operational in the Muslim republics (Central Asia, Kazakhstan, Azerbaidzhan) and are applied almost as strongly in the three Baltic republics and in Moldavia. However, in the "brotherly" Slavic republics, as well as in Georgia and Armenia, the above scheme is not operational and local native communists are entrusted with controlling their own citizenry.

This variation in methods of control visibly divides the non-Russian republics into five "reliable" and nine "unreliable." The reliable republics are either Slavic or those whose incorporation into the old Russian Empire had been more or less voluntary (even as a "lesser evil choice"). Most of their inhabitants profess the Orthodox faith, have strong cultural and historical ties with Russia, and were already relatively privileged (after the Russians themselves) during the times of the tsars.

The "unreliable" nationalities were conquered (or reconquered) rather recently, are either of Islamic or Scandinavian culture, mostly Muslim by religion (some Protestant and Catholic), and their incorporation into the Russian Empire was visibly contrary to the wishes of their people. Many were classified as *inorodsty* in tsarist times. The Moldavians are a special case since their "republic" is an artificial concoction (like the old Karelo-Finnish Republic), created to justify the annexation of a chunk of Rumanian territory.

Because the three Baltic nations are small and present no visible threat to Russia's future, the most serious control problem is in the Muslim republics, with their large territories, rapidly growing population, and rising nationalism fed by a dangerous combination of racial, national, and religious feelings. This is not to underestimate, however, the upsurge of nationalism in the Ukraine or Georgia, whose ties with Russia, however unsatisfactory, lack the colonial elements present in the Moscow-Central Asian relationship.

Aware of the danger, Moscow has been eager to appease local nationalist feelings by offering selective concessions, most of which are very limited in scope. Already under Stalin, *pro-forma* republican ministries of defense and foreign affairs had been created. The latter operates as a type of state tourist bureau, the former merely as window dressing with no clear functions whatsoever. Later under Khrushchev (and especially before 1962), a few genuine concessions were made. Several ministries were moved from Moscow into the local regions, some large enterprises were shifted to local control, and more economic leeway in general was given to individual republics.[38]

Post-Khrushchev reforms combine minor concessions with publicity-oriented phraseology. The number of control-sharing ministries (existing both in Moscow and at the local levels) has been increased at the expense of other types.[39] Control-sharing (subordination in reality) seems to be the new motto. Since 1965 the Councils of Ministers of individual republics have been allowed to "look into" Moscow's economic plans for enterprises of all-Union importance located in their territory and to make "suggestions" (only) in these matters.[40] Finally, permanent missions of individual republics to the USSR Council of Ministers in Moscow are being opened in order to improve economic, scientific and cultural contacts,[41] a renewal of an earlier practice started in the 1920's.

These moves are of limited practical importance, but they give the appearance of increased autonomy for the individual republics. They follow the old policy of making concessions to non-Russian nationalities as long as no transfer of real power is involved. Moscow shows no willingness, for example, to share the power of taxation with the individual republics. At the same time, the non-Russians are reminded of the primacy of "all-union, international tasks." They are advised that strict delimitation of federal jurisdiction on one hand, and Republican jurisdiction on the other, and coordination between the two, is neither contradictory nor mutually exclusive, but in close "dialectical unity."[42] The word "dialectic" is used as a "code name" for anything the Party promotes and would like to see people accept without too much explanation. What Moscow really means is that it reserves the prerogative of deciding what rights the individual republics are to receive.

MODERN NATIONALISM AND SOCIALIST THEORY

The idea of modern nationalism had very limited circulation in pre-revolutionary Central Asia outside the Jadid movement. "The concept of nation state or even of nationalism barely penetrated either the steppe region or Turkestan until after the abrupt ending of the tsarist regime in 1917."[43] One of the Bukharan proponents of modern Turkestani nationalism, Abd ar-rauf Fitrat, considered that being a good Muslim and a good patriot (i.e., nationalist) were closely connected notions.[44] During the Soviet period this concept grew and matured among the Muslims of Central Asia, becoming "internally defined." A number of historical events helped the Central Asians to come to this realization. The nationalist Basmachi revolt provided the initial bloodletting necessary in nursing a nationalist cause. The liquidation of the formerly autonomous principalities of Khiva and Bukhara removed the remnants of feudal state frameworks, which were obstructing the formation of modern national entities. National delimitation, the proud achievement of the Soviet nationality policy of the mid-1920's, started the newborn national units on the road to modern national consciousness. Collectivization, an unpopular measure imposed from the outside, consolidated common resentment against Moscow. The purges of original national-communists (Khodzhaev, Ikramov and others) reinforced local nationalist feelings. Social reforms, economic development and educational progress resulted in the widespread training of local cadres, but the latter resented the limitations imposed on their political powers. The modernization itself provided the indispensable spark for the emerging nationalist spirit. By the middle of the twentieth century, a group of nations, mainly Turkic speaking, Muslim inspired, oriental in life style, finally had emerged. The strongest and most advanced among them, the Uzbek nation, was the core of this group. Some Soviet experts even envisage the possibility of a Central Asian fusion of nationalities around the Uzbek nation.[45]

Soviet nationality policy promulgates the idea of "one Soviet nation" gradually emerging all over the USSR and forming around the Russian national core, with the Russian culture predominant and the Russian language accepted as the *lingua franca*. This process supposedly goes through several stages. First, the creation of a common politico-economic base, then the triumph of socialist uniformity, with borders between the republics losing their importance, and finally the establishment of one socialist culture with common Soviet national characteristics.[46]

With "one Soviet nation" as the official final goal, the problem lies in finding proper methods of achieving this end. Here three theories conflict: that of *sliianie* (fusion), *sblizhenie* ("rapprochement"), and *rastvet* (flourishing). Proponents of pure *rastvet* were quite vocal until the end of the 1960's. They attempted to avoid the unpleasant subject of "one Soviet nation" and saw the existing nationalities of the USSR as essentially formed and only in need of more prosperity.[47] Lately, however, such opinions are seldom heard.

While "rapprochement" is the official policy,[48] distinction is made between "rapprochement" per se and "rapprochement" leading to eventual fusion—i.e., the intermediate process sometimes labeled "integration." Extreme "integrationists" not only reject the right of individual nationalities to choose their own road to socialism, but even question the basic Soviet constitutional guarantee of the sanctity of national territory of the individual republics.[49] They regard separate roads to socialism as leading to national socialism, hence, fascism. The "integrationists" promote linguistic assimilation and have reintroduced the old Stalinist idea that national self-determination is to be exercised by toilers only.[50]

Attempts to reject the principle of territorial inviolability and to reintroduce class criteria in self-determination violate the basic, albeit theoretical, right of the Union Republics to secede from the USSR. Moreover, the idea that class struggle continues under socialism, a pet Stalinist conception, has been consistently rejected, until recently, by all post-Stalin Soviet leaders.

Proponents of a non-Integrationist "rapprochement" argue that the republics did transfer to the USSR a part of their inherent rights, but still preserve those which guarantee them a sovereign existence. For instance, they insist that all republics have equal rights and obligations, since representatives of all the republics participate in "the realization of all-Union sovereignty" by sharing in federal functions. Individual republics keep the right to alter their own jurisdiction by constitutional changes, and this is supposed to be the mainstay of their sovereignty.[51] However, major unilateral changes in the constitutions of individual republics cannot be accomplished under present-day Soviet conditions and the participation, for example, of Soviet Muslims in key Party, government, army and security positions in Moscow has always been minimal. Membership in such entities as the Supreme Soviet is of too limited a value to be considered.

Deprived of an effective voice in the decision-making process in Moscow, individual republics have no choice but to press for increasing roles at home and to avoid giving more than lip service to officially promoted concepts of "fusions" and "integrations."

The new direction Soviet nationality policy is supposed to take was defined by Leonid Brezhnev in his speech on the occasion of the fiftieth anniversary of the formation of the USSR. Brezhnev endorsed the theory of *sblizhenie* ("rapprochement") and repeated traditional Soviet arguments about the extent of socio-economic progress achieved by the individual republics, the emergence of the "common Soviet culture" with Russian as *the* language of communication between the nationalities, and the close interrelation between Soviet patriotism and socialist internationalism. He underscored the extent of intermarriage between the nationalities and repeated that the national question "has been solved" in the USSR.[52] But this was not all. Emphasizing, as usual, the leading role of the Russian republic among other republics of the USSR, Brezhnev used the expression "first among equals" (*pervaia sredi ravnykh*),[53] equivalent to the latin papal *primus inter pares*. He not only stressed the emergence of a "Soviet nation, a new historical community of peoples," but warned that the Party would not tolerate obstacles toward the "rapprochement" among the nationalities.[54]

The important question is the degree of implementation of Brezhnev's *primus inter pares* policy and his warnings to opponents of "rapprochement." The removal of Alexander Iakovlev, head of the Central Committee's Agitation and Propaganda Department, is especially worrisome.[55] In November 1972, Iakovlev took a strong stand against the so-called "Russity" (Slavophile-inspired Great Russian chauvinists), growing increasingly influential within Russia. Among other things, he criticized them for spreading Slavophile literature, such as nineteenth century writings setting "our people" against "not ours" (*ne nashi*), obviously meaning non-Russians, and for lauding men like General Skobelev, one of the tsarist conquerors of Central Asia.[56]

In 1923 Stalin warned that Great Russian chauvinism "constitutes the chief danger tending to undermine the confidence of the formerly oppressed peoples in the Russian proletariat," and considered it responsible for "nine-tenths of the nationalism which has survived and which is developing in certain republics."[57] At present, however, all Party attacks are directed against "local nationalism," while critics of Russian chauvinism, if they take their task seriously, may expect Iakovlev's fate.

The crucial point in dispute is the same one which constantly obstructs Moscow's relationship with China and other socialist countries. This is the "own road to socialism" idea so vehemently denounced in Moscow since the intervention in Prague. Since, in communist jargon, "road to socialism" equals "road to the future," then "own road" means that of sovereignty and equality. No nation, whether independent or part of a larger federation, is willing to renounce it voluntarily, unless on a share and share alike basis within a well-balanced federal system, which the Soviet Union is not. How long the increasingly nationalistic Russian leadership will be able to maintain a minimally credible pretense of commitment to "socialist internationalism" without making far-reaching concessions to non-Russians, both inside the USSR and outside in the "socialist bloc," remains to be seen.

NOTES

[1] Hans Kohn, *The Idea of Nationalism* (New York: Collier Books, 1969), p. 15.

[2] See N. Ashirov, "Izmeneniia v kul'te. Evoliutsiia Islama SSSR," *Nauka i Religiia*, No. 9 (1971), p. 18, for the usage of "European" as opposite to Muslim.

[3] Alexandre Bennigsen and Chantal Lemercier-Quelquejay, *Islam in the Soviet Union* (New York: Praeger, 1967), p. 138.

[4] M. Dzhunusov, "Obshchestvo internatsionalistov—obshchestvo massovogo ateizma," *Nauka i Religiia*, No. 9 (1972), p. 23.

[5] Maxime Rodinson, *Marxisme et le monde musulman* (Paris: Ed. du Seuil, 1972), pp. 154-55.

[6] *Ibid.*, pp. 152-53.

[7] Israel Zangwill, *The Principle of Nationalities* (London: Watts, 1917), p. 39.

[8] Hans Bräker, *Kommunismus und Weltreligionen Asiens*, I, 1, 2. *Religionsdiskussion und Islam in der Sovjetunion* (Tübingen: J. C. B. Mohr [Paul Siebeck], 1969), pp. 91 ff.

[9] Lt. Colonel Jean Prautois, "Islam et nationalisme en Asie Centrale soviétique," *Revue de défense nationale* (Paris, December 1971), pp. 1847-48.

[10] Dzhunusov, p. 10.

[11] Alexandre Bennigsen et Chantal Quelquejay, *Les mouvements nationaux chez les musulmans de Russie. Le Sultangalievisme au Tatarstan* (Paris: La Haye, 1960), pp. 226 ff.

[12] Hélène Carrère d'Encausse, *Reforme et révolution chez les musulmans de l'empire russe. Boukhara 1867-1924* (Paris: Armand Collin, 1966), p. 169.

[13] Rodinson, pp. 158-59 and 179.

[14] K. Kh. Khanazarov, "Nekotorye voprosy natsional'nykh iazykov v sovetskom obshchestve," *Voprosy filosofii*, No. 12 (1972), p. 44.

[15] Sh. Rashidov, "Moguchee sredstvo obshcheniia i internatsional'nogo vospitaniia," *Kommunist*, No. 7 (1972), p. 23.

[16] "Population of the Soviet Union," Report by the Central Statistical Board under the USSR Council of Ministers, *Moscow News* (supplement to issue No. 17), 1-8 May 1971, p. 6.

[17] James Critchlow, "Signs of Emerging Nationalism in the Moslem Soviet Republics," *The Soviets in Asia*, Proceedings of a symposium held at George Washington University, 19-20 May 1972 (Maryland: Cremona Foundation, 1972), pp. 21-22.

[18] S. I. Bruk, "Etnodemograficheskie protsessy v SSSR (po materialam perepisi 1970 goda)," *Sovetskaia etnografiia*, No. 4 (1971), p. 28.

[19] "Population of the Soviet Union," p. 6.

[20] Bruk, pp. 14-15.

[21] *Ibid.*, p. 24.

[22] Rein Taagepera, "National Differences Within Soviet Demographic Trends," *Soviet Studies*, XX, 4 (Glasgow, April 1969), 486.

[23] Bruk, p. 16. Bruk is a deputy-director of the Institute of Ethnography, USSR Academy of Science.

[24] Prautois, p. 1853.

[25] Roman Szporluk, "The Nations of the USSR in 1970," *Survey*, No. 81, (Autumn 1971), pp. 68-69.

[26] L. Chizhova, "Nekotorye voprosy planirovaniia trudovykh resursov," *Planovoe khoziaistvo*, No. 4 (1971), pp. 37 and 41.

[27] *Trudovye resursy Uzbekistana Problemy raspredeleniia i ispol'zovaniia* (Tashkent: Akademiia Nauk Uzb. SSR. Institut Ekonomiki, 1970), p. 45.

[28] See papers by Rosen, Clem and others read at the Central Asian Conference, Columbia University, 7-8 April 1972, in E. Allworth, ed., *The Nationality Question in Central Asia* (New York: Praeger, 1973).

[29] See V. Perevedentsev, "Migratsiia naseleniia i ispol'zovanie trudovykh rezervov," *Voprosy ekonomiki*, No. 9 (1970).

[30] *Ibid.*, p. 41.

[31] *Trudovye resursy Uzbekistana* . . . , p. 128.

[32] S. Daulenov, "Ekonomika Kazakhstana v deviatoi piatiletke," *Planovoe khoziaistvo*, No. 12 (1971), p. 42.

[33] V. Kistanov, "Leninskaia natsional'naia politika i ekonomicheskoe raionirovanie v SSSR," *Voprosy ekonomiki*, No. 12 (1972), p. 64.

[34] *The New York Times*, 4 May 1973.

[35] Prautois, p. 1851.

[36] A. Chotonov, "Mesto traditsii v strukture natsional'noi gordosti," *Izvestiia Akademii Nauk Kirgizskoi SSR*, No. 6 (1971), p. 71.

[37] For more details, see Michael Rywkin, "Some Changes in the Administrative and Political Structure of Central Asia during and after Khrushchev," *International Review of History and Political Science* (Meerut, India, August 1968); and "Moscow Versus the Minority Nationalities: Trends for the New Decade," *Bulletin* (Institute for the Study of the USSR, October 1970).

[38] For more details see Borys Lewickyj, *Polityka narodowościowa ZSSR w dobie Chruszczowa* (Paris: Institut Literacki, 1966), pp. 196 ff.

[39] M. A. Shafir, "Kompetentsiia Soiuza SSR i soiuznykh respublik v sovetskom gosudarstve," *Sovetskoe gosudarstvo i pravo*, No. 10 (1970), pp. 14 and 16.

[40] S. N. Dosymbaev, "Uchastie soiuznoi respubliki v upravlenii promyshlennosti soiuznogo podchineniia," *Sovetskoe gosudarstvo i pravo*, No. 2 (1971), p. 64.

[41] A. A. Agzamkhodzhaev, "Sotsialisticheskii federalizm i printsip ravnopraviia narodnov," *Sovetskoe gosudarstvo i pravo*, No. 12 (1972), p. 57. The Uzbek mission to Moscow was approved 12 March 1971.

[42] "Editorial," *Kommunist*, No. 14 (1972), p. 9.

[43] Geoffrey Wheeler, *The Modern History of Soviet Central Asia* (New York: Praeger, 1966), pp. 52-53.

[44] Carrère d'Encausse, p. 177.

[45] K. Hallik, "Rol' kulturnykh sviazei v ukreplenii druzhby sovetskikh liudei," *Kommunist Estonii*, No. 9 (Tallin, 1969), p. 35.

[46] A. M. Gindin and S. G. Markin, "Tvorcheskoe razvitie leninskoi natsional' noi politiki v resheniiakh XXIV s'ezda KPSS," *Vosprosy istorii KPSS*, No. 7 (1971), pp. 18-19.

[47] I. P. Tsamerian, "Mezhdunarodnoe znachenie opyta KPSS po reshenii natsional'nogo voprosa v SSSR," *Vosprosy istorii KPSS*, No. 9 (1968), p. 44.

[48] M. Suslov, "Obshchestvennye nauki—boevoe oruzhie partii v stroitel'stve kommunizma," *Kommunist*, No. 1 (1972), p. 24.

[49] S. S. Agadzanian, *K voprosu o prirode i perspektivakh razvitiia sotsialisticheskikh natsii v SSSR* (Erevan: Aiastan, 1972), pp. 67 and 74.

[50] *Ibid.*, pp. 92 and 183.

[51] V. S. Shevtsov, "Suverenitet v sovetskom gosudarstve," *Sovetskoe gosudarstvo i pravo*, No. 6 (1972), pp. 52-53.

[52] L. I. Brezhnev, "Doklad . . . o piaditesiatiletii Soiuza Sovetskikh Sotsialisticheskikh Respublik," *Kommunist*, No. 18, 18 December 1972, pp. 15-17.

[53] *Ibid.*, p. 10.

[54] *Ibid.*, pp. 14 and 18.

[55] *The New York Times*, 7 May 1973.

[56] A. Iakovlev, "Protiv antiistorizma," *Literaturnaia gazeta*, 15 November 1972.

[57] Joseph Stalin, *Marxism and the National Question. Selected Writings and Speeches* (New York: International Publishers, 1942), p. 156.

IF THE NAVAJO WERE INSIDE THE SOVIET UNION: A COMPARATIVE APPROACH TO THE RUSSIAN NATIONALITY POLICY

Rein Taagepera and Ralph Michelsen
University of California, Irvine
Irvine, California

Soviet treatment of national minorities is all too often measured against an ideal standard of fairness, rather than against a humanly achievable one. Soviet claims that they have completely solved their "minorities" problems are, at best, questionable. But impartial scholarship should compare the Soviet performance to that of other states. Because there are similarities in American and Russian geographical expansionism, it might be of special interest to compare their practices.

Even within the same systemic framework the treatment of a minority may vary depending on its relative size, compactness, racial and cultural distinctiveness, native or immigrant origin, etc. Therefore, we will first identify minority groups in both countries which are inherently amenable to comparison because they resemble each other in the aforementioned respects. Furthermore, since minority practices themselves have an impact on a minority's size, distinctiveness, and compactness, no instant snapshot of the present scene will suffice—the whole evolution of minority practices would have to be taken into account, from Moscovy to the present USSR, and from the Thirteen Colonies to the present United States.

POLICIES TOWARD VOLGA-SIBERIAN AND AMERICAN NATIVES

The United States won the West (and the East) predominantly from preliterate tribes who had not developed levels of political organization that could cope with the invaders. This Western expansion of the Americans offers many similarities with the Eastern expansion of the Russians, from the Volga to the Pacific Ocean. In both cases the native population was rather sparse and consisted of linguistically and culturally diverse tribes with many uncoordinated social organizations (except for the fragile political superstructure imposed by the Spanish and Tatar empires in some areas). While the belief systems of the Hopis or the Khantis may be as complex as that of Americans or Russians, the material culture of the American Indians and of the Volga-Siberian populations was simpler than that of the conquerors. (However, the differences in cultural complexity between the Iroquois and the pioneers, or between the Mordvins and the Cossacks, may have been smaller than they seem in hindsight.)

Our further discussion will concentrate on the comparison of the American and Russian policy (and its implementation) toward these politically less cohesive non-European populations. In the United States this scope involves all American Indians. In Russia-USSR it involves populations east and southeast of the original Slavic lands, with the exception of the organized and literate Volga Tatar, Caucasian, and Central Asian states. Within this scope, efforts on the part of the dominant cultures to acculturate the minorities offer some striking parallels. There seems to be a behavioral continuum from relatively friendly contact to overt hostilities, to conquest, to attempted forced acculturation, to partial autonomy, and finally to some accommodation to cultural differences. This behavioral continuum can be reduced to a succession of attitudes: 1) benevolent coexistence; 2) frustration and hostility; 3) benevolent paternalism; 4) compromise. These patterns are presented here very tentatively. On the one hand, they may apply to most cases where a technologically complex population penetrates the territory of a technologically simpler population; thus, we are not suggesting that the Americans and the Russians share a pattern that is unique to them. On the other hand, the model is bound to oversimplify an intricate panorama. We are concentrating on pointing out similarities, without asserting that similarities exceed the differences. After discussing the four stages proposed, we will present a more detailed case study of two nations: the Navajo and the Khakassians.

1) **Benevolent coexistence.** Initial contacts with indigenous groups tend to be friendly, with both sides working toward maximization of their own interests. This usually takes the form of trade, with the natives supplying raw materials in exchange for new technological items. If a strong symbiotic relationship is established, such as fur trade, this initial period of benevolence may last for generations.

Private penetration frequently precedes state action. New settlements in America were often created by fortune seekers or dissident groups, and the pioneers in the West often were people who disliked the organized state power in the East. The first Russian pioneers in the Volga-Siberian area often were runaway serfs and groups in temporary conflict with the tsar (e.g., the Ural Cossacks), or Cossacks only nominally under the tsar's authority.[1] Being largely on their own, the early settlers have no numerical and little technological advantage over the natives, and must depend on the natives' goodwill. At this stage the British/U.S. and Russian governments sometimes unsuccessfully tried to discourage further penetration of the continent (e.g., in Bashkiria and trans-Appalachia) because it provoked costly native rebellions. But in case of trouble the settlers would ask and receive the armed support of the government.

While the natives tend to have no desire to convert the newcomers to their life style, the settlers tend to offer their technology and/or religion to the natives. But early settlers also occasionally go native (e.g., in Yakutia).[2] Governments tend to conclude loosely worded submission treaties which the natives may interpret as mere peace or alliance treaties, and a fur tribute (in Russia) which the natives may mistake for a trade agreement in exchange for protection and foreign goods. Treaties often are concluded with native "chiefs" who have no such authority, leading to "treaty breaking" by the natives.

2) **Frustration and hostility.** Peaceful contacts eventually lead to shifts toward some of the new values introduced by the foreigners. Adjustments must be made in the subsistence role played by the producers of raw materials, and these lead to other shifts in social organization. Some old values deteriorate and must be adjusted to the new environment. Because the native populations usually have no traditional methods for dealing with the new economic system, the foreign modernizers, with their more sophisticated political, economic, and military technology, move into the void; and they assume control once they have established a sufficiently strong power base.

As the full impact of increasing numbers of settlers, of loss of land, and of the burden of the fur tribute (a general practice of the Russians but not of Americans) becomes clear, the natives react more violently than during the early contacts and in some cases try to eliminate the foreign presence for good; this is the period of wars such as the King Philip War (1672-1676) in New England and those of Shamil in Daghestan. The natives often split into factions friendly and hostile to the foreigners. Prevention of raids on previously "pacified" tribes and territories by the still independent natives becomes an important motive or pretext for a never-ending further penetration, especially in the Asian steppes and the American West.

If a viable symbiotic relationship does not exist (as it did in Yakutia), the natives are decimated, removed, or superficially forced into the political, social, and economic mold of the dominant society. These efforts lead to more warfare, even with natives who already are resigned to foreign rule but not to physical or cultural annihilation. But finally, survivors are forced to accept the dictates of the foreign rulers.

3) **Benevolent paternalism.** When the modernizers have established military-political control and when there is no serious threat of native rebellion, the dominant society reassumes its benevolence in a paternalist way. This second round of benevolence focuses on initiating modernization as perceived by the conquerors. Native values, customs, social order, and religion are indiscriminately condemned as evil or obsolete. The conquerors' education, religion, and national language are forcibly imposed with the best of intentions but often with results disastrous to the natives and expensive for the conquerors. Schools serve as centers of acculturation and are often run by the religious-ideological arm of the dominant group. Native-language texts and teaching are disfavored or viewed as a necessary temporary evil.

The natives surviving the conquest are encouraged or forced to adopt new ways of life that are in such conflict with their traditions that they resist many of the innovations. Christianization and individualization in the United States paralleled Christianization, then Marxianization, in Russia/USSR. The forced collectivization of lands and herds in Siberia compares with the forced individualization of tribal lands in the United States, at least with respect to its disruptive effect on natives: in both cases the land often ended up under Russian/Anglo control because the individual Indian would cheaply sell or lease his individual parcel (which was bound to be culturally meaningless to him as private property), while the early native collective farm chairmen were not culturally prepared to run those European constructs and "had" to be put under Russian supervision.

Among other alien concepts the democratic administrational structure (including decision-making by majority vote) was imposed on the Indians, although it was completely antithetical to their values schemas: used to decision-making by unanimity (through slow consensus-building), they viewed voting as a stronghand method doing violence to the minority. The Soviet administrational structure (including decision-making through unanimous vote not necessarily based on personal conviction) might not be considered more (or less) strange than the American system, by the Indians (or the Siberian natives).

The paternalistic disruption of native social structure increases political and cultural fractionalization—Christianized versus non-Christianized, Communist versus non-Communist, traditionalist versus modernizing, related ethnic groups who are given separate literary languages or territorial divisions, etc. Certain territories are specifically left under nominal native control—the Indian reservations and the Soviet Autonomous Republics and Oblasts and National Districts. But through immigration (in USSR) and through leasing (in the USA), the erosion of native sanctuaries starts often as soon as they are proclaimed, and the provisional nature of these territories is recognized openly: "termination" of their reservations has recently become a fact for some Indian groups deemed sufficiently developed to enter the white man's world unprotected; and the Soviet administrational boundaries are expected to be revamped according to economic needs once the technologically underdeveloped national areas catch up economically (either by assimilation or by out-crowding of the titular nationality).

People subjected to paternalism must try to catch up with the dominant society but must never actually make it to a point of effective competition. While complete acculturation is the openly stated goal, in reality only acculturation into the lower strata of the dominant society is acceptable. Truly full acculturation (including a show of political, economic, and educational skill and initiative on a level equal to that of the dominant group) is as likely to bring heavy repression as refusal to be acculturated. In the United States, the prime example is the Cherokee nation, who in the early nineteenth century performed an almost Japan-like feat of adopting Western technology and political organization. The Cherokees patterned their government after that of the United States, had well-tended farms, schools, and newspapers in Northern Georgia. Under the pressures of their covetous white neighbors, President Jackson ordered and carried out their deportation (1839), in spite of a Supreme Court decision which would effectively have protected the Cherokee treaty rights.[3] In their new location in Oklahoma, the Cherokees once more managed to reorganize, only to have their autonomy shattered again when the Oklahoma territory achieved statehood. Native communist elites in the Soviet Union have suffered repeated purges, and it would seem that excessive initiative in modernization has been as deadly as excessive foot-dragging; the safe way for native cadres is to confirm continuously the leading role of the Russian big brother by following orders passively. Stalin's deportation of several non-European nations from their ancestral grounds has later been condemned by the Soviets as a violation of socialist legality, but the return to ancestral territory has been denied to one of the nations— namely, to the most developed one, the Crimean Tatars. Jackson's Supreme Court and Stalin's successors have wept, but the USSR and the USA have kept the lands of the Crimean Tatars and the Cherokee nation.

The most fundamental cross-cultural conflict involves the goals of the different societies. The dominant society's goal is to integrate their subject groups into the mainstream, thereby creating unity and reducing problems and the concomitant costs of separateness. The goal of the natives is to maintain their separate identity and to control their own destiny, either by rejecting modernization (when it clashes with valued traditions) or by selectively accepting those innovations perceived to be useful and integrating them into the traditional framework. The period of adjustment to benevolent paternalism usually involves covert hostilities, but there may be occasional outbreaks of rebellion. The dominant society enforces its own rules of conduct by punishing individuals rather than groups. However, if the threat is perceived to be great, the policy may regress to mass action, such as deportation or massacre.

4) **Compromise based on disparity in size.** In the final stage the policies shift to compromise. As a result of long and often bitter learning experiences, the dominant society realizes the futility of achieving complete integration: covert hostility, often in the form of resentful apathy, prolongs the acculturative process and increases costs. Also, the dominant group can afford to be tolerant after the natives have been reduced to a tiny minority. At that stage the disinterested curiosity is no more blocked by fright, and larger segments of the population become sympathetic to preserving and studying the "endangered species." Innocuous culture traits (such as folk costumes, festivities, arts and crafts) begin to be tolerated, encouraged, and even imitated (such as the present Indian jewelry craze in the United States). In some cases this policy even includes toleration of native language, religion, and political organization. Allowing certain cultural differences to persist makes political and economic goals more compatible and attainable. However, the dominant society will never allow complete independence of the minorities (this, of course, is a prediction, not a fact).

The four phases postulated may be of unequal duration, depending on the local geographical and historical circumstances. Often their features are intertwined in long transition periods. In several aspects, the Russian/Soviet pattern shows a phase lag compared to the American pattern. The last wholesale deportations of nations took place in the United States a century ago, but in the USSR only 30 years ago. After a number of treaties and legislative acts an unstable peak was reached in reservation land in 1887, while in the USSR "stable" national areas (stable so far) were delineated around 1930. The American Indians felt the full impact of paternalism before the turn of this century in the West (and much earlier on the East Coast); the Siberian natives felt it most strongly during the Soviet period (and much earlier in the Volga area). In native-language education and literary activity the Soviet record is clearly superior to what the United States has ever accomplished. It could be said that in this respect the Soviet Union already has accomplished a great leap forward into the final compromise phase. But there are recurring Soviet statements about future fusion of nationalities and about Russian being "the second maternal language" of every Soviet citizen, and these make one wonder whether the language concessions are not part of the reluctant temporary concessions of a "phase 4" period, which is to be followed by an attempted phase 5, absorption—perhaps no more than a replay of phases 2 and 3.

CASE STUDY I: THE NAVAJO

Initial attempts at friendly relations with Indians had worn thin by the time the United States government inherited the "Navajo problem" from the Spaniards and Mexicans. Spanish territorial claims were claims in name only, as they had little direct contact with the Navajo (although the Navajo had adopted some of the Spanish material culture through their Pueblo neighbors). The Navajo had acquired horses and sheep by raiding Spanish villages and ranches, and this had had a profound effect on the Navajo culture. They became more mobile, and raiding became a way of life for most of the Navajo bands. These bands were the core of Navajo social organization. They consisted of extended families, some of whom occasionally banded together under a successful "war chief" for purposes of raiding or self-protection. The Navajo never reached a level of tribal organization where any one chief could influence more than a small percentage of the whole population.

When the Americans took over the administration of the territory in 1846, as an outcome of the war with Mexico, the benevolent coexistence ("Phase 1") concept was attempted, using the traditional American treaty-making process; but it failed. Raids continued to the extent that between 1846 and 1850 it is estimated that nearly 8,000 sheep and cattle and 20,000 horses and mules were taken.[4] Direct military intervention ("Phase 2") followed, although peaceful attempts at treaty-making were not abandoned. Fort Defiance was established near the heart of Navajo territory. Another peace treaty was signed by a nearby chief, with the Americans still laboring under the mistaken idea that they were dealing with the chief of all the Navajo. Raids continued under other leaders. Finally, in 1863, Colonel Kit Carson adopted a scorched earth policy. On the one hand, he destroyed the Navajo's sheep and crops, and on the other, he promised no bodily harm, plus food and shelter for those who surrendered themselves at Fort Defiance. Eventually 8,000 starving Navajo were moved to Fort Sumner, where the government gave them rations and where an attempt at culture change was begun ("Phase 3"). However, the Indians made little effort to adopt the white man's ways. A few drifted back to their homeland to join those few who had remained free. After four years the government accepted failure and allowed the remaining Indians to return also. About one-fourth of their former terrain was allocated as a reservation and the Navajo were given rations, sheep, goats, and ploughs to start them on the road to modernization. This was not without setbacks for both cultures. There were occasional raids and the Navajo were to face a long struggle to maintain and expand their reservation in order to sustain an ever-increasing population (12,000 in 1880; 90,000 in 1960; 135,000 in 1973).

The year 1868 can be considered the beginning of the reservation period. The Navajo continually overflowed from the prescribed reservation area to occupy former homelands. This was partially alleviated by enlarging the reservation, but there were frequent and sometimes bloody confrontations with ever-growing numbers of new white settlers. The Navajo herds grew and the peripatetic Navajo clung to his former life styles. Although schools had been promised by the government, the idea met with little enthusiasm from the Navajo. Several years after the first school was established at Fort Defiance, only eleven students were enrolled. In 1887 the Bureau of Indian Affairs (BIA) passed a compulsory school-attendance regulation. This effort at forced acculturation resulted in further strained relations. Children were rounded up and put into boarding schools where they were not allowed to use their native language, had their long hair cut, and generally were not allowed to be Indians. But even as late as 1919, barely one-fifth of the children who were eligible for school were actually attending.[5] Meanwhile, the government introduced improved breeding stock for Navajo herds and also financed irrigation projects in order to build up a viable economy, which was increasingly threatened by a growing population. Management and administration was almost entirely in the hands of the BIA.

The lack of tribal development during this period probably rested on two factors. The first was the aboriginal, and hence traditional, social organization, which did not include any real authority figure. People in such band level societies are slow to accept authority. The second factor was rooted in the economic base of the people: herding forced the bands to disperse ever more widely in order to maintain pasturage for their animals. Overgrazing and overpopulation brought about a need to expand the subsistence pattern and also the need for political centralization.

Meanwhile, public awareness of Navajo problems had developed through civic-minded Anglo-American organizations such as the Indian Rights Association. Hence it was no longer politically expedient for the government to ride roughshod over their Indian wards. In 1923 the BIA handpicked a tribal council by choosing two men from each of five reservation districts. This council was practically power-less and was used by the federal government to make oil leases in the name of the Navajo people. However, it gave the council members the opportunity to express their views. By 1936 the national political mood had shifted under President Roosevelt, and the New Deal was extended to the Indians. Encouraged by a con-gressional act, the tribal council was reorganized along democratic lines. This resulted in a gradual but steady move on the part of the Navajo to administer their own affairs. The role of the BIA became less authoritarian and more advisory.

Another traumatic experience faced by the Navajo illustrates the changing roles of the Navajo Tribal Council and the Bureau. Until the early 1930s, the Navajo had grazed their sheep wherever they could find pasturage. Economic conditions, as a result of over-grazing, had deteriorated. In 1934 the BIA instituted a program of stock reduction aimed at reducing the herds by 40 percent. In order to accomplish balanced land use, the reservation was divided into districts which limited the individual's grazing area. The Navajo resisted and once again the government had to apply force. However, the final outcome resulted in the Navajo Council making and enforcing its own grazing rules in 1956. Navajo autonomy was beginning to bloom.

Several outside factors have contributed to Navajo adaptation to change since the 1930s. World War II not only brought many young men into the armed forces but it also offered off-reservation opportunities for employment. Wage work began to replace traditional subsistence patterns. Natural resources have been exploited both by outsiders and by the Navajo themselves. Oil alone contributed over a million dollars a month to tribal funds in 1960. In addition, there are large royalties from coal, uranium, and natural gas. The government has provided over 88 million dollars for roads, schools, and hospitals. The Tribal Council is now beginning to assert itself more and more in educational policy. Full scholarization was claimed by 1970. The Navajo administer their own college and there is an experimental grade school with an all-Navajo school board.

The curriculum at this school includes native leaders teaching traditional Navajo culture in the Navajo language. Other courses, however, are taught in English. Some school books (by BIA) are bilingual, with the Navajo portion in a modified Latin script. The "Navajo Times" is published by the Navajo, but in English. There are some radio programs in the Navajo language.

CASE STUDY II: THE KHAKASSIANS

The 67,000 Khakassians (1970) speak a Turkic language and live in Central Siberia rather close to the borders of Mongolia and of Kazakhstan. Like the post-contact Navajo, they were originally nomadic herdsmen and hunters, and some of their octagonal houses bear a remarkable similarity to the Navajo hogan. More numerous than the Navajo until 1940, they are now only half as numerous. Their habitat consists of forested mountains and steppes with a severely continental climate not unlike that of the Navajo country.

The Russians first appeared in the Khakass area in the early seventeenth century (simultaneously with the first Navajo-Spanish contacts). They imposed their usual fur tribute relatively peacefully and built outposts. But refusal to pay the tribute developed, and during the latter part of the seventeenth century Russian fortresses were under constant attack. Originally the area was inhabited by people with three totally distinct languages (Turkic, Samoyed and Ket), but during the eighteenth century all other groups became Turkicized. At the same time Russian conquest was completed, and mining prospects started to attract Russian settlers. During the nineteenth century this immigration continued and reached a peak around 1850. Besides being crowded out of some of the land, the Khakass life style apparently was not much altered. They were converted to Greek Orthodoxy, but Shamanist practices lasted well into the twentieth century.

In 1930 a Khakass Autonomous Oblast was created, with an area of 24,000 square miles, about one quarter of Arizona's area and about equal to the combined area of the Navajo reservations (28,000 sq. mi.). Its population (446,000 in 1970) also is about one quarter of Arizona's. In Soviet practice, larger nations (over 100,000) tend to have their own republics, while smaller ethnic groups have autonomous oblasts or (if very sparsely settled) national districts with less cultural autonomy. The Khakassians, who numbered around 60,000 in the 1930's, may seem to have been definitely in the autonomous oblast range. But the Khakassian tribes are linguistically and culturally related to the adjacent Oirots (later renamed the "Altaians"), so that a common autonomous oblast or (since the combined population was over 100,000) republic could have been envisaged and, indeed, was briefly promised by Soviet Russia in 1921.[6] In the early thirties, some Khakassian officials had informal merger talks not only with the Oirots but also with Kazakhs, before they were purged. From this viewpoint, it could be said that the Soviets needlessly splintered populations into units too small to have the critical mass for cultural development, possibly in order to better control and assimilate them. On the other hand, in 1921 there was not even a Khakassian literary language common to all the Khakassian tribesmen. The five tribes fused completely only later, and the dialect differences may have been sufficiently large to make even the construction and popular acceptance of a single Khakassian literary language quite a challenge. Be that as it may, the ultimate decision on merger was not left with the Khakass and Oirot leaders.

The Khakass Autonomous Oblast initially included about equal numbers of Khakassians and of Russians, but a new massive wave of immigration soon gave the Russians an overwhelming majority: from 1926 to 1932 the population almost doubled, from 88,000 to 173,000. Intensive immigration continued until 1959, when the Khakassians (whose number remained stationary, in contrast to the rapid Navajo population growth) formed only 12 percent of the total population of 411,000. In the 1960s the trends changed: between the 1959 and the 1970 censuses the oblast's population increased only 8.5 percent (Arizona: 40 percent), while the number of ethnic Khakassians increased by 18 percent (the Navajo: 45 percent). About 85 percent of Khakassians live in their own Oblast.

The economic development of the Khakass Autonomous Oblast has been considerable since its creation 40 years ago. Coal, iron, molybdenum, copper, gold, and gypsum are being mined. There is some lumber, wool, and food processing industry. Wheat growing seems to be on the increase, to complement the traditional sheep and cattle. In this aspect Khakassia would seem to be more developed than the Navajo reservations. But practically all this development is being carried out by European labor and largely for the benefit of the European population. In this sense, the development of Khakassia should not be compared to that of the Navajo reservations alone but to that of the whole of Northern Arizona. Then extensive development can be seen in both cases, and in both cases it is largely irrelevant to the question of minority treatment and opportunities. By the mid-fifties "many hundreds" of Khakassians were working in industry,[7] at a time when industry was already asserted to be extensively developed and must have occupied many tens of thousands of Russians. Like the Navajo, the Khakassians seem to have remained predominantly rural; a recent Soviet encyclopedia characterizes them as cattle raisers and wheat growers, with no mention of industrial occupations.[8] The industrial development in Khakassia's and Arizona's mines and cities has basically bypassed the native population in both cases. In agrarian development the Khakassian oblast has perhaps—if the cited wheat-growing is extensive—surpassed the Navajo reservation: but then the reservation is quite unsuited to the growing of wheat.

Native-language education may be better developed in Khakassia than among the Navajo. In the mid-fifties, 20 percent of the Oblast's 400 schools used the Khakass language at a time when 15 percent of the population was Khakassian. This indicates that the Khakass-language schools were predominantly small rural schools, but also that most Khakass children probably received a few years of native-language primary schooling. There were 10 seven-year schools and two high schools using the Khakass language, indicating that intermediate-level education was largely either missing or used Russian. In the Oblast pedagogical institute, instruction was in Russian. All this compares rather favorably with the educational opportunities the Navajo had, in the 1950's, either in their own language or in English. The educational level of the Khakassians can be expected to have risen considerably since then, in conformity with the general Soviet pattern. But the trend in the USSR also has been toward less national language and more Russian instruction for smaller nationalities; we do not know whether Khakass-language primary schooling has been maintained. However, there does not seem to be any crippling loss of national identity or language; the total number of Khakassians increased by 18 percent between the 1959 and 1970 censuses (compared to a 13 percent increase in the number of

Russians in the Soviet Union as a whole, and about 8 percent in the Khakass AO). The percentage of those Khakassians who considered Khakass language as their main language remained well over 80 percent, and 35 percent of these did not consider themselves fluent in Russian. (About 40 percent of the Navajo are not fluent in English.)

At the start (1930) of the new Khakassian literary language, Latin script was used. As in many Soviet areas, a switch to the Russian alphabet was ordered in 1939. In 1970, 13 books and booklets were published, with a total of 19,000 copies. Of these, 11 (with 14,000 copies) were originally written in Khakass; the remainder were translations.[9] A Khakass-language newspaper also existed, apparently.

Although actual decision-making in Khakassia is predominantly in Russian hands (largely due their numerical and educational superiority), some ceremonial top jobs are most likely reserved for Khakassians, in line with USSR-wide practice. The five deputies sent by the Autonomous Oblast to the USSR Supreme Soviet also are likely to include a couple of Khakassians. While the role of these deputies is rather passive, one can imagine what moral boost to the Navajo identity it would be if there were a Navajo even among the back-benchers in the U.S. Congress (where possible Indian participation was last considered in 1778!).

RESERVATION VERSUS AUTONOMOUS OBLAST

There is a major difference between the criteria used to delineate the U.S. reservations and the Soviet Autonomous Oblasts (and Autonomous and Union Republics, and National Districts).

The reservations represent areas that are effectively inhabited by Indians, where white settlement is restricted (except in case of long-term land leasing); thus, reservations tend to be small and scattered, with the same or related people often cut into several non-contiguous reservations. Indians seeking city jobs are obliged to leave the reservation. The disadvantage of this system for the development of a viable modernized culture is the fractionalization of tribes and the loss of tribal and linguistic identity of those who go into the white man's world; an appreciable fraction of the tribe members live outside the reservation. The advantage is that within reservations Indians have the absolute majority and have been encouraged to dominate in local decision-making. The reservations have taken advantage of this in varying degrees. However, decisions are sometimes subject to BIA approval, especially in cases of land leasing.

In contrast, the Soviet national republics, oblasts, and districts include the whole area inhabited by a given nation, along with numerous Russians who often form the majority of the national area's population. The disadvantage of this system for development of a viable modernized culture is that the native population is a minority in its (supposedly) own country and is outweighed even in decisional areas left to local control. The advantage is that nearly all Khakassians, say, are included in the same territory that bears their name, and this fosters a common identity for all dialectal groups and also for those who have gone to the cities. Perhaps even more importantly, the territory is not uniformly rural: it offers "city jobs." While the capital city of Khakassia, Abakan (90,000 inhabitants in 1970), may be as Russian as Flagstaff, Arizona, is Anglo-American, a Khakassian taking a menial job in Abakan still remains mentally in Khakassia, in a city which has (or had, in 1950) a Khakass-language high school with 300 students and which harbors the Oblast government in which a number of ceremonial top jobs go to Khakassians. In contrast, a Navajo going to Flagstaff is an immigrant.

Thus, there are advantages and disadvantages to both the American and the Soviet approaches to the territorial delineation of scattered native areas penetrated by immigrants. Given the force of habit, both the Navajo and the Khakassians might prefer, if given the choice, to maintain their present status—a Navajo might be as horrified at the thought of his present reservation being submerged in a larger Navajo-land controlled by an Anglo majority as a Khakassian might be at the thought of giving up symbolic claim to the industrial city of Abakan and being reduced to isolated rural reservations in the mountains.

TENTATIVE CONCLUSIONS

In sum, it would seem that as far as low-technology native groups are concerned, neither the Russian/Soviet nor the U.S. system has a clear superiority over the other. Conquest methods were rather similar. The U.S. and the tsarist policies may have shown more benign neglect, and the Soviet policies may have shown more well-meant disruption during the paternalist phase. Compared to the United States, life in the Soviet Union is rather highly regimented, with extensive security regarding the basic needs and with heavy suppression of deviation from the officially prescribed norms of behavior. This applies to individuals and also to natural groups. Under conditions of underdevelopment, security may have highest priority, and the Soviets have a comparatively good record in preserving the secular aspects of native cultures and in supplying primary education in the native language. The spiritual aspects of native cultures have been ruthlessly destroyed, in order to instill Marxist values; however, the Soviet record is no worse than the American practice during the Christianization and individualization of the natives. While getting "civilized," many Soviet peoples are being crowded out, and many a smaller group faces imminent oblivion in this sea of immigrants; the American Indians had the same experience, at an earlier date. Modern technology has penetrated the Soviet autonomous republics and oblasts much faster than the American Indian reservations; but most of it is handled by Russians for the Russians, and more-than-symbolical native participation remains to be demonstrated, especially on the level of skilled jobs and decision-making. As far as political nation-building is concerned, the Soviet autonomous republics and oblasts have more outer trappings but less effective native self-government than many of the more organized Indian reservations.

If the Navajo were inside the Soviet Union, they would have a rather large national oblast or even a Navajo autonomous republic, with an Uncle-Tomahawk-type republic president and five to eleven docile deputies in the Moscow Supreme Soviet. But over one half of these deputies would be non-Navajo, because more than one half of the republic's population would be white people. There would be extensive industry, run by the whites. The Navajo would have universal literacy based on a network of Navajo-language grade schools, and there would be state-supported original Navajo literature and a few translations of world classics. But the Navajo would have no say about the exploitation of their territory's mineral wealth, and all Indian dissidents would be buried before they could finish saying "Bury my heart at Wounded Knee."

If the Khakassians were inside the United States, they might have five scattered reservations for the five original tribes, with no common standard literary language and practically no printed publications, except in the conqueror's language. As a group, they would have a low formal political status, and educational facilities would be limited. The paternalistic hand of the BIA would be lighter than that of the Soviets, but still heavy. But they would have some freedom to criticize and protest—in spectacular and ineffective ways.

The choice between the two systems would be hard. If the Navajo or the Khakassians had any choice.

NOTES

[1] Alton S. Donnelly, *The Russian Conquest of Bashkiria 1552-1740: A Case Study in Imperialism* (New Haven: Yale University Press, 1968), pp. 30, 48.

[2] Terence Armstrong, *Russian Settlement in the North* (Cambridge: University Press, 1965), p. 96.

[3] Frances Svensson, *The Ethnics in American Politics: American Indians* (Minneapolis: Burgess Publishing Co., 1973), p. 19.

[4] E. H. Spicer, *Cycles of Conquest* (Tucson: University of Arizona Press, 1962), p. 216.

[5] Lawrence C. Kelly, *The Navajo Indians and Federal Indian Policy* (Tucson: University of Arizona Press, 1968), p. 172.

[6] Walter Kolarz, *The Peoples of the Soviet Far East* (London: George Philip, 1954), p. 174.

[7] M. G. Levin and L. P. Potapov, eds., *The Peoples of Siberia* (Chicago: University Press, 1964), p. 373.

[8] *Eesti Nõukogude Entsüklopeedia*/Estonian Soviet Encyclopedia/ (Tallinn, 1970), Vol. 2, p. 497.

[9] *Petshat' SSR v 1970 godu* (Moscow: Kniga, 1971), p. 11.

PART V

THE CASE OF SOME PERSECUTED MINORITIES

MODERNIZATION, HUMAN RIGHTS, AND JEWISH NATIONALISM IN THE USSR

Zvi Gitelman
The University of Michigan
Ann Arbor, Michigan

Many have assumed that there exists a worldwide long-term secular trend whereby even larger ethnic groups are constituted, eventually reaching the point where they begin to merge with each other. Projecting such a trend, one arrives at the conclusion that the number of ethnic groups will decrease, since particularistic ethnic consciousnesses tend to fade and a more universal consciousness begins to dominate the minds of men. Some have merged "is" and "ought" and have seen this kind of development not only as ineluctable but also as desirable. Nationalism is viewed as an evil force, dividing men from each other, and internationalism, which is presumed to lessen conflict and promote understanding, is assumed to depend on the loss of parochial national identities. This secular trend is associated with the process of "modernization," another concept that has frequently been presented as an objective process but that has been burdened with subjective connotation.

This general view, widely accepted in Western liberal thought, at least until recently, is also consonant with the outlook of Karl Marx and his followers. Marx saw nations as the transient phenomena of the capitalist historical epoch and fully expected the consciousness of nation and ethnic group to fade as the consciousness of class rose to preeminence. The injustices of this world were economic and class-determined and would be corrected by revolutionary political means. If there existed ethnic tensions and national prejudices, these would be eradicated when their root cause, which lay in the material realm and the manipulation of unconscious proletarians by capitalist exploiters, would be appreciated and eventually eliminated. While Rosa Luxemburg persisted in a literal adherence to this view, the political environment in which Lenin operated made a greater impact on his tactical program, and by 1913 he had come to the realization that national sentiment might well persist even after a political revolution had done away with the capitalist order. The behavior of the European proletariat during World War One, when only a minority adhered to the orthodox socialist interpretation that the war was an internal dispute of the capitalist-imperialists, shocked socialists into recognizing the power of national sentiment and identification. Nevertheless, Soviet Marxists have persisted to this day in adhering to the thesis that in the long run there is bound to be an amalgamation of nations and nationalities. It may be true that the long run has turned out to be surprisingly long, but the theory still holds that as time goes on in socialist societies different ethnic groups "draw closer together," and this rapprochement should eventuate into the merger of one group into another. The Soviets differentiate between the process of *sblizhenie*, or the drawing closer of peoples, and *sliianie*, their eventual amalgamation into a homogeneous entity. *Sblizhenie* is said to describe ongoing processes in the Soviet Union and is hailed as a progressive force, while *sliianie* is acknowledged to be a future stage of higher development. The modernization of the USSR has been accompanied by *sblizhenie*, as the difference between the more and less modernized peoples has been progressively reduced, while *sliianie* will be achieved, perhaps not all at once, with the further development of Soviet society.

All of this rests on an assumption made explicit by the Bolsheviks in the early part of the century—namely, that nationalism and ethnic tensions are characteristic only of capitalist societies and that, with the aid of some reeducation and propaganda, the political revolution should automatically solve whatever "national questions" may exist. The assumption derives from a more basic one, which is that social and political phenomena are explicable in materialist, class terms. A materialist conception of history and society cannot accept the view that nationalism has existence independent of class and of a particular economic system. It cannot agree with the contention that in discussing the concept of "nations" or nationalism we deal with

> undefined and undefinable subjects. . . . We . . . are dealing with the shadowy realm of collective psychology, which eludes rational consciousness. Every attempted definition of "the nation," the "nationalist idea," or "national feeling" ends in mysticism or mystifications; it can only be expressed in images and symbols.[1]

Stalin's attempt to define a nation, in the course of which he ruled that the Jews were not one, has raised serious theoretical and practical problems for Soviet and other socialist policy makers and theorists. One Polish sociologist has explicitly rejected the Stalinist formula and has concluded that "if we do not want to arrive at a purely arbitrary, synthetic formula but an analytic one, we have to deal with highly varied social phenomena which cannot be comprehended within a unified and identical definition."[2] Soviet scholars, too, have raised doubts about Stalin's definition,[3] and Hugh Seton-Watson, no stranger to nationality problems, concludes that "a nation exists when an active and fairly numerous section of its members are convinced that it exists. Not external objective characteristics, but subjective conviction is the decisive factor."[4] Denying a group the status of a nation raises some questions of human rights, since national status confers certain rights and privileges upon a group that is defined as a nation. Because the Jews are denied national status in the USSR, they are denied some of the symbols of nationhood—a parliament, a flag, a government—as well as some of the practical cultural benefits accruing to those with nation status. When Jews argue that they are entitled to national rights since they perceive of themselves as members of a nation, they are raising an issue of individual and group rights.

That Jews in the USSR should raise such issues in a militant and dramatic way came as a great surprise not only to Soviet officials but also to people outside the Soviet Union. After all, the Jews seemed to bear out the general thesis of a secular trend to assimilation and merger with other peoples. The results of the 1970 census showed that the number of Jews had declined from 2,268,000 to 2,151,000 (94.4 percent of the 1959 figure), and this at a time when the overall Soviet population had increased by 15.8 percent. Of the 91 nationalities (plus "others") for whom 1970 census data were reported, only Jews, Mordovians, Karelians, Poles, Finns, Czechs, and Slovaks declined in number.[5] Moreover, among all Soviet nationalities Jews display the greatest degree of linguistic assimilation. While in 1970 93.9 percent of the Soviet population gave their mother tongue as that of their nationality, only 17.7 percent of the Jews listed a Jewish language (mainly Yiddish) as their mother tongue (in 1926 71.9 percent and in 1959 21.5 percent of the Jews had listed a Jewish language as their mother tongue).[6] In an earlier period, Soviet analysts as well as others would have concluded that this linguistic assimilation could be taken as an indicator of general loss of national identity. But as the Soviet sociologist I. Kon notes, "not every linguistic assimilation is voluntary." He goes on to assert that "even complete linguistic assimilation . . . the loss of one's native tongue . . . is not tantamount to the disappearance of other ethnic differences. A person may speak the language of the majority and yet consider himself a member of the national minority."[7] Another Soviet scholar specifically mentions the Jews when he points out that "even while losing the mother tongue and even cultural characteristics national consciousness is often preserved (Russianized Germans and Jews, Tatarified Bashkirs)."[8] Nevertheless, it is generally assumed that a necessary step on the long road to amalgamation is taken when a nation ceases to use its own language and adopts that of another. The Jews in the USSR seem to have taken a longer step in this direction than any other nationality.

SOVIET MODERNIZATION AND THE DECLINE IN JEWISH NATIONAL CONSCIOUSNESS

The thesis that economic and cultural modernization would be accompanied by the decline of national consciousness and the drawing together of nations seems to have been confirmed by the Jewish experience in the USSR during the 1920's and the 1930's. In the 1920's the Bolsheviks, retreating somewhat from their earlier rejection of the idea of a Jewish nation, tried to reach the Yiddish-speaking majority of the Soviet Jewish population and imbue them with the ideals and ideology of Bolshevism. In line with this aim, and in accordance with the general Soviet policy of the 1920's of "socialist in content, national in form," the Party's Jewish Sections conducted political, cultural, and social activity among the Jews, using the Yiddish language as the medium of communication.[9] This policy of *korenizatsiia*, or "nativization," led to the establishment of Party cells, schools, trade union cells, courts, and artisanal cooperatives operating in Yiddish. Indeed, whole regions were established where Yiddish was the official language, and some Jewish activists explicitly stated that in due course efforts to settle Jews in compact masses on the land would gain for the Jews the attributes of a nation: Jews would have a recognized, definable territory within the boundaries of the USSR, and because of compact settlement and the existence of Yiddish language institutions within it, they would share a common language. This policy offered the Jews the possibility of being politically integrated into the Soviet system while continuing to maintain, and indeed enhance, their ethnic identity and distinctiveness. It was recognized that there were national cultural rights, apart from freedom from persecution, that Jews should enjoy, even though long-term developments would make those rights superfluous.

By and large, the Jewish population was not enthusiastic about this combination of political integration and ethnic maintenance. The kind of ethnic maintenance offered did not appeal to the traditional elements of the Jewish community, since the Party explicitly and militantly rejected the Jewish religion, Hebrew culture, and Zionist ideology, and attempted to substitute a secular Yiddish culture whose content was "socialist." Many saw this as an artificial product, a foreign body grafted on to Jewish culture, having little in common with that culture, except the externality of language. Russian culture was generally regarded as a "higher" culture than Yiddish, and it was recognized that Russian was the key to economic and cultural advancement. Therefore, Russian culture attracted precisely those elements most interested in modernization and self-development, as well as the development of Soviet society as a whole. Those Jews who were interested in maintaining the ethnic heritage and identity were those who valued traditional culture and who were unwilling to accept Soviet substitutes for it, even if this meant that they would be politically and socially unintegrated into the mainstream of Soviet society and left in the backwaters of the *shtetl* culture while other Jews were advancing into the forefront of modern, technological culture.

These attitudes were manifested in a variety of forms. While by 1930 there were 1,000 Yiddish language schools in the USSR, and almost half of all Jewish children attending schools in the Belorussian and Ukrainian Republics were enrolled in Yiddish schools, in the RSFSR—a republic opened to the Jews only in 1917 and one which tended to attract the upwardly mobile to its industries, academies, and institutions—only 16.8 percent of Jewish school children were enrolled in Yiddish schools.[10] Jewish parents, even in Belorussia and the Ukraine, the former Pale areas, apparently preferred to send their children to Russian schools, and a leading Jewish activist criticized "the tendency [of cultural activists] to drag all Jewish children into Yiddish schools by force. . . Gross distortions occurred in some cities where people who do not need Yiddish schools were forced—by use of terror—to attend them."[11] A visitor to the Ukraine found that Jewish children in a Yiddish school preferred to use Russian texts. He explained this by the fact that "Russian is the language of a culture stronger than the secular non-Hebrew culture conveyed by the Yiddish language in the Soviet Union; Russian is also the language spoken in Moscow and generally throughout the USSR; and all those pupils, and parents, too, who ever expect to move freely about the Union must have complete mastery of the Russian language."[12] The prestige of Russian, as well as its practical value, was rated as much higher than that of Yiddish. In 1927 36.5 percent of all Jewish members of the Communist Party gave Yiddish as their mother tongue, but only 4.4 percent conducted their work in Yiddish.[13] Even some activists of the Jewish Sections spoke Russian among themselves and sent their children to Russian schools. Among Jewish workers, there was an admiration for things Russian and a disdain for Yiddish. A Yiddish newspaper reports: "The Jewish worker does not want to read a [Yiddish] newspaper. He will break his teeth, he will not understand a word, but give him Russian. A Jewish comrade begins to speak in Yiddish at a workers' meeting—they don't want to listen. And when she finishes, they translate her [speech] even though you couldn't find a non-Jew here for love or money."[14]

This attitude toward Yiddish grew out of the association of Yiddish with the backward *shtetl* and out of the desire to acquire Russian culture as a prerequisite to social mobility. "A meeting of the transport workers. One comrade, a porter, takes the floor and comes out categorically against any work in Yiddish. When challenged, he answered: the matter is quite simple. . . For many years I have carried hundreds of pounds on my back day in and day out. Now I want to learn some Russian and become a *kontorshchik* [office worker]."[15]

Objective developments, as well as subjective desires, seemed to be leading the Jews to *sblizhenie* and even *sliianie*. Marriages of Jews to non-Jews increased in the Ukraine and Belorussia, and in the RSFSR well over 20 percent of Jews intermarried in the late 1920's.[16] By 1926 82.4 percent of the Jewish population was considered urban, and a Soviet Jewish sociologist, Yankl Kanton, remarked that "the large city creates certain conditions for assimilatory processes and certain segments of the Jewish population become assimilated."[17] A Soviet Jewish demographer concluded that assimilation among Jews was not "a gradual fading away, but . . . a massive development of the post-war period." He pointed out that the Jewish birth rate, "one of the basic elements of the concept of 'national growth,' " was declining.[18] These trends were accelerated in the 1930's when "socialist content" gained the upper hand over "national form." The intensive collectivization-industrialization campaigns, the strategic elements of the USSR's drive toward modernization, could not brook such diversions of energy and attention as the development of national cultures, and the entire population was mobilized in the drive to achieve rapid modernization. Political integration was no longer as compatible with ethnic pluralism as it had been in the previous decade. The interpretation of "proletarian internationalism" was that the common socialist aim of all the nationalities was far more important than the secondary cultural characteristics which might distinguish among them. Jews, like others, were gripped by enthusiasm for the great tasks of industrialization and modernization which Stalin had set for them, and they could not worry about such petty matters as Yiddish culture and Jewish identity. The spirit of "internationalism" seems to have pervaded much of the Jewish population, which welcomed the de-emphasis of ethnic identification as a means of reducing anti-Semitism and making it possible for the Jew to be fully accepted into Soviet society. "This generation thought that antisemitism had been done away with forever, like all forms of oppression and injustice, that national differences were a survival of capitalism, and to follow national traditions was absurd and reactionary."[19] Mixed marriages became more frequent. The social structure of the Jewish population changed dramatically, with a rise in the proportion of workers and white collar employees, the emergence of an educated professional class, and the decline of the petty traders and the unemployed of the *shtetl*, as well as the disappearance of the traditional community and its functionaries and institutions. Jews seemed to be in the forefront of the drive toward the supra-national future. They were in the vanguard of the urban proletariat and intelligentsia, of those who were eradicating the differences among peoples and who were leading the way to the amalgamation of all peoples into one large socialist family. At the same time, their human rights were being safeguarded as they had never been under the tsars, for discrimination and anti-Semitism were illegal, and all cultural, political, economic, and social opportunities seemed to be open to the Jews.

MODERNIZATION AND ACCULTURATION
WITHOUT ASSIMILATION

Today it is clear that the trends of the 1920's and 1930's have been halted, and even reversed, and the notion that there is a linear progression toward diminishing ethnic prejudices and assimilation has proved false. National consciousness has not been eradicated, and in the case of many Jews, has been aroused only recently. The stimuli for such consciousness are various, but their cumulative effect has resulted in the feeling on the part of many that their "Jewish problem" has not been solved and, indeed, cannot be solved within the Soviet system. This conviction has been brought about by developments within and without Soviet society.

World War II was the first great shock for those who were well on their way to assimilation. The Jewish tragedy and Soviet attempts to minimize or ignore it shocked some into a Jewish consciousness which they could express fully only years later. As Meir Gelfond, a leader of the movement to emigrate to Israel, said: "We arrived at the idea [of Zionism] ourselves, that Jews should live in a country of their own. This was our conclusion after we learned what happened under Hitler."[20] When the Soviet poetess Margarita Aliger asked her mother why she had kept the fact of her Jewish origin from her, and why it was left to Hitler to tell her that she was Jewish, she was expressing the feelings of many Soviet Jews. One of the founders of the *aliyah* (emigration to Israel) movement in Kharkov stated: "My national conscience was awakened in 1942-43 because of the war, Hitler, and genocide. Already at the age of 16, in 1944, together with a young Riga girl I had met and with whom I talked about Palestine, I tried to organize youth groups."[21]

In 1939-40 the USSR incorporated the Baltic republics, Eastern Poland, and Bessarabia-Bukovina, with over a million Jews from these areas now absorbed into the Soviet population. Many of them retained allegiance to Jewish traditions, Hebraic culture, and Zionist ideology. These "zapadniki" revived national consciousness among Soviet Jews and enabled them to reestablish contact with the mainstream of world Jewry. In many instances the newcomers taught Soviet Jews Hebrew, Zionism, and the Jewish religion.[22] It is not accidental that the emigration movement of the 1960's began in the Baltic cities of Riga and Vilnius and that it is particularly strong in such places as Kishinev and Chernovtsy. From these areas the movement spread eastward into the older areas of the USSR, with the "zapadniki" continuing to act as teachers and leaders.

A third stimulus to the reawakening of national consciousness was the establishment of the state of Israel in 1948. Coming on the heels of the holocaust, the establishment of the Jewish state, initially supported and encouraged by the USSR, fired the imagination of many Jews in the Soviet Union, some of whom believed that free emigration to Israel would now be permitted.[23] The well-known spontaneous reception given to Golda Meyerson (Meir), Israel's first ambassador to Moscow, attests to the importance an independent Jewish state had for Soviet Jews.

While anti-Semitism had surfaced in the 1930's in the USSR and had emerged quite clearly in the course of World War II, its greatest impact came during the "black years," 1948-1952. While it could have been argued that anti-Semitism was a purely social phenomenon unsanctioned by the government, by 1948 it became clear that it was also official policy. The last vestiges of Jewish culture were erased, the leading figures of that culture arrested and then liquidated, and the anti-Semitic campaign threatened the entire Jewish population when the battle against "cosmopolitanism," climaxed by the "doctor's plot" of 1952, was being waged.[24] The events of those years, including the spontaneous hostility displayed toward Jews by ordinary Soviet citizens, led some to try to hide their national identity to solve their "Jewish problem" by assimilating, while others concluded that assimilation was a chimera and yet to be a Jew in the USSR was intolerable. The trial of Adolf Eichmann in 1960 aroused memories of the holocaust and instructed a younger generation in some of the history of that period. According to one of the *aliyah* movement's activists in Riga, "The news made a strong impression in the Soviet Union" and led to the first organized public actions by Jews in Latvia.[25]

As in other Jewish communities, the Arab-Israeli war of 1967 and its aftermath aroused among many Soviet Jews a realization of how personally catastrophic an Israeli defeat would be, and later, a feeling of relief and pride at the Israeli victory. Most crucial was the realization that the Soviet government supported those forces whose declared intention it was to destroy the Israeli state and its inhabitants.

> Until June, 1967, Soviet Jews had illusions about co-existence with the regime, despite the fact that it wanted to spiritually destroy the Jews. But suddenly they realized that the Soviet government identifies itself with those who wish to destroy the Jewish state, the sole hope left for the Jewish people. Russia spat on the Jewish people "and then we knew that we would never be able to live under such a regime."[26]

Following the war Soviet propaganda became so shrill and one-sided that it could not but arouse the attention of the most indifferent Jew, especially as it began to interchange the terms "Zionist" and "Jew" rather freely. As cartoons, articles, books, and broadcasts continued to deal with the "international Zionist danger," Jews took a greater interest in the entire subject and began to draw their own conclusions. A young engineer, now in Israel, reports that until 1967 he had been completely indifferent to Israel and Zionism. But Soviet propaganda made him wonder at "the internal contradictions and exaggerations of this propaganda. The authors seemed to be accusing me of being a Jew. So I began to be interested in Soviet Middle Eastern policy."[27] The first Leningrad trial in November 1970 aroused memories of the late Stalinist period and forced still others to ponder the meaning of being a Jew in the USSR.

The Soviet Jew finds himself in a permanent identity crisis. Soviet policies have made it impossible for Jews to express themselves culturally as Jews, and so they have become thoroughly acculturated into Russian culture, being producers as well as consumers of that culture. At the same time, Soviet society has refused to allow the Jew to assimilate into it, while the government has set up legal barriers to the assimilation of the Jews. Soviet Jews are acculturated—they have adopted the culture of another group, mainly the Russians—but they are not assimilated—they have not adopted that other group's culture to such an extent that they no longer have any characteristics identifying them with their former culture and no longer have loyalties to it.[28] Most Soviet Jews consider themselves culturally Russian.

However, since their internal passports designate them as Jews, and since the surrounding society tends to regard them as Jews rather than Russians, they are in the uncomfortable position of being culturally Russian but legally and socially Jewish. This split identity creates an internal dissonance whose resolution can be achieved by becoming either wholly Jewish or wholly Russian. Either Jews assimilate and become Russian in every sense, or they change their cultural and social identities and attempt to leave for the Jewish homeland, concluding that the position of the Jew in the USSR is destined to remain acculturation without assimilation, that *sblizhenie* for them means simply the loss of their culture, while *sliianie* is nowhere to be seen on the horizon. Naturally, this identity crisis is solved differently by different people, and for some it is not even felt. Larissa Bogoraz-Daniel tells how until the age of eight she was totally unaware of her nationality, but that during and immediately after the war she felt keenly that she was Jewish. During the "black years," "Jews of my generation began to choose their path. A minority tried to convince themselves that they, or at least their children, were Russians. Others reacted in the opposite way—they insisted on being identified as Jews, and this was an act of defiance." Bogoraz-Daniel herself says that "Unfortunately, I do not see myself as a Jew" because despite her "genetic ties" to the Jewish people her culture is Russian. "Still and all I am not a Russian. Today I am a stranger in this land . . . I now have the sad feeling in my heart that I have no homeland, no nation, no suitable environment. And I am not alone in this."[29]

Those who decided that their homeland is in Israel constituted a heterogeneous group, with no unifying program or organizational structure. As Zilberberg says, "Those taking part in the movement for emigration to Israel were united and guided by one thing alone—the desire to leave."[30] There were differences of opinion on the tactics to be used in order to achieve the common aim. Most people simply went through normal channels, applying—and, where necessary, reapplying—for permission to leave. A small group resorted to illegal means. In between these extremes are those who appealed to Soviet and international authorities and organizations on the grounds of receiving their human rights. There is no doubt that the example of the "Democratic Movement," as Amalrik labels it, had a profound influence especially on this group of Jewish activists. Composed largely, but not exclusively, of Soviet intelligentsia, the very element which was the most "modernized" and hence supposed to be the most highly assimilated, these Jews often had close personal ties with members of the Soviet dissenting community. In fact, some of the Jewish activists had been directly involved in dissent and opposition on general political grounds, but had concluded that the only viable personal solution for them was emigration. To be sure, there were what some called the "old guard" or "traditional" Zionists, who abjured any connection with the Democratic Movement and refused to become involved in criticisms of the Soviet system on general grounds, but even they were directly and profoundly influenced by the tactics of the Democratic Movement—namely, the appeal to fundamental human rights and the direct appeal to the United Nations and its Human Rights Commission. The emphasis was on legal means and the appeals were made to international and national law. Article 13/2 of the Universal Declaration of Human Rights, to which the USSR is a signatory, states that "Everyone has the right to leave any country, including his own, and to return to his country." This was the basis of the argument by *aliyah* activists that they be allowed to leave the USSR and "return" to "their own" original homeland, Israel. The right to leave was reaffirmed and elaborated in a 1963 study by a UN organ, the Sub-Commission on Prevention of Discrimination and Protection of Minorities.[31] Though not widely known in the USSR, the Universal Declaration of Human Rights was studied by Soviet dissenters, including Boris Tsukerman, who was a legal adviser to the unofficial Committee on Human Rights of the Soviet Union (Sakharov, Chalidze, *et al.*) and who became a prominent activist in the *aliyah* movement.[32] The importance of international standards to Soviet Jewish activists is reflected in the fact that of 220 petitions for the right to emigrate to Israel received in the West between 1968 and 1970, 56, or one quarter, were addressed to the United Nations, its officers, and its organs, including the Commission on Human Rights.[33] This is precisely what Soviet dissenters were doing, especially in 1968, which was International Human Rights Year. Though there were points of friction between the Democratic Movement and the *aliyah* movement, there was constant contact and some mutual support. The Soviet Committee on Human Rights, and Andrei Sakharov in particular, have several times called for the recognition of the right of Jews to emigrate, and the Leningrad and Riga trials have been criticized.[34] The well-known organ of the opposition, the *Khronika tekushchikh sobytii*, began in 1969 to report on the Jewish movement and was clearly the inspiration for a number of *samizdat* Jewish publications.[35]

CONCLUSION

It is clear that modernization cannot be equated with the mutual assimilation of nationalities, for it is not modernization in and of itself which determines the fate of a nation, but the specific circumstances in which it finds itself. Soviet Jews shared with others the expectation that the modern age would bring with it a diminution of national differences and that, as different peoples came in contact with each other, understanding would grow and there would be a mutual interpenetration. This has not turned out to be the case; Soviet Jews, like Ukrainians, Crimean Tatars, Balts, and others have found it necessary to assert the human rights granted to them by the Soviet constitution and by international conventions to which the USSR is a signatory. It seems that individual and national rights are not the automatic by-product of modernization, and modernization does not appear to eliminate the need for national rights and the protection of minorities. Insofar as modernization makes international communication more rapid and more effective, it does contribute to worldwide consciousness of human rights and facilitates the struggle for these rights which seemingly must go on even beyond the modern age.

NOTES

[1] Herbert Lüthy, "A Rehabilitation of Nationalism?" in K. A. Jelenski, ed., *History and Hope* (London: Routledge and Kegan Paul, 1962), p. 85.

[2] Jerzy Wiatr, in *Z Pola Walki* IX, 3 (1967), 87.

[3] See the series of "discussion articles on the concept of nation," in *Voprosy istorii* for 1966 and 1967. See also Grey Hodnett, "The Debate over Soviet

Federalism," *Soviet Studies* XVIII, 4 (1967), and his "What's in a Nation," *Problems of Communism* XVI, 5 (September-October, 1967).

[4] *Nationalism New and Old* (Sydney, 1965), p. 3.

[5] Data from the 1970 census are taken from G. M. Maksimov, "Dvizhenie naselenie SSSR (1959-1970 gg.)," *Istoriia SSSR*, No. 5, 1971.

[6] *Ibid.*, pp. 14-15.

[7] I. Kon, "Dialektika razvitiia natsii," *Novyi Mir* No. 13 (1970), p. 145.

[8] I. S. Gurvich, "Nekotorye problemy etnicheskogo razvitiia narodov SSSR," *Sovetskaia Etnografiia* No. 5 (1967), p. 63.

[9] On the Jewish Sections of the Party, see my *Jewish Nationality and Soviet Politics* (Princeton: Princeton University Press, 1972).

[10] Sh. Klitenik, *Kultur arbet tsvishn di yidishe arbetndike inem Ratnfarband* (Moscow-Kharkov-Minsk: Tsentrfarlag, 1931), p. 9.

[11] M. Kiper, "Oifgabn in der kultur-oifkler arbet," *Shtern* June 28, 1927.

[12] Harold R. Weinstein, "Language and Education in the Soviet Ukraine," *The Slavonic Yearbook*, Vol. XX of *The Slavonic and East European Review* (1941), p. 138.

[13] A. Brakhman and Y. Zhiv, eds., *Yidn in FSSR* (Moscow-Kharkov-Minsk: Tsentrfarlag, 1930), p. 107.

[14] *Der Veker*, February 16, 1923. For other examples of workers' hostility to Yiddish, see *Der Odeser Arbeter*, January 6, 1930, and Menakhem Nadl, "Sher un eizn," *Asufot*, No. 2 (15) (November 1971), p. 81.

[15] *Der Emes*, April 16, 1924.

[16] For data from the Ukraine, see I. I. Veitsblit, *Di dinamik fun der Yidisher bafelkerung in Ukraine far di yorn 1897-1926* (Kharkov: Literatur un Kunst, 1930), p. 50. The RSFSR data is in *Natsional'naia politika VKP (b)* (Moscow: Gospolitizdat, 1930), p. 41.

[17] *Di Yidishe bafelkerung in Ukraine* (Kharkov: Melukhe Farlag, 1929), p. 33. On urbanization and assimilation, see Robert Le Vine, "Political Socialization and Culture Change," in Clifford Geertz, ed., *Old Societies and New States* (New York: The Free Press, 1963), pp. 284-285.

[18] Veitsblit, p. 53.

[19] Ilya Zilberberg, "From Russia to Israel: A Personal Case-History," *Soviet Jewish Affairs* No. 3 (May 1972), p. 44.

[20] Dr. Meir Gelfond in *Haaretz*, April 9, 1971.

[21] Quoted in *Jews in Eastern Europe* V, 1 (April 1972), pp. 23-24.

[22] Gelfond describes this in "Tiurmenye vstrechi," *Sion* No. 1, 1972, pp. 11-19.

[23] See, for example, Mikhael Margulis, "Tokhnit Batum shel shlosha studentim," *Maariv*, January 28, 1972, p. 30.

[24] See Yehoshua A. Gilboa, *The Black Years of Soviet Jewry* (Boston: Little, Brown, 1971). On the widespread fear among Soviet Jews at this time, see "Ben Khorin," *Mah Koreh Sham* (Tel Aviv: Am Oved, 1970).

[25] M. Perakh, "Pepel Rumbuli probudil serdtsa zhivykh," *Nasha strana*, November 25, 1971.

[26] David Giladi, summarizing statements by Soviet immigrants to Israel at the World Zionist Congress, in *Haaretz*, January 25, 1972.

[27] Ephraim Feinblum, quoted in *Jews in Eastern Europe, op. cit.*, p. 25.

[28] On the difference between acculturation and assimilation, see Arnold Rose, *Sociology: The Study of Human Relations* (New York, 1956), pp. 557-558.

[29] From a *samizdat* pamphlet, "The Jews in the Soviet Union," quoted in *Maariv*, March 23, 1973.

[30] Zilberberg, p. 53.

[31] For details, see William Korey, *The Soviet Cage: Anti-Semitism in Russia* (New York: Viking, 1973), pp. 184-190.

[32] *Ibid.*, p. 346, n. 6. For examples, see Letter from 59 Moscow Jews in *Exodus* No. 4 (Institute of Jewish Affairs, London, June 1971); Letter of 18 Georgian Jewish families in *Bulletin on Soviet and East European Jewish Affairs*, No. 4 (December 1969); and *Iskhod* (Exodus), Nos. 1 and 2 in *Possev*, Seventh Special Issue, March 1971.

[33] *Ibid.*

[34] For full documentation, see *ibid.*, chapter 14.

[35] See Peter Reddaway, ed., *Uncensored Russia* (New York: American Heritage Press, 1972), ch. 15.

THE STRUGGLE OF THE CRIMEAN TATARS*

Peter J. Potichnyj
McMaster University
Hamilton, Ontario, Canada

The twentieth Party Congress, and especially Khrushchev's famous secret speech, are considered by many to be directly responsible for the vigor with which the non-Russian people of the Soviet Union have begun to voice their accumulated resentment against the injustices suffered at the hands of Great-Russian chauvinists. Of all the non-Russian groups, the Crimean Tatars have organized the most vigorous protest—a protest supported by the fact that other deported nationalities have been rehabilitated, permitted to return to their former territories, and granted once again autonomous status within the Soviet federation.[1]

Because of the publicity which surrounded the deportation, the partial rehabilitation, and the present condition of the Crimean Tatars, it is sometimes forgotten that the story of their suffering began long before Stalin, Khrushchev, and Brezhnev came on the scene. As Walter Kolarz observed, "the liquidation of the Crimean Tatars as an ethnic group and their removal from their Crimean homeland by the Soviet government was but the last act of a long process which had started when the Empress Catherine II established a Russian Protectorate over the Crimea in 1774 and annexed it in 1783."[2] Thus, in order to place the struggle of the Crimean Tatars in proper perspective, one must recall briefly the history of this unfortunate and persecuted nationality.

RUSSIAN-TATAR RELATIONS

The tragedy of the Crimean Tatars began immediately upon their conquest by the Russians. The country which these people had built and which had flourished from the fifteenth century onward began to decline rapidly because of the

---

*Reprinted with the kind permission of the *Canadian Slavonic Papers* (Vol. XVII, Nos. 2 and 3, 1975).

gradual exodus of the Tatars. Between 1784 and 1790, out of a total population of
one million, about 300,000 Tatars left the peninsula for Turkey.[3] This voluntary
emigration was supplemented by forcible transfers instituted by the Russian government under the pretext of defense requirements. Thus, a large number of native
inhabitants were transferred from the sea coast or strategically important positions where they lived to other areas in the interior of the Crimean peninsula where
they could be better controlled. The years 1807 to 1811, the time of the Russo-
Turkish war, witnessed a further outflow of the Crimean Tatar population. In the
years 1859 to 1863, during and after the Crimean War, still another large emigration took place.[4] This large exodus of Tatars from the Crimean peninsula reduced
the native population to 34.1 percent of the total by 1897.[5]

The Tatar migration was a direct result of the oppressive rule the Russian
authorities had exercised over the Tatars from the time of the annexation of their
peninsula to the period immediately preceding and following the Crimean War.
It was at that time the idea arose of removing the Tatars altogether from the
Crimea. Robert Conquest quotes an article from volume XXXV of the 1937 edition of the *Bol'shaia Sovetskaia Entsiklopedia* stating that "in the autumn of 1854
there followed a decree of the Minister of War to the effect that the Emperor has
ordered all inhabitants of the Muslim faith living in the coastal area to be removed
from the coast into inland provinces."[6] This policy was suggested by Prince
Menshikov, the Commander-in-Chief of the Russian military. The government
deemed it too difficult an undertaking, and so only the inhabitants of several
villages were forcibly removed to the Kursk region.[7]

On the other hand, however, because of its mild climate and long-established
horticultural traditions, it was easier for the tsarist administration to promote migration to the Crimea. The new settlers who came included Russians, Ukrainians, Jews,
Germans, as well as Bulgarians, Czechs and even Estonians. Although strongly
supported by the government, this colonization effort did not have a serious impact
until the end of the nineteenth century.

By 1917 only slightly over one-fourth of the total population of the peninsula were Crimean Tatars. Russians accounted for nearly 50 percent, while
Ukrainians and other nationalities made up the remaining 25 percent.[8] Between
1926 and 1936 the proportion of Tatars in the Crimea was further reduced to
23.1 percent.[9] In 1936 Russians composed 43.5 percent and Ukrainians 10 percent
of the population of the Crimean A.S.S.R.,[10] while other large groups included
the Jews (7.4 percent) and the Germans (5.7 percent). In short, according to the
first edition of the *Bol'shaia Sovetskaia Entsiklopedia*, the Tatars comprised only
202,000 of the total 875,000 inhabitants of the autonomous republic.[11] More
recent population changes are discussed below.

THE REVOLUTION OF 1917 AND THE
STRUGGLE FOR NATIONHOOD

The fall of the Russian Empire raised hopes among the Crimean Tatars of
regaining a measure of self-government. This objective, however, was not easily
achieved in the confused situation of World War I and the Revolution. The strategic
position of the Crimea made it a battleground for nationalist Tatars, Germans,
Bolsheviks, the Ukrainian governments in Kiev, and the White Russian armies. On

5 May 1917 a "National Assembly" at Simferopol proclaimed the autonomy of the Crimean Tatars. In October, a *Kurultai* (assembly) proclaimed a Crimean Democratic Republic. This creation, however, was rapidly suppressed by the communists, and Chlebiev, its president, was shot in February 1918. Under the well-known Hungarian Communist Bela Kun, a Crimean Revolutionary Committee instituted a reign of terror, which was met by a determined partisan movement. Lenin opposed this policy and in 1921 an amnesty was proclaimed.[12] Between 1917 and 1920 it was uncertain whether the Crimea would be incorporated with the Ukraine or the Russian Republic. The various Ukrainian national governments asserted their claims to the Crimea, and even communist Ukrainian leaders were loathe to relinquish Ukrainian demands, if only because of their concern with maintaining the overall territorial integrity of the Ukraine.[13] From the standpoint of the Crimean Tatars, however, there were distinct advantages associated with not being subordinated to the Ukrainian Republic. Under the conditions existing at the time, more autonomy was to be enjoyed from a government located afar. At the same time, inclusion of the Crimea within the Russian Republic facilitated direct Russian control over the northern coast of the Black Sea and thus over the Ukraine. Hence, Lenin advanced both Tatar and Russian interests when he insisted, against the wishes of local communists, on the establishment of the Crimean Autonomous Soviet Socialist Republic within the Russian Federation.[14] There was reason, therefore, for the Crimean Tatars to consider Lenin a benefactor. "This administrative structure provided the Tatars especially in the twenties, with a good measure of cultural-linguistic autonomy."[15]

However, collectivization and the overall shift in the Soviet nationality policy that took place in the late 1920's destroyed the promising national renaissance of the Crimean Tatars (which grew out of an important pre-revolutionary Tatar modernizing nationalist movement). Waves of purges struck the Crimean national leaders. As early as 1928 Veli Ibrahim, the top Crimean leader, was executed for "bourgeois nationalism," and several thousand Crimean Tatars were also executed or deported.[16] In the following years Soviet authorities continued a policy of repression and intimidation. As one eyewitness relates, during the forced collectivization of 1929-1930 some 30,000 to 40,000 Crimean Tatars were deported either to the Urals or to Siberia, where many of them perished.[17] Many thousands more died during the famine of 1931-1934, which resulted from the collectivization of agriculture.[18] Crimean political leaders protested, but in vain. Mehmed Kubay, who replaced Veli Ibrahim, openly stated that "Moscow destroys the Republic of Crimea, carries away all its natural riches without giving bread to the starving population of the peninsula."[19] For this act he was removed, as was his successor Ilias Tarakhan; and the head of government, Ibrahim Samedin, fell to the Yezhov mass terror of 1936-1938.

Throughout the late thirties several campaigns were aimed at destroying "the roots of nationalism" among the Tatar's population, resulting in mass purges among scientists, educators, and writers.[20] This destruction of native cultural and political leaders was followed, here as elsewhere in non-Russian areas, by a policy of radical Russification. In 1938 the Cyrillic alphabet was introduced and a large part of Crimean Tatar literature was declared non-proletarian and non-Soviet. All of these undertakings were accompanied by large numbers of victims among the Crimean Tatars. It is hardly surprising, therefore, that news of the outbreak of war with Germany and the arrival of German forces in the Crimea at the beginning of November 1941 was openly welcomed by many Tatars—although they were not alone in this respect.

COLLABORATION

As Walter Kolarz has correctly pointed out, it is indeed "quite difficult to say to what extent the Crimean Tatars remained loyal to the Soviet regime and to what extent they betrayed it when living under German occupation."[21] Because the deportation of Crimean Tatars from the peninsula and the liquidation of the Crimean Tatar A.S.S.R. was justified on the grounds of collective disloyalty, it is necessary to address this problem directly. As stated, grounds for collaboration existed from the outset.

Contemporary Crimean Tatar leaders admit that approximately 0.5 percent of the population was involved in anti-Soviet activities.[22] Edige Kirimal talks in his book about six battalions of guard units which were organized at the beginning of 1942 from volunteers and former Tatar Soviet soldiers who had been captured by the Germans and kept in prisoner-of-war camps in Simferopol, Kherson, and Nikolaev.[23] In addition, there were small defense units organized by the inhabitants of Tatar villages whose number is not easily determined. Kirimal estimates that from 1942 to 1944 between 8,000 and 20,000 men were actively involved in the fight against Soviet partisans.[24]

Where the truth lies is difficult to assess. It is possible that Soviet, German, and Crimean Tatar émigré nationalist sources all exaggerate the number of disloyal Tatars—the Germans for propaganda reasons, the émigrés to show the strength of the nationalist movement, and the Soviets to justify their repressive measures against the Crimean Tatar population. The official Soviet statement on the matter offers no statistics. On 25 June 1946 the Secretary of the Presidium of the Supreme Soviet of the R.S.F.S.R., Bakhmurov, explained the repressive measures against the Tatars in the following way: many Crimean Tatars, instigated by German agents, joined German volunteer detachments and waged armed struggle against Red Army units; they set up saboteur gangs to fight against the Soviet power in the rear; the bulk of the Crimean Tatar population did not offer opposition to the traitors.[25]

What constitutes "many" Tatars is vague as far as precise figures are concerned. Certainly "many" Crimean Tatars formed partisan units to fight the invading Germans. Quite often, as Soviet Crimean Tatar sources show, those who fought against the Germans were treated with suspicion by the Soviet partisan command in the Crimea and quite often they were liquidated.[26] Furthermore, it is important to bear in mind that just as "many" (probably even more) Russians worked hand in glove with the Germans, as testified to by many documentary sources.[27] But Russian collaboration was overshadowed by Russian heroism in the defense of Sevastopol, while the remnants of the once famous warriors of the Crimean Khans, though contributing disproportionately to the anti-German struggle (according to Pisarev), had to pay the supreme penalty for the sins of some of their members. The decree of June 1946 also confirmed the abolition of the Crimean A.S.S.R. and legalized the change of the Autonomous Republic into an ordinary administrative *oblast* of the Russian Republic.[28] Later, in 1954, the *oblast* was transferred from the Russian to the Ukrainian Republic as Russia's "gift" to the Ukraine on the occasion of the 300th anniversary of the Treaty of Pereiaslav between the Ukraine and Russia.

This act opened a new chapter in the triangular relations among the Tatars, Ukrainians, and Russians. The Tatars had played an important role as allies of the Ukrainian Cossacks in the revolution of 1648-1654 and, at one time or another, supported Ukrainian interests *vis-à-vis* Poland and Russia. Yet they were also considered in Ukrainian historiography and popular lore to have engaged in plunder and destruction of Ukrainian communities. However, both Ukrainians and Tatars had suffered a common incorporation into the Russian empire. Both nationalities thus shared certain common relationships with the Russians; but at the same time there always existed grounds for conflict between the two. By transferring the Crimea to Ukrainian jurisdiction, the Soviet leadership made Ukrainians responsible for the Crimean Tatar problem, whether they liked it or not. Today this fact is clearly recognized by both the Crimean Tatars and the Ukrainian dissenters in the U.S.S.R.[29]

DEPORTATION

In April 1944 the Red Army recaptured the Crimea from the Germans, and a month later the N.K.V.D. moved in. During the night of 18-19 May 1944 the Crimean Tatars were given only five to fifteen minutes to collect what belongings they could carry (in some cases not even food was allowed), and then loaded into freight cars and deported to special reservations in Central Asia (mainly Uzbekistan and Kazakhstan) and Eastern Siberia.[30] No exceptions were allowed; even "members of the small pro-Soviet partisan movement, including its leader, Khaurullakh," and later, those Tatars who at the time were serving in the Soviet Army, were banished from the Crimea.[31] Thus, a population of approximately 250,000 was made homeless and transferred great distances at a very high cost in human life. "This deportation, which seems to have been carried out with an accompaniment of much killing and brutality, was supervised by Marshal Voroshilov,"[32] who in 1954, as Chairman of the Presidium of the Supreme Soviet, stated that the Crimea was strategically important and that its transfer to the Ukrainian Republic showed Russia's trust in its Ukrainian partner.[33]

CASUALTIES

The casualties the Crimean Tatars suffered were indeed great. Crimean Tatar sources quote the figure of 46.3 percent deaths in the deportations and eighteen months following. This figure generally is accepted by such prominent Russians as Academician Sakharov, and defended by General Grigorenko and other dissenters.[34] Some Crimean Tatar documents refer to the deportation of the whole population as genocide. During the 1968 Crimean investigations and trials, these assertions were contrasted with official K.G.B. reports, which show a smaller number of deaths than those claimed by the Crimean Tatars. According to one of the two key K.G.B. documents, "Of the people from the Crimea who were living under the 'special settlement' regime, 13,592 died between May 1944 and January 1945, to January 1st, 1946, 13,183 people died, of which 2,562 were men, 4,525 women, and 6,096 children under 16."[35] These figures are certainly an underestimate. Moreover, they do not take into account all those who died during the journey. Basing their statements on the mutual census and registration, Tatars speak of heavy casualties on the trains, in some of which no food was available on journeys lasting not less than eleven days, and often more. "Entire trains are reported as abandoning the journey after the death of all the deportees aboard."[36] Nevertheless, as one Crimean Tatar defendant at the Tashkent trial in 1969 stated, even the 10 percent figure implied by the first K.G.B. document is evidence of a terrible crime—proof of genocide.[37]

REHABILITATION

On 5 September 1967 the Supreme Soviet of the U.S.S.R. decreed that the "citizens of Tatar nationality who formerly lived in Crimea" were henceforth considered rehabilitated.[38] The decree was based on the argument that the "groundless charges" that all Crimean Tatars had "collaborated with the Germans" must be withdrawn, especially inasmuch as "a new generation in the meantime has taken up working and political life."[39] The act of rehabilitation meant a lifting of all decisions which contained indiscriminate charges against the Tatars; reestablishment of all the rights and privileges of Soviet citizenship in public and political life; and the reestablishment of radio programs and newspapers in the Tatar national language. The decree, however, failed to provide for the return of the Tatars to the Crimea. Instead, it assured them that the councils of ministers of the union republics in which they had "taken root" were instructed to "continue rendering help and assistance" in their "economic and cultural construction, taking account of their national interests and peculiarities." Thus, of all deported peoples, only the Tatars and Volga Germans were denied the right to national autonomy. This decision did not discourage the Tatars. On the contrary, in a display of courage and determination unequalled by larger nationalities, the Tatars organized themselves for a long and difficult struggle aimed at resurrecting their national autonomy and returning to their Crimean homeland.

Prior to the act of rehabilitation, the Tatars had started gathering signatures and petitioning various highly placed Soviet politicians in writing and through delegations. But their survival as a nationality was based as much upon their determination, courage, and organization as upon changes in the political climate in the Soviet Union. The death of Stalin and subsequent de-Stalinization did lift oppressive controls and individual harassment from the Tatars. For example, they no longer had to report every two weeks to the local militia.[40] Also, beginning in 1956 an attempt was made to revive their cultural life, first in Uzbekistan, where they lived in a more or less compact mass, and then gradually in other areas of the U.S.S.R. In the same year, in Tashkent, Uzbek authorities began publishing *Lenin Baigary* (Leninist Banner), a newspaper in the literary Crimean Tatar language which, despite its politically orthodox line, played an important part in the Crimean Tatar revival.[41] The establishment of the Crimean Tatar division in the Uzbek Gafur Guliam Publishing House in Tashkent was another important event in the life of Crimean Tatars. It was through the efforts of this division, managed by two poets,

Cherkez Ali and Seitumer Emin, that a number of literary works and children's books were published. Contemporary authors as well as known writers of the twenties and thirties are represented in published selections of this division. A third important cultural institution in Uzbekistan is the Department of Crimean Tatar Language and Literature at the Nizami Pedagogical Institute in Tashkent. This department prepares teachers of the Crimean Tatar language for secondary schools.

The importance of these establishments for the cultural and political renaissance of the Crimean Tatars cannot be overemphasized. The newspaper functions not only as a forum for cultural and social activities but also as a very potent tool in the struggle for Tatar national rights. In its pages information has been systematically published about Tatar contributions to the war against the Germans, in this way helping to clear the Crimean Tatars of the accusation of collaboration and treason.[42] Thus, entirely within the permitted framework of the official line, the Crimean Tatars started receiving more balanced information about events in the Crimea during World War II and, at the same time, the moral fortitude and determination to rectify once and for all the unjust punishment meted out to the entire population for the sins of some of its members. One can see in the *samizdat* documents how horribly unjust (in the light of the above facts) the policy of the Soviet government has appeared to a new generation of Crimean Tatars born in exile.

To strive for the future one must first remember the past. And here the publishing activities were of particular importance to Crimean Tatars. Their ability to organize themselves initially was also evident in the existence of numerous dance ensembles and choirs, which preserved and perpetuated Crimean Tatar folklore both in live performances and on record. But it took the Crimean Tatars a decade to organize themselves for political action.

THE FIGHT TO RETURN HOME

In 1964 came the beginnings of such an organization. Its aims were to gain political rehabilitation for the Tatars, regain their Crimean homeland, and reestablish their "status of administrative autonomy." The visible organization was composed of Crimean Tatar representatives elected by Tatar settlements and maintained by them in Moscow for the purpose of lobbying with the government. This group, of course, was not official because the Soviet government does not recognize such special interest representation. Nevertheless, the group continues to exist to this day, despite increasing harassment by the Soviet establishment. For a long time, this group published an unofficial information bulletin, and in its activities with the government was able to rely on information from all the Tatar settlements, including statistics dealing with casualties during deportation and discrimination against the Crimean Tatars both in their present settlements and in the Crimea. The mode of electing and maintaining the representatives is the best indicator of the organic ties between the Crimean Tatar leadership and their population. It is quite difficult even for the Soviet leadership to deny legitimacy to Tatar representatives, especially as their demands are always strongly supported by written petitions and the personal signatures of thousands of people. In this way the Crimean

Tatars were able to create enough pressure at home and enough publicity abroad to be taken seriously by the top Soviet leadership.

Georgadze, the Secretary of the Presidium of the Supreme Soviet, Andropov, Chairman of the K.G.B. and member of C.P.S.U. Politburo, Rudenko, the Prosecutor General, and Shchelokov, the Minister of Public Order, received the Crimean Tatar representatives on 21 July 1967 and promised them political rehabilitation while at the same time hinting at further concessions. It was at this meeting that Andropov supposedly stated that the Crimean Tatar movement could continue, but only if it did not overstep legal bounds. Most importantly, the Tatar delegates were told that their problem was being considered by the authorities and was still on the agenda of the Politburo. This news raised hopes among the Tatars that their demands to return to the Crimea would also be granted. This feeling was further reinforced when the Uzbek authorities evidently intimated in 1968 that the Tatars could return to the Crimea, but that resettlement would be conducted in a planned manner and arrangements would be made jointly by the authorities of Uzbekistan and the Crimean *Oblast.*

However, this turned out to be an empty promise. By the end of 1968 only 148 families had been allowed to return to the Crimea, and it then became clear to all concerned that "the legal and orderly way" of returning to the Crimea was nothing but a bureaucratic subterfuge to discourage, if not completely bar, the Tatars' return. Impatiently, the Tatars began to move to the Crimea without government permission. The Crimean authorities turned them back in a brutal and cruel fashion.[43] The Tatars claim that some 12,000 people were ejected from the Crimea in this manner. It is likely that the local administration, on its own authority, would not undertake to persecute the returning Tatars in this manner, and complaints to higher powers did not help. In a petition addressed to the Central Committee and Supreme Soviet, the Crimean Tatar representatives bitterly complained about this continued repression, noted that those who tried to return were persecuted, and observed that *agents provocateurs* were being used to destroy Tatar solidarity and to suppress their movement.[44] They also complained that the rehabilitation decree of 5 September 1967 implicitly sanctioned their deportation to Uzbekistan and other republics. It was in this letter that the Tatar representatives rejected the argument of the Soviet authorities that the Crimea was overpopulated, pointing out that emigration from the Ukraine to the Crimea continued unabated and that, furthermore, it also made economic sense to have the Tatars back in their homeland. If their legitimate appeals were disregarded, they indicated, they would have no recourse but to appeal to world opinion.

At this point one must backtrack briefly to indicate what happened to the population of the Crimea following the removal of the Tatars. In 1945 and 1946 the exiled Tatars were replaced by Ukrainians who had been forcibly removed from that part of Galicia retained by Poland.[45] It should be noted that one of the key officials the Crimean Tatars were petitioning from 1967 on, the Chairman of the Presidium of the Supreme Soviet, Nikolai Podgorny (a Ukrainian), was the very official responsible for the exchange of Polish and Ukrainian populations at the end of the war. It may be surmised that these Ukrainians, forcibly evacuated from their homes in Poland, may have been especially fearful of a second displacement following the return of the Tatars. As a group, these Ukrainians were especially aware of their national identity because of their historic struggle against the Poles and their resentment of the Russians. This factor, combined with the satisfaction given in 1954 to historic Ukrainian territorial claims to the Crimea, may well have provided grounds for charges by the Crimean Tatars of Ukrainian nationalist chauvinism.[46]

It should be pointed out that according to the 1959 census, Russians constituted a large majority of the population of the Crimea (71.4 percent), although their relative strength declined to 67.3 percent in 1970. This change was caused by a large emigration of Ukrainians to the Crimea in the 1960's, raising the number of Ukrainians from 268,000 to 481,000 (22.3 to 26.5 percent of the total population).[47] However, the Russians inhabiting the Crimea have historically constituted the main threat to Tatar interests. The circumstances associated with their original settlement as a conquering force in the Crimea, and their oppression of the Tatars during the wars with Turkey, the Revolution and Civil War, and then during collectivization, impressed on them attitudes resembling those of the French *colons* in Algeria.[48] These attitudes remain to this day a potent influence on ethnic relations in the Crimea.

Overall population growth in the Crimea appears to be part of a broader process of southward migration in the USSR. Although Soviet and non-Soviet demographers alike argue that this movement is largely spontaneous and unplanned, it cannot be denied that the Soviet government has a practical as well as programmatic interest in promoting "correct" patterns of ethnic migration.[49] From the Tatar standpoint the migration of Russians and Ukrainians very definitely has been a deliberate act on the part of the Soviet government, indicating that a labor shortage has in fact existed in the Crimea, and rendering hypocritical the official assertion that no room is left for the Crimean Tatars in their homeland.

The Tatars' petition to the Central Committee and Supreme Soviet represented a new and more militant phase in their struggle to return to the Crimea. The prevarications of the authorities were one force in propelling the Crimean Tatars in this direction. Another factor probably was the link between the Crimean Tatars and the other dissent movements in the USSR, which appears to have come into being at this time. Among those who took on the task of fighting for Tatar rights was Alexei Kosterin, a Russian writer with a long and outstanding record as a defender of deported nationalities. Upon Kosterin's death in November 1968, the fight was taken up by a Ukrainian, Major General P. Grigorenko. Such prominent dissenters as A. D. Sakharov, P. Iakir, A. A. Volpin, and many others also came to the support of Tatar demands. However, it was Grigorenko, more than anybody else, who stimulated a stronger expression of Tatar feelings when on 17 March 1968 he proclaimed in Moscow, on the occasion of A. Kosterin's birthday, that the Tatars should "stop begging" and "take back that which was taken from you unlawfully."[50]

The Tatars, who felt that their more subdued efforts had failed, followed Grigorenko's advice and began to organize demonstrations in Tashkent, Andizhan, Bekabad, and Fergana—the areas of Tatar concentration. But the largest of the demonstrations took place on 21 April 1968 in Chirchik, a small town not far from Tashkent. The Crimean Tatars gathered there in large numbers to celebrate the ninety-eighth birthday of Lenin, in this way underscoring once more the legitimacy of their demands to return to the Crimea and reestablish the Crimean Tatar Autonomous Republic (created originally upon Lenin's orders). The local authorities to whom the Tatars applied for permission to hold the meeting not only refused but called out the police and military forces in order to suppress it. When the Tatars persisted they were attacked again and again by police forces wielding high pressure hoses, poisonous liquid spray, and truncheons. The Crimean Tatars hold the Russian Secretary of the *gorkom Iakubov*, Major-General Sharliev, the Uzbek commandant of the local troops, and the Russian Second Secretary of the Uzbek Communist Party, Lomonosov, directly responsible for the Chirchik repressions. About 300 Crimean Tatars were arrested, but most were released soon thereafter. In the end only twelve persons were charged with "breach of public order" and sentenced from six months to two-and-a-half years in labor camps. The majority of those prosecuted did not even take part in the demonstrations.[51]

It was clear that the demonstration was used as a pretext for proceeding against a select and potentially dangerous (from the Soviet point of view) group of individual Tatar leaders. At the same time the Soviet authorities, in a time-honored method worthy of the "black hundreds," attempted to isolate the Tatars from potential supporters among other nationalities by spreading wild rumors about Crimean Tatar activities. It appears, for example, that the Samarkand local authorities were guilty of spreading rumors that the Crimean Tatars had desecrated an Armenian cemetery.[52] The reaction of the Tatars to this repression was instantaneous. Ayder Bariev, a Tatar tractor driver, flew to Moscow to protest, but his telegram to Prosecutor General R. Rudenko went unanswered.[53] A petition from the Tatar representatives in Moscow addressed to the Politbureau, Presidium of the Supreme Soviet, and Prosecutor General demanding the release of people arrested in Chirchik also evoked no response. The government reacted in a different manner. Tatars living in Moscow were rounded up and deported by baggage train back to Central Asia. Some eight hundred were expelled from Moscow in this fashion.[54] The Moscow Assistant Prosecutor, Stasenkov, informed the Tatars that their question had been decided "fully and finally" and that there would be no more concessions.[55] In his letter to the Prosecutor, General Grigorenko accused him of failing to fulfill his constitutional duties not only by not checking on illegal policy actions in this case, but by not even receiving complaints in the first place.[56]

It thus came to pass that the Crimean Tatars had to appeal to world public opinion sooner than they may have anticipated. Besieged from all sides, the 118 representatives of Tatar communities issued their appeal to "World Public Opinion" on 21 July 1968 calling again for help to bring about a return to their homeland.[57] More petitions and arrests followed. As Vardys rightly points out, "the Kremlin had apparently decided that the Tatars needed to be restrained by decapitating their leadership."[58] Not only Crimean Tatar leaders but also their supporters among other dissenters were silenced. The most vociferous and articulate, Major General Grigorenko, was arrested, tried for "slandering the Soviet Union" and sent to an insane asylum—procedure reserved for particularly troublesome political dissenters under both the tsarist and communist leadership. The appeal on 22 May 1969 by Grigorenko and fifty-five leading Moscow figures to the United Nations Commission on Human Rights fell on deaf ears. The decision to proceed with prosecution against the Tatars was not changed.

That the Kremlin tried to control the Tatar movement by removing their leaders is shown best by the trials held in 1969 and 1970. The most well known is the one staged in Tashkent from 1 July to 5 August 1969.[59] The trial of the "Tashkent Ten," as it is also known, involved the leading Crimean Tatars accused of anti-Soviet propaganda (in their underground publications and petitions they had referred to Soviet policy toward the Tatars as "racist" and the forced deportation of the Tatars as "genocide"). The defendants pleaded not guilty to the charges of slander but all were convicted. One of the ten, Rollan K. Kadiev, a promising young nuclear physicist, was sentenced with three others to three years in a labor camp. The remainder received one-year sentences but were released because they had been in prison before the trial.

Thus, the Tatars' struggle to regain their homeland has been unsuccessful. Although under severe pressure from the Soviet authorities, they have not given up the fight. Their plight is becoming increasingly known not only in the Soviet Union but also abroad. Within the USSR the Tatars succeeded in gaining support among dissenters of all nationalities, especially among Ukrainian dissidents who, although fighting for their own rights, recognize the suffering of the Crimean Tatars and their right to regain their homeland. This attitude of liberally minded Ukrainians is of vital importance, since the Crimea is administratively a part of the Ukraine. Russian dissidents, and particularly other Turkic people, are also aware of the struggle of the Crimean Tatars and watch it with interest and sympathy. The wave of purges in the national republics is strong evidence that the nationality problem in all its forms is very much alive, and that the Tatars are not an isolated case, even though they have gone further than all other non-Russian groups in giving mass expression to their national demands.

CONCLUSION

In studying something as rich in drama as the recent history of the Crimean Tatars, one is apt to lose sight of the enduring features of the plight of this small national group. Here the attempt has been made to show that the conflict between the Russians and Crimean Tatars goes back for centuries, and that the "ultimate solution" of the Crimean Tatar problem carried out by Stalin and tacitly continued by his successors was first proposed by the Tsarist colonial officials. Russian distrust of the Crimean Tatars long predates the Second World War, as does the Russian concern with the strategic and security aspects of the Crimea and its population. Soviet policy toward the Crimean Tatars, especially during World War II and afterwards, must be understood within this broad historical framework.

The Soviet leaders have not simply been following historical precedents in some mechanical fashion but have been dealing with a situation endowed with its own social and political dynamics. At the local level a triangular relationship has existed among Tatars, Ukrainians, and Russians in which each group has experienced strife but also limited cooperation with each of the others. However, the fact that the Russian majority of the population has dwelt predominantly in the towns, while Ukrainians have lived mainly in the countryside, at present provides the basis for a potentially sharper conflict of interest between Tatars and Ukrainians than between Tatars and Russians.

While it is clear that the Soviet leaders have taken into consideration, and indeed have exploited, these ethnic group cleavages in the Crimea, it is probable that they have based their actions upon their impressions of the Crimean Tatars as political dissidents. In fact, the Crimean Tatars represent a unique phenomenon in the dissident movement of the 1960's and early 1970's; their only counterpart has been another small nationality, the Meshketians. The Crimean Tatar movement has enjoyed both a high degree of overt organization and manifest mass participation. No other dissident group has been able to mobilize as high a percentage of its natural constituency as the Crimean Tatars. Their petitions have repeatedly been signed by thousands of individuals, and it is probable that few Crimean Tatar families have not been touched by this struggle. The Soviet security police have always been worried by real or imagined links bridging different deviant groups, and the Crimean Tatar movement has provided some genuine grounds for concern on this score. The contacts which developed between the main Moscow-based dissident movement, represented by Major General Grigorenko and others like him, is well known and thus requires no further comment; but mention must be made of the less publicized interest of Ukrainian dissidents like Chornovil, Dzyuba, Karavans'kyi and others in the Crimean Tatar cause. In a sense, the sympathy of Ukrainians and other non-Russians for the Crimean Tatars may be potentially more serious than their tie with the liberal Russian intelligentsia, because it raises implicitly the prospect of a common opposition to the regime. And in this connection the Soviet leadership cannot help but fear that larger and politically more significant Muslim nationalities, above all the Uzbeks, Azerbaidzhanis, and Volga Tatars, may be affected by the example of the Crimean Tatars. Although anticipation of possible contagion among the Soviet Muslim people tends to promote a policy of repression (which has in fact been the policy pursued by the Soviet leadership), it is conceivable that this may be moderated by considerations of Soviet foreign policy in the developing world in general and in Muslim countries in particular if the Crimean Tatar cause continues to receive sufficient publicity.

NOTES

[1] It should be pointed out that the Tatar Autonomous Soviet Socialist Republic, situated on the Volga with its capital city of Kazan, and representing one of the constituent units of the Russian Federation (R.S.F.S.R.), is not the home of all Tatar peoples of the USSR.

[2] Walter Kolarz, *Russia and Her Colonies* (New York: F. A. Praeger, 1955), p. 76.

[3] See the article on the Crimean A.S.S.R. in *Bol'shaia Sovetskaia Entsyklopedia*, first edition, XXXV (1937), 279-324.

[4] Some scholars estimate that over 150,000 Tatars legally left the Crimea between 1859 and 1863, while a large number (at least several thousand more) departed illegally. See Edige Kirimal, *Der nationale Kampf der Krimturken* (Emsdetten: Lechte, 1952), pp. 1-2 and 7-8; Kolarz, pp. 76-77. Robert Conquest has convincingly shown that from 1860 to 1862 about 231,177 Tatars left the Crimea, *The Nation Killers* (London: Macmillan, 1970), p. 57.

[5] V. Stanley Vardys, "The Case of Crimean Tatars," *Russian Review*, XXX, 2 (April 1971), 101.

[6] Conquest, p. 56.

[7] Kolarz, p. 77.

[8] See "Iz istorii krymskikh tatar (Po materialam S. P. Pisareva)," *Politicheskii Dnevnik* (Samizdat publication) (April 1970), p. 30. Hereafter referred to as "Iz istorii . . . " An important document entitled "Obrashchenie 60,000 krymskikh tatar Presidiumu 24 S'ezda KPSS i vsem delegatam s'ezda" (probably of March 1971) lists thirty-two other documents bearing thousands of signatures of Crimean Tatars and addressed to various State and Party institutions and other Soviet mass organizations. Most of them, unfortunately, are not available in the West.

[9] Kolarz, p. 79.

[10] *Ibid.*

[11] Vardys, p. 102.

[12] Kirimal, p. 28.

[13] Majstrenko, "National'no-vyzvol'nyi rukh kryms'kykh tatar i ikh vzaiemyny z Ukrainoiu," *Ukrains'kyi Samostiinyk*, Nos. 7-8 (1971), pp. 561-62.

[14] Kirimal, p. 287.

[15] Vardys, p. 102.

[16] Kirimal, p. 292 and sources cited in his footnote 1229.

[17] G. Aleksandrov, "Istreblenie Krymskikh Tatar," *Sotsialisticheskii Vestnik* (Paris, March 1950), pp. 51-52.

[18] Kirimal, p. 294.

[19] *Ibid.*, p. 295.

[20] *Ibid.*, p. 296.

[21] Kolarz, p. 80.

[22] "Iz istorii . . . ," p. 32.

[23] Kirimal, p. 305.

[24] *Ibid.*, p. 305. Robert Conquest is inclined to agree with Kirimal. Conquest, p. 64.

[25] See Kolarz, footnote on p. 80, or Conquest, p. 47.

[26] "Iz istorii . . . ," p. 31. The most important source of the Crimean Tatar participation in the war against the Germans which is referred to in various Crimean Tatar protest documents "Dokumenty ob uchastii krymskotatarskogo naroda v Velikoi Otechestvennoi Voine 1941-45gg" in six volumes and two photographic albums, unfortunately, is not available in the West. The letter of former partisans—the Crimean Tatars—is also unavailable.

[27] Kirimal, footnote 1289 on p. 305 and footnote 1317 on p. 314.

[28] Conquest, p. 47.

[29] See especially the letters of Iu. B. Osmanov of 21 December 1967 to Brezhnev and the Politburo "Prodolzhenie Istorii" in which he attacks both Russian chauvinism and Ukrainian nationalism. The letter, "Krym-arena razgula velikodezhavnogo shovinizma i ukrainskogo natsionalizma," with 32,000 signatures, is not available in the West. Among Ukrainian dissenters, Viacheslav Chornovil,

Sviatoslav Karavans'kyi and others expressed strong support of Tatar demands for return to the Crimea. See: V. Chornovil, *Lykho z Rozumu* (Paris, 1968), p. 146; S. Karavans'kyi, "Petition to Soviet of Nationalities," *Ukrainian Quarterly*, 24 (Summer 1968) and *The New Leader* 6, 15 January 1968. The *Chronicle of Current Events*, No. 11, tells of the arbitrary actions of the local authorities and police authorities against the homes of Crimean Tatar returnees. The reports also quote protests made by Russian and Ukrainian workers on collective farms in the Crimea against the inhuman persecutions of their Tatar neighbors.

[30] Robert Conquest, *op. cit.*, pp. 105-107. Edige Kirimal claims that Stalin was planning to remove the Tatars from the Crimea in 1941 but that war with Germany interfered with these plans. Kirimal, p. 325.

[31] A Crimean Tatar source puts the number serving in the Soviet Armed Forces at 20,000. "Iz istorii . . . ," p. 32.

[32] Conquest, p. 105.

[33] Vardys, p. 103.

[34] See P. G. Grigorenko's address in English translation in *Problems of Communism*, XVII, 4 (July-August 1968), 94. See also "Otkrytoe pismo Russkikh druzei krymskikh tatar," *Novoe Russkoe Slovo*, 28 March 1969, pp. 3, 8. Also, A. E. Kosterin, "Uvazhaemye tovarishchi," a letter addressed probably to the Politburo. See also P. G. Grigorenko, ed., *Sbornik "Pamiati Alekseia Evgrafovicha Kosterina,"* (Moscow, November 1968). The text of this document was smuggled out of the USSR and published by the Flemish Committee on Eastern Europe and reprinted by *Posev*, No. 4 (1969), pp. 47-61.

[35] Conquest carefully analyzed the two documents as well as all of the available information on the subject and observed: "the first K.G.B. document states that the Crimean deportees started to reach Uzbekistan on 29 May 1944 and had in the main arrived by 8 June 1944. Figures at the beginning of July 1944 were: 35,750 families, with a total of 134,742 members comprising of 21,619 men, 47,537 women, and 65,568 children under 16. The document adds that from 1 January 1945 to 1 January 1946 death accounted to 13,183, comprising 2,562 men, 4,525 women, and 6,096 children." Conquest adds that "General Grigorenko, commenting on this document, notes that the 151,424 figure of July 1944 had lost 16,682 dead by January 1945 in spite of reinforcement of 818 families, and that if we subtract the estimated numbers of the latter from the January 1945 total alive, the deaths come out 3,468 higher—i.e., 20,150 for the first six months. Adding the 13,183 for the following year, we have a total of 33,333 deaths. This figure is thus an official one of around 22 percent dead." Conquest further points out that a second document, "from the Deputy Head of the First Special Department of Uzbek K.G.B., dated 5 February 1968, states that no exact figures are available of deportees, but cites a report on the economy of the N.K.V.D. 'special settlements' giving deaths there from May-June 1944 to 1 January 1945 as 13,592, and saying that this is 9.1 percent dead. That is, the figure is based on the 151,424 arrivals in Uzbekistan. The year 1945 is not covered, but if we add the 13,592 of Document II to the 1945 deaths of Document I we get 26,775—a total of about 18 percent—i.e., lower than the other 'official figure,' but in the same region." Conquest, pp. 161-62.

[36] Conquest, p. 162.

[37] Peter Reddaway, ed., *Uncensored Russia: Protest and Dissent in the Soviet Union* (New York: American Heritage Press, 1972), p. 262.

[38] See *Vedomosti Verkhovnogo Soveta SSSR*, No. 37, 8 September 1967. Already in 1955 an unpublished decree of the Presidium of the Supreme Soviet stated that the Crimean Tatars were "removed from the conditions of Special Settlement," and freed from the control of M.V.D. but that they had no "right to the return of the property confiscated at the deportation . . . [or] the right to return to the places from which they were deported." See translation of the decree in Conquest, p. 185.

[39] See *Vedomosti . . . , ibid.*

[40] "Iz istorii . . . ," p. 31.

[41] Vardys, p. 104. As late as 1966 the Crimean Tatar language was described as an "unwritten language" in *Iazyki Narodov SSSR*, II (Moscow, 1966) cited in Conquest, footnote 5, chapter 12, p. 217.

[42] For a different assessment see P. G. Grigorenko, p. 95.

[43] See *Khronika Tekushchikh Sobytii . . .* and *Novoe Russkoe Slovo*, 5 October 1968. The struggle of the Crimean Tatars to return to Crimea is very well told by Borys Lewytzkyj in his excellent study *Politische Opposition in der Sowjetunion 1960-1972* (Munchen: Deutschen Taschenbuch Verlag Gmbtl and Co. Kg, 1972).

[44] *Novoe Russkoe Slovo*, 5 October 1968.

[45] *Entsyklopediia Ukroinozhavstva*, II, 3 (Paris-New York: Shevchenko Scientific Society, 1959), 1179.

[46] For example, the Ukrainian Soviet Encyclopedia praises the liquidation of the Crimean Khanate by Russia as a progressive event and praises the unification of the Crimea with the Ukraine as a "historical act" which "shows the limitless faith and love of Russian and Ukrainian people," and "the historic ties of the Crimea with the Ukraine." *Ukrainians'ka Radians'ka Entsyklopediia*, VII (Kiev: Academy of Sciences, 1959-1965), 382 and 391. The volume on the Crimean *oblast* of the multi-volume *Istoriia Mist i Sil Ukrains'koi RSR* published by the Institute of History of the Academy of Sciences of the Ukrainian SSR echoes this analysis. The Ukrainian scholarly publications outside the USSR, on the contrary, do present a more objective treatment of the Crimean-Tatar question. See *Entsyklopediia Ukrainoznavstva* cited above and *Ukraine: A Concise Encyclopedia*, I-II (Toronto: University of Toronto Press, 1963-1971).

[47] Roman Szporluk, "The Nations of the U.S.S.R. in 1970," *Survey*, No. 4 (81) (Autumn 1971), p. 89.

[48] It was Ivan Dzyuba who first pointed out this resemblance. Ivan Dzyuba, *Internationalism or Russification* (London: Weidenfeld and Nicholson, 1968).

[49] Szporluk has convincingly shown elsewhere that "Russian immigration to the Ukraine, Uzbekistan, etc., is officially encouraged, sponsored and organized." Roman Szporluk, "Dissent and the Non-Russian Nationalities," in P. J. Potichnyj, ed., *Dissent in the Soviet Union* (Hamilton: McMaster University, 1972). See also V. I. Naulko, "Heohrafichne rozmichchennia Narodiv v U.R.S.S.," (Kiev: Academy

of Sciences, 1966). For an excellent treatment of the Soviet nationality policy see Borys Lewytzkyj, *Die sowjetische Nationalitaten politik nach Stalins Tod, 1953-1970* (Munchen: Ukrainische Freie Universitat, 1970), and his "Sovetskij Narod," *Osterreichische Osthefte*, XV, 2 (May 1973).

[50] *Problems of Communism* (July-August 1968), pp. 93-95.

[51] Conquest, p. 204.

[52] *Ibid.*

[53] *Ibid.*

[54] General Volkov, head of the Moscow branch of MVD (MOOP at that time) was in charge of this operation.

[55] Conquest, p. 204.

[56] *Posev*, January 1969.

[57] The appeal revealed that since 1959 more than 200 Crimean Tatars had been sentenced to up to seven years imprisonment "although they have always acted within the framework of the Soviet Constitution." Conquest, p. 205.

[58] Vardys, p. 107.

[59] Detailed information on the trial including extracts from documents, KGB archives, and a reconstructed transcript of the trial is contained in the *samizdat* publication known as *Tashkentskii protses* which is in possession of the Alexander Herzen Foundation, Amsterdam.

LIST OF CONTRIBUTORS

Yaroslav Bilinsky is Professor of Political Science at the University of Delaware, Newark. His fields of specialization are nationality politics in the USSR and Soviet foreign policy. Among others, he published *The Second Soviet Republic: The Ukraine after W.W.II* (1964) and *Changes in the Central Committee; Communist Party of the Soviet Union 1960-66* (1967). Also, he is a contributor to *Ukraine in the Seventies* (1975).

Jurij Borys is Professor of Political Science at the University of Calgary, Canada. His publications include *The Communist Party and the Sovietization of Ukraine; A Study in the Communist Doctrine of the Self-Determination of Nations* (1960), and (with Nils Andren, *et al.*) *Foreign Governments* (1965). Also, he has published numerous articles on Soviet nationality problems.

Oleh Fedyshyn is Associate Professor of Politics at Richmond College (City University of New York). He is the author of *Germany's Drive to the East and the Ukrainian Revolution, 1917-1918* (1971), and he has published a number of articles and reviews in American and European professional journals, mostly in the field of Soviet nationality policy.

Zvi Gitelman is Associate Professor of Political Science at the University of Michigan. He is the author of *Jewish Nationality and Soviet Politics* (1972) and published articles and monographs on Soviet Jewry and on East European politics.

Stephan Horak is Professor of History at Eastern Illinois University, Charleston, Illinois. He is author of *Poland and Her National Minorities 1919-1939* (1961), *Poland's International Affairs, 1919-1960* (1964), and *Junior Slavica: A Selected Annotated Bibliography* (1968). Also, he has published many articles in American, Canadian, and European journals, and is Editor of the journal *Nationalities Papers*.

Ihor Kamenetsky is Professor of Political Science at Central Michigan University. In addition to various articles and monographs, he has published *Hitler's Occupation of Ukraine: 1941-44* (1957), *Secret Nazi Plans for Eastern*

Europe; A Study of Lebensraum Policies (1961) and the bibliography *Guide to the Dag Hammarskjöld Collection on Developing Nations* (3 vols.: 1968; 1970; 1977).

Borys Lewytskyj resides in Munich and is the author of numerous books and scholarly articles. Some of his recent publications are: *Die Marschälle und die Politik* (1971), *Die Gewerkschaften in der Sowjetunion* (1970), *Politische Opposition in der Sowjetunion* (1960-72), *The Stalinist Terror in the Thirties* (1973), *Die linke Opposition in der Sowjetunion* (1974), *Die sowjetische Nationalitätenpolitik nach Stalins Tod: 1953-1970* (1970), and *Sowjetische Entspannungspolitik heute* (1975).

Vasyl Markus is Professor of Political Science at Loyola University of Chicago, Illinois. He has published mostly on Soviet nationalities and religious policies, East European national minorities, and Soviet law and foreign policy. Besides his contributions to a number of periodicals in various languages, he has published *L'Ukraine soviétique dans les relations internationales et son statut en droit international* (1959) and *Nationalities Policy of the CPSU* (1961). Also, he is a member of the editorial board of *Ukraine: A Concise Encyclopedia* (1963, 1971).

Ralph C. Michelsen is a Ph.D. candidate in anthropology at the University of California, Irvine, and he also teaches in this field at the School of Social Sciences there. He has published in the *Journal of American Folklore* and *The Masterkey*, and he has contributed numerous articles to *The Pacific Coast Archaeological Society Quarterly*. In 1975, he produced a film entitled: "The Kiliva Indians: Hunters and Gatherers of Baja California."

Peter Potichnyj is Professor of Political Science at McMaster University, Hamilton, Ontario. Among some of his publications are: *On the Current Situation in the Ukraine* (1970), editor; *Ukraine in the Seventies* (1975); and *From Cold War to Detente* (1976), co-editor.

Thomas Remeikis is Associate Professor and Chairman of the Political Science Department at Calumet College, Chicago. His fields of specialization are comparative systems and Soviet nationality policy, and he has written on Soviet government and Lithuanian affairs. Among other work, he has edited *Proceedings of the Institute of Lithuanian Studies* (1972).

Michael Rywkin is Professor and Chairman of the Department of Germanic and Slavic Studies, and Head of the Russian Area Studies at City College of the City University of New York. He has published various articles in the field of Soviet nationality problems and Russian colonization, and is the author of *Russia in Central Asia* (1963).

Rein Taagepera is Associate Professor of Political Science at the University of California, Irvine. He is co-editor of *Problems of Mininations: Baltic Perspectives* (1973) and published the bimonthly newsletters *Estonian Events* (1967-1972) and *Baltic Events* (1973-1975).

Peter Vanneman teaches political science at the University of Arkansas. One of his recent publications is *The Supreme Soviet: Politics and the Legislative Process in the Soviet Political System* (1973).